S0-CCZ-426

The

FEDERAL

APPOINTMENTS

PROCESS

Constitutional Conflicts

A Series with the Institute

of Bill of Rights Law at the

College of William and Mary

Neal Devins, series editor

The

FEDERAL

APPOINTMENTS

PROCESS

A Constitutional and

Historical Analysis

Michael J. Gerhardt

WITHDRAWN
UTSA LIBRARIES

DUKE UNIVERSITY PRESS

Durham and London

2003

Library
University of Texas
at San Antonio

© 2000 Duke University Press

All rights reserved

Printed in the United States

of America on acid-free paper ∞

Designed by Rebecca Giménez

Typeset in Adobe Caslon by

Tseng Information Systems, Inc.

Library of Congress Cataloging-

in-Publication Data appear on the

last printed page of this book.

Paperback edition © 2003

Library
University of Texas
at San Antonio

I dedicate this book to
my loving wife, Deborah,
without whose support, faith,
and patience nothing I do would
have meaning; and to our son,
Benjamin Samuel, whom
we love beyond measure
forever and always.

CONTENTS

Part Two

EVALUATING THE ROLES OF THE MAJOR PLAYERS IN THE FEDERAL APPOINTMENTS PROCESS

Part Three

REFORMING THE FEDERAL APPOINTMENTS PROCESS

INTRODUCTION TO
THE PAPERBACK EDITION

THE RECENT HISTORY of the federal appointments process suggests, contrary to Abraham Lincoln's famous declaration, that ours is a government of men and not of laws. In the two years since the original edition of this book was published, conflicts between presidents and senators have intensified over federal appointments generally and with particular ferocity over judicial nominations. For six of Bill Clinton's eight years as president, Republican senators subjected his judicial nominees to unprecedented delays and obstruction in the hopes of barring the appointment of liberal activists to the federal bench. In the final year of Clinton's presidency, Republicans blocked final Senate action on forty-one pending judicial nominees to enable the next president to fill the positions instead. Once it became clear the next president would be George W. Bush, many Democrats threatened to block any conservative ideologues whom he might attempt to appoint as federal judges, in retaliation for the Supreme Court's controversial opinion in *Bush v. Gore*,[1] which short-circuited Vice President Albert Gore's challenge to the vote count in Florida and effectively awarded Bush the presidency. After retaking control of the Senate roughly midway through Bush's first year in office, Democrats made good on their threat. They slowed down the confirmation process for his judicial nominees as payback for both *Bush v. Gore* and Republicans' blockage of many of President Clinton's judicial nominees. Democrats were especially effective at preventing President Bush from appointing anyone they suspected of being a conservative ideologue to the federal courts of appeals. Near the end of President Bush's second year in office, the Senate Judiciary Committee had rejected two of his circuit nominees; the president had a lower proportion of judicial nominees confirmed during his first year in office than any previous president; and his judicial nominees had taken longer to get confirmed than those of any other president. When the Senate recessed for the 2002 midterm elections, fifty-one judicial nominations were pending before the Senate, including thirty-three awaiting hearings before the Judiciary Committee. The obstruction angered the president. He retaliated by successfully campaigning in the 2002 midterm elections for Republicans to regain control of the Senate. In the week before election day, the President repeatedly asked voters — seventeen times in fifteen campaign stops — for a Republican majority in the Senate to ensure favorable and speedy confirmation of his judicial nominees. At the same time, he asked voters to elect Republicans to Congress to get around the Democrats' opposition to his historic plans for a new Department of Homeland Security whose employees would serve at the President's pleasure. No sooner had he achieved his objective than the White House signaled, with the support of the then-incoming Republican Majority Leader Trent Lott, that it would renominate some judicial candidates blocked by the Democratic Senate, including the two circuit court nominees whom the Judiciary Committee had rejected. Through these and other actions, Presidents Clinton and Bush and senators from both parties demonstrated the primacy of their concerns for which people should enforce and interpret the laws.

IF ABRAHAM LINCOLN was wrong about the nature of our government, it is because of two significant themes in the federal appointments process. I discuss each in the original edition of this book, and each is evident from the history of the federal appointments process. Both individually and collectively, these themes provide useful frameworks for making sense of recent developments in the federal appointments process.

The first theme is the peculiar dynamic emanating from the Appointments Clause of the United States Constitution. One element of this dynamic is that the clause creates a realm of shared authority that plainly invites conflict. Anyone familiar with federal judicial selection over the past few decades knows just how combative contests over judicial appointments can be. Though not always short, their nastiness and brutality seem otherwise to exemplify the conditions that Thomas Hobbes had described as existing within the state of nature. The structure of the Constitution pits presidents and senators against each other in the federal appointments process, and the framers fully expected (even hoped) that conflicts would ensue from this design. Their expectation was that the checks and balances of the Constitution, including the distribution of authority on judicial appointments, were designed, in Madison's famous phrasing, so that "ambition must be made to counteract ambition." The framers viewed conflicts as inevitable and even desirable, as each branch sought to aggrandize its powers at the expense of the other. The ensuing friction would prevent one branch from becoming tyrannical. Consequently, one should not be surprised to find, particularly in times of divided government, presidents and senators at odds over their shared responsibility for federal appointments. Indeed, a common view is that the Senate's "Advise and Consent" authority constitutes the only significant political check on a president's nominating authority.

Another aspect of the special dynamic created by the Appointments Clause is that it invites accommodations at least as much as it invites conflicts. In relatively short order after ratification of the Constitution, presidents and senators developed informal accommodations to reduce the inevitability of conflict and yet preserve some realm of discretion for presidents and senators with respect to judicial appointments. These practices constitute the most important driving forces in the federal appointments process. Thus President Clinton often went well out of his way to appease leading Republicans in making judicial nominations. This was especially true with respect to his two Supreme Court nominees. Shortly after taking office, President Bush tried to curry good will with Democrats by renominating two people whom Clinton had boldly made judges through recess appointments after the Republican-led Senate had blocked their confirmation. Moreover, Democratic leaders in the lame duck session in November 2002 tried in turn to curry President Bush's good will by enabling the full Senate to approve two judicial nominations on which they had refused to act before the 2002 midterm elections.

Still another element of the special dynamics created by the Appointments Clause is that to the extent conflicts over appointments do get resolved, the structure tends to work to the advantage of the president. By fixing the power to nominate in a single person, the Appointments Clause gives presidents a substantial edge over the diffuse Senate in maximizing their net influence over appointments, since it is very difficult for a critical mass of senators to remain united over a long period in opposition to a president's nominees. On appointments matters, the Senate occupies a defensive posture in which it is confined to exercising vetoes. To counter the president's structural advantages in the appointments process, the Senate has delegated substantial authority to committees and individual senators, so that many final decisions about appointments are made in settings in which only one or a small number of senators have made the critical decisions. Thus, most of the obstruction of both Clinton's and Bush's judicial nominees was the result of the Judiciary chair's refusal to schedule hearings or final Committee votes, the Senate Majority Leader's refusal to allow floor votes, and individual senators' exercising temporary, often fatal holds on judicial nominations that were offensive to them.

The second theme in the federal appointments process that provides a useful perspective on recent conflicts and accommodations within the system is the patterns and practices of the major institutions responsible for federal appointments. It is tempting to think that current crises are worse than those experienced at other times. A major theme in the original edition of this book was the importance of resisting this temptation and adopting an alternative perspective known as historical institutionalism. Historical institutionalism is especially helpful for putting recent developments within the federal appointments process into a broader perspective than merely viewing them as the consequences of the personal desires, objectives, and characteristics of presidents and senators. To be sure, leaders' personal traits and agendas are pertinent to understanding their performance in office. For instance, a popular view is that President George W. Bush does not want to make the same mistakes that his father is thought to have made. Some speculate that one reason for George H.W. Bush's failure to win reelection was that he had not done enough as president to accommodate the far right wing of his party by fighting over judicial appointments rather than seek accommodation with Democrats. Hence, since his earliest days in office one priority of President George W. Bush has been to appoint as judges people closely identified with the conservative wing of the party, whose support will be essential for his reelection. Moreover, George W. Bush is reputed to have felt that his father's administration and reelection effort were hurt by a lack of loyalty from party leaders and political appointees, so he has placed a premium on loyalty as a criterion for service within his administration. Yet, there is a great deal that occurs within the federal appointments process that cannot be explained by focusing on a president's or senator's personal strengths or shortcomings. Institutional analysis helps to illuminate more fully the institutional consequences of the choices made by national political leaders as well as the internal and external pressures influencing presidents' and senators' decision-making on appointments matters. Indeed, this perspective helps to show, among other things, that even President Lincoln, given his intense commitment to political patronage, might not have believed his own rhetoric about our government being one of laws and not of men. The past two years fit neatly into four significant institutional patterns of practices evident from the history of the federal appointments process.

The first such pattern is the set of informal accommodations or arrangements developed by the Senate to guide the federal appointments process. I refer to these as institutional norms. Following institutional norms generally produces a relatively peaceful appointments process. Hostilities, or war, can break out over appointments when the president, senators, or nominees violate the institutional norms applicable to the federal appointments process or such norms are in flux. One of these norms is senatorial courtesy, according to which a president who fills a vacant federal office in a given state will defer to the preferences of one or both senators from that state if they belong to president's party. During the six years in which they controlled the Senate during the Clinton administration, Republican senators attempted to expand the traditional, intraparty scope of this prerogative by stalling any nominations made to offices in their states that the president had not cleared with them beforehand. The more President Clinton resisted making accommodations with Republican senators, the more some of them resisted his nominations. Once Democrats regained control of the Senate in 2001, Democratic senators tried in vain to pressure President Bush to consult with them before making nominations to offices in their states. President Bush generally resisted their invitations, but he was careful to accept Republican senators' choices for federal offices in their states. Thus, his nominees, even embattled ones, generally have enjoyed the support of sponsoring senators. Such was the case, for instance, with the two circuit court nominees whom Democrats allowed the full Senate to confirm during the lame duck session in 2002 — Michael McConnell, sponsored by Senator Orrin Hatch (the incoming chair of the Judiciary Committee), and Dennis Shedd, sponsored by retiring Strom Thurmond (whom Shedd once served as chief counsel on the Judiciary Committee).

President Bush has also demonstrated his respect for other forms of senatorial courtesy. One involves presidential deference to senators' recommendations regarding federal offices of special concern to them or in areas in which they profess some expertise. So, President Bush nominated one former aide of Senator Hatch to the Federal Circuit Court of Appeals and two others to the United States Claims Court. President Bush also took advantage of another form of senatorial courtesy: the deference shown by senators toward present and former colleagues nominated to some confirmable office. (Table 1 lists the eighty-eight senators who have later served in the cabinet, table 2 the seventy-three senators who later served as ambassadors or in other diplomatic posts, table 3 the fifteen senators who also served on the Supreme Court, and table 4 the seven former senators who failed to be confirmed for major confirmable positions.) He nominated two former senators to his cabinet: John Ashcroft as attorney general and Spencer Abraham as energy secretary. Abraham was confirmed after meeting little resistance, while Ashcroft's nomination met strong opposition because many Democratic senators were concerned about how vigorously he would enforce laws he had opposed as a senator. The Senate eventually confirmed him by the closest vote yet for a successful nominee for attorney general, with the critical difference provided by senators skeptical of Ashcroft who nonetheless voted to confirm because of senatorial courtesy.

A second significant pattern within the appointments process is the degree to which senatorial deference toward presidential nominations varies, depending on the level of the appointment. Various statistics suggest that the Senate is most deferential to subcabinet nominations, next-most deferential to nominations to cabinet offices, third-most deferential to lower court nominations, and least deferential to Supreme Court nominations. For example, one survey indicates that the Senate as a whole or in committee has formally rejected or forced the withdrawal of fewer than two hundred of the more than two million executive nominations made since 1932. It is noteworthy that every president has had some subcabinet nominees rejected and forced to be withdrawn. (see table 5). It is noteworthy as well that one of the most common reasons for opposing such nominees are problems with their political or constitutional views or their abilities or temperament, as judged by the Senate, to fulfill their duties fairly and evenhandedly in the offices to which they have been nominated. Senators care about these problems because the officials are expected to function with little daily supervision (and almost never by the presidents who nominated them) and because they are expected to work more closely with members of Congress and their staffs in monitoring the effectiveness of the laws in their fields. Thus, it was not surprising that President Bush's choice for solicitor general, Ted Olson, who had been active in trying to oust Bill Clinton from office and in other partisan causes throughout his career, was confirmed by the slimmest of margins only because a floor vote had been arranged on his nomination by Trent Lott in one of his last acts as majority leader before Democrats retook control of the Senate in 2001. Subsequently, Democrats blocked several of President Bush's subcabinet nominees, some of whom President Bush nevertheless appointed either by means of recess appointments or as acting appointments. One of these was none other than Justice Scalia's son, Eugene, whom the president had appointed as acting solicitor to the labor department. Not long after the midterm elections of 2002, Bush indicated that he would renominate Scalia for a permanent appointment to the position. Moreover, the Senate has formally rejected only nine cabinet nominations (see table 6), only two of which were of senators, and all but one of which occurred during periods of divided government. In addition, the Senate forced the withdrawal of nine other cabinet nominations (including that of Linda Chavez, President George W. Bush's initial choice as labor secretary), confirmed over seven hundred cabinet officers, and on several occasions confirmed cabinet officers after close votes or contentious hearings. These statistics reflect an apparent acceptance of the principle that a president must have his preferred team in place if he is to discharge his constitutional responsibilities, a belief that the close working relationship between cabinet and president will generally keep the cabinet officers in line, and senators' awareness they will have the means by which to make these officials (unlike federal judges) accountable through congressional oversight and informal interaction. The statistics suggest that cabinet nominees effectively enjoy a presumption of confirmation, which may be overcome only by serious problems: conflicts of interest (Charles Warren's close professional associations with the industry he was expected to monitor through enforcement of the antitrust laws as President Coolidge's attorney general), questionable ethics or integrity (Zoë Baird's failure to comply with tax laws she was expected to enforce as President Clinton's attorney general), failure to abide by certain standards of behavior (John Tower's engaging in personal misconduct that military personnel under his supervision as President Bush's defense secretary would have been discharged for committing), or commitment to problematic political or constitutional views (Roger Taney's actions to dismantle the National Bank as President Jackson's acting treasury secretary, Henry Stanberry's support for President Johnson's Reconstruction policies and help in securing Johnson's acquittal in his impeachment trial).

Supreme Court nominations have always been the most hotly contested. Twenty-eight Supreme Court nominees have failed to be confirmed by the Senate, including five senators (see table 7), and the Senate has approved at least fourteen other Supreme Court nominees only after close votes or intense, contentious confirmation proceedings.[2] At least ten of the twenty-eight nominees who failed did so primarily because of their constitutional or political views, which the opposition viewed as signaling how the nominees would likely have performed in office if confirmed; and with the fourteen successful but closely contested nominations, the nominees' political or constitutional views were the most commonly cited basis for opposition. Many of the most contentious Supreme Court nominations occurred during periods of divided government: the opposition party controlled the Senate when ten of the twenty-eight failed Supreme Court nominations were rejected by the Senate and during all but one of the fourteen closely contested nominations.[3] Nevertheless, concerns about Supreme Court nominees' ideology generally tend to transcend rigid party loyalty. The Senate is disposed to treat Supreme Court nominees with less deference than other nominees because once confirmed they wield unique power, have life tenure, and are generally immune to political retaliation.

These statistics further reflect the general view that the stakes involved ments. In his second term, President Cleveland got his third chance to make a Supreme Court appointment. Because the retiring justice was from New York, the expectation was that Cleveland would fill a seat with a New Yorker agreeable to the senior senator from his party, David Hill. President Cleveland turned twice to New Yorkers, both widely considered eminently qualified but neither approved by Hill, who gathered his colleagues to defend the prerogative of senatorial courtesy. President Cleveland had been willing to cater to the prevailing practice of filling a vacancy with someone from the retiring justice's state, but he was not disposed to cater to Hill, a leader of the anti-Cleveland faction among New York Democrats. Rather than nominate yet another New Yorker after the Senate at Hill's bidding had rejected two of his nominees, President Cleveland turned to a different norm to defeat Hill's resistance: he nominated Senator Edward Douglass White of Louisiana, whom the Senate quickly confirmed.

The battle was not over. When Justice Howell Jackson, a Southerner, died unexpectedly in 1895, President Cleveland did not nominate a Southerner to replace him but instead turned to a New Yorker. This time, he asked Hill's approval, which Hill gladly gave. In so doing, Cleveland was able to diminish the strength of the longstanding expectation that a president would replace a retiring justice with a nominee from the same state. In other words, Cleveland had found a way to employ existing norms to divide and conquer expected opposition.

A few other presidents since have similarly employed institutional norms to alter others norms or create new ones. Of particular significance, Presidents Reagan through Clinton have helped to establish a new norm of prior judicial experience as a prerequisite to Supreme Court selection More recently, President Clinton acted as a norm entrepreneur when he made a recess appointment of a federal judge in the closing days of his administration. In doing so, he deviated from the practice accepted for more than twenty years in which presidents did not make recess appointments of federal judges. The deviation was a response to the efforts of Senator Jesse Helms of North Carolina to put holds on all four of Clinton's nominees, three of whom were African American, to a seat on the Fourth Circuit that had traditionally gone to a North Carolinian. Helms's holds thwarted Clinton's objective to appoint the first African American to the Fourth Circuit. To maneuver around Helms's assertion of privilege, Clinton nominated for the seat an African American from a different state in the Fourth Circuit—Roger Gregory of Virginia. In late December 2000, Clinton named Gregory as a recess appointment to the Fourth Circuit, which would allow Gregory to serve until the end of the next congressional session.

The recess appointment put the onus on the incoming president, George W. Bush, to risk alienating African American voters by nominating someone other than Gregory to the vacancy that Gregory was filling as a recess appointee. Bush demurred by declaring he would defer to the preferences of Virginia's two Republican senators, John Warner and the newly elected George Allen. By late January 2001, Warner and Allen both asked President Bush to nominate Gregory. With both of Virginia's senators on record as supporting Gregory, there was enormous pressure on President Bush to renominate him, particularly in light of Senator Warner's admonition that "[w]hen two senators take the initiative as we have done, despite the unusual nominating process, I am confident the president will accede to our wishes." In May 2001, President Bush included Gregory among the first eleven people he nominated to the federal courts of appeals.

President Bush acted as a norm entrepreneur by jettisoning the longstanding norm of allowing the American Bar Association (ABA) to prescreen judicial nominees before their formal nominations by the President.[13] Beginning at the end of the Truman administration and extending through the first two years of Clinton's, both presidents and Senate leaders routinely requested and received formal ratings from the ABA on all judicial nominations. Ever since the ABA gave a mixed rating to Robert Bork as a Supreme Court nominee, many prominent Republicans challenged the organization's claim that its ratings are based on neutral, professional credentials and not on the ideologies of judicial nominees. In 1997 Senator Orrin Hatch, then chair of the Senate Judiciary Committee, concluded that these challenges had sufficient merit to justify doing away with the ABA's privileged status in testifying to the quality of judicial nominees. Thus he too acted as a norm entrepreneur. In spite of Hatch's edict, President Clinton continued to consult informally with the ABA before making his judicial nominations. President George W. Bush's decision not to restore the ABA to its privileged status in rating nominees provoked criticism from many Democratic senators, who after regaining control of the Senate in May 2001 slowed down all pending judicial nominations so that the ABA could rate the president's nominees, at least informally.[14] President Bush moved faster than his predecessors in making judicial nominations because his staff did not wait for the ABA to rate prospective nominees before their formal nominations, but his nominees from mid-2001 until the end of 2002 had to wait for an ABA rating for roughly six weeks after their nominations nonetheless, because the ratings were still used by Democrats on the Judiciary Committee. With Republicans back in control of the Senate as of January 2003, the expectation is that the ABA will lose even its informal role in rating judicial nominees for the foreseeable future.

Circumventing the ABA is only one of the innovations President Bush has made in the federal appointments process. His proposal to bring 170,000 existing federal workers from twenty-two agencies into his newly proposed Department of Homeland Security is the most ambitious reorganization plan for the federal government since President Truman created the Defense Department. Many Democratic senators had opposed the plan after the president proposed it in July 2001, in part because it contained provisions allowing his administration to bypass civil service rules in hiring, firing, promoting, and demoting employees of the new department. Democrats worried that these provisions would give the president carte blanche in removing career civil service employees whose replacements would be picked solely on the basis of political patronage. Congress approved the proposal nevertheless and substantially reduced civil service protections for the employees of the new department to a degree arguably unparalleled in any other federal agency.

President Bush's other innovation, announced shortly after the midterm elections, has been his executive order to place as many as 850,000 government jobs—nearly half the civilian work force—up for competition from private contractors in coming years. The stated reasons for the initiative are to save money and improve the quality of some government services. Critics worry that this innovation, like the new Department of

Homeland Security, might further weaken the civil service system and facilitate hiring based solely on political patronage.

President Bush's innovations in the federal appointments process call to mind some other presidents who turned to the American people to break critical impasses with the Senate. His campaign for his party to regain control of the Senate in midterm elections was not unlike the efforts of President Jackson: Stung by the Senate's rejections of many important nominations (including the nominations of his loyal lieutenant Roger Taney as treasury secretary and as an associate justice), Jackson campaigned in 1834 for more Democratic majorities in state legislatures, which at the time chose U.S. senators. His campaign was successful, and culminated in his renominating several people whom the Senate had previously rejected, including Roger Taney as chief justice of the United States. Similarly, President Franklin Roosevelt successfully campaigned around the country in 1934 and again in 1936 to increase the number of Democrats in the Senate to ensure more favorable receptions for his judicial nominees, his court-packing plan, and his New Deal initiatives. He got most of what he wanted, including a Senate which quickly and easily confirmed every one of his nine appointments to the Supreme Court.

Senators, too, have frequently acted as norm entrepreneurs. Thomas Walsh and Charles Curtis did so when they (and others) pressured Harlan Fiske Stone to become the first Supreme Court nominee to testify before the Senate Judiciary Committee in 1925. In 1979 Ted Kennedy initiated several other practices, most of which remain in effect to this day. He announced that senators who withheld the "blue slips" of persons nominated for judgeships from their states could no longer rely on the committee chair to kill the nominations. Senator Kennedy also directed that every nomination would be discussed by the full committee, and that the committee would determine whether to proceed with a nomination by holding a hearing. In addition, Kennedy arranged for the committee to adopt a questionnaire that all nominees would be required to complete and that would be made available to the public (with the exception of answers to a few questions). The committee also began to routinely publish its confirmation proceedings. Moreover, Kennedy invited various groups to testify before the committee and to rate judicial nominees. An especially important innovation was the establishment of the committee's own investigatory staff to examine the backgrounds of judicial nominees apart from Justice Department inquiries.

IN CLOSING, I hasten to clarify the focus and perspective of this book. First, it is tempting to wonder about the extent to which comparisons of presidential and senatorial activity in different historical periods are useful, because so much has changed in the federal appointments process over time. For instance, Senate committees have wielded significant authority over appointments decisions, particularly since the Second World War. Their influence extends far beyond judicial appointments, as reflected in the events of the fall of 2002, when the threats of a Senate investigation forced both the resignation of Harvey Pitt as the head of the Securities and Exchange Commission and the withdrawal of William Webster as his choice to lead a new board in charge of overseeing the accounting industry. It is true that committees are more powerful now than ever before, but there were various means in the late eighteenth century and the nineteenth, as now, by which individual senators might be able to prevent final Senate action on nominations. In the end, what is critical is not how much senatorial power has changed over time; what is critical, and I hope I am sufficiently sensitive to this point, is how, or to what extent, differences in power are relevant to the operations of the federal appointments process.

Second, my hope is that the focus in the book roughly approximates presidents' and senators' relative preoccupation with judicial appointments. Their preoccupation stems from their recognition that a president's judicial appointments can have enormous impact on the future direction of constitutional law and that once confirmed his appointees perform largely beyond their means to control. Because there is little common ground among Republicans and Democrats over the appropriate qualifications for federal judicial nominees, senators from both parties end up having to expend a great deal of energy monitoring judicial selection. I leave it to individual readers to decide if either the Congress or I should pay more (or less) attention to the quality of federal appointments besides those to the federal courts.

Third, the historiography in this book is admittedly not original. Much if not all of the historiography undertaken by institutionalists does not purport to be original, and I claim to be no exception among these schol-ars. While I would note some novel revelations about James Polk, James Garfield, and Grover Cleveland, among others, novelty is not my objec-tive. Instead, my objective has been more modest, namely to provide a framework for understanding the operation of the federal appointments process. I defer to readers' judgments on the utility of this framework, as described more fully in the introduction to the original edition of this book.

Last but not least, I wish to acknowledge the many people who have given me useful assistance and feedback in completing this edition. To begin with, this edition benefits from the hard work of Paul Dame, Wil-liam & Mary Law School Class of 2003, who helped to put together the new tables included in this edition. These tables include useful informa-tion on the apparent reasons for failed nominations as well as the com-position of the Senate at the time of the president's cabinet, judicial, and other nominations.

I am also particularly grateful to Tom Baker, Stephen Carter, Sheldon Goldman, Carl Tobias, and Keith Whittington for setting me straight on a few details of notable incidents discussed in the original edition of this book and now corrected. The remaining errors are, alas, my own.

Most importantly, I wish to acknowledge the people without whose support this book, like everything else I do, would not be possible. First and foremost, I thank my wife Deborah, particularly for her incessant desire to spend more rather than less time with me. Second, I am grateful to my three sons, Benjamin, Daniel, and Noah, who are the three best men I know.

December 1, 2002
M.J.G.
Williamsburg, Virginia

TABLE I Senators Who Later Served as Cabinet Members, 1789–2002

Name and Party Affiliation in Senate	Position	Nominating President	Party Breakdown in Senate at Confirmation[1]	Years of Cabinet Service	Years of Senate Service
Abraham, Spencer (R-Mich.)	Energy	George W. Bush (R)	R-50 D-50	2001–	1995–2001
Adams, John Quincy (F-Mass.)	State	Monroe (DR)	DR-34 F-10	1817–25	1803–8
Armstrong, John, Jr. (R-N.Y.)	War	Madison (DR)	DR-27 F-9	1813–14	1800–2, 1803–4
Ashcroft, John (R-Mo.)	Atty. general	George W. Bush (R)	R-50 D-50	2001–	1995–2001
Barbour, James (R/CrR-Va.)	War	J. Q. Adams (DR)	AD-26 J-20	1825–28	1815–25
Barry, William T. (R-Ky.)	Postmaster general	Jackson (D)	D-26 NR-22	1829–36	1814–16
Bayard, T.F., Sr. (D-Del.)	State	Cleveland (D)	R-43 D-34	1885–89	1869–85
Bentsen, Lloyd (D-Tex.)	Treasury	Clinton (D)	D-57 R-43	1993–94	1971–93
Berrien, John M. (J/W-Ga.)	Atty. general	Jackson (D)	D-26 NR-22	1829–31	1825–29, 1841–45, 1845–52

TABLE I (continued)

Name and Party Affiliation in Senate	Position	Nominating President	Party Breakdown in Senate at Confirmation[1]	Years of Cabinet Service	Years of Senate Service
Bibb, George M. (R/J-Ky.)	Treasury	Tyler (W)	W-28 D-25	1844–45	1811–14, 1829–35
Blaine, James G. (R-Me.)	State	Garfield/ Arthur (R)	R-37 D-37	1881	1876–81
Brady, Nicholas F. (R-N.J.)	Treasury	G. H. W. Bush (R)	D-55 R-45	1989–93	1982
Branch, John (CrR/ J-N.C.)	Navy	Jackson (D)	D-26 NR-22	1829–31	1823–29
Breckinridge, John (R-Ky.)	Atty. general	Jefferson (DR)	DR-27 F-7	1805–6	1801–5
Brock, William E., III (R-Tenn.)	Labor	Reagan (R)	R-53 D-47	1985–87	1971–77
Browning, Orville H. (R-Ill.)	Interior	A. Johnson (R)	U-42 D-10	1866–69	1861–63
Buchanan, James (J/D-Pa.)	State	Polk (D)	D-31 W-25	1845–49	1834–45
Byrnes, James F. (D-S.C.)	State	Truman (D)	D-56 R-38	1945–47	1931–41

TABLE I   (continued)

Name and Party Affiliation in Senate	Position	Nominating President	Party Breakdown in Senate at Confirmation[1]	Years of Cabinet Service	Years of Senate Service
Calhoun, John C. (N/D-S.C.)[2]	State	Tyler (W)	W-28 D-25	1844–45	1832–43, 1845–50
Cameron, Simon (R-Pa.)	War	Lincoln (R)	R-31 D-10	1861–62	1845–49, 1857–61, 1867–77
Campbell, George W. (R-Tenn.)	Treasury	Madison (DR)	DR-27 F-9	1814	1811–14, 1815–18
Carlisle, John G. (D-Ky.)	Treasury	Cleveland (D)	D-44 R-38	1893–97	1890–93
Cass, Lewis (D-Mich.)[3]	State	Buchanan (D)	D-36 R-20	1857–60	1845–48, 1849–57
Chandler, Zachariah (R-Mich.)	Interior	Grant (R)	R-45 D-29	1875–77	1857–75, 1879
Chase, Salmon P. (FS/R-Ohio)	Treasury	Lincoln (R)	R-31 D-10	1861–64	1849–55, 1861
Clay, Henry (R/AJ/ W-Ky.)	State	J. Q. Adams (DR)	AD-26 J-10	1825–29	1806–7, 1810–11, 1831–42, 1849–52
Clayton, John M. (AJ/W/ Op-Del.)	State	Taylor (W)	D-35 W-25	1849–50	1829–36, 1845–49, 1853–56

TABLE I (continued)

Name and Party Affiliation in Senate	Position	Nominating President	Party Breakdown in Senate at Confirmation[1]	Years of Cabinet Service	Years of Senate Service
Cohen, William S. (R-Me.)	Defense	Clinton (D)	R-55 D-45	1997–2001	1979–97
Conrad, Charles M. (W-La.)	War	Fillmore (W)	D-35 W-25	1850–53	1842–43
Corwin, Thomas (W-Ohio)	Treasury	Fillmore (W)	D-35 W-25	1850–53	1845–50
Crawford, William H. (R-Ga.)	War	Madison (DR)	DR-27 F-9	1815–16	1807–13
Crawford, William H. (R-Ga.)	Treasury	Madison/ Monroe (DR)	DR-25 F-11	1816–25	1807–13
Creswell, John A. J. (UU-Md.)	Postmaster general	Grant (R)	R-56 D-11	1869–74	1865–67
Crittenden, John J. (R/AJ/W/ Op/Am-Ky.)	Atty. general	W. Harrison/ Tyler (W) and Fillmore (W)	W-28 D-22	1841, 1850–53	1817–19, 1835–41, 1842–48, 1855–61
Davis, Jefferson F. (D-Miss.)	War	Pierce (D)	D-38 W-22	1853–57	1847–51, 1857–61

TABLE I   (continued)

Name and Party Affiliation in Senate	Position	Nominating President	Party Breakdown in Senate at Confirmation[1]	Years of Cabinet Service	Years of Senate Service
Dexter, Samuel (F-Mass.)	War	J. Adams (F)	F-19 DR-13	1800–1801	1799–1800
Dexter, Samuel (F-Mass.)	Treasury	J. Adams (F)/Jefferson (DR)	DR-18 F-13	1801	1799–1800
Dickerson, Mahlon (R/CrR/ J-N.J.)	Navy	Jackson/Van Buren (D)	NR-26 D-20	1834–38	1817–29, 1829–33
Dix, John A. (D-N.Y.)	Treasury	Buchanan (D)	D-36 R-26	1861	1845–49
Dulles, John Foster (R-N.Y.)	State	Eisenhower (R)	R-48 D-47	1953–59	1949
Eaton, John H. (R/JR/ J-Tenn.)	War	Jackson (D)	D-26 NR-22	1829–31	1818–21, 1821–29
Ewing, Thomas (AJ/W-Ohio)	Treasury	W. Harrison/ Tyler (W)	W-28 D-22	1841	1831–37, 1850–51
Ewing, Thomas (AJ/W-Ohio)	Interior	Taylor/ Fillmore (W)	D-35 W-25	1849–50	1831–37, 1850–51
Fall, Albert B. (R-N.M.)	Interior	Harding (R)	R-59 D-37	1921–23	1912–21

TABLE I   (continued)

Name and Party Affiliation in Senate	Position	Nominating President	Party Breakdown in Senate at Confirmation[1]	Years of Cabinet Service	Years of Senate Service
Fessenden, William P. (W/Op/ R-Me.)	Treasury	Lincoln (R)	R-36 D-9	1864–65	1854–64, 1865–69
Fish, Hamilton (W/Op-N.Y.)	State	Grant (R)	R-56 D-11	1869–77	1851–57
Forsyth, John (R/J-Ga.)	State	Jackson/Van Buren (D)	D-20 NR-20	1834–41	1818–19, 1829–34
Frelinghuysen, F.T. (R-N.J.)	State	Arthur (R)	R-37 D-37	1881–85	1866–69, 1871–77
Garland, Augustus H. (D-Ark.)	Atty. general	Cleveland (D)	R-43 D-34	1885–89	1877–85
Graham, William A. (W-N.C.)	Navy	Fillmore (W)	D-35 W-24	1850–52	1840–43
Grundy, Felix (J/D-Tenn.)	Atty. general	Van Buren (D)	D-30 W-18	1838–39	1829–38, 1839–40
Harlan, James (Op/R-Ia.)	Interior	A. Johnson (R)	U-42 D-10	1865–66	1855–57, 1857–65, 1867–73
Howe, Timothy O. (R-Wis.)	Postmaster general	Arthur (R)	R-37 D-37	1882–83	1861–79

TABLE I (continued)

Name and Party Affiliation in Senate	Position	Nominating President	Party Breakdown in Senate at Confirmation[1]	Years of Cabinet Service	Years of Senate Service
Hull, Cordell (D-Tenn.)	State	F. D. Roosevelt (D)	D-60 R-35	1933–44	1931–33
Johnson, Reverdy (W/U/ D-Md.)	Atty. general	Taylor/ Fillmore (W)	D-35 W-25	1849–50	1845–49, 1863–68
Kellogg, Frank B. (R-Minn.)	State	Coolidge (R)	R-56 D-39	1925–29	1917–23
Key, David M. (D-Tenn.)	Postmaster general	Hayes (R)	R-39 D-36	1877–80	1875–77
Kirkwood, Samuel J. (R-Ia.)	Interior	Garfield/ Arthur (R)	R-37 D-37	1881–82	1866–67, 1877–81
Knox, Philander C. (R-Pa.)[4]	State	Taft (R)	R-61 D-32	1909–13	1904–9, 1917–21
Lamar, Lucius Q. C. (D-Miss.)	Interior	Cleveland (D)	R-43 D-34	1885–88	1877–85
Livingston, Edward (J-La.)	State	Jackson (D)	D-25 NR-21	1831–33	1829–31
McGrath, James H. (D-R.I.)	Atty. general	Truman (D)	D-54 R-42	1949–52	1947–49

TABLE I (continued)

Name and Party Affiliation in Senate	Position	Nominating President	Party Breakdown in Senate at Confirmation[1]	Years of Cabinet Service	Years of Senate Service
McLane, Louis (J-Del.)	Treasury	Jackson (D)	D-25 NR-21	1831–33	1827–29
McLane, Louis (J-Del.)	State	Jackson (D)	D-20 NR-20	1833–34	1827–29
Marcy, William L. (J-N.Y.)	War	Polk (D)	D-31 W-25	1845–49	1831–33
Marcy, William L. (J-N.Y.)	State	Pierce (D)	D-38 W-22	1853–57	1831–33
Meigs, Return J., Jr. (R-Ohio)	Postmaster general	Madison/ Monroe (DR)	DR-27 F-9	1814–23	1808–10
Monroe, James (Anti-Admin-Va.)	State	Madison (DR)	DR-30 F-6	1811–17	1790–94
Monroe, James (Anti-Admin-Va.)	War[5]	Madison (DR)	DR-27 F-9	1814–15	1790–94
Morrill, Lot M. (R-Me.)	Treasury	Grant (R)	R-45 D-29	1876–77	1861–69, 1869–76
Muskie, Edmund S. (D-Me.)	State	Carter (D)	D-58 R-41	1980–81	1959–80

TABLE I (continued)

Name and Party Affiliation in Senate	Position	Nominating President	Party Breakdown in Senate at Confirmation[1]	Years of Cabinet Service	Years of Senate Service
New, Harry S. (R-Ind.)	Postmaster general	Harding/ Coolidge (R)	R-51 D-43	1923–29	1917–23
Niles, John M. (J/D-Conn.)	Postmaster general	Van Buren (D)	D-28 W-22	1840–41	1835–39, 1843–49
Ramsey, Alexander (R-Minn.)	War	Hayes (R)	D-42 R-33	1879–81	1863–75
Saxbe, William (R-Ohio)	Atty. general	Nixon/Ford (R)	D-56 R-42	1974–75	1969–74
Schurz, Carl (R/LR-Mo.)	Interior	Hayes (R)	R-39 D-36	1877–81	1869–75
Schweiker, Richard (R-Pa.)	Health & Human Services	Reagan (R)	R-53 D-46	1981–83	1969–81
Schwellenbach, L. B. (D-Wash.)	Labor	Truman (D)	D-56 R-38	1945–48	1935–40
Seaton, Frederick A. (R-Neb.)	Interior	Eisenhower (R)	D-48 R-47	1956–61	1951–52
Seward, William H. (W/Op/ R-N.Y.)	State	Lincoln/ A. Johnson (R)	R-31 D-10	1861–69	1849–61

TABLE I (continued)

Name and Party Affiliation in Senate	Position	Nominating President	Party Breakdown in Senate at Confirmation[1]	Years of Cabinet Service	Years of Senate Service
Sherman, John (R-Ohio)	Treasury	Hayes (R)	R-39 D-36	1877–81	1861–77, 1881–97
Sherman, John (R-Ohio)	State	McKinley (R)	R-47 D-34	1897–98	1861–77, 1881–97
Southard, Samuel L. (R/AJ/W-N.J.)	Navy	Monroe/ J. Q. Adams (DR)	DR-44 F-4	1823–29	1821–23, 1833–42
Southard, Samuel L. (R/AJ/W-N.J.)	Treasury	J. Q. Adams (DR)	AD-26 J-20	1825	1821–23, 1833–42
Southard, Samuel L. (R/AJ/W-N.J.)	War	J. Q. Adams (DR)	J-28 AD-20	1828	1821–23, 1833–42
Swanson, Claude A. (D-Va.)	Navy	F. D. Roosevelt (D)	D-60 R-35	1933–39	1910–33
Teller, Henry M. (R/SR/ D-Colo.)	Interior	Arthur (R)	R-37 D-37	1882–85	1876–82, 1885–97, 1897–1903
Toucey, Isaac (D-Conn.)[6]	Navy	Buchanan (D)	D-36 R-20	1857–61	1852–57
Van Buren, Martin (R/CrR/ J-N.Y.)	State	Jackson (DR)	D-26 NR-22	1829–31	1821–28

TABLE I (continued)

Name and Party Affiliation in Senate	Position	Nominating President	Party Breakdown in Senate at Confirmation[1]	Years of Cabinet Service	Years of Senate Service
Walker, Robert J. (J/D-Miss.)	Treasury	Polk (D)	D-31 W-25	1845–49	1835–45
Webster, Daniel (Adams/AJ/ W-Mass.)	State	W. Harrison/ Tyler (W) and Fillmore (W)	W-28 D-22	1841–43, 1850–52	1827–41, 1845–50
Weeks, John W. (R-Mass.)	War	Harding/ Coolidge (R)	R-59 D-37	1921–25	1913–19
Weeks, Sinclair (R-Mass.)	Commerce	Eisenhower (R)	R-48 D-47	1953–58	1944
Wilkins, William (J-Pa.)	War	Tyler (W)	W-28 D-25	1844–45	1831–34
Williams, G. Henry (R-Oreg.)	Atty. general	Grant (R)	R-52 D-17	1872–75	1865–71
Windom, William (R-Minn.)	Treasury	Garfield/ Arthur and B. Harrison (R)	R-37 D-37	1881, 1889–91	1870–71, 1871–81, 1881–83
Woodbury, Levi (J/D-N.H.)	Navy	Jackson (D)	D-25 NR-21	1831–34	1825–31, 1841–45

TABLE I (continued)

Name and Party Affiliation in Senate	Position	Nominating President	Party Breakdown in Senate at Confirmation[1]	Years of Cabinet Service	Years of Senate Service
Woodbury, Levi (J/D-N.H.)	Treasury	Jackson (D)	D-20 NR-20	1834–41	1825–31, 1841–45

1. Majority party and largest minority party only. For senators who were nominated twice for the same position, only the party breakdown at the time of the first confirmation is given.

2. Also served as secretary of war under President Monroe from 1817 to 1825 before his service in the Senate.

3. Also served as secretary of war under President Jackson from 1831 to 1836 before his service in the Senate.

4. Served as attorney general in McKinley's and Theodore Roosevelt's administrations from 1901to 1904 before being elected to the Senate.

5. While also continuing as secretary of state.

6. Served as attorney general under President Polk from 1848 to 1849 before being elected to the Senate.

AJ: Anti-Jackson
Am: American (Know-Nothing)
Anti-Admin: Anti-Administration
CrR: Crawford Republican
D: Democrat
DR: Democratic-Republican
F: Federalist

FS: Free Soil
J: Jacksonian
JR: Jacksonian Republican
LR: Liberal Republican
N: Nullifier
NR: National Republican

Op: Oppositions
R: Republican
SR: Silver Republican
U: Unionist
UU: Unconditional Unionist
W: Whig

SOURCES: 2 *Congressional Quarterly, Guide to Congress* 1094–96 (5th ed., 2000); Senate Historical Office, *Senators Who Have Served as Cabinet Members* (November 2002); U.S. Congress, Senate, *Biographical Directory of the United States Congress, 1774–1989*, S. Doc. 100–34, 100th Cong., 2d sess., 1989.

TABLE 2   Senators Who Later Served as Diplomats, 1789–2002

Name and Party Affiliation in Senate	Position	Nominating President	Party Breakdown in Senate at Confirmation[1]	Years of Senate Service
Adams, John Quincy (F-Mass.)[2]	Russia, 1809–14 (MP); United Kingdom, 1815–17 (EE/MP)	Madison (DR)	DR-28 F-6; DR-27 F-9	1803–8
Armstrong, John, Jr. (R-N.Y.)	France, 1804–10 (MP)	Jefferson (DR)	DR-25 F-9	1800–1802, 1803–4
Austin, Warren R. (R-Vt.)	United Nations, 1947–53 (representative)	Truman (D)	R-51 D-45	1931–46
Bagby, Arthur P. (D-Ala.)	Russia, 1848–49 (EE/MP)	Polk (D)	D-36 W-21	1841–48
Baker, Howard H., Jr. (R-Tenn.)	Japan, 2001– (ambassador)	George W. Bush (R)	R-50 D-50	1967–85
Barbour, James (R/CRR-Va.)	United Kingdom, 1828–29 (EE/MP)	J. Q. Adams (DR)	J-28 AD-20	1815–23, 1823–25
Bayard, Richard H. (AJ/W-Del.)	Belgium, 1850–53 (CdA)	Fillmore (W)	D-35 W-25	1836–39, 1841–45
Bayard, Thomas F. (D-Del.)	Great Britain, 1893–97 (AEP)	Cleveland (D)	D-44 R-38	1869–85
Borland, Solon (D-Ark.)	Central America, 1853–54 (EE/MP)	Pierce (D)	D-38 W-22	1848–53
Brock, William E., III (R-Tenn.)	U.S. trade representative, 1981–85	Reagan (R)	R-53 D-46	1971–77

TABLE 2   (continued)

Name and Party Affiliation in Senate	Position	Nominating President	Party Breakdown in Senate at Confirmation[1]	Years of Senate Service
Brown, Ethan Allen (R-Ohio)	Brazil, 1830–34 (CdA)	Jackson (DR)	D-26 NR-22	1822–25
Buchanan, James (J/D-Pa.)	Russia, 1832–33 (EE/MP); United Kingdom, 1853–56 (EE/MP)	Jackson (D); Pierce (D)	D-25 NR-21; D-38 W-22	1834–45
Cameron, Simon (D, R-Pa.)	Russia, 1862 (EE/MP)	Lincoln (R)	R-31 D-10	1845–49, 1857–61, 1867–77
Campbell, George W. (R-Tenn.)	Russia, 1818–20 (EE/MP)	Monroe (DR)	DR-34 F-10	1811–14, 1815–18
Cheney, Person C. (R-N.H.)	Switzerland, 1892–93 (EE/MP)	B. Harrison (R)	R-47 D-39	1886–87
Christiancy, Isaac P. (R-Mich.)	Peru, 1879–81 (EE/MP)	Hayes (R)	D-42 R-33	1875–79
Clark, Richard C. (D-Ia.)	Ambassador at large, 1979	Carter (D)	D-58 R-41	1973–79
Clayton, Powell (R-Ark.)	Mexico, 1897–1905 (EE/MP, AEP)	McKinley (R)	R-47 D-34	1871–77
Cooper, John Sherman (R-Ky.)	India and Nepal, 1955–56 (AEP); German Democratic Republic, 1974–76 (AEP)	Eisenhower (R); Nixon (R)	D-48 R-47; D-56 R-42	1946–49, 1952–55, 1956–73

1

TABLE 2 (continued)

Name and Party Affiliation in Senate	Position	Nominating President	Party Breakdown in Senate at Confirmation[1]	Years of Senate Service
Corwin, Thomas (W-Ohio)	Mexico, 1861–64 (EE/MP)	Lincoln (R)	R-31 D-10	1845–50
Crawford, William H. (R-Ga.)	France, 1813–15 (MP)	Madison (DR)	DR-27 F-9	1807–13
Dallas, George M. (J-Pa.)	Russia, 1837–39 (EE/MP); United Kingdom, 1856–61 (EE/MP)	Van Buren (D); Pierce (D)	D-30 W-18; D-40 R-15	1831–33
Dayton, William L. (W-N.J.)	France, 1861–64 (EE/MP)	Lincoln (R)	R-31 D-10	1842–51
Dix, John A. (D-N.Y.)	France, 1866–69 (EE/MP)	A. Johnson (R)	U-42 D-10	1845–49
Dodge, Augustus C. (D-Ia.)	Spain, 1855–59 (EE/MP)	Pierce (D)	D-38 W-22	1848–55
Dominick, Peter H. (R-Colo.)	Switzerland, 1975 (AEP)	Ford (R)	D-60 R-37	1963–75
Eaton, John H. (R/JR/J-Tenn.)	Spain, 1836–40 (EE/MP)	Jackson (D)	D-27 W-25	1818–29
Edge, Walter E. (R-N.J.)	France, 1929–33 (AEP)	Hoover (R)	R-56 D-39	1919–29
Ellis, Powhatan (J-Miss.)	Mexico, 1836 (CdA); Mexico, 1839–42 (EE/MP)	Jackson (D); Van Buren (D)	D-27 W-25; D-30 W-18	1825–32

TABLE 2 (continued)

Name and Party Affiliation in Senate	Position	Nominating President	Party Breakdown in Senate at Confirmation[1]	Years of Senate Service
Eustis, James B. (D-La.)	France, 1893–97 (AEP)	Cleveland (D)	D-44 R-38	1876–79, 1885–91
Ferguson, Homer (R-Mich.)	Philippines, 1955–56 (AEP)	Eisenhower (R)	D-48 R-47	1943–55
Forsyth, John (R/J-Ga.)	Spain, 1819–23 (MP)	Monroe (DR)	DR-34 F-10	1818–19, 1829–34
Fowler, Wyche, Jr. (D-Ga.)	Saudi Arabia, 1997– (ambassador)	Clinton (D)	R-55 D-45	1987–93
Hale, John P. (ID/FS/Op/ R-N.H.)	Spain, 1865–69 (EE/MP)	A. Johnson (R)	U-42 D-10	1847–53, 1855–65
Hamlin, Hannibal (D/R-Me.)	Spain, 1881–82 (EE/MP)	Garfield (R)	R-37 D-37	1848–61, 1869–81
Hannegan, Edward A. (D-Ind.)	Prussia, 1849–50 (EE/MP)	Polk (D)	D-36 W-21	1843–49
Hecht, Chic (R-Nev.)	Bahamas, 1989–94 (AEP)	G. H. W. Bush (R)	D-55 R-45	1983–89
Hendrickson, Robert C. (R-N.J.)	New Zealand, 1955–56 (AEP)	Eisenhower (R)	D-48 R-47	1949–55
Hunter, William (F-R.I.)	Brazil, 1834–43 (CdA, EE/MP)	Jackson (D)	D-20 NR-20	1811–21
Johnson, Reverdy (W/U/D-Md.)	England, 1868–69 (EE/MP)	A. Johnson (R)	R-42 D-11	1845–49

TABLE 2 (continued)

Name and Party Affiliation in Senate	Position	Nominating President	Party Breakdown in Senate at Confirmation[1]	Years of Senate Service
Jones, George W. (D-Ia.)	New Granada,[3] 1859–61 (MR)	Buchanan (D)	D-36 R-26	1848–59
Keating, Kenneth B. (R-N.Y.)	India, 1969–72 (AEP); Israel, 1973–75 (AEP)	Nixon (R)	D-57 R-43; D-56 R-42	1959–65
Kellogg, Frank B. (R-Minn.)	Great Britain, 1923–25 (AEP)	Coolidge (R)	R-51 D-43	1917–23
King, Rufus (Pro-Admin/F-N.Y.)	Great Britain, 1796–1803 (MP); United Kingdom, 1825–26 (EE/MP)	Washington (F); J. Q. Adams (DR)	F-19 DR-13; AD-26 J-20	1789–96, 1813–25
King, William R. (R/JR/J/D-Ala.)	France, 1844–46 (EE/MP)	Tyler (W)	W-28 D-25	1819–44, 1838–52
Krueger, Robert C. (D-Tex.)[4]	Burundi, 1994–95 (ambassador); Botswana, 1996– (ambassador)	Clinton (D)	D-57 R-43	1993
Livingston, Edward (J-La.)	France, 1833–35 (EE/MP)	Jackson (D)	D-25 NR-21	1829–31
Lodge, Henry C., Jr. (R-Mass.)	United Nations, 1953–60 (representative); Vietnam, 1963–64, 1965–67 (AEP); Ambassador at large, 1967–68; Germany, 1968–69 (AEP); Vatican, 1970–77 (personal representative)	Eisenhower (R); L. B. Johnson (D); L. B. Johnson (D); L. B. Johnson (D); Nixon (R)	R-48 D-47; D-67 R-33; D-68 R-32; D-64 R-36; D-57 R-43	1937–44, 1947–53

TABLE 2   (continued)

Name and Party Affiliation in Senate	Position	Nominating President	Party Breakdown in Senate at Confirmation[1]	Years of Senate Service
Mansfield, Michael J. (D-Mont.)	Japan, 1977–88 (AEP)	Carter (D)	D-61 R-38	1953–77
Mattingly, Mack F. (R-Ga.)	Seychelles, 1992– (AEP)	G. H. W. Bush (R)	D-56 R-44	1981–87
McGee, Gale (D-Wyo.)	OAS, 1977–81 (permanent representative)	Carter (D)	D-61 R-38	1959–77
McLane, Louis (J-Del.)	United Kingdom, 1829–31 (EE/MP)	Jackson (DR)	D-26 NR-22	1827–29
Mondale, Walter F. (D-Minn.)	Japan, 1993–96 (AEP)	Clinton (D)	D-57 R-43	1964–76
Monroe, James (Anti-Admin-Va.)	France, 1794–96 (MP); Great Britain, 1803–7 (MP)	Washington (F); Jefferson (DR)	F-17 DR-13; DR-18 F-13	1790–94
Moseley-Braun, Carol (D-Ill.)	New Zealand, 1999–2001 (ambassador)	Clinton (D)	R-55 D-45	1993–99
Palmer, Thomas W. (R-Mich.)	Spain, 1889–90 (EE/MP)	B. Harrison (R)	R-39 D-37	1883–89
Pendleton, George H. (D-Ohio)	Germany, 1885–89 (EE/MP)	Cleveland (D)	R-43 D-34	1879–85

TABLE 2 (continued)

Name and Party Affiliation in Senate	Position	Nominating President	Party Breakdown in Senate at Confirmation[1]	Years of Senate Service
Piles, Samuel H. (R-Wash.)	Colombia, 1922–28 (EE/MP)	Harding (R)	R-59 D-37	1905–11
Pinckney, Charles (R-S.C.)	Spain, 1801–4 (MP)	Jefferson (DR)	DR-18 F-13	1789–1801
Poindexter, Miles (R/PR-Wash.)	Peru, 1923–28 (AEP)	Coolidge (R)	R-51 D-43	1911–23
Ransom, Matt W. (D-N.C.)	Mexico, 1895–97 (EE/MP)	Cleveland (D)	R-43 D-39	1872–95
Rives, William C. (J/D/W-Va.)[5]	France, 1849–53 (EE/MP)	Taylor (W)	D-35 W-25	1832–34, 1836–39, 1841–45
Sackett, Frederic M. (R-Ky.)	Germany, 1930–33 (AEP)	Hoover (R)	R-56 D-39	1925–30
Sargent, Aaron A. (R-Calif.)	Germany, 1882–84 (EE/MP)	Garfield (R)	R-37 D-37	1873–79
Sasser, James R. (D-Tenn.)	China, 1995–99	Clinton (D)	R-53 D-47	1977–95
Saxbe, William B. (R-Ohio)	India, 1975–76 (AEP)	Ford (R)	D-56 R-42	1969–74
Soulé, Pierre (D-La.)	Spain, 1853–55 (EE/MP)	Pierce (D)	D-38 W-22	1847, 1849–53
Stone, Richard B. (D-Fla.)	Ambassador at large, 1983–84	Reagan (R)	R-54 D-46	1975–80

TABLE 2 (continued)

Name and Party Affiliation in Senate	Position	Nominating President	Party Breakdown in Senate at Confirmation[1]	Years of Senate Service
Van Buren, Martin (R/CRR/J-N.Y.)	United Kingdom, 1831–32 (EE/MP)[6]	Jackson (D)	D-25 NR-21	1821–28
Weller, John B. (D-Calif.)	Mexico, 1860–61 (EE/MP)	Buchanan (D)	D-36 R-26	1852–57
Wilkins, William (J-Pa.)	Russia, 1834–35 (EE/MP)	Jackson (D)	D-20 NR-20	1831–34
Williams, John (R-Tenn.)	Central America, 1825–26 (CdA)	J. Q. Adams (DR)	AD-26 J-20	1815–23
Wright, Joseph A.(U-Ind.)[7]	Prussia, 1865–67 (EE/MP)	A. Johnson (R)	U-42 D-10	1862–63

1. Majority party and largest minority party only. For senators who were nominated twice for the same position, only the party breakdown at the time of the first confirmation is given.
2. Also served in the following capacities before his service in the Senate: Netherlands, 1794–97 (MR); Prussia, 1797–1801 (MR).
3. Colombia.
4. Before his service in the Senate, was ambassador at large from 1979 to 1981.
5. Before his service in the Senate, was a diplomat in France from 1829 to 1832.
6. Nomination rejected by the Senate in January 1832 after he had begun his service.
7. Before his service in the Senate, held the same diplomatic post in Germany from 1857 to 1861.

AEP: Ambassador Extraordinary and Plenipotentiary	EE/MP: Envoy Extraordinary and Minister Plenipotentiary	MR: Minister Resident
CdA: Chargé d'affaires	MP: Minister Plenipotentiary	OAS: Organization of American States

AJ: Anti-Jackson	FS: Free Soil	PR: Progressive
Anti-Admin: Anti-Administration	ID: Independent Democrat	Pro-Admin: Pro-Administration
CrR: Crawford Republican	J: Jacksonian	R: Republican
D: Democrat	JR: Jacksonian Republican	U: Unionist
DR: Democratic-Republican	NR: National Republican	W: Whig
F: Federalist	Op: Opposition	

SOURCES: 2 *Congressional Quarterly, Guide to Congress* 1094–96 (5th ed., 2000); Senate Historical Office, *Senators Who Served as Ambassadors or Held Diplomatic Appointments* (May 2001); U.S. Department of State, *Principal Officers of the Department of State and United States Chiefs of Mission, 1778–1990,* available at http://www.state.gov/r/pa/ho/po/ (last visited 24 Nov. 2002).

TABLE 3　Senators as Supreme Court Justices

Name and Party Affiliation in Senate	Nominating President	Party Break-down in Senate at Confirmation[1]	Year of Confirmation
William Patterson (Adams-N.J.)	Washington (F)	F-17 DR-13	1793
Oliver Ellsworth (Adams/ F-Conn.)*	Washington (F)	F-19 DR-13	1796
John McKinley (J/D-Ala.)	Van Buren (D)	D-30 W-18	1837
Levi Woodbury (J/D-N.H.)	Polk (D)	D-31 W-25	1846
David Davis (I-Ill.)[2]	Lincoln (R)	R-31 D-10	1862
Salmon P. Chase (R-Ohio)*	Lincoln (R)	R-36 D-9	1864
Stanley Matthews (R-Ohio)	Garfield (R)	R-37 D-37	1881
Lucius Q. C. Lamar (D-Miss.)	Cleveland (D)	R-43 D-34	1888
Howell E. Jackson (D-Tenn.)	B. Harrison (R)	R-47 D-39	1893
Edward D. White (D-La.)	Cleveland (D)	D-44 R-38	1894
Edward D. White (D-La.)*	Taft (R)	R-61 D-32	1910
George Sutherland (R-Utah)	Harding (R)	R-59 D-37	1922

TABLE 3 (continued)

Name and Party Affiliation in Senate	Nominating President	Party Break- down in Senate at Confirmation[1]	Year of Confirmation
Hugo L. Black (D-Ala.)	F. D. Roosevelt (D)	D-76 R-16	1937
James F. Byrnes (D-S.C.)	F. D. Roosevelt (D)	D-66 R-28	1941
Harold H. Burton (R-Ohio)	Truman (D)	D-56 R-38	1945
Sherman Minton (D-Ind.)	Truman (D)	D-54 R-42	1949

Total: 16 (including White twice)

1. Majority party and largest minority party only.
2. Only justice who served in the Senate after his term on the Court.

* denotes chief justice.

D: Democrat   I: Independent
DR: Democratic-Republican   R: Republican
F: Federalist

SOURCES: 4 Robert C. Byrd, *The Senate, 1789–1989: Historical Statistics, 1789–1992* 253, 692–98; 2 *Congressional Quarterly, Guide to Congress* 1094–96 (5th ed., 2000).

TABLE 4 Former Senators Not Confirmed for Major Confirmable Positions, 1789–2002

Name	Position	Nominating President	Party Breakdown in Senate[1]	Year of Final Action	Major Reason
John J. Crittenden	Associate justice	John Quincy Adams (DR)	J-28 Admin-20	1829	Democratic Senate wanted Jackson to appoint next justice
Martin Van Buren	Ambassador to United Kingdom	Jackson (D)	D-25 NR-21	1832	Political infighting in Jackson's cabinet; Vice President Calhoun cast deciding vote against nomination
George E. Badger[2]	Associate justice	Fillmore (W)	D-35 W-24	1853	Nominee considered too partisan
Thomas Ewing, Sr.	Secretary of war	A. Johnson (R)	R-42 D-11	1868	Senate resistance to end of military Reconstruction
George H. Williams	Chief Justice	Grant (R)	R-49 D-19	1874	Widely viewed as unqualified
Stanley Matthews	Associate justice	Hayes (R)	D-42 R-33	1881	Nominated too close to election and alleged to be too closely aligned with corporate interests
John G. Tower	Secretary of defense	George H. W. Bush (R)	D-55 R-45	1989	Questions regarding personal behavior

Total: 7

1. Majority party and largest minority party only.
2. Was a sitting senator at the time he was nominated.

TABLE 4 (continued)

Admin: Administration
D: Democratic
DR: Democratic-Republican
J: Jacksonian

NR: National Republican
R: Republican
W: Whig

SOURCES: Cabinet Nominations Rejected or Withdrawn, at http://www.senate.gov/learning/brief_26
.html (last visited Oct. 22, 2002); Advise and Consent – and Rejections, at http://www.appointee.brook
ings.org/sg/a2.htm (last visited Oct. 22, 2002); Richard Allen Baker, *Legislative Power over Appointments
and Confirmations,* in 3 *Encyclopedia of the American Legislative System* 1605-19 (1994); 4 Robert C. Byrd,
The Senate, 1789–1989: Historical Statistics, 1789–1992 688-91, 699-723; 2 *Congressional Quarterly, Guide to
Congress* 1094-96 (5th ed., 2000); Senate Executive Journal; 1, 2 Charles Warren, *The Supreme Court in
United States History* (rev. ed. 1937).

TABLE 5   Cabinet Nominees Rejected or Withdrawn, 1789–2002

Name of Nominee and Cabinet Office	Nominating President	Party in Control of Senate	Year of Final Action	Disposition	Major Reason
Lucius Stockton (War)	John Adams (F)	F-19 DR-13	1801	Withdrawn	Nominee's request
Henry Dearborn (War)	Madison (DR)	DR-27 F-9	1815	Withdrawn[1]	Lack of support in Senate
Roger B. Taney (Treasury)	Andrew Jackson (D)	D-20 NR-20	1834	Rejected	Disagreement over Bank of the United States
Caleb Cushing (Treasury)	Tyler (W)	W-28 D-22	1843	Rejected[2]	Political feud between Tyler and Senate Whigs
David Henshaw (Navy)	Tyler (W)	W-28 D-25	1844	Rejected	Political feud between Tyler and Senate Whigs
James M. Porter (War)	Tyler (W)	W-28 D-25	1844	Rejected	Political feud between Tyler and Senate Whigs
James S. Green (Treasury)	Tyler (W)	W-28 D-25	1844	Rejected	Political feud between Tyler and Senate Whigs
Edwin D. Morgan (Treasury)	Lincoln (R)	R-36 D-9	1865	Withdrawn	Nominee declined appointment

TABLE 5 (continued)

Name of Nominee and Cabinet Office	Nominating President	Party in Control of Senate	Year of Final Action	Disposition	Major Reason
Thomas Ewing, Sr. (War)*	A. Johnson (R)	R-42 D-11	1868	Not reported from committee	Senate resistance to end of military Reconstruction
Henry Stanbery (Atty. general)	A. Johnson (R)	R-42 D-11	1868	Rejected	Senate retaliation for nominee's representation of Johnson in his impeachment trial
Benjamin Bristow (Atty. general)	Grant (R)	R-49 D-19	1874	Withdrawn	Nominee declined appointment
Charles B. Warren (Atty. general)	Coolidge (R)	R-56 D-39	1925	Rejected[3]	Nominee's close ties to sugar industry
Lewis L. Strauss (Commerce)	Eisenhower (R)	D-64 R-34	1959	Rejected	Senatorial enmity stemming from nominee's term as head of Atomic Energy Commission
Robert C. Wood (Housing & Urban Development)	L. B. Johnson (D)	D-64 R-36	1969	Not reported from committee	Appointment came late in Johnson administration
John G. Tower (Defense)*	G. H. W. Bush (R)	D-55 R-45	1989	Rejected	Questions regarding personal behavior

TABLE 5   (continued)

Name of Nominee and Cabinet Office	Nominating President	Party in Control of Senate	Year of Final Action	Disposition	Major Reason
Zoë E. Baird (Attorney General)	Clinton (D)	D-57 R-43	1993	Withdrawn	Failure to pay Social Security taxes on illegal nanny and chauffeur
Bobby Ray Inman (Defense)	Clinton (D)	D-57 R-43	1994	Withdrawn	Nominee requested withdrawal
Hershel W. Gober (Veterans Affairs)	Clinton (D)	R-55 D-45	1997	Withdrawn	Nominee requested withdrawal
Linda Chavez (Labor)	G. W. Bush (R)	D-50 R-49 I-1	2001	Withdrawn	Failed to disclose employment of illegal alien as nanny

Total: 19

1. The Senate actually voted to reject Dearborn's nomination but allowed President Madison to withdraw the nomination.

2. Cushing was rejected again after President Tyler renominated him on the same day of his initial rejection by the Senate.

3. Warren was successively rejected by the Senate, renominated by President Coolidge, and again rejected.

* denotes former senator.

D: Democratic	NR: National Republican
DR: Democratic-Republican	R: Republican
F: Federalist	W: Whig
I: Independent	

SOURCES: Cabinet Nominations Rejected or Withdrawn, at http://www.senate.gov/learning/brief_26 .html (last visited Oct. 22, 2002); Advise and Consent – and Rejections, at http://www.appointee.brook ings.org/sg/a2.htm (last visited Oct. 22, 2002); Richard Allen Baker, *Legislative Power over Appointments and Confirmations*, in 3 *Encyclopedia of the American Legislative System* 1605–19 (1994); 4 Robert C. Byrd, *The Senate, 1789–1989: Historical Statistics, 1789–1992*, at 699–723; 2 *Congressional Quarterly, Guide to Congress* 1094–96 (5th ed., 2000).

TABLE 6 Subcabinet Nominees Not Confirmed by the Senate, 1945–2002
(Table is not comprehensive, because of incomplete records and nominations
withdrawn before formal submission.)

Name of Nominee and Position	Nominating President	Party Breakdown in Senate	Year of Final Action	Disposition	Major Reason
Aubrey Williams (Rural Electrification Administration)	Truman (D)	D-56 R-38	1945	Rejected	Deemed unqualified
Edwin W. Pauley (under secretary of the navy)	Truman (D)	D-56 R-38	1946	Withdrawn	Withdrawn at nominee's request after allegations of bribery surfaced
Carl A. Ilgenfritz (chair, Munitions Board)	Truman (D)	R-51 D-45	1949	Rejected	Nominee lobbied for retaining private executive salary
Leland Olds (Federal Power Commission)	Truman (D)	R-51 D-45	1949	Rejected	Allegedly "socialistic" writings and opposition from private utility and fuel interests
Martin A. Hutchinson (Federal Trade Commission)	Truman (D)	D-54 R-42	1950	Rejected	Senatorial courtesy
Frank E. Hook (Motor Carrier Claims Commission)	Truman (D)	D-54 R-42	1950	Rejected	Senatorial courtesy

TABLE 6 (continued)

Name of Nominee and Position	Nominating President	Party Breakdown in Senate	Year of Final Action	Disposition	Major Reason
Frank A. Waring (board of directors, Tennessee Valley Authority)	Truman (D)	D-49 R-47	1951	Withdrawn	Nominee declared "personally obnoxious" to Sen. McKellar of Tennessee
Philip C. Jessup (delegate to United Nations meeting in Paris)	Truman (D)	D-49 R-47	1951	No action	Accused of communist sympathies by Sen. Joseph McCarthy
Gen. Mark W. Clark (ambassador to the Vatican)	Truman (D)	D-49 R-47	1951	No action	Opposition to creating diplomatic mission to the Vatican
B. Bernard Greidinger (Renegotiation Board)	Truman (D)	D-49 R-47	1952	No action	Nomination stalled and withdrawn because of nominee's desire to maintain substantial personal involvement in business interests
Tom Lyon (Bureau of Mines)	Eisenhower (R)	R-48 D-47	1953	Withdrawn	Nominee received irrevocable pension from a mining company
Timothy J. Murphy (Interstate Commerce Commission)	Eisenhower (R)	D-64 R-34	1960	No Action	Democratic credentials questioned because of seconding nomination of Vice President Nixon at 1956 GOP convention

TABLE 6 (continued)

Name of Nominee and Position	Nominating President	Party Breakdown in Senate	Year of Final Action	Disposition	Major Reason
Patrick V. Murphy (Law Enforcement Assistance Administration)	L. B. Johnson (D)	D-64 R-36	1968	No action	Criticism of police conduct during civil disorder in D.C. in 1968
William J. Casey (president, Export-Import Bank)	Nixon (R)	D-56 R-42	1973	Postponed indefinitely	Alleged improprieties while at the SEC
L. Patrick Gray III (director, Federal Bureau of Investigation)	Nixon (R)	D-56 R-42	1973	Withdrawn	Nominee requested withdrawal after questions regarding handling of Watergate affair
Robert H. Morris (Federal Power Commission)	Nixon (R)	D-56 R-42	1973	Rejected	Nominee had been an attorney for Standard Oil for fifteen years
Stanton D. Anderson (ambassador to Costa Rica)	Nixon (R)	D-56 R-42	1974	Withdrawn	Withdrawn at nominee's request
James M. Day (Mine Enforcement and Safety Administration)	Ford (R)	D-56 R-42	1974	No action	Opposition from United Mine Workers

TABLE 6 (continued)

Name of Nominee and Position	Nominating President	Party Breakdown in Senate	Year of Final Action	Disposition	Major Reason
Peter M. Flanigan (ambassador to Spain)	Ford (R)	D-56 R-42	1974	Withdrawn	Involvement in Nixon's "sale" of diplomatic posts and ITT antitrust settlement
Andrew E. Gibson (Federal Energy Administration)	Ford (R)	D-56 R-42	1974	Withdrawn	Nominee requested withdrawal after *New York Times* reported his severance package of $800,000 from oil company
Daniel T. Kingsley (Federal Power Commission)	Nixon (R)	D-56 R-42	1974	Withdrawn by Ford after Nixon's resignation	Involvement in Nixon's "respon-siveness program" to reward campaign donors
Ben B. Blackburn (Federal Home Loan Bank Board)	Ford (R)	D-60 R-37	1975	Rejected	Nominee's opposition to civil rights legislation and public views on blacks and public housing tenants
Isabel A. Burgess (National Transportation Board)	Ford (R)	D-60 R-37	1975	Rejected	Nominee had abused position since appointment by Nixon
Joseph Coors (Corporation for Public Broadcasting)	Ford (R)	D-60 R-37	1975	Tabled	Fears of censorship and nominee's refusal to resign as director of independent news service

TABLE 6   (continued)

Name of Nominee and Position	Nominating President	Party Breakdown in Senate	Year of Final Action	Disposition	Major Reason
James F. Hooper III (Tennessee Valley Authority)	Ford (R)	D-60 R-37	1975	Postponed Indefinitely[1]	Questionable business dealings
William J. Kendrick (Equal Employment Opportunity Commission)	Ford (R)	D-60 R-37	1975	No action	Nominee had worked as consultant to National Association of Manufacturers
Thomas L. Longshore (Tennessee Valley Authority)	Ford (R)	D-60 R-37	1976	Rejected	Close alignment with private utility interests
Graham A. Martin (presidential representative to talks on political status of Micronesia)	Ford (R)	D-60 R-37	1976	Postponed indefinitely	Criticism of nominee's performance as ambassador to South Vietnam in 1975
George F. Murphy, Jr. (Nuclear Regulatory Commission)	Ford (R)	D-60 R-37	1976	No action	Questions regarding long service as staff member of congressional committee and lack of opportunity to explore nominee's views fully

TABLE 6 (continued)

Name of Nominee and Position	Nominating President	Party Breakdown in Senate	Year of Final Action	Disposition	Major Reason
Warren B. Rudman (chairman, Interstate Commerce Commission)	Ford (R)	D-60 R-37	1976	Withdrawn	Nominee requested withdrawal after accusations that nomination was made to assist Ford in New Hampshire primary
Marion Edey (Council on Environmental Quality)	Carter (D)	D-61 R-38	1977	Postponed indefinitely	Perceived lack of qualifications
Kent F. Hansen (Nuclear Regulatory Commission)	Carter (D)	D-61 R-38	1977	Rejected	Potential conflicts of interest
Robert Mendelsohn (assistant secretary of the interior)	Carter (D)	D-61 R-38	1977	Withdrawn	Pending civil suit for violation of California campaign disclosure law
Theodore C. Sorensen (director, Central Intelligence Agency)	Carter (D)	D-61 R-38	1977	Withdrawn	Nominee requested withdrawal after massive opposition by Republicans
Donald L. Tucker (Civil Aeronautics Board)	Carter (D)	D-61 R-38	1977	Withdrawn	Questionable financial dealings

TABLE 6   (continued)

Name of Nominee and Position	Nominating President	Party Breakdown in Senate	Year of Final Action	Disposition	Major Reason
Irby Turner, Jr. (Corporation for Public Broadcasting)	Carter (D)	D-61 R-38	1977	No action	Alleged insensitivity to need for minority-oriented programming
Norval Morris (Law Enforcement Assistance Administration)	Carter (D)	D-61 R-38	1978	No action	Opposition from National Rifle Association based on nominee's position on gun control
Robert S. Gershon (ambassador to Uruguay)	Carter (D)	D-58 R-41	1980	No action	Blocked by Sen. Jesse Helms
F. Keith Adkinson (Federal Trade Commission)	Reagan (R)	R-53 D-46	1981	Withdrawn	Nominee requested withdrawal after allegations of abuse of former position with Senate committee
William M. Bell (Equal Employment Opportunity Commission)	Reagan (R)	R-53 D-46	1981	No action	Unqualified, no experience in government
Ernest W. Lefever (assistant secretary of state for human rights)	Reagan (R)	R-53 D-46	1981	Withdrawn	Withdrawn at nominee's request after Senate committee rejected nomination based on questions regarding commitment to human rights

TABLE 6 (continued)

Name of Nominee and Position	Nominating President	Party Breakdown in Senate	Year of Final Action	Disposition	Major Reason
Warren Richardson (assistant secretary of health and human services)	Reagan (R)	R-53 D-46	1981	Withdrawn	Nominee requested withdrawal after charges of anti-Semitism surfaced
John R. Van de Water (National Labor Relations Board)	Reagan (R)	R-53 D-46	1981	Rejected	Opposition of AFL-CIO
Robert T. Grey, Jr. (deputy director, Arms Control and Disarmament Agency)	Reagan (R)	R-53 D-46	1982	Withdrawn	President withdrew nomination in the face of opposition from Senate conservatives led by Sen. Jesse Helms
Rev. Sam B. Hart (U.S. Civil Rights Commission)	Reagan (R)	R-53 D-46	1982	Withdrawn	Opposition from civil rights groups
Norman Terrell (Arms Control and Disarmament Agency)	Reagan (R)	R-53 D-46	1982	Withdrawn	Opposition from conservative senators based on nominee's service in previous administrations

TABLE 6 (continued)

Name of Nominee and Position	Nominating President	Party Breakdown in Senate	Year of Final Action	Disposition	Major Reason
Leslie Lenkowsky (U.S. Information Agency)	Reagan (R)	R-54 D-46	1984	Rejected	Questions regarding a USIA "blacklist" of speakers who disagreed with the Reagan administration
William Bradford Reynolds (associate attorney general)	Reagan (R)	R-53 D-47	1985	Rejected	Performance as assistant attorney general
Edward A. Curran (chairman, National Endowment for the Humanities)	Reagan (R)	R-53 D-47	1985	Rejected	Lack of qualifications and experience
Donald J. Devine (director, Office of Personnel Management)	Reagan (R)	R-53 D-47	1985	Withdrawn	Nominee requested withdrawal in the face of almost sure rejection because of stormy relationship with Congress
James L. Malone (ambassador to Belize)	Reagan (R)	R-53 D-47	1986	Postponed indefinitely	Nominee requested postponement after Sen. Edward Zorinsky threatened a filibuster

TABLE 6 (continued)

Name of Nominee and Position	Nominating President	Party Breakdown in Senate	Year of Final Action	Disposition	Major Reason
Robert E. Rader, Jr. (review panel, Occupational Safety and Health Administration)	Reagan (R)	R-53 D-47	1986	Rejected	Opponents argued that as a lawyer nominee had blocked OSHA workplace inspections
Jeffrey Zuckerman (general counsel, Equal Employment Opportunity Commission)	Reagan (R)	R-53 D-47	1986	Rejected	Opposition of civil rights advocates
Robert M. Gates (director, Central Intelligence Agency)	Reagan (R)	D-55 R-45	1987	Withdrawn	Fallout from Iran-contra scandal
Dorothy L. Strunk (Mine Safety and Health Administration)	Reagan (R)	D-55 R-45	1987	Rejected	Opposition from United Mine Workers and Teamsters
Richard N. Viets (ambassador to Portugal)	Reagan (R)	D-55 R-45	1987	No action	Opposition from Senators Jesse Helms and Robert Byrd

TABLE 6 (continued)

Name of Nominee and Position	Nominating President	Party Breakdown in Senate	Year of Final Action	Disposition	Major Reason
Robert B. Fiske, Jr. (deputy attorney general)	G. H. W. Bush (R)	D-55 R-45	1989	Withdrawn	Conservative criticism of conduct as chairman of American Bar Association
James E. Cason (assistant secretary of agriculture)	G. H. W. Bush (R)	D-55 R-45	1989	No action	Questionable record on environmental issues
Frederick M. Bush (ambassador to Luxembourg)	G. H. W. Bush (R)	D-55 R-45	1989	Withdrawn	Nominee requested withdrawal after being linked to federal housing projects under investigation
William Lucas (assistant attorney general for civil rights)	G. H. W. Bush (R)	D-55 R-45	1989	Rejected	Lack of experience
Debra R. Bowland (Wage and Hour Division, Department of Labor)	G. H. W. Bush (R)	D-55 R-45	1989	Rejected	Opposition from organized labor
Joy A. Silverman (ambassador to Barbados)	G. H. W. Bush (R)	D-55 R-45	1990	No action	Complaints regarding reward of diplomatic posts to donors

TABLE 6 (continued)

Name of Nominee and Position	Nominating President	Party Breakdown in Senate	Year of Final Action	Disposition	Major Reason
Victor Stello, Jr. (assistant secretary of energy)	G. H. W. Bush (R)	D-55 R-45	1990	Withdrawn	Ties to industry and conduct while employed by the Nuclear Regulatory Commission
Frederick Vreeland (ambassador to Myanmar)	G. H. W. Bush (R)	D-55 R-45	1990	Withdrawn	Refusal by Myanmar to accept nominee and Senate concern about misrepresentation in nominee's official biography
George Fleming Jones (ambassador to Guyana)	G. H. W. Bush (R)	D-55 R-45	1990	No action	Opposed by Sen. Jesse Helms
John Bushnell (ambassador to Costa Rica)	G. H. W. Bush (R)	D-55 R-45	1990	No action	Nomination was delayed by Sen. Jesse Helms until the waning hours of the 101st Congress
Robert L. Clarke (comptroller of the currency)	G. H. W. Bush (R)	D-56 R-44	1991	Rejected	Opposition to nominee's deregulatory views
Lani Guinier (assistant attorney general)	Clinton (D)	D-57 R-43	1993	Withdrawn	Nominee's academic writings on race and political power

TABLE 6 (continued)

Name of Nominee and Position	Nominating President	Party Breakdown in Senate	Year of Final Action	Disposition	Major Reason
Morton H. Halperin (assistant secretary of defense for democracy and peacekeeping)	Clinton (D)	D-57 R-43	1994	Withdrawn	Nominee requested withdrawal because of resignation of his sponsor, Secretary of Defense Les Aspin, and conservative opposition
Robert A. Pastor (ambassador to Panama)	Clinton (D)	D-57 R-43	1994	No action	Opposed by Sen. Jesse Helms
Sam Brown (ambassador to the Conference on Cooperation and Security in Europe)	Clinton (D)	D-57 R-43	1994	No action	Republican filibuster
Michael P.C. Carns (director, Central Intelligence Agency)	Clinton (D)	D-53 R-47	1995	Withdrew	Brought illegal immigrant to United States from Philippines
Henry W. Foster, Jr. (surgeon general)	Clinton (D)	D-53 R-47	1995	No action	Opposition from anti-abortion groups and failure to invoke cloture

TABLE 6 (continued)

Name of Nominee and Position	Nominating President	Party Breakdown in Senate	Year of Final Action	Disposition	Major Reason
William F. Weld (ambassador to Mexico)	Clinton (D)	R-55 D-45	1997	Withdrawn	Withdrawn at nominee's request in the face of opposition from Sen. Jesse Helms
Bill Lann Lee (assistant attorney general for civil rights)	Clinton (D)	R-55 D-45	1997	No action	Conservative opposition
Anthony Lake (director, Central Intelligence Agency)	Clinton (D)	R-55 D-45	1997	Withdrawn	Nominee requested withdrawal
Daryl Jones (secretary of the air force)	Clinton (D)	R-55 D-45	1998	Rejected	Criticism from fellow air force officers
Carol J. Parry (Federal Reserve Board of Governors)	Clinton (D)	R-55 D-45	2000	No action	Senate refused to consider nomination before next presidential election
Mary Sheila Gall (chair, Consumer Product Safety Commission)	G. W. Bush (R)	D-50 R-49	2001	Rejected	Ten-year record as member of commission

TABLE 6   (continued)

Name of Nominee and Position	Nominating President	Party Breakdown in Senate	Year of Final Action	Disposition	Major Reason
Donald R. Schregardus (Enforcement Division, Environmental Protection Agency)	G. W. Bush (R)	D-50 R-49	2001	Withdrawn	Nominee requested withdrawal after nomination stalled in Senate

1. President Ford resubmitted Hooper's nomination in 1976 and the Senate again postponed it indefinitely.

SOURCES: 4 Robert C. Byrd, *The Senate, 1789–1989: Historical Statistics, 1789–1992,* at 725–29; 1–10 *Congress and the Nation* (1965, 1969, 1973, 1977, 1981, 1985, 1989, 1993, 1997, 2002); *Congressional Quarterly, Guide to Congress,* 1094–96 (5th ed., 2000).

TABLE 7 Supreme Court Nominees Rejected or Withdrawn, 1789–2002

Name of Nominee and Position	Nominating President	Party Breakdown in Senate	Year of Final Action	Disposition	Major Reason
William Patterson*	Washington (F)	F-16 DR-13	1793	Withdrawn; later renominated and confirmed	Nominee was a member of the Senate when the Judiciary Act was enacted and at the time of his nomination: Washington therefore viewed his candidacy as unconstitutional
John Rutledge (Chief Justice)	Washington (F)	F-19 DR-13	1795	Rejected	Nominee's opposition to the Jay Treaty
Alexander Wolcott	Madison (DR)	DR-28 F-6	1811	Rejected	Lack of experience and judicial temperament
John J. Crittenden*	John Quincy Adams (DR)	J-28 Admin-20	1829	Postponed indefinitely	Democratic Senate wanted Jackson to appoint next justice
Roger B. Taney	Jackson (D)	D-20 NR-20	1835	Postponed indefinitely	Nomination viewed as political reward
John C. Spencer	Tyler (W)	W-28 D-25	1844	Rejected then renominated and withdrawn	Feud between Tyler and Senate Whigs
Reuben H. Walworth	Tyler (W)	W-28 D-25	1845	Tabled (1844); renominated and withdrawn (1845)	Feud between Tyler and Senate Whigs

TABLE 7 (continued)

Name of Nominee and Position	Nominating President	Party Breakdown in Senate	Year of Final Action	Disposition	Major Reason
Edward King	Tyler (W)	W-28 D-25	1845	Postponed (1844); renominated (1844); withdrawn (1845)	Feud between Tyler and Senate Whigs
John M. Read	Tyler (W)	W-28 D-25	1845	No action	Feud between Tyler and Senate Whigs
George W. Woodward	Polk (D)	D-31 W-25	1846	Rejected	Personal opposition of Sen. Cameron of Pennsylvania
Edward W. Bradford	Fillmore (W)	D-35 W-24	1852	No action	Senate refused to fill seat in election year
George E. Badger[1]	Fillmore (W)	D-35 W-24	1853	Postponed indefinitely; withdrawn	Nominee considered too partisan
William C. Micou	Fillmore (W)	D-35 W-24	1853	No action	Democratic Senate refused to confirm Whig nominee before election
Jeremiah S. Black	Buchanan (D)	D-36 R-26	1861	Rejected	Republican Senate refused to confirm Democratic nominee before election
Henry A. Stanbery	Andrew Johnson (R)	U-42 D-10	1866	No action	Senatorial opposition to Johnson's agenda

TABLE 7 (continued)

Name of Nominee and Position	Nominating President	Party Breakdown in Senate	Year of Final Action	Disposition	Major Reason
Ebenezer Hoar	Grant (R)	R-56 D-11	1870	Rejected	Nominee had offended senators with his brusque manner as attorney general
George H. Williams (Chief Justice)*	Grant (R)	R-49 D-19	1874	Withdrawn	Widely viewed as unqualified
Caleb Cushing	Grant (R)	R-49 D-19	1874	Withdrawn	Correspondence surfaced between nominee and Confederate President Jefferson Davis in 1861
Stanley Matthews*	Hayes (R)	D-42 R-33	1881	No action[2]	Nominated too close to election and alleged to be too closely aligned with corporate interests
William B. Hornblower	Cleveland (D)	D-44 R-38	1894	Rejected	Senatorial courtesy
Wheeler H. Peckham	Cleveland (D)	D-44 R-38	1894	Rejected	Senatorial courtesy
John J. Parker	Hoover (R)	R-56 D-39	1930	Rejected	Alleged racism and opposition to organized labor
Abe Fortas (Chief Justice)	L. B. Johnson (D)	D-64 R-36	1968	Withdrawn	Financial improprieties

TABLE 7 (continued)

Name of Nominee and Position	Nominating President	Party Breakdown in Senate	Year of Final Action	Disposition	Major Reason
Homer Thornberry	L. B. Johnson (D)	D-64 R-36	1968	Withdrawn	Fortas seat not vacated
Clement Haynsworth	Nixon (R)	D-57 R-43	1969	Rejected	Ethical improprieties
G. Harrold Carswell	Nixon (R)	D-57 R-43	1970	Rejected	Mediocre judicial credentials; hostility to civil rights
Robert Bork	Reagan (R)	D-55 R-45	1987	Rejected	Massive resistance from interest groups
Douglas Ginsburg	Reagan (R)	D-55 R-45	1987	Withdrawn (before nomination formalized)	Marijuana use while a law professor at Harvard

Total: 28

1. Was a sitting senator at the time he was nominated.
2. Later renominated and confirmed under President Garfield.

* indicates former senator.

Admin: Administration	NR: National Republican
D: Democratic	R: Republican
DR: Democratic-Republican	U: Unionist
F: Federalist	W: Whig
J: Jacksonian	

SOURCES: 4 Robert C. Byrd, *The Senate, 1789–1989: Historical Statistics, 1789–1992*, at 688–91; 2 *Congressional Quarterly, Guide to Congress*, 1094–96 (5th ed., 2000); Senate Executive Journal; 1, 2 Charles Warren, *The Supreme Court in United States History* (rev. ed. 1937); David Yaloff, *Pursuit of Justices* (1999).

TABLE 8 Lower Federal Court Nominees Not Confirmed by the Senate, 1939–2002

Name	Court	Nominating President	Party Breakdown in Senate[1]	Year of Final Action and Disposition	Major Reason
Floyd H. Roberts	W.D. Va.	F. D. Roosevelt (D)	D-69 R-23	1939 Rejected	Breached senatorial courtesy
M. Neil Andrews	N.D. Ga.	Truman (D)	D-54 R-42	1950 Rejected	Senatorial courtesy
Carroll O. Switzer	S.D. Ia.	Truman (D)	D-54 R-42	1950 Rejected	Senatorial courtesy
Joseph Jerome Drucker	N.D. Ill.	Truman (D)	D-49 R-47	1951 Rejected	Senatorial courtesy
Cornelius J. Harrington	N.D. Ill.	Truman (D)	D-49 R-47	1951 Rejected	Senatorial courtesy
Frieda Hennock	S.D.N.Y.	Truman (D)	D-49 R-47	1951 No action	Gender and allegations of improper relationship with married federal judge
Francis X. Morrisey	D. Mass.	L. B. Johnson (D)	D-68 R-32	1965 Withdrawn	Nominee requested withdrawal after allegations that he was unqualified
William B. Poff	W.D. Va.	Ford (R)	D-60 R-37	1976 No action	Senatorial courtesy

TABLE 8 (continued)

Name	Court	Nominating President	Party Breakdown in Senate[1]	Year of Final Action and Disposition	Major Reason
Carin Ann Clauss	D.D.C.	Carter (D)	D-61 R-38	1978 No action	ABA opposition, Criticism by judges of 3rd Cir. on performance as solicitor of Labor Department
Charles B. Winberry	E.D.N.C.	Carter (D)	D-58 R-41	1980 No action	Ethical violations and lack of experience
Jefferson B. Sessions III	D. Ala.	Reagan (R)	R-53 D-47	1986 Withdrawn	Alleged racial insensitivity and lack of qualifications
Bernard H. Siegan	9th Cir.	Reagan (R)	D-55 R-45	1988 Withdrawn	Lack of courtroom experience and radical views
Susan W. Liebeler	Fed. Cir.	Reagan (R)	D-55 R-45	1988 No action	Political ideology
Kenneth L. Ryskamp	11th Cir.	G. H. W. Bush (R)	D-56 R-44	1991 No action	Racial insensitivity and lack of judicial qualifications
Charles Stack	11th Cir.	Clinton (D)	R-53 D-47	1996 Withdrawn	Nominee requested withdrawal after questions surfaced regarding qualifications

TABLE 8 (continued)

Name	Court	Nominating President	Party Breakdown in Senate[1]	Year of Final Action and Disposition	Major Reason
Frederica Massiah-Jackson	E.D. Pa.	Clinton (D)	1998 Withdrawn	Question regarding judicial temperament and conduct as a state judge in Pennsylvania	
Ronnie L. White	E.D. Mo.	Clinton (D)	R-55 D-45	1999 Rejected	Views on capital punishment and allegations of judicial activism
Barbara Durham	9th Cir.	Clinton (D)	R-55 D-45	1999 Withdrawn	Nominee requested withdrawal to deal with family illness
Charles W. Pickering	5th Cir.	G. W. Bush (R)	R-50 D-50	2002 Rejected	Problems with judicial record
Priscilla R. Owen	5th Cir.	G. W. Bush (R)	D-50 R-49	2002 Rejected	Problems with judicial record

1. Majority party and largest minority party only

SOURCES: 1-10 *Congress and the Nation* (1965, 1969, 1973, 1977, 1981, 1985, 1989, 1993, 1997, 2002); *Congressional Quarterly, Guide to Congress* 1094-96 (5th ed., 2000).

INTRODUCTION

FEW AREAS AT the intersection of constitutional law and politics generate more controversy or opinions than the federal appointments process. It has become like the weather: almost all commentators and many participants gripe about it, but no one seems able (or at least willing or prepared) to do anything about it. Indeed, for most of the history of this republic the federal appointments process has been pilloried. If a government agency had gotten the repeatedly bad ratings that the federal appointments process has received, it almost certainly would have been dismantled (just as the Independent Counsel Act recently was) or radically overhauled by now. Yet, in spite of the extensive and repeated criticism of the performance of national political leaders in the federal appointments process, the institutions responsible for federal appointments have successfully resisted significant reform of the process. Just the opposite. And the resistance to change speaks volumes about the agendas, interests, and practices of the institutional and other actors perennially involved in the federal appointments process.

Just as national political leaders have developed vested interests in their respective institutional prerogatives in the federal appointments process, many scholars have developed vested interests in their opinions or theories about this process and do not easily abandon or broaden their thinking about it. Legal scholars in particular have largely been time-bound in their study of the federal appointments process. That is, they have tended to view single incidents in a vacuum or as unique events without regard to their possible relationships to other incidents in the process; other pending or past legislative matters; or broader social, political, and historical developments.

More often than not, legal scholars have narrowed their coverage of the federal appointments process to focus on dramatic incidents that suit their particular purposes. For instance, in the hope of insulating the federal judiciary as much as possible from partisan politics, most legal scholars have focused primarily if not exclusively on Supreme Court appointments, and specifically on Senate confirmation hearings. This focus has become especially popular among legal scholars since the Senate's rejection of President Ronald Reagan's nomination of Robert Bork to the Supreme Court in 1987, because of the perceived risk posed to judicial independence by Senate inquiries into judicial nominees' predispositions and viewpoints on pending constitutional issues.[1] The problem is that such inquiries conceivably have pressured judicial nominees (especially those to the Supreme Court) to conform their views to those held by a majority of senators for the sake of securing confirmation.

To be sure, such coverage has produced significant insights into and analyses of particular episodes or controversies, particularly the personalities or personal ambitions, quirks, and qualities of the presidents, senators, nominees, and other major figures involved in notorious incidents. Yet, such analyses have generally failed to provide lasting insights into the federal appointments process, to clarify the social, political, and historical contexts in which appointments controversies arise, and to develop appropriate criteria for analyzing the performances of the major participants in the appointments process from different historical periods.[2]

It is the purpose of this book to offer a different way of thinking about the federal appointments process, one that entails focusing on and illuminating the historical patterns and practices in the process (including the reasons for and the nature of its general resistance to significant reform). The perspective suggested here is by no means the only or even the preferred way of explaining and evaluating the federal appointments process, but it is a useful way to expand academic and popular understanding of its dynamics. The book's historical focus should not be viewed as a liability. While the book does not purport to provide comprehensive overviews, applications, or analyses of all the most current social science and economic theories regarding presidential or congressional decision making, it does make available information that other theorists can use within their own frameworks in the course of developing or promoting their own special perspectives on the federal appointments process.

The broader perspective urged in this book is that of so-called historical institutionalism, a term that refers to the work undertaken over the past decade by social scientists who have rediscovered the value of studying how institutional arrangements shape and direct political behavior.[3] As applied to the federal appointments process, this perspective focuses on the institutional contexts in which federal appointments have taken place throughout U.S. history. Viewing the federal appointments process from the perspective of historical institutionalism illuminates the patterns and practices that have developed within the process. These patterns and practices reflect the different ways in which the leaders of national political institutions — namely, presidents and senators — have tried to influence or shape the appointments process as well as the ways their internal organizations or decision-making processes have been shaped by their own and others' actions and experiences in the process.

Moreover, historical institutionalism integrates history and institutional analysis with an appreciation of the strategies constitutional actors use to cultivate or develop legal and other norms to protect their respective prerogatives and to achieve their desired objectives. An important purpose of this book is to demonstrate that the Constitution establishes a very loose framework that provides little constraint on the institutional actors empowered to make decisions on federal appointments. Consequently, the driving force of the appointments process are the norms developed by presidents and senators to constrain or guide their decision making. Historical institutionalism further suggests that institutional norms also can change the behavior of actors, who develop strategies for using existing norms to their advantage and for developing new or different ones.

Two viewpoints of the federal appointments process are particularly important to historical institutionalists. The first is the inside view of the system. This internal viewpoint is concerned with the interaction — both formal and informal — between the major actors who routinely participate in the appointments process, their respective organizations for decision making on appointments matters, their perceptions of the norms constraining or affecting their behavior,[4] and the degree to which the performances of these actors in the appointments process have facilitated their achievement of the political or constitutional objectives of greatest concern to them.

Introduction

3

The second viewpoint important to historical institutionalists examines the external forces—the social, political, economic, and historical developments or influences originating from outside the formal or constitutional structure—pressuring or constraining presidential and senatorial decision making and actions taken on appointments matters. The outside viewpoint is concerned with the multilayered, complex contexts in which the power structure for dealing with appointments has developed and in which nomination and confirmation decisions have been made.

Combining the inside and outside perspectives helps to illuminate many aspects of the federal appointments process largely overlooked in prior studies of the system. The outside perspective leads to such important questions as, How have social, political, and economic developments shaped the institutions centrally involved in the appointments process—namely, the presidency and Senate—as well as the performances of presidents and senators in this system? And does constitutional structure matter; permit accountability; produce competent appointments in terms of the fit between talent, ability, and experience and the particular responsibilities of an office; and allow capture of the appointments process by factions? The outside perspective also allows an evaluation of the quality of the discourse between the president and the Senate and examines whether the president or the Senate wields too much or too little power on appointments matters. The development of an outside view of the presidency and the Senate would allow scholars to develop standards for evaluating presidential and senatorial contributions and performances in the appointments process that cut across different historical periods.

The inside perspective of the federal appointments process leads to a different set of questions, including, among others, Why or how were particular nominations made and why did certain nominations succeed or fail? What is the nature of presidential-senatorial interactions within the appointments process? And what kind of relationship exists between judicial and other kinds of nominations and confirmation, and between certain appointment decisions and other presidential choices and senatorial activities? By looking at both internal and external perspectives scholars can consider the fundamental question of how presidents and senators coordinate or perceive their different powers or restructure their respective offices in response to, as well as in anticipation of, social, economic, political, and other outside developments or changes.

This book sketches answers to some of the basic questions raised by the inside viewpoint of the federal appointments process,[5] drawing on law and particularly history to illuminate the internal perspective of the system, including the patterns and practices different institutions and actors have developed for dealing with appointments. The book consists of three parts. Part 1 examines the origins, constitutional structure, and evolution of the federal appointments process. It reviews the original understanding; the different aspects or implications of the basic constitutional design (particularly those characterizing the modern operations); and the degree to which certain historical, social, and political developments have shaped the operations or dynamics of the federal appointments process.

Part 2 analyzes the powers available to and the criteria appropriate for evaluating the performances of or contributions made by each of the major actors routinely involved in the federal appointments process. Individual chapters are devoted to analyzing the roles performed in the appointments process (including the patterns or practices developed and the lessons learned) by presidents, senators, nominees, the media, interest groups, and the public.

Part 3 analyzes proposals for reforming the federal appointments process. In particular, this part examines several modest recommendations for altering some Senate procedures to streamline the appointments process as well as some radical proposals for amending the Constitution to reduce presidential or senatorial input or to diminish the (perceived if not proven) negative consequences of factional dominance within the appointments process (though there is, even with respect to judicial selection, widespread disagreement among scholars and political analysts about whether or to what extent such dominance is undesirable). This part also examines the strategies for developing new norms (or informal arrangements) and fortifying deteriorating norms that might be important (to the extent one agrees with this objective) for reducing delays in judicial confirmation proceedings.

Based on its analysis of the federal appointments process from the perspective of historical institutionalism, the book reaches several conclusions. The first is that clarifying the social, political, and historical contexts in which appointments decisions are made or controversies arise is indispensable for understanding and evaluating the operations of this special system. Elucidating the complex contexts in which presidents and senators make decisions on appointments helps to explain the external forces that affect the process. Further, clarifying such contexts also helps to explain the system's internal dynamics and operations, including the motivations of key participants, the actors' understanding of their respective authorities in this arena, and executive and legislative institutional arrangements for formulating appointments decisions and strategies. In constructing this perspective, both history and political science are extremely useful disciplines, the latter because it helps to inform our judgments, analyses, and understandings of how institutions such as the presidency and the Senate take shape and operate; and the former because it is the repository of useful lessons and comparative data, including more than two hundred years worth of meaningful examples, demonstrations, and analogies of presidential and senatorial performances in the venue of appointments.

For example, studying past practices and patterns of decision making and activity in the federal appointments process allows participants and observers to predict confirmation conflicts, failures, and successes, and their spillover effects. Some of these effects include the increased likelihood or intensity of confirmation skirmishes over nominations made to federal offices with substantial responsibilities in especially sensitive areas such as national security, civil rights, and the environment. Outcomes also turn on the degree of fallout from very contentious or unpopular policies and the relative quality of presidential or senatorial preparation, organization, strategizing, and coordination of interest group support or opposition.

The book concludes further that institutional analysis of the federal appointments process has comparative advantages over the conventional mode (particularly popular with legal scholars) of understanding the system in purely personal terms. The major problem with the latter approach is that it fails to provide meaningful comparative analysis of different presidents' and senators' decisions or actions regarding appointments because it treats every difference in performance as resulting from personal characteristics or attachments and neglects to explain the most significant trends in the process.

In contrast, historical institutionalism evaluates the performances of major political leaders in terms of their power (or their duties and available resources) and authority (or their warrants) for changing the constitutional order. Historical institutionalism illuminates the extent to which outcomes are attributable to personal actions or traits and to governmental structure, management, and organization. Historical institutionalism also allows a comparison of the performances of different presidents and senators, because the institutional concerns of the presidency have remained relatively constant over the course of U.S. history.

By providing for the direct election of senators, the Seventeenth Amendment altered the institutional dynamics of senatorial operations regarding appointments. Historical institutionalism illuminates the implications of this alteration. For example, in the form of public choice theory, it helps to demonstrate the necessity of examining the motivations and actions of individual senators for understanding Senate operations.

Institutional analysis also illuminates the learning curve of each of the major actors routinely involved in the federal appointments process. The lessons learned are passed down or shared within (and across) the executive and legislative branches by means of the institutional memories each branch has cultivated or developed. For example, in the Senate, veteran senators overlap with junior members, parliamentarians span several Congresses, and party organizations and interest groups can serve as repositories of learning. Executive branch officials foster institutional memory through such means as internal memoranda, career civil servants, the employment of people with substantial prior experience in the executive or legislative branches (or both), official opinion letters, memoirs or diaries, and personal interaction or communications.

Among the most important lessons learned by presidents and senators (as well as other unofficial participants routinely involved in the process, including interest groups) is that, much like the recent impeachment proceedings against President Clinton,[6] confirmation skirmishes often reflect the increasingly prevalent phenomenon of "postelection politics," in which the major political parties continue to wage in a variety of fora (including but by no means limited to confirmation proceedings) the fights they began in presidential contests.[7]

In addition, through their interaction in the federal appointments process, presidents and senators have learned about their respective authorities and abilities to influence outcomes as well as the actions and performances of other important actors, the significance of formal constraints and informal arrangements, and the preconditions for change. They have learned from their own experiences or those of other institutional actors about the factors they need to control in order to cultivate support for or opposition to various nominations, including the popularity of presidents or their policies, the potential for nominees' private traits to be transformed into public liabilities or strengths, and the need and the ways in which to develop good press as well as solid internal institutional support or organization. In short, the performance of each institutional actor within the appointments process provides examples for other actors to avoid or follow in accordance with their particular objectives (and, of course, within the contexts or constraints of their particular circumstances).

Institutional analysis clarifies further that institutional norms (such as the rule of law and precedent), informal practices (such as senatorial courtesy), and social norms (regarding, e.g., homosexuality, free speech, privacy, and lying) also fit into the learning process. Individual actors do not act independently of everything else in the political process; rather they attempt to influence and are affected by the various norms they have developed for their own benefit and around which they learn to maneuver or with which they try to align themselves in order to achieve their desired objectives. Reform recommendations should fit the structure of this learning curve in order to correspond or conform to the actors' short- and long-term interests or needs, formal constraints and informal arrangements, persistent (and perhaps irreconcilable) conflicts, potential for accommodation, common ground, and feasible objectives.

For example, it is noteworthy that some norms that goven the federal appointments process are in flux (such as the practice of allowing senators to put nominations on temporary rather than indefinite hold). The flux suggests that perhaps norms, more so than structure or formal Senate procedures, are malleable. How much a given norm is amenable to change depends on the degree to which presidents and senators can be convinced change is in their mutual interest.

To be sure, it is by no means certain that significant reform of the appointments process (at least of any formal aspects) is possible. Innovation (such as President Carter's efforts to bypass senators and use special commissions to recommend candidates for circuit court appointments) is generally resisted (at least by many of the principal actors), and the last significant structural changes that have affected performance within the system date back to Civil Service reform, the opening of congressional hearings, and the adoption of the Seventeenth Amendment. Such resistance to change suggests that the structure and formal practices might not be the proper focus of reform efforts. Instead, norms might constitute more appropriate targets. For example, a notion that has become popular with some legal theorists who study the relationship between law and social norms is the use of shaming penalties to ensure compliance with community norms.[8] Indeed, President Clinton attempted just such a strategy when in the fall of 1997 he publicly rebuked the Republican leadership for allowing inordinate delays of his judicial nominations. Not long thereafter, in his annual report on the state of the federal judiciary, Chief Justice Rehnquist also denounced the Senate's delays in processing judicial nominations. These rebukes helped to break (at least temporarily) the logjam in the judicial selection process. Consequently, the media (or other public leaders), drawing on the Rehnquist and Clinton models, might consider asking public officials (such as the president or senators) whether they favor significant reform of the federal appointments process (if so, why? if not, why not?). The media or interest groups or interested senators could pressure public officials to defend their failure to give serious consideration to recent proposals for streamlining the appointments process made by two highly respected bipartisan organizations, The Century Foundation and the Miller Center for the Study of Public Affairs at the University of Virginia.[9] Moreover, the media might consider asking presidents and senators whether they would support legislation defining the qualifications for different confirmable offices (and if they wouldn't, why not?). Alternatively, presidents and senators could be asked to define or set forth the requisite qualifications for certain officials, particularly federal judges. Or presidents or senators could be asked whether it is possible

Introduction

9

to define qualifications of federal judges without mentioning ideology (if so, how? if not, why not?). Refusal to answer such questions would give the public some clear understanding of the reasons for resistance to change in the federal appointments process. Given the vested interests of key players in the status quo, serious or significant change is not likely to occur without altering or changing the incentives or vested interests of these institutional actors. Hence, one might ask, What is likely to change the institutional orientation of presidents or senators with respect to particular nominations or appointments generally? (Relying on some of the recent insights of theorists who study social norms,[10] one might figure out the particular kinds of information or data that are important to the relatively close-knit community responsible for federal appointments and tailor messages accordingly.)

In examining this book's basic themes and argumentation, readers should keep three caveats in mind. The first relates to the organization of the book. The chapters are designed to provide overlays for viewing the different dimensions of particular incidents in or aspects of the federal appointments process. To underscore the multidimensional aspects of appointments matters, I examine more than once some of the more controversial nominations and confirmation contests in American history. For instance, the Senate's rejections of President Andrew Jackson's nominations of Roger Taney as secretary of the treasury and as an associate justice and subsequent confirmation of Taney as Chief Justice illustrate how a president learns from his (and his predecessors') past mistakes in the appointments process and adapts or responds to the ways senators try to achieve their own (often opposing) agendas through the exercise of their confirmation authority. Taney's rejections as secretary of the treasury and associate justice and confirmation as Chief Justice illustrate further a nominee's limited ability to exert direct influence over the outcome of his or her confirmation proceeding. These rejections also illustrate how senators try to shape the president's agenda in the appointments process (and on other legislative matters). Other incidents that reveal similarly complex lessons about the federal appointments process include the Senate's rejection of President Lyndon Johnson's nomination of then-Associate Justice Abe Fortas to be Chief Justice, the Senate's rejection of President Reagan's nomination of Robert Bork as an associate justice,

Clarence Thomas's narrow confirmation as an associate justice, and President Clinton's forced withdrawals of his nominations of Zoë Baird as attorney general and Lani Guinier as assistant attorney general to head the Justice Department's Civil Rights Division.

The second caveat is that it is practically impossible to develop comprehensive statistical or empirical data on the actions of presidents and senators in the federal appointments process. To begin with, presidents in the late eighteenth century and nineteenth century did not maintain comprehensive or detailed records on their nominations or appointments. Nor did the Senate maintain records on its actions regarding presidential nominations during that period, a period that coincided with the Senate's general rule against open hearings. Collecting data has not become easier in this century. There is no central clearinghouse on pending nominations, vacancies, or confirmations. No single statute specifies all confirmable offices. There are hardly any formal requirements for making available to the public data on pending or prospective nominations. The few include the General Accounting Office's mandate to monitor payment to all salaried federal officers, the Congressional Research Service's limited studies of the federal appointments process undertaken at the request of members of Congress or their staffs, and the *Congressional Record*'s transcriptions of formal confirmation proceedings and votes. Otherwise, there are gaps in the information that can be collected. For instance, one can only speculate about the total number of temporary or nonconfirmed officials now occupying confirmable offices throughout the federal government. Neither the executive branch nor the Senate keeps track of all of the vacancies in confirmable offices (or if they do, as required by statute, they refuse to release such data). Even if one were to call every single confirmable office in the country to determine if its occupant has been confirmed or not, many offices would not respond (as my research assistants discovered in their contacts with the Office of Personnel Management and the General Accounting Office, among others). Nor have presidents or senators ever systematically maintained records on forced withdrawals of presidential nominations. Thus, the desire to quantify fully the activities within the federal appointments process, even for the most recent presidents, needs to be balanced against the relative paucity of collected *and* collectable data on such activities.

Introduction

The third caveat relates to the book's methodology and endnotes. I have undertaken some original historical and empirical research as well as relying on a wide range of secondary sources, but I have restricted my citations in the endnotes to quotes from primary sources or secondary materials, including, in some cases, past empirical studies of certain aspects of the federal appointments process.

In my analysis of post–World War II appointments controversies and developments, I rely to some extent on the results of an informal survey that I conducted of fifty-nine officials with firsthand experiences with the federal appointments process because of their service in one or more administrations.[11] I have complied with the requests of virtually all of these respondents to keep their identities confidential but have made use of their (and of course other respondents') insights throughout the book. I am most grateful for their public service as well as their candor in sharing their experiences and insights with me.

Part One

THE ORIGINS, STRUCTURE,

AND EVOLUTION OF THE FEDERAL

APPOINTMENTS PROCESS

Chapter One

THE ORIGINAL UNDERSTANDING OF THE

FEDERAL APPOINTMENTS PROCESS

IT IS CUSTOMARY to gloss over the original understanding of the federal appointments process because the relevant portion of the Constitution—the Appointments Clause—is relatively succinct and straightforward: "[The president] shall nominate, and by and with the Advice and Consent of the Senate, shall appoint Ambassadors, other public Ministers and Consuls, Judges of the supreme Court, and all other Officers of the United States, whose Appointments are not herein otherwise provided for, and which shall be established by Law."[1] By its plain language the clause empowers the president to nominate certain federal officials whose final confirmation is left for the Senate to decide. The clause also authorizes Congress to establish other offices to be filled by people nominated by the president, subject to the confirmation of the Senate.

Some other appointment matters, though not explicitly provided for by the clause, are also relatively easy to determine from the plain meaning of the constitutional text and reasonable inferences from the structure. For instance, the Constitution plainly does not require the full Senate to conduct hearings on the nominations of each of the officials covered by the clause and to confirm or reject each of those nominees by a majority vote. The Senate's authority to devise rules for its own proceedings has been commonly construed as permitting it to delegate to appropriate committees (or subcommittees) the functions of gathering relevant evidence, taking testimony (such as that of nominees), and making recommendations on nominations.[2] Such delegation has become common for numerous reasons. For instance, it has helped to streamline the Senate's decision making in a number of areas (including appointments), thereby making it possible for senators to distribute or allocate their time and energies as each sees fit. Moreover, delegation allows members to specialize in areas of particular concern to their constituents and provides an environment for more senior members to pass on institutional knowledge to more junior members and to inculcate in them norms of reciprocity, apprenticeship, and the like.[3] The Senate has also implemented safeguards or mechanisms to prevent any abuses resulting from the delegation of responsibility to committees. One important check on committee authority is the fact that the Senate's rules governing proceedings may be set aside in several ways, including by unanimous consent of the Senate, the substitution of a different rule adopted by a majority vote, or a judgment made by the Senate leadership or the whole body that further action is unnecessary in light of the committee's recommendation.

Other questions about the allocation of power over federal appointments do not have clear answers. One vexing question, for instance, is who precisely qualifies as an "officer of the United States" such that his or her nomination should be made by the president and subsequently approved or rejected by the Senate. Nor is it crystal clear whether the Appointments Clause requires the president to consult with the Senate before making a nomination by virtue of its grant to the Senate of the power to give advice on certain appointments. Yet another issue is whether the Constitution limits or defines the criteria that the president must follow in choosing which people to nominate or that the Senate must consider in approving or rejecting presidential nominees for certain offices.

The delegates at the constitutional convention, and later the ratifiers, discussed some of these questions. For all practical purposes, however, the record is silent on the question of whether the phrase "advice and consent of the Senate" was meant to have the same meaning in the contexts of treaty ratifications and the appointments of ambassadors, cabinet officers, inferior federal judges, and Supreme Court justices. The discussion never approached that level of detail. The debates over the structure of the federal appointments process focused instead on a much broader question: whether the power should be vested in the entire legislature, as proposed in the original Virginia Plan; in the Senate alone; in the president alone;

or in the president with the advice and consent of the Senate—the plan that was adopted in the closing days of the constitutional convention.

The latter proposal, advanced most persistently by Alexander Hamilton of New York and Nathaniel Gorham of Massachusetts, was twice defeated before its ultimate approval by the constitutional convention. The final approval, pursuant to a motion by James Madison of Virginia, displaced a prior vote vesting the authority in the Senate.[4] The different proposals reflected a serious division at the convention between two groups, each with different concerns about how to design the federal appointments process. One group, consisting of Oliver Ellsworth and Roger Sherman of Connecticut, Elbridge Gerry of Massachusetts, Benjamin Franklin of Pennsylvania, George Mason of Virginia, and John Rutledge of South Carolina, feared that granting the appointment power to the executive would lead to monarchy. The other group, consisting of Gouverneur Morris and James Wilson of Pennsylvania, Madison, Gorham, and Hamilton, primarily worried that granting the appointment power to the national legislature would produce cabals, intrigue, and factions. Ultimately, the final compromise giving rise to the Appointments Clause sought to avoid abuse rather than to guarantee a specific outcome, such as the appointment of the best-qualified people to important posts.

THE FOUNDERS' DELIBERATIONS ON ALLOCATING THE FEDERAL APPOINTMENTS AUTHORITY

The need for the federal Constitution to provide some mechanism for the appointments of certain officials in the new national government was obvious to the constitutional convention's delegates from the start. Their respective state experiences informed their judgments considerably. They knew firsthand that "[n]o state constitution granted to the governor an independent appointing power. [Moreover, i]n several states the governor had little or no appointing power; in those states in which he exercised a limited appointing power, it was always with the advice and consent either of a council appointed by the legislature, or by the legislature itself. Only in Massachusetts, Maryland, New Hampshire, and Pennsylvania were judges appointed by the governor, and in three of the states he shared the appointing power with a council."[5] For example, Virginia's constitution of 1776, reflecting the national trend, permitted the legislature to choose judges, the secretary of state, the attorney general, the governor's cabinet (styled the "Privy Council"), and even the governor himself. The Massachusetts Constitution, despite a clause that provided for virtually absolute separation of powers between the branches of the state government, required the legislature to select a host of executive officers.

Many of the delegates from states with little or no gubernatorial involvement in the appointments process regarded their states' practices in this area as failures. These practices had originated as responses to fears of monarchic power and as efforts to sacrifice some energetic government in exchange for greater accountability and representation. Most representative legislatures, however, had fallen easy prey to demagogues, provincialism, and factions. Consequently, in spite of the sharp restrictions imposed by most of the states on the appointment powers of governors, the delegates at the constitutional convention quickly accepted the desirability of a significant presidential role in making certain federal appointments. This agreement tracked their common understanding that the Articles of Confederation had failed to grant sufficient authority to the national government. Consistent with this understanding, they voted early in the convention's deliberations to establish presidential authority to appoint all officers "not otherwise provided for."[6] This vote took place without debate and with all of the states in agreement except Connecticut, which divided on the issue.

Subsequently, the debate over federal appointments in the convention followed two tracks: the delegates did not agree on which appointments required coverage in the Constitution, nor on where to vest the authority to appoint federal judges. Only at the end of the convention did the two tracks converge in the compromise that led to the Appointments Clause. Even then, some delegates complained that because of the eagerness of many delegates to complete their deliberations on the new constitution and leave Philadelphia, some issues, such as where to vest the authority to make federal appointments, had not been resolved.[7] At the very least, these disagreements indicate that some of the delegates had wanted to vest, or had seriously considered vesting, the authority for making different kinds of appointments in places other than those approved in the final draft of the Constitution.

Origins, Structure, and Evolution

Indeed, the very first plan for the new national government considered by the convention, the Virginia Plan introduced by Edmund Randolph on May 29, 1787, placed the appointment authority in two different places, depending on the kinds of appointments involved. Subsequent debate accepted this division. Consequently, the focus of the initial discussion on federal appointments was on the Virginia Plan's proposal to make the president alone responsible for such appointments. The operative provision empowered him "to enjoy the executive rights vested in Congress by the Confederation."[8] James Wilson understood the powers given to the president by virtue of this provision to include "those of executing the laws, and appointing officers, not (appertaining to and) appointed by the Legislature."[9] James Madison tried to clear up any misunderstanding by moving to insert the words "with power to carry into effect the national laws, to appoint to offices in cases not otherwise provided for."[10] The convention approved Madison's motion. Afterward, Madison stated that he did not think the words "to appoint to offices" were really necessary, but he thought that their inclusion would help "to prevent doubts and misconstructions."[11]

As an alternative to the Virginia Plan, William Paterson proposed the New Jersey Plan on June 15, 1787. It provided for, *inter alia,* a plural executive with the power "to appoint all federal officers not otherwise provided for."[12] On June 18, Alexander Hamilton introduced a plan far more sympathetic to the establishment of a very strong chief executive. His proposed constitution would have vested the executive with the sole power to appoint "the heads or chief officers of the departments of Finance, War, and Foreign Affairs" and to nominate "all other officers[,] subject to the approbation or rejection of the Senate."[13] Hamilton's plan, though it did not attract any discussion or comment at the time it was proposed, was the first to suggest the method of appointment ultimately adopted by the convention. He proposed that the Senate should have only the power of rejecting or approving nominees suggested by the president, reflecting his view that the Senate should not participate in exercising the nominating power. Yet another plan, proposed by Charles Pinckney of South Carolina, vested the appointment power in Congress.[14]

The next discussion of any proposed procedures for administrative or other nonjudicial appointments occurred as part of a series of resolutions in late July. The latter were referred on July 23 by the convention sitting as a Committee of the Whole to the Committee on Detail, which was responsible for putting all formal recommendations and suggestions into draft form. One resolution provided "that a national Executive be instituted, to consist of a single person," who would have the power "to appoint to all offices in Cases not otherwise provided for."[15] This resolution clearly vested the president with some appointment powers, and even with respect to those that remained with Congress the president was given the "right to negative any legislative act, which shall not be afterwards passed, unless by two-third parts of each branch of the national Legislat[ure]."[16] By exercising this "negative" privilege, the president could at least have held up any appointment by Congress until such time as it confirmed its previous nomination or proposed another more to the liking of the president.[17] On August 6, the Committee on Detail issued a report proposing, *inter alia,* a clause giving the Senate the additional power to appoint ambassadors and Supreme Court justices and another providing for the appointment of the treasurer by both houses of the legislature.[18]

On August 23, the convention considered the proposal to vest the appointment authority for ambassadors in the Senate. Gouverneur Morris argued against it. He viewed "the [Senate] as too numerous for the purpose; as subject to cabal; and as devoid of responsibility."[19] Wilson strongly agreed.[20] On the next day, however, the convention again considered the provision that the president should "appoint officers in all cases not otherwise provided for by the Constitution."[21] Roger Sherman objected that many officers, such as general officers in the army in peacetime, should not be appointed by the president, and he moved to add the words "or by law," which would have allowed Congress to determine the scope of the president's appointment power.[22] The motion lost, with only Sherman's home state, Connecticut, voting for it.[23]

On August 17, the convention separately considered the proposal to vest in Congress the authority to appoint the national treasurer. Opposing this proposal, George Read of Delaware moved to leave the appointment of the treasurer to the president. "The Legislature," he suggested, "was an improper body for appointments. Those of the State legislatures were a proof of it. The Executive being responsible would make a good choice."²⁴ Mason opposed the motion on the ground that "the legislature representing the people ought to appoint the keepers" of the public's money.²⁵ The motion lost, but on September 14, the final day on which the convention considered the text of the Constitution, the delegates adopted Rutledge's motion to delete the special provision and let the treasurer be appointed in the same manner as other officers.²⁶

A parallel but even more heated debate had focused on the Virginia Plan's proposal that the national legislature should choose federal judges.²⁷ When this provision came before the convention for consideration on June 5, James Wilson led the opposition. He explained: "Experience sh[o]wed the impropriety of such appointments by numerous bodies. Intrigue, partiality, and concealment were the necessary consequences. A principal reason for unity in the Executive was the officers might be appointed by a single, responsible person."²⁸ John Rutledge responded that he "was by no means disposed to grant so great a power to any single person. The people will think we are leaning too much towards Monarchy."²⁹

At this point, Benjamin Franklin, who was sometimes prone to make his points through humorous jabs, asked the delegates to consider other possible mechanisms for judicial appointments. One possibility he suggested was the method used in Scotland, "in which the nomination proceeded from the Lawyers,"³⁰ for they would have an incentive to divide the appointee's practice amongst themselves. Though Franklin's comment may only have been a jest, his suggestion foreshadowed the practice prevalent during the Carter administration and still popular in some states of designating special commissions, largely consisting of lawyers, to recommend judicial nominees to those with final appointing authority.

Ignoring Franklin's comment, James Madison, considered by many the chief architect of the Virginia Plan, expressed his agreement with Wilson's concerns about legislative "intrigue and partiality."³¹ However, Madison "was not satisfied with referring the appointment to the Executive."³² Instead, he proposed placing the power of appointment in the Senate, "as numerous en[ough] to be confided in—as not so numerous as to be governed by the motives of the other branch; and as being sufficiently stable and independent to follow their deliberate judgments."³³ When the question finally came to a vote, the convention voted nine to two to defer consideration until a time of "maturer reflection."³⁴

The convention next considered the matter of judicial appointments on June 13. Charles Pinckney and Roger Sherman moved to restore the original provision in the Virginia Plan for the appointment of the Supreme Court by the entire Congress.[35] Madison objected to this motion on the ground that many members of Congress were not competent "[j]udges of the requisite qualifications. They were too much influenced by their partialities. The candidate who . . . had displayed a talent for business in the legislative field, who perhaps had assisted ignorant members in business of their own, or of their Constituents, or used other winning means, would without any of the essential qualifications for an expositor of the laws prevail over a competitor not having these recommendations but possessed of every necessary accomplishment."[36] As an alternative Madison proposed that the Senate, a more elite and less numerous body, be empowered to appoint federal judges. Pinckney and Sherman ultimately withdrew their motion, and the convention accepted Madison's suggestion without comment.[37]

Not long thereafter, two other proposals were made for empowering the president to make judicial appointments. As part of the New Jersey Plan, William Paterson suggested that the executive appoint all federal judges,[38] while New York's Alexander Hamilton proposed that judges should be among those offices nominated by the executive, subject to approval or rejection by the Senate.

The subject resurfaced on July 18, when the convention considered a resolution (based on Madison's proposal) "that a national judiciary be established to consist of one supreme tribunal the judges of which [shall] be appointed by the [Senate]."[39] Nathaniel Gorham opened the debate, expressing concern that the Senate was "too numerous, and too little personally responsible, to ensure a good choice."[40] He proposed instead that the president should appoint the justices, with the advice and consent of the Senate—following the model set by his home state of Massachusetts.[41] Wilson responded that the president should be able to make appointments on his own, but that he would accept the Gorham proposal as a less appealing alternative.[42] Luther Martin of Maryland, an ardent Anti-Federalist, and Roger Sherman both endorsed judicial appointments by the Senate. Martin approved appointment by the Senate, because "being taken from all the states it w[oul]d be best informed of characters and most capable of making a fit choice."[43] Sherman agreed that the Senate would be more likely to choose properly than the executive, because "it would be composed of men nearly equal to the Executive, and would of course have . . . more wisdom. They would bring into their deliberations a more diffusive knowledge of characters. It would be less easy for candidates to intrigue with them, than with the Executive Magistrate."[44] With Gouverneur Morris's concurrence, Mason objected that the president should not be empowered to appoint judges if these were going to be authorized to try presidential impeachments as the judges would be tempted not to convict the person who had appointed them. Mason complained that the president, because of his residence at the seat of government for a period of years, would be unduly influenced to make appointments from that state. Gorham dismissed the complaint: "As the Executive will be responsible . . . for a judicious and faithful discharge of his trust, he will be careful to look through all the States for proper characters. The Senators will be as likely to form their attachments at the seat of Gov[ernmen]t where they reside, as the Executive. If they cannot get the man of the particular State to which they may respectively belong, they will be indifferent to the rest. Public bodies feel no personal responsibility, and give full play to intrigue and cabal."[45]

As a compromise Madison proposed that the national executive appoint federal judges subject to the concurrence of at least one-third of the Senate.[46] This proposal, Madison claimed, would "unite the advantage of responsibility in the Executive with the security afforded in the [Senate] ag[ain]st any incautious or corrupt nomination by the Executive."[47] Splitting ranks with Madison, Edmund Randolph advocated instead that the Senate should have the power to appoint federal judges. Randolph "thought the advantage of personal responsibility might be gained in the Senate by requiring the respective votes of the members to be entered on the Journal. He thought too that the hope of (receiving) app[ointmen]ts would be more diffusive if they depended on the Senate, the members of which w[oul]d be diffusively known, than if they depended on a single man who could not be personally known to a very great extent."[48] Gorham responded that the Senate was in no better position than the president to find good judicial candidates from around the country and that ultimately the president "would certainly be more answerable for a good appointment, as the whole blame of a bad one would fall on him alone."[49]

In the end, the delegates rejected Gorham's proposal by a vote of six to two. Consequently, Gorham suggested an alternative that would authorize the president to nominate and appoint judges with the advice and consent of the Senate. The delegates divided four to four on this proposal's merits.[50] Madison then proposed presidential nomination with an opportunity for Senate rejection, by a two-thirds vote, within a specified number of days.[51] The convention tabled the motion for later discussion.

Three days later, on July 21, Madison defended his change of positions, suggesting that the executive would be more likely than any other branch "to select fit characters," and that "in case of any flagrant partiality or error, in the nomination, it might be fairly presumed that [two-thirds] of the [Senate] would join in putting a negative on it."[52] It is conceivable that Madison's different proposals were part of a strategy to move the convention "toward presidential participation in the appointment process. In any event, the [later] motion eliminated the House of Representatives from [this] process and paved the way for nomination of justices by the executive."[53] Madison's fellow Virginian, Edmund Randolph, agreed with the latter practice because he saw "the responsibility of the Executive as a security for fit appointments."[54] Morris also supported the motion.[55] George Mason opposed the proposal because he believed "appointment by the Executive [to be] a dangerous prerogative. It might even give him an influence over the Judiciary department itself."[56]

The delegates rejected Madison's motion for executive appointment "unless disagreed to by the Senate" by a vote of six to three. By the same vote, the convention accepted his other proposal for the Senate to appoint Supreme Court justices.[57]

The convention next considered the question of where to vest the authority to make judicial appointments in early September. This was the first time it openly considered a proposal virtually identical with the Appointment Clause's current form.[58] Furthermore, on September 4, the Committee of Eleven, specially charged to deal with all postponed matters, issued a report including a provision for executive nomination of Supreme Court justices with the advice and consent of the Senate.[59] The discussion on this provision occurred on September 6 and 7, at which time

Origins, Structure, and Evolution

several delegates, including Charles Pinckney and James Wilson,[60] opposed it. Gouverneur Morris, who had consistently favored appointment by the executive, was the sole speaker on its behalf. He explained, "[A]s the President was to nominate, there would be responsibility, and as the Senate was to concur, there would be security."[61] The convention unanimously agreed on the language of the proposed Appointments Clause pertaining to the mechanism for judicial appointments and, by a vote of nine to two, on the insertion of the phrase "And all other officers of the United States" into the clause.[62]

The discussion about the Appointments Clause in the ratification campaign tended to follow the arguments made in the constitutional convention, albeit sometimes with more passionate rhetoric. Not surprisingly, opponents of the new Constitution criticized and opposed the division of authority in the Appointments Clause, while the Constitution's proponents tended to defend it. The broad outlines of the process established by the clause were repeatedly acknowledged in pamphlets and articles defending it throughout ratification. Alexander Hamilton made the most prominent defense in *The Federalist Papers*. In explaining the clause's division of authority, Hamilton argued that the real power of appointment would reside with the president. He maintained that "one man of discernment is better fitted to analyze and estimate the peculiar qualities adapted to particular offices, than a body of men of equal or perhaps even of superior discernment."[63] He explained further that "a single well directed man . . . cannot be distracted and warped by that diversity of views, feelings and interests, which frequently distract and warp the resolutions of a collective body."[64] A multimember body, such as the one responsible for appointments in his own state of New York, was a less attractive alternative. Such a council acting in secret would be "a conclave in which cabal and intrigue will have their full scope. . . . [T]he desire of mutual gratification will beget a scandalous bartering of votes and bargaining for places."[65]

It is also not surprising, given Hamilton's preference for a strong executive, that he took the position that the constitutional procedure for making federal appointments did not envision a dominant or significant role for the Senate. He expected the Senate to defer to the president's choices of nominees. The Senate's function was not to reject a nominee because the senators preferred someone else, for they could not be sure "that the subsequent nomination would fall upon their own favorite, or upon any person in their estimation more meritorious than the one rejected."[66]

Although Hamilton preferred a strong national executive, he acknowledged that the Senate was not supposed to be a rubber stamp. The Appointments Clause, he explained, provided for the Senate's concurrence as "an excellent check upon a spirit of favoritism in the President, and would tend greatly to prevent the appointment of unfit characters from State prejudice, from family connection, from personal attachment, or from a view to popularity."[67] Indeed, Hamilton expected that the president "would be both ashamed and afraid to bring forward . . . candidates who had no other merit than that of coming from the same State to which he particularly belonged, or of being in some way or other personally allied to him, or of possessing the necessary insignificance and pliancy to render them the obsequious instruments of his pleasure."[68]

In the ratification conventions, the opponents of the new Constitution objected that the Appointments Clause made the president or the Senate or both too powerful. For example, George Mason told the Virginia ratifying convention that the failure of the Constitution to establish an executive council to provide formal advice to the president (something he had advocated but failed to convince the constitutional convention to adopt) was "a fatal defect,"[69] and that the "improper power of the Senate in the appointment of public officers" resulted in dangerously blending the Executive and Legislative powers."[70] Similarly, Luther Martin told the Maryland legislature that there had been considerable opposition to the Appointments Clause on the ground that it would make the president "king, in everything but name," for he would have "a formidable host, devoted to his interest, and ready to support his ambitious views."[71]

Participants in ratifying conventions in several other states complained that the proposed Constitution deprived the president of an independent appointing authority, which he ought to enjoy as chief executive, and made him dependent on the Senate. Some denounced the fusion of legislative and executive powers as violating the principle of separation of powers, while others expressed the fear that the Senate would become too powerful and would wield its power along aristocratic lines.

Origins, Structure, and Evolution

For example, in his "Letters of a Federal Farmer," Richard Henry Lee of Virginia maintained that "the President is connected with or tied to the Senate; he may always act with the Senate, but he can never effectually counteract its views. The President can appoint no officer, civil or military, who shall not be agreeable to the Senate."[72] Samuel Spencer expressed a similar objection to the North Carolina ratifying convention: "The President may nominate, but [the Senate will] have a negative on his nomination, till he has exhausted the number of those he wishes to be appointed. He will be obliged, finally, to acquiesce in the appointment of those whom the Senate shall nominate, or else no appointment will take place."[73]

William Davie, who had been a delegate from North Carolina to the constitutional convention, defended the Appointments Clause at the North Carolina ratifying convention on a basis not expressly claimed prior to the ratification campaign. He explained that the clause had been adopted as a compromise between the large and small states. "The small states," he said, "would not agree that the House of Representatives should have a voice in the appointment to offices; and the extreme jealousy of all the states would not give it to the President alone."[74] Roger Sherman and Oliver Ellsworth made a similar point in their report to the governor of Connecticut urging ratification of the Constitution: "The equal representation of the States in the Senate and the voice of that branch in the appointment to offices will secure the rights of the lesser as well as the greater states."[75]

The weight of authority suggests, however, that these arguments were slightly overstated. To be sure, the smaller states had generally supported strengthening the role in the federal appointments process of the Senate, in which they had been guaranteed equal representation with the larger states by virtue of the Great Compromise of July 16. It is also fair to say that after the Great Compromise, the smaller states "continuously eyed the larger states for signs [that] they were attempting to construct a system that benefitted them inordinately, while the larger states were under a constant temptation to do precisely that."[76] Yet, the adoption of the Appointments Clause was less a compromise (at least explicitly) between larger and smaller states than it was a compromise ultimately between those who believed in and those who feared a strong executive. Each of the latter two groups had some members from large states and some from small states.[77]

In Pennsylvania, the major objection to the Appointments Clause was that the Constitution had placed too much power in the hands of the Senate and made the president into an instrument of that body. James Wilson led the defense, stating that the Appointments Clause was not his "favorite part of the Constitution" but that in it "the Senate stands controlled. If it is that monster which it is said to be, it can only show its teeth; it is unable to bite and devour. . . . With regard to appointment of officers, the President must nominate before they can vote."[78] He denied that the Appointments Clause made the president subservient to the Senate, for, in his opinion, the Senate could do nothing until the president had made the first move: "Clearly, [the president] holds the helm, and the vessel can proceed in neither one direction nor another without his concurrence."[79]

In retrospect, the Appointments Clause was not an unusual compromise given the framers' general understanding of the Constitution's scheme of separation of powers. The basic goals of the whole scheme were to ensure balance, accountability, and energy.[80] These objectives are apparent in the compromise embodied in the Appointments Clause. The latter allows the president to make nominations because he is more accountable for his choices than the multimembered body of the Senate, he can act more efficiently in making nomination decisions, he is likely to be less provincial than the Senate in nominating people because he is expected to be more familiar than any senator with qualified people from around the country, and he is less prone than senators to make secret deals on appointments. The clause includes the Senate in the federal appointment process because that body is sufficiently independent from the president and protective of the public welfare to prevent the president from nominating his cronies or other unfit people to important governmental positions, to make the president account relatively swiftly for his bad judgment in making nominations, and can otherwise check the president's abuse of his nominating authority.

Neither the constitutional convention and ratification debates nor the Appointments Clause indicated that the clause's division of authority or that any senatorial deference (or the absence thereof) depended on the kind of appointment involved. Although one might suppose that some appointments might have justified more Senate scrutiny or involvement than others, the proponents of the Constitution never said so. Nor, of course, did they suggest anything to the contrary. Their concern in dividing the authority over federal appointments between the president and the Senate was to reduce or check abuse by either or both. The rest, it seems, was to be worked out between the two in practice.

THE SENATE'S PRENOMINATION ROLE

One aspect of the Appointments Clause on which the constitutional and various state ratifying conventions featured virtually no debate was the precise meaning of the term "advice." Yet, the meaning of that term is significant for clarifying whether the Appointments Clause permits or requires the Senate to participate in the prenomination phase of an appointment.

The first place to look for guidance in resolving this issue is obviously the constitutional text, but it is not dispositive. On the one hand, Charles Black argues that while the term "consent" in the Appointments Clause could denote a perfunctory task, the term "advice," according to its plain meaning and common usage, requires someone or some body to perform the function of an adviser, thereby authorizing the Senate to give or withhold "advice on the basis of all the relevant considerations bearing on the decision." [81]

On the other hand, John McGinnis construes the term "advice" far more narrowly, suggesting that it contemplates only a postnomination act because "[t]he very grammar of the clause is telling: the act of nomination is separated from the act of appointment by a comma and a conjunction. Only the latter act is qualified by the phrase 'advice and consent.' Furthermore, it is not at all anomalous to use the word 'advice' with respect to the action of the Senate in confirming an appointment. The Senate's consent is advisory because confirmation does not bind the President to commission and empower the confirmed nominee." [82] Black agrees, citing *Marbury v. Madison*,[83] that "the President's 'appointment,' after the Senate's action is still voluntary, so that in a sense the action of the Senate even under settled practice may be looked on only as 'advisory' with respect to a step from which the President may still withdraw. [Moreover,] nominations are occasionally withdrawn after public indications of Senate sentiment (and probable action) which may be thought to amount to advice."[84]

There is ample early historical practice to support the latter view. For instance, William Cushing, President Washington's second choice to succeed John Jay as Chief Justice, in 1795 declined the post, but only after Washington had formally nominated him and the Senate had confirmed his appointment.[85] Cushing instead remained an associate justice until his death in 1810. Two of President Madison's top choices to fill the vacancy arising on the Court as a result of Cushing's death—Lincoln Levi and John Quincy Adams—declined the appointment, but only after each had already been formally nominated by President Madison and confirmed by the Senate for the position.[86] Similarly, John Jay declined a second appointment to serve as Chief Justice even though President John Adams had formally nominated Jay without his knowledge to succeed the outgoing Chief Justice Oliver Ellsworth in 1800 and the Senate had confirmed him.[87] John Marshall, who accepted his nomination by President Adams to become Chief Justice, had previously declined an appointment to be U.S. attorney for Virginia in 1798, but not before having been nominated by President Washington and confirmed by the Senate for the position.[88] Marshall had also rejected Washington's offer a few years earlier to join his cabinet as attorney general. Regardless of the many instances in which people declined their appointments to high office after having been formally nominated and confirmed, it is not clear why, if the word "advice" meant only that the Senate's consent to a nomination did not bind a president or nominee to take a particular office, the framers placed it before the word "consent" in the Appointments Clause rather than the other way around.

The only framer who directly addressed this quandary—George Mason—did so only once and did not seem to be bothered by it. Mason, an ardent Anti-Federalist who opposed the Constitution's ratification, commented on the meaning of "advice" in the midst of a debate in the Senate regarding the confirmation of three of President Washington's nominees to be ministers to foreign capitals. Reasoning from the text of the Appointments Clause, Mason suggested that "[t]he Word 'Advice' here clearly relates in the Judgment of the Senate on the Expediency or

Inexpediency of the Measure, or Appointment; and the word 'Consent' to their Approbation or Disapprobation of the Person nominated; otherwise the word 'Advice' has no meaning at all."[89] Professor McGinnis construes this comment to mean that the term "advice" "called on the Senate to advise as to the prudence of appointing anyone to this kind of office, whereas the word 'Consent' called on the Senate to consider the fitness of the person nominated."[90]

Moreover, several framers seemed to agree during the constitutional and state ratification conventions that the power to nominate belonged solely to the president. For example, in *The Federalist Papers*, Alexander Hamilton maintained that "[i]t will be the office of the President to *nominate*, and, with the advice and consent of the Senate, to *appoint*. There will, of course, be no exertion of *choice* on the part of the Senate. They may defeat one choice of the Executive, and oblige him to make another; but they cannot themselves *choose*—they can only ratify or reject the choice he may have made."[91] Likewise, James Wilson suggested that the nominating authority under the Constitution "should be . . . unfettered and unsheltered by counsellors."[92]

It is important to understand, however, that those who spoke during the constitutional and state ratifying conventions in favor of the view that the nominating power belonged solely to the president supported a strong presidential role in the appointments process and objected to an equally strong or dominant role for the Senate.[93] This is not to say that their views are irrelevant or unilluminating, but their opinions must be put into perspective. Recognizing that the Appointments Clause might have been based on a view of the nomination power as belonging solely to the president is not the same thing as reading it to preclude *any* role for the Senate or some senators to provide input on the making or choice of nominations. No one disputes that the president alone has the formal authority to nominate people to confirmable posts—that is, to make the final judgments about whom to nominate; however, it is a far different thing—and not at all inconsistent with the existence of such presidential authority nor with the language of the Appointments Clause—to say that the Senate may be constitutionally permitted to give counsel to the president before he formally announces his choices for confirmable offices.

Historical practices subsequent to the ratification of the Constitution shed further light on the meaning of the term "advice." Every U.S. president (including George Washington) has faced considerable pressure to consult with senators on his nominations to confirmable offices. Indeed, most presidents have undertaken such consultation, and often have deferred to senators' suggestions (particularly for federal offices in their respective states). While such consultation and deference do not necessarily confirm that a president is constitutionally compelled to consult with the Senate as a body or with any group of senators prior to making formal nominations, they do reflect the fact that presidents, as a matter of prudence or comity, have found it expedient at least sometimes to seek the advice of senators and to respect some senators' choices of particular candidates for certain positions. No president has ever said that the Constitution *required* him to consult formally with the Senate prior to making a nomination;[94] however, virtually every president has understood that failure to do so, at least informally, would likely be costly to himself, his nominee, or both.

Ultimately, reading the term "advice" restrictively in the manner attributed to Mason and supposedly implied by some framers' comments about the exclusivity of the president's nominating power makes little sense. Congress has, and frequently exercises, the power to create the offices to which the president's nomination power applies. Consequently, any question about whether anyone at all should be appointed to the office already created by Congress has already been resolved to some extent by the time the president nominates someone to fill it. It is absurd to think that the Senate, which will have approved of the creation of the position, will as a matter of constitutional law need to continue to debate the necessity of an office's creation or existence again not just later but every single time the president nominates someone to it.

To be sure, in the circumstances giving rise to Mason's comment — President Washington's nomination of Gouverneur Morris to be minister to France — the Senate had not had the chance to consider the basic question about whether anyone should have been nominated to that particular office because the offices of ambassador being filled by President Washington at the time had been created by the Constitution itself rather than by legislative enactment.[95] Even so, it makes little sense to think that the term "advice" had to be added to the Appointments Clause to allow the Senate to raise a specific objection to a president's attempt to fill an office not yet authorized by it, because the Senate could simply refuse to "consent" to any nomination until it had determined whether or not the position should be filled. The need for the Senate to offer such "advice" would be extremely rare, given that the framers fully expected the specific offices to which the nomination and confirmation powers would apply would be left to the discretion of and established by Congress. A president's deviation from that basic understanding might become a source of conflict between himself and the Senate; however, the debate over Washington's nominees that gave rise to Mason's comment covered no such ground. Rather, Mason thought Morris was the wrong person for the job, and thus he insisted on a construction of the Appointments Clause that supported the outcome he desired—namely, the Senate's rejection of Morris as the minister to France.

A more sensible reading of the term "advice" is that it means that the Senate is constitutionally entitled to give advice to a president on whom as well as what kinds of persons he should nominate to certain posts, but this advice is not binding. The use of "advice" in the Appointments Clause suggests that the Senate has authority to give advice as to how a president should exercise his nominating power either generally or in particular cases. In addition, the Appointments Clause authorizes the Senate to "consent" to the nomination of the particular person proposed. In other words, the Constitution does not mandate any formal prenomination role for the Senate to consult with the president; nor does it impose any obligation on the president to consult with the Senate prior to nominating people to confirmable posts. The Constitution does, however, make it clear that the president or his nominees may have to pay a price if he ignores the Senate's advice. Whether or not a president has consulted with senators before formally nominating someone to a confirmable post, he still must get the Senate's consent to the nomination made. If the word "advice" were not in the Appointments Clause, the president could object on separation-of-powers grounds to the attempt of one or more senators to give him advice on the kinds of nominations he should make. He could argue that the Senate's formal role in the process does not begin until after he has formally made a nomination and that such advice injects the Senate or the senator(s) improperly into a realm that is exclusively the president's. Instead, the Constitution allows a president to object on the narrower ground that he is not bound to take any advice from the Senate regarding nominations generally or in particular cases, and the Senate can respond that a president makes such a refusal at the risk of having his nominee(s) rejected. The president might still win, but not without having been made aware beforehand of the price his action may entail. Such consultation would, at least in theory, work to the advantages of both parties in that it could lead to the development of some consensus (or the reduction of some tension) between the two branches and the opportunity for the president and Senate to check each other's judgments in this important area.

THE CONSTITUTIONAL LIMITS ON PRESIDENTIAL AND SENATORIAL DISCRETION IN THE APPOINTMENTS PROCESS

Does the Constitution impose any special obligation(s) on the president in making his nominations or on the Senate in evaluating them? Put slightly differently, does the Constitution impose any criteria directing or otherwise constraining how the President or the Senate may exercise their respective discretion in this area?

There are three conceivable answers to this question. First, the oath the president takes to "preserve, protect and defend the Constitution of the United States of America"[96] may be construed as requiring him to nominate, particularly to judicial offices, only those people who share his view of how the Constitution should be interpreted. To do otherwise would arguably mean he had put someone in office who would be likely to wield authority in an unconstitutional manner (at least as measured against the president's own views on the matter).

This first argument is flawed for several reasons. First, it rests on the mistaken premise that once a president takes his oath of office, his views of how the Constitution should be interpreted are necessarily transformed into law of the same magnitude, order, or status as the Constitution itself. There is nothing about the oath that would support such a conclusion. The oath taken by a president obliges him to take actions consistent with

Origins, Structure, and Evolution

the Constitution; it does not establish any separate standard by which to measure the constitutionality of his actions (or those of his appointees).

Moreover, none of the framers' comments on the nomination power as belonging strictly to the president illuminates whether or not the Constitution constrains his choice of whom to nominate. Such a determination depends on the applicability and content of other, separate provisions of the Constitution. Neither the Appointments Clause nor any other part of the Constitution sets forth any such limitation. The only constraint on a president's judgment in making nominations is purely practical. Thus, for instance, the Constitution does not preclude a president from nominating nonlawyers to key Justice Department posts or federal judgeships (as President Reagan mused about doing during the 1980 presidential election). The delegates to the constitutional convention and the ratifiers did occasionally express their expectation that a president would nominate qualified people to federal judgeships and other important governmental offices; but those comments were expressions of hope and concern about the consequences of and the need to devise a check against a president's failure to nominate qualified people, particularly in the absence of any constitutionally required minimal criteria for certain positions.

In addition, enforcing the idea that the president's oath constrains his choice of nominees would lead to absurd results. For instance, it would mean that senators, who take a similar (though somewhat less elaborate) oath, would be similarly constrained to reject any nominee whose constitutional views did not comport with their own. This would suggest that whenever a president and the Senate had different constitutional philosophies, the Constitution would require a stalemate until such time as one persuaded the other to change its views or a different president or senators became involved. It is hard to imagine that any constitutional or state ratifying convention delegates shared this interpretation; no evidence exists that anyone at the time of the drafting and ratification of the Constitution mentioned the possibility of such conflict. Even if it were possible to find a constitutional constraint on the president's or Senate's actions on the basis of their respective oaths of office, any deviation from those limits would be treated by the federal courts as a nonjusticiable, political question based on constitutional and prudential considerations. These include but are not limited to the absence of any clear authority for judicial review of such matters, serious conflicts between the political branches and the judiciary, and uncertainty about the finality and validity of federal appointments.

A second conceivable answer to the question of whether the Appointments Clause imposes a constraint on how the president and the Senate may exercise their respective appointment authorities is that the original understanding and basic structure of the federal appointments process support Senate opposition to important presidential nominees only for very good or compelling reasons. Various aspects of the constitutional structure were designed to facilitate this outcome, including the president's power of repeated nomination, which will enable him sooner or later to get his way unless the Senate has a sufficiently good reason that can persuade or move a majority to put its own political capital repeatedly on the line against it; the unitary nature of the office of the presidency, enabling its occupant to make decisions more efficiently and easily than those made by the more politically diverse body of the Senate; and the likelihood that the president can rely on a greater mandate for his choice than the Senate can for its opposition based on his election by the whole nation (and almost assuredly in part based on his representations about the likely nature of his judicial appointments).

Several framers also indicated their belief that the Senate should reject a president's nominees only for compelling reasons. Given that the Senate was not to exercise the nominating power at least formally, Alexander Hamilton, for example, supposed that a nominee should be rejected only for "special and strong reasons."[97] In explaining the division of authority in the Appointments Clause to the North Carolina ratifying convention, James Iredell, whom President Washington would later appoint an associate justice on the Supreme Court, agreed with Hamilton's view that the Senate should reject a presidential nominee only if that person was "positively unfit" for the post to which he had been nominated.[98]

Of course, too much should not be made out of these comments and inferences. At most, some framers' comments reflect their expectations or hopes that the Senate would reject presidential nominees only for important or compelling reasons. They made these statements to assuage concerns expressed in the ratifying conventions that the Appointments Clause might allow senators to reject nominees arbitrarily or repeatedly in the hope of eventually forcing a president to nominate someone more to their liking. Their comments did not describe or assert the existence of any constitutional mandate specifying guidelines or standards for the rejection of nominees.

The third view on whether the Appointments Clause constrains a president's or senator's judgment in any particular way is the simplest and most sensible. The clause says nothing about the criteria on which the president and the Senate may base their decisions. This silence implies that either actor may make a choice in this context for any reason. Indeed, as George Washington suggested when he was the nation's first chief executive, "As the President has a right to nominate without assigning his reasons, so has the Senate a right to dissent without giving theirs."[99]

This understanding of the dynamics of the appointments process treats the most meaningful checks as consisting of some kind of external political pressure. Alexander Hamilton described how this would operate in practice. The need for Senate approval of a president's nominees would have, in his opinion, "a powerful, though, in general, a silent operation. It would be an excellent check upon a spirit of favoritism of the President, and would tend greatly to prevent the appointment of unfit characters from state prejudice, from family connection, from personal attachment, or from a view to popularity."[100] If the president still proceeded to choose poorly, Hamilton predicted that "[t]he blame of a bad nomination would fall upon the President singly and absolutely."[101] And if the Senate acted unwisely or without sufficient justification, then Hamilton expected that the "censure of rejecting a good [nomination] would lie entirely at the door of the Senate."[102] In other words, the check on a president's or senator's abuse of his or her discretion in making final judgments about appointments is the political fallout from such abuse.[103]

Moreover, the framers largely left unexplored the matter of what would qualify as very good or compelling reasons for rejecting a nomination, leading to the conclusion that they did not intend for the Constitution to limit the bases for presidential or senatorial action in this area. For example, although one might imagine that simply being unqualified would constitute a reasonable basis for rejection, the delegates and ratifiers never discussed the qualifications required for various confirmable offices.[104] Such silence might have reflected any number of things. For instance,

Original Understanding of Appointments Process

the framers might have thought (but never explicitly said) that rejection based on the absence of minimal qualifications was so obvious that it required no discussion. Or they might have thought the subject was not sufficiently important to discuss; or perhaps they simply neglected to discuss it. In addition, the framers might have expected (but again never expressed their expectation) that the president and the Senate would make determinations regarding qualifications as (and when) each saw fit, and perhaps some framers hoped that the minimally necessary qualifications for certain positions would be obvious.

In any event, the early practice confirms that the Constitution allows the president and the Senate to base their decisions or actions regarding appointments on whatever grounds they deem appropriate. The practice further demonstrates the significance of the delegations of authority made to the president and Senate by the Appointments Clause to the Constitution's general scheme of checks and balances. In fact, every president has faced serious opposition from the Senate with respect to some of his nominees, both judicial and nonjudicial. The remainder of this book explores the nature and significance of these conflicts in greater detail.

Chapter Two

THE STRUCTURE OF THE

FEDERAL APPOINTMENTS PROCESS

THE ORIGINAL UNDERSTANDING of the federal appointments process does not fully illuminate the system's essential purposes and potential. Inferences from the design and various postratification developments and practices are also important for clarifying the balance of power effectuated by the Appointments Clause. This chapter considers the implications for the balance of power posed by the inferences that can be reasonably drawn from the allocations of power and relationships created by the Appointments Clause. Understanding the basic structure of the federal appointments process and its evolution in history is crucial for developing the proper perspective for analyzing the institutional dynamics of the system.

THE SIGNIFICANCE OF A SINGLE APPOINTMENTS CLAUSE

The Constitution establishes a single mechanism for the appointment of "officers of the United States" requiring presidential nomination and Senate confirmation. To borrow Justice Stevens's comment from another context,[1] there is only one Appointments Clause. The same clause and the same constitutional structure are applicable to the appointments of all "officers of the United States."[2]

The uniformity of the constitutional language and design has at least two significant implications for the balance of power between the president and the Senate. First, the structure does not provide explicit recognition of any exceptions, particular procedures, or special accommodations that must be reached between the president and the Senate in making different kinds of federal appointments. The Appointments Clause plainly sets forth one basic mechanism—for the president to make nominations and the Senate to confirm or reject his nominees—that applies broadly, regardless of the kind or extent of power of the officials being appointed. Although the president and the Senate are free to develop to their mutual satisfaction special procedures for appointing different kinds of federal officers, such arrangements are not binding on subsequent presidents, senators, or generations. If, for example, some senators think that Supreme Court nominees should meet some special burden of proof to be confirmed because of the special powers they will wield in office,[3] the only recourse left to them is to get a critical mass of senators to concur with the special procedure they prefer. Even so, no formal mechanism ensures that each senator will apply the appropriate burden of proof, so that the enforcement of such a standard would appear to be practically impossible even if it violated no constitutional stricture.[4]

Moreover, the uniformity of the constitutional design for federal appointments raises a question about the comparative competency of presidents and senators to select different kinds of officials. By virtue of its allocation of appointments authority, the Appointments Clause clearly rests on the implicit assumptions that a president will be able efficiently to make nominations (or devise a scheme for facilitating the making of nominations) and that senators both individually and collectively will be proficient at making confirmation decisions about the fitness of presidential nominees to serve. The clause's allocation of authority necessarily implies that both political actors will be involved with a wide variety of appointments.

The critical question is whether the underlying assumption of the Appointments Clause regarding the comparative institutional operations, performances, or functions of the president and the Senate makes sense. Many of the people the president and the Senate share responsibility for appointing exercise very specialized functions, and it is unlikely that presidents and senators will be experts themselves in the fields in which these nominees will perform their specialized tasks. Nor is it likely that presidents or senators will be able to give each federal appointment the same degree of attention. Consequently, presidents and senators must rely on others to advise them on the fitness of people to perform certain specialized tasks. The Constitution is silent as to who should perform these advisory functions. Yet, it is obvious that a president's (or a senator's) choice of advisers is as important as the choice of whom to nominate.

Moreover, a serious issue arises as to the advantages of making the president, the Senate, or both responsible for all federal appointments. The question entails figuring out whether, or to what extent, it is worth the time and energy (and political capital) for presidents and senators (or their respective subordinates) to become involved with the logistics or technicalities of filling certain positions.

THE PRESUMPTION OF CONFIRMATION

The Constitution also establishes a presumption of confirmation that works to the advantage of the president and his nominees. First, by requiring only a bare majority of the Senate for approval, the Constitution sets a relatively low threshold for the president's nominees. Virtually all other significant legislative action must satisfy much stiffer procedural requirements: the passage of laws requires the concurrence of both houses of Congress and the president's signature (or, if vetoed, a two-thirds override), treaties require the agreement of at least two-thirds of the Senate, and the removal of high-level political officers and federal judges requires a majority of the House for impeachment and at least two-thirds of the Senate for removal and disqualification.[5] As a practical matter, the constitutional structure would appear to make it difficult for a small number of senators (generally consisting of some number less than one-half of the Senate) to stop a presidential nomination in the absence of some special Senate procedures empowering individual senators or subsets with some special authority to obstruct. (Of course, the development and cultivation of such procedures have become very significant features of the Senate regarding appointments.)

Second, by fixing the power to nominate in a single person who (arguably) has a mandate of national scope and includes within that power the ability to make successive nominations, the Appointments Clause gives the president a substantial advantage over the diffuse Senate in disagreements over appointments. The Appointments Clause puts a "political burden on the Senate [that] makes it difficult [for the Senate] to successfully oppose a President of ordinary political strength for narrow or partisan reasons."[6] The problem for the Senate is one of sustaining opposition; as a large collegial body, it faces a much more difficult hurdle in organizing itself repeatedly in a prolonged contest with the unitary executive over the latter's choices to fill a certain position. The Senate's job is made more difficult because it occupies a defensive posture in the appointments process in which it is largely confined to exercising a veto. As a structural matter, it lacks the means to formally take the lead in making nominations or in the initial stages of the appointments process.

Furthermore, once a nomination is made, it is likely, by virtue of having been formally made by the president of the United States, to be clothed with an aura of respectability, credibility, and presumptive merit unless a critical mass of senators can show otherwise. Consequently, the focus in the Senate necessarily is less on a nominee's merits than on potentially disqualifying factors.[7] If the case against confirmation cannot be made to the satisfaction of a majority of senators, a nominee normally is confirmed.

The existence of this presumption suggests further that evaluating presidential performance on the basis of the percentage of nominees actually confirmed is pointless because the structure is designed to ensure a relatively high success rate. Thus, the issue is not whether most of a president's nominees will be confirmed but rather which ones will encounter difficulties. Because it is not possible for the Senate to give all presidential nominees the same degree of scrutiny, senators carefully choose those worth contesting.[8] A president's uncertainty as to which nominees will encounter confirmation difficulties is the most important leverage senators have in the federal appointments process. On the one hand, obstructing presidential nominees will almost certainly be at some cost to the Senate (for it might provoke a negative or retaliatory response from the president or some of the nominee's supporters), but, on the other hand, it is likely that a president need not lose more than a few confirmation contests with the Senate before he sustains (or is depicted by his political foes or some segment of the media as having sustained) potentially serious political damage.

Origins, Structure, and Evolution

The federal appointments process is a mirror image of the traditional law-making structure. Whereas Article I empowers the Congress to set the agenda on lawmaking, the Appointments Clause grants this power to the president on appointments. The president's nomination power enables him to be proactive in trying to fill influential federal offices with people committed to his political or constitutional views.

This distribution of power by the Appointments Clause has the potential to give presidents enormous influence over the direction of judicial decision making. Obviously, the president's nomination power allows him to take the initiative in filling judicial vacancies within the federal system.[9] The Senate's primary recourse is to accept or veto the president's choices, but by virtue of the presumption of confirmation and the president's authority to make successive nominations, a president holds the structural advantage for influencing the exercise of judicial power.

Moreover, the president's nomination power plainly allows him to insinuate his priorities or views into the lawmaking process. For every non-judicial position that Congress creates and whose occupant qualifies as an "officer of the United States" with policymaking influence, the president potentially has a unique opportunity to set the direction or tone for how the powers wielded by such nominees will be exercised. For instance, through his nominations of all U.S. attorneys the president exercises considerable influence over the enforcement of federal criminal laws. Moreover, presidents are potentially able to dominate the policymaking functions performed within a wide range of administrative agencies by virtue of their powers to nominate the heads of those agencies.

Of course, it is the goal of every president to use his power to staff the executive and judicial branches so that his policies are implemented (or supported). With respect to the independent judiciary, however, a president's influence is limited primarily to appointing judges. A president can suggest to Congress changes in the substantive law or in the structure of the judicial branch (including changes in the appellate process and new judgeships), but he has no other relatively direct method to affect judicial outcomes, though a president might conceivably be able to affect outcomes by signaling to lower-court judges who desire elevation to higher

Structure of the Federal Appointments Process

courts the kinds of decisions that he would likely reward through elevation. Moreover, judges are appointed for life, so a president can affect policies well after his term through his judicial appointments.

In contrast, a president has a number of tools through which he can exert continuing influence over policies implemented by executive branch officials. He can directly order changes in policy, he can structure decision making through executive orders, he can meet with officials privately to persuade them, and he can remove them (although he is limited in this power with respect to some officials). Of course, such actions are likely to be costly for a president, so he is likely to prefer to appoint agents who will carry out his wishes without requiring much additional oversight or subsequent discipline. And obviously a president may use his nominating authority to reward appointees or staffers for their loyal service or to encourage or entice appointees or staffers to implement his preferences faithfully.

CONSENSUS

Another noteworthy feature of the constitutional structure for making federal appointments is that its allocation of authority puts pressure on presidents and senators to reach some accord on how to fill most federal offices and thereby to ensure the continued functioning of the national government. Consensus is conceivable as long as the president and the Senate each recognize two needs. First, each actor must recognize that it may be held politically accountable for taking action that slows down the functioning or efficiency of the national government, such as frustrating or complicating agreement on filling various federal offices. The more powerful or high-profile a vacant office, the greater the potential costs to the party responsible for keeping it empty. Second, senators tend to recognize (as a consequence of the presumption of confirmation) that they must deliberate carefully about whether to obstruct a president's choices (particularly for high-profile positions), because the odds of failure and the costs of failure to both the institution and individual senators are potentially high.

Chapter Three

HISTORICAL CHANGES AND PATTERNS

THE HISTORY OF the federal appointments process can enrich our understanding of the system's operations in several ways. First, it provides an important lens through which to view and understand the operations of the federal appointments process both generally and in particular cases. Second, history illuminates social and political developments that have helped to transform or shape the institutional arrangements or power relationships in the federal appointments process. These developments have turned modern confirmation proceedings into multitextured events. Third, a close reading of past practices reveals important patterns in the ways political institutions have approached and formulated decisions regarding some federal appointments.

THE INDISPENSABILITY OF CLEAR CONTEXT

Clarifying comprehensively the context in which appointments arise is crucial for fully explaining the operations of the federal appointments process. Defining the context helps to reveal the changes, developments, or movements in society or the polity that presidents and senators are trying to control or to which they are reacting in the course of exercising their respective appointment authorities. In other words, context is indispensable for developing a coherent external perspective on the federal appointments process. Indeed, fully examining the historical, social, political, and economic contexts in which presidents and senators have operated clarifies the various forces (and norms) that have shaped the institutions of the presidency and the Senate (including their interaction on appointments matters), such as the growth of and partial demise of political parties, the rise of interest groups and the phenomenon of identity politics (the tendency of members of the electorate to vote for or against candidates depending on whether the latter are closely identified or associated with causes, interests, issues, or symbols the voters approve of or dislike), and the proliferation of mass communications technology. In the course of dealing with these different forces (and, of course, with each other), presidents and senators have tried to be both proactive and reactive in defining or wielding their respective powers. These external influences have helped to transform the institutions of the presidency and the Senate in ways that have little to do with the formal constitutional structure but still must be understood for full and fair evaluation of presidential and senatorial decision making on appointments.

Moreover, context helps to clarify the internal dynamics of the federal appointments process, including presidents' or senators' strategies for making decisions regarding appointments and their interactions with each other and other actors routinely involved in appointments. The interaction among these actors often leads to or includes informal arrangements or accommodations that must also be understood for a full or fair assessment of the efficacy or limits of the relevant constitutional structure.

A few examples involving some of President Abraham Lincoln's most important appointments should illustrate this basic perspective. A particularly revealing illustration of the importance of context is President Lincoln's nomination of Samuel Freeman Miller of Iowa to the Supreme Court. Jeffrey Tulis argues that the Miller appointment is an excellent example of the Senate's energetic assertion of its constitutional role in the appointment of Supreme Court justices.[1] And so it is. Yet, the context of the Miller appointment demonstrates that it was not simply a case of presidential passivity or Senate aggression in the appointments process. On the one hand, the norm for nineteenth-century presidents was, admittedly, to defer generally to congressional demands or recommendations regarding appointments. Moreover, President Lincoln's exercise of his appointment authority was influenced by extraordinary external pressures, including the needs to manage and ultimately win the Civil War, to keep the Union together, and to nurture and unify his fledgling political party, including the coalition that had brought him into office. None of these was a small matter; each required considerable time, attention, and energy. Lincoln was not disposed to jeopardize any of these goals at the time the vacancy to which Miller was ultimately nominated arose.

On the other hand, President Lincoln appreciated the stakes involved in Supreme Court nominations, and he had his own standards for selecting nominees, including loyalty to his party and to the preservation of the Constitution, opposition to slavery, geographic suitability (as was true for all nineteenth- and early twentieth-century presidents), and demonstrated professional ability or judicial experience. By all accounts, Miller met these criteria. Moreover, Miller enjoyed the support of virtually all the western governors and the entire western delegation in Congress. In addition, a unique congressional petition containing the names of 129 of the 140 members of the House and almost every senator was submitted to the president on Miller's behalf. This unprecedented lobbying effort, never again matched in size or intensity in U.S. history, grabbed Lincoln's attention. Certainly it signaled clearly the extraordinary political support that Miller enjoyed (and that Lincoln would have to flout if he nominated another candidate). It also grabbed his attention because the effort had been made on behalf of a person whose credentials were impeccable and whose constitutional views were plainly consistent with those of the president for Supreme Court nominations. In the end, Lincoln's choice of Miller was remarkably straightforward, for it fully satisfied the short- and long-term interests of both the president and Congress.

President Lincoln took a different tack in finding a replacement for Chief Justice Taney, who died in October 1864, shortly before the presidential election.[2] Lincoln deliberately postponed announcing his choice until after his reelection campaign was over. By then, the circumstances for making the nomination were different from those that had existed at the time of Justice Miller's appointment. The Union's prospects for winning the Civil War had vastly improved, and the president had received a solid majority of support for his reelection bid. Although the president retained the same selection criteria for the Court, he had the additional concern that the Republican party had suffered some significant losses in the 1864 congressional elections and needed serious mending. He wanted to nominate his longtime friend and political ally, Postmaster General Montgomery Blair, but Lincoln doubted that Blair's nomination could unify the Republican party. Instead, after eight weeks of deliberation, President Lincoln settled on his former treasury secretary and longtime political adversary, Salmon Chase. He did so because, as Henry Abraham suggests in his monumental study of the Supreme Court appointments process, "first, he had no doubt that Chase's policy views on the war and future reconstruction were sound and reliable[;] second, if anyone could heal the widening breach in the Republican party, it would be Chase[; and] third, Chase [had] campaigned hard and effectively for Lincoln's [re]election."[3] Whereas the broader list of potential candidates for Chief Justice was based on a variety of significant factors, including constitutional philosophy and commitment to the preservation of the Union and Lincoln's reconstruction policies, the president chose Chase because he believed that Chase could best satisfy both those concerns and the immediate, important need to keep the Republican party unified.

President Lincoln's concerns about keeping both the Union and the Republican party unified also influenced his nonjudicial appointments. Of course, in his first term the external pressures competing for his time and attention and constraining or imposing challenges on his exercise of presidential powers were largely the same as those he had to confront in nominating Justice Miller, and the internal pressures were almost identical as well, with a few exceptions. For one thing, the president made patronage appointments for people who had assisted his presidential campaigns.[4] His agenda for his first term included, however, putting less emphasis on appointing people who had been personally loyal to him and more emphasis on (1) acknowledging and rewarding party leaders who had been instrumental to his initial election as president, (2) maintaining different constituencies' support for his administration, and (3) ensuring the success of his reelection campaign. Consequently, President Lincoln brought into his first administration some of his most ardent political rivals, who were then put in the uncomfortable position of either having to do his bidding as president or appearing to be disloyal to his administration or the Union. President Lincoln often deferred to his cabinet secretaries in their choices of subordinates, and it was not unusual for the former to choose their most loyal political supporters to serve under them. The obvious disadvantage of this practice was that it resulted in the choice of a cabinet that was doomed from the start to lack harmony and loyalty to Lincoln and his policy objectives.[5]

In his second term Lincoln adopted a different strategy for making high-level nonjudicial appointments because he had support from the American people and because the prospects appeared to be much stronger for keeping the Union together and resolving the Civil War favorably. Lincoln's eminent biographer David Herbert Donald suggests that

> In contrast to the members of the original cabinet, none of the [new] appointees was a major political leader and none had aspirations for the presidency. Lincoln now felt so strong that he did not have to surround himself with the heads of the warring Republican factions. He did not require ideological conformity of the men he chose. . . . Unlike his original cabinet — like his holdovers, [William] Seward [secretary of state], [Edwin] Stanton [secretary of war], and [Gideon] Welles [navy secretary] — [his second-term appointees] were warmly attached to Lincoln personally. He could now afford the luxury of a loyal cabinet.[6]

As the internal and external pressures on Lincoln's presidency changed, so did his plan for dealing with them. Lincoln's coordination of various presidential powers, including his appointment authority, to deal with virtually unparalleled challenges and to facilitate the achievement of certain constitutional and political objectives is the hallmark of his presidency. To appreciate why this is so, it is necessary to do more than just describe the historical, political, and social contexts in which Lincoln — or, for that matter, any president or senator — acted. Context helps to elucidate the challenges confronting the different actors involved in the federal appointments process, but it does not suggest appropriate ways for measuring how well different presidents and senators operating under different circumstances and in different time periods have dealt with the internal and external pressures confronting them. The next section examines in greater detail the different social and political forces influencing the operations of the federal appointments process.

Several significant postratification developments have helped to shape the allocation of power among, the relationships between, and the internal organizations of the actors and institutions routinely involved in the appointments process. These developments include the rise and partial decline of political parties, the increase in the size and influence of the national government, the evolution of senatorial accountability and Senate operations, the growth of organized interest groups, and expanding media coverage of the federal appointments process. Each of these developments has had ramifications for the operations of the appointments process and the performances of the principal governmental actors in it. More precisely, each development has influenced how presidents and senators have interacted on and constructed their internal decision-making processes regarding federal appointments.

The Rise and (Partial) Decline of Political Parties

The rise of political parties in the United States has had enormous influence on the federal appointments process. In almost every era of U.S. history, two political parties have dominated the national political landscape. These parties have served many functions. For example, national political parties have been instrumental in choosing the two leading contenders in every presidential election; no independent candidate has ever won the presidency. Political parties have also served an integrating function in political history, linking together the lives and interests of local, state, and national party members. In addition, state and local political organizations have been instrumental in electing senators, introducing people aspiring to national office to politics, and supplying the names of appropriate people for presidents and senators to tap for federal offices in their respective states.

The rise of national political parties coincided with—and, indeed, helped to shape fundamentally—presidents' and senators' conceptions and exercises of their prerogatives regarding appointments. For example, President George Washington maintained that merit was a prime consideration for any appointment, along "with service during the Revolution, firm support of the new Constitution, and equity among the states."[7]

Origins, Structure, and Evolution

Consequently, all twelve of Washington's Supreme Court appointments came from the political party of the Federalists, who, in the words of Jean Edward Smith, "embraced the idea of a strong national government and saw the broad words of the Constitution as a means to that end. Their opponents, increasingly known as Republicans, were led by [Thomas] Jefferson, [James] Madison, and [James] Monroe. The Republicans favored states' rights and sought to restrict the growth of national power by insisting on a narrow reading of the constitutional text."[8] Washington's successor, John Adams, also a Federalist, came into office as the victor of a bitterly partisan campaign. He rewarded party loyalty whenever he had an open position to fill and extended Washington's criteria for awarding federal appointments to subordinate offices.

There are many reasons for the early and persistent dominance of party loyalty as a criterion in presidential choices for key federal offices, including recognition of the utility of appointments as excellent rewards for loyal followers. In many cases, presidents and senators have seen party loyalty as a cue to the ideology of the nominee. Just as many voters have used party identification as a cue to ideology when electing members of Congress who will be their faithful agents, so have presidents and senators used political views as a proxy to determine the ideology of a candidate and as information about the policies the nominee is likely to support.

For example, allegiance to a core component of a party's political agenda was at the center of the Senate's first rejection of a Supreme Court nominee, John Rutledge. In 1795, the Senate, by a vote of fourteen to ten, rejected President Washington's nomination of Rutledge to become the nation's third Chief Justice. Many of Rutledge's qualifications were beyond question: he had been an influential delegate at the constitutional convention; he had previously been nominated and confirmed as an associate justice of the Supreme Court, though he had resigned from this position before the Court had ever convened in order to become chief justice of the South Carolina Supreme Court; and he had served in the post of Chief Justice of the United States on a recess appointment,[9] presiding over the Supreme Court's August 1795 term.

Nevertheless, loyalty to party platform played a major role in Rutledge's rejection. Just days before Rutledge had accepted his recess appointment as Chief Justice, he had vigorously denounced the Jay treaty.

This proved to be a grave mistake because the treaty had become a major source of division between Federalists and Republicans. The Jay treaty was a conciliatory agreement negotiated by the Washington administration to ease tensions with Great Britain and thus was supported by Federalists; Republicans, however, viewed it as an affront to France and to American interests at home, particularly those of American citizens still indebted to British creditors. The treaty's backers in the Senate, the Federalists, had endured widespread public criticism for their support of the treaty. Consequently, they felt betrayed by Rutledge, whom they had expected as a fellow Federalist to follow the party line. Despite President Washington's support for Rutledge, thirteen of the sixteen Federalists in the Senate voted to reject his nomination. In a possible move to deflect criticism that the opposition to Rutledge had been based on his public disapproval of a critical aspect of their party identity and program, some Federalist senators explained their rejection on the ground that Rutledge was mentally unstable and thus was not fit for high office (based on the "intemperate" and impolitic nature of his comments about the Jay treaty).[10]

Another early example of the significance of party loyalty as a criterion for making federal appointments is the fallout from President John Adams's attempt to pack the federal judiciary with more than fifty loyal Federalists on the eve of the inauguration of his vice president and Republican rival, Thomas Jefferson. President Jefferson's refusal to honor what he called Adams's "midnight appointments" precipitated one of the most famous, if not the most famous, constitutional law decisions of all time, *Marbury v. Madison*.[11] Six days after *Marbury* was decided, the Supreme Court in *Stuart v. Laird*[12] upheld the Republican Congress's abolition of the judgeships created by the prior Federalist majority.

Subsequent presidents throughout the remainder of the nineteenth century used patronage to accomplish many ends, not just to reward party and personal loyalty. They employed it to gain further control over the exercise of executive power, the making or implementation of national policy, and the direction of the federal judiciary, particularly the Supreme Court. President Andrew Jackson took this practice to new heights and is generally credited with being the first president to implement the spoils system. Under Jackson, this system, according to the distinguished historian Arthur Schlesinger Jr., became "an indispensable means of unifying administration support[,] . . . brought to power a fresh and alert group which had the energy to meet the needs of the day[,]" and helped to "narrow the gap between the people and the government—to expand popular participation in the workings of democracy."[13]

Presidents prior to Jackson had been unsure that they had the constitutional authority to remove appointments made to confirmable positions by their predecessors and appoint the people they wanted to occupy those positions. President John Adams retained Washington's cabinet in full, in spite of the fact that three of the four cabinet officers had no personal allegiance to Adams and ultimately proved disloyal to him. Although Thomas Jefferson declared in his first inaugural address that his administration would tolerate differences in party allegiance, he later amended his statements to clarify that the "will of the nation calls for an administration of government according with the opinions of those elected."[14] Jefferson proceeded cautiously in trying to remove Federalists so that it might "injure the best men least, and effect the purposes of justice and public utility with the least private distress; that it may be thrown, as much as possible, on delinquency, on oppression, on intolerance, on anti-revolutionary adherence to our enemies."[15] It is unclear how many Federalists Jefferson removed because of their party affiliations (and thus their likely antipathy to his political agenda), but by the end of 1803 he had appointed Republicans to one-half of the major offices in the national government. Partly because they were Republicans and ideologically aligned with Jefferson, the next two presidents—James Madison and James Monroe—each removed only twenty-seven officials from the federal government.[16] Nevertheless, in 1820 President Monroe signed into law the Tenure in Office Act (sponsored surreptitiously by Monroe's secretary of the treasury, William Crawford, in anticipation of his own election as president). It provided that district attorneys and the principal officers who had responsibility for collecting and disbursing money should thenceforth be appointed to serve fixed terms of four years.[17] In spite of the new legislation, the fifth president, John Quincy Adams, like his father before him, expended little effort to appoint people who were personally loyal to him. Instead, he stitched together a cabinet of disparate elements and removed only twelve officials. In contrast, his successor,

Historical Changes and Patterns

Andrew Jackson, embraced the Tenure in Office Act as embodying "a leading principle [of reform] in the republican creed."[18] During his presidency, Jackson removed between 10 and 20 percent of federal officials and replaced them with loyal political supporters or allies.[19]

The spoils system was just as important to the political survival and success of almost every other nineteenth-century president. An enormous turnover in personnel occurred every four years from 1840 through 1860 because control of the presidency changed parties in every election but one in that period. The nation's first Whig president, William Henry Harrison, vowed at the outset of his administration to defer completely to Whig congressional leaders in awarding patronage but died before he could implement the policy.[20] Harrison's successor, John Tyler, was not a Whig; nor did he share Harrison's philosophy of government. Hence, he removed or accepted the resignations of many federal officials, including all of Harrison's cabinet appointees with the sole exception of Secretary of State Daniel Webster. Tyler tried to name his political allies and friends to the vacated offices, but he had few allies in the Senate, which rejected the majority of his nominees.[21] In keeping with the practice of his mentor Andrew Jackson, President James K. Polk sought to realize fully the value of patronage. In trying to use patronage to ensure the faithful implementation of his policy objectives while also trying to oversee a Democratic party rife with factions, President Polk made as many enemies as friends with his appointments. Maintaining this balance was an enormous strain for Polk, who complained about the pressures of patronage in his diary on an average of at least once a week.[22]

President Zachary Taylor removed nearly two-thirds of his predecessors' appointees during his first year in office.[23] In choosing the people to fill these vacated offices, Taylor followed the counsel of the northern Whigs who had helped to get him elected. When Taylor died after only two years in office, Vice President Millard Fillmore assumed the presidency. Fillmore, who had been excluded from decisions on patronage and from participation in any of President Taylor's councils, accepted the resignations of all of Taylor's cabinet officers and replaced them with Whigs who shared his penchant for moderation and compromise.[24] The next president, Franklin Pierce, largely bypassed moderates in the Democratic party to replace most of Fillmore's appointments with representatives from other factions in the party, with the exception of strident abolitionists.[25] Although he had served as Pierce's ambassador to Great Britain, the next president, James Buchanan, purged the civil service of all of Pierce's appointments in the hope of replacing them with people closely aligned to his political orientation.[26]

President Lincoln effected the largest turnover in office of any pre–Civil War president, including 1,457 removals from the 1,639 offices to which he was entitled to make nominations. Like Jackson before him, President Lincoln understood, as David Herbert Donald has observed, "that in a democratic, federal government like ours, patronage is one sure way of binding local political bosses to the person and principles of the President, and for this reason [Lincoln] used and approved the spoils system. [Indeed,] Lincoln's entire administration was characterized by astute handling of patronage."[27] Contrary to the belief of some that Lincoln was above the demands of party politics or using federal offices to reward party loyalists, Lincoln proudly declared as president that his administration "had distributed to it's [sic] party friends as nearly all the civil patronage as any administration ever did."[28]

The spoils system dominated federal appointments until several presidents, including Rutherford B. Hayes, Chester Arthur, Grover Cleveland, and Benjamin Harrison, championed civil service reform as a means for reducing the Senate's control of the appointments process and increasing the professionalism of a significant realm of government service.[29] Presidents Teddy Roosevelt and Woodrow Wilson tried especially hard in the early twentieth century to extend civil service reform by insisting on high standards (in addition to ideological compatibility) for most of their appointments. Nevertheless, the spoils system had not been discarded by any means, and it regained some momentum under President Warren G. Harding. Subsequently, it has remained viable for a wide range of non–civil service positions because of the persistent needs to repay political or personal debts, provide incentives to supporters, secure party support for reelection, and ensure the faithful implementation of a president's preferred policy objectives and the success of legislative initiatives.

Perhaps nothing more clearly illustrates the influence of political parties on federal appointments, especially during the nation's first hundred years, than the fact that only three of the fifty-eight Supreme Court justices appointed in the nineteenth century were members of a different political party than that of the president who appointed them. The three presidents who diverged from the norm did so for compelling reasons.

John Tyler was the first president to nominate someone to the Court from a party other than his own. Tyler was an unusually unpopular and weak president. In the last two years of his term, the Senate rejected the majority of his nominations, including four nominees to his cabinet, four nominees to the Supreme Court, and his choices to become the ministers to France and Brazil.[30] Indeed, President Tyler had only one successful nomination in six attempts to fill two vacancies on the Court. Tyler's poor record on appointments was largely due to the fact that he had alienated the mainstream of both of the major political parties. He had alienated Democrats by leaving their party to become Whig candidate William Henry Harrison's running mate in 1840. When Tyler became president due to Harrison's death only a month into his term, he alienated the Whigs by opposing their key legislative proposals. Hence, the Whig majority in the Senate did not trust Tyler, and the Democrats resented him because he had abandoned their party. Moreover, the Whigs were eager to oppose President Tyler's attempt in 1843 to fill the vacancy on the Court left by the death of Justice Smith Thompson of New York, hoping to save the appointment for the man they expected to win the next presidential election in 1844 — Senator Henry Clay of Kentucky.

In December 1843, President Tyler nominated John Spencer of New York, a scholarly lawyer who had served as Tyler's secretary of war and secretary of the treasury, to fill the Thompson vacancy.[31] Spencer was also a political enemy of Senator Clay and his supporters, and Clay easily organized a faction in the Senate to defeat the nomination. Subsequently, Tyler nominated Reuben Walworth of New York, but this nomination ran into early trouble because Walworth was not the preferred candidate of the New York state political machine. Walworth withdrew his nomination after the Senate postponed action on it. In the meantime, another vacancy had arisen on the Court and Democrat James K. Polk had become the surprise victor over Clay in the presidential election of 1844. Though a lame duck, Tyler persisted in trying to fill at least one of the vacancies. Having broken with the Whigs, Tyler felt little compulsion to please them with his next nomination. Hence, his third nomination to replace Thompson was Samuel Nelson, a Democrat, who at the time of his nomination was chief justice of the New York Supreme Court and a renowned expert on commercial law, an area then thought to constitute a significant portion of the Court's workload. The Senate quickly confirmed Nelson. His qualifications were sterling, the Democrats were disposed to approve one of their own, and the Whigs regarded him as a less offensive choice than any of the Democrats Polk was likely to pick.

Twenty years later, President Abraham Lincoln reached outside his political party for a Supreme Court nominee under quite different circumstances. Unlike those of Tyler, Lincoln's nominations met with little resistance, because the members of the opposition party had largely abandoned their seats and thus his party dominated the Senate throughout his presidency. President Lincoln made five appointments to the Court in a little more than four years; all except for one came from within the ranks of his own Republican party. The sole exception was his third appointment, which he made in 1863. Because Congress had just created a Tenth Circuit consisting of California and Oregon, the common expectation at the time was that Lincoln would name someone who came from that region who would be familiar with its particular needs *and* could be counted on to back the cause of the Union in the Civil War litigation then on the docket. Lincoln's choice was Stephen Field from California.[32] Although Field was a Democrat, he had significant backing from the state's powerful governor, Leland Stanford. Even more important, Lincoln believed that Field's real political beliefs were quite similar to his own and to those of most senators. Hence, Lincoln figured, correctly, that the nomination would sit well with the full Senate. The Senate unanimously confirmed Field three days after his nomination.

It was not until 1893 that another president, Benjamin Harrison, a Republican, looked outside his political party for a Supreme Court nominee. Generally, President Harrison preferred to appoint only Republicans to federal offices.[33] One major exception was his appointment of Justice Howell Jackson to the Court. A critical factor in Jackson's appointment was the timing. Harrison had already made three successful appointments to the Court but had become a lame duck by the time a fourth vacancy had arisen as a result of the death of Justice L. M. Q. Lamar, a Democrat from Mississippi appointed by President Grover Cleveland. Hence, Harrison looked for a southerner who would be ideologically agreeable to him and to a majority of the Senate (which was about to become Democratic). He settled on Jackson, a Tennessean whose political views were well known to Harrison because he was an old family friend and had served with Harrison in the Senate. Harrison figured the Senate was unlikely to turn down one of its own, and indeed, the Senate confirmed Jackson within minutes of receiving his nomination.

Whereas political parties functioned as an organizational framework for Senate action for most of the nineteenth century, the influence of major political parties declined in the twentieth century,[34] with concomitant consequences for presidential nominations. Perhaps the most dramatic illustration of party dominance in the nineteenth century occurred in the waning days of John Tyler's presidency when the Whig majority in the Senate helped to ensure the rejection of five of the six nominations made by the onetime Democrat Tyler to fill two seats on the Court. Almost as dramatic was the Senate's rejection of three of President Millard Fillmore's nominations to fill a single Supreme Court vacancy in 1852.[35] Although the Senate in 1851 had confirmed Fillmore's nomination of fellow Whig Benjamin Curtis to the Court, the Senate had a different disposition a year later. By then, the Whig party had a majority, and the Whigs believed Fillmore's chances for reelection (and their own political fortunes if they continued to support him) were nil. Consequently, the Senate adjourned to avoid action on Fillmore's choice to fill the new vacancy. Fillmore had become a lame duck and the Democrats had taken control of the Senate by the time Fillmore made his next two nominations to fill the vacancy, both of which failed because the new Democratic majority wanted to preserve the vacancy for the incoming Democratic president, Franklin Pierce, to fill. The degree of sustained opposition to both Tyler's and Fillmore's nominees would have surprised many framers, but then many of them had not anticipated the rise of political parties.[36]

The Senate has not been able to sustain opposition to a president's Supreme Court nominations to any remotely similar degree in the twentieth century. Only two streaks come anywhere close. In the early 1970s, the Senate rejected two of President Richard Nixon's Supreme Court nominations in succession before it approved a third.[37] In 1987, the Senate rejected President Reagan's nomination of Robert Bork to the Court and helped to force the withdrawal of his next nominee, Douglas Ginsburg, before approving his third, Anthony Kennedy.

The decline in the control of political parties over federal appointments has coincided with the rise in influence of a much broader range of factors, including personal and other kinds of allegiances and factional interests in the political process. Consequently, although political parties have declined in influence, partisanship—the degree to which party allegiances dictate or influence choices and results—retains vitality. In other words, partisanship or loyalty to some factional or special interest still remains a strong factor in the appointments process. In making federal appointments, presidents (and senators too, for that matter) have increasingly looked to other indicators of a candidate's agreement with essential aspects of their political philosophy; these include professional accomplishments, speeches or articles, interest group support, the nominee's patrons, and personal vouching from trusted advisers. An especially striking illustration of this shift is the fact that eight presidents in the twentieth century appointed a total of eleven Supreme Court justices who were not members of their political parties, as opposed to three such nominations in the preceding century.[38] Nor has it been unusual in the twentieth century for presidents to reach outside their political parties (or even outside politics altogether) for other important appointments.

For instance, Dwight D. Eisenhower, who became the first Republican elected to the presidency in two decades when he was elected in 1952, did not accede to the intense pressure to make party affiliation a uniform criterion of his most important appointments. Eisenhower came to the presidency with a reputation and image that transcended party politics and with no formal affiliation with the Republican party prior to 1952. Hence, he was not disposed to appease traditional party leaders or the party's most conservative elements. Eisenhower wanted people from outside government, and he trusted only those who had proven themselves in leading large organizations, particularly businesses.[39] His initial cabinet choices included few prominent Republicans and two Democrats, and one of his five Supreme Court appointees was a Democrat.[40] Whereas Presidents Jackson and Lincoln had proudly used patronage to solidify their support and to unite their administrations and had viewed it as instrumental in democratizing the federal government, President Eisenhower "did not want to make appointments that would be political pay-offs." "Patronage," he complained, "is almost a wicked word. . . . By itself, it could well-nigh defeat democracy."[41]

Even in decline, political parties have remained among the most powerful organizations contending for control of the federal appointments process. Next to close personal association with the president or others to whom he feels indebted, significant stature in the president's political party has been a consistent feature of nominees for most federal appointments. In the twentieth century the norm has been for at least 82 percent of a president's appointees, regardless of the offices to which they have been appointed, to claim his political party as their own.

The question is, has the prominent, persistently important, and sometimes decisive role played by political parties in shaping the federal appointments process somehow frustrated the framers' original aspirations or design? The answer to this question depends largely on whether political parties qualify as the kinds of factions whose influence the framers sought to check through the creation and implementation of a variety of constitutional mechanisms. The framers' obsession with preventing factions from corrupting or frustrating their primary goals of devising a balanced, energetic, and accountable national government led them to include such devices in the Constitution as federalism, checks and balances, separation of powers, bicameralism, equal representation of the states in the Senate, judicial review, and the reservation of some of the most important political questions for Senate deliberation—and even then, depending on the question, sometimes by supermajority vote. The issue boils down to whether or not political parties pose any greater or similar danger to the constitutional order than did the factions from which the framers had hoped to safeguard the national political process. Whatever the answer, political parties have served as useful proxies for political beliefs and obvious sources of prospective nominees and political supporters.

The Expansion of the National Government

The national government and the scope of presidential authority have expanded dramatically since 1787. To most political scientists and historians this is quite old news. Nevertheless, a good deal of legal scholarship in the 1980s and 1990s analyzed the congruity between the original conception of the presidency and its present status.[42] Regardless of how one answers this question, two related facts are clear. The first is that the president now exerts much more influence (and initiative) in formulating national policy than he did in the nineteenth century (with the obvious exceptions of Andrew Jackson and to a lesser extent Abraham Lincoln).[43] The second is that the Appointments Clause has provided a venue for other shifts in authority to become dominant. As the range of responsibility for the national government has grown, Congress has created more offices requiring presidential nomination and Senate confirmation. For instance, the Kennedy administration had 196 positions at the secretary, deputy secretary, assistant secretary, and deputy assistant secretary levels, while there were more than 1,000 positions requiring Senate confirmation (excluding military appointments) at the midpoint of President Bill Clinton's second term. Whereas President Kennedy appointed 123 federal judges in his abbreviated term of office,[44] President Clinton had appointed 205 federal judges by the end of his first term and another 168 by mid-July 2000 (for a total of 373 judicial appointments as of that time). The president is also entitled to nominate and the Senate to consider the confirmations of thousands of officers in the armed forces. (For instance, in the first five months of the 106th Congress, 98 percent of presidential nominations—9,868 of 10,071—were for military offices.) As confirmable offices have grown in number, so too has the president's supervisory and administrative authority, for he has had the primary duty of both choosing the people occupying such offices and overseeing those officials' actions.

The growth of presidential power has not gone unnoticed by Congress. After all, Congress has authorized much of the expansion through its power to create new federal offices. In creating such offices, Congress has assiduously preserved the Senate's authority to confirm or reject presidential nominees. As a practical matter, the more offices created by Congress, the more chances senators have to consult and the more bargaining chips they have to use in consulting with the president on federal appointments and related legislative matters. In other words, the potential number of contestable nominations has expanded considerably. While the Senate has not rejected or otherwise blocked Supreme Court nominations to the same degree in this century as it did in the previous one,[45] far more presidential nominations are potentially available for senators to oppose. As both a practical matter and a consequence of the constitutional design, senators largely occupy a defensive posture in the confirmation process, so that it is difficult, if not impossible, for them to oppose *all* presidential nominations consistently and still expect to keep the federal government operating effectively or to maintain credibility in claiming purely non-partisan motivations for all of their actions. Consequently, many senators are disposed largely to defer to presidential nominations. For instance, between 1981 and 1994, the Senate confirmed 706,187, or 98 percent, of the 720,162 persons nominated by the president for all positions requiring Senate approval. (The overwhelming majority of presidential nominations—well over 90 percent—were for military offices.)

Although most senators might be disposed to defer to presidential nominees, many have not been disposed to defer absolutely. Substantial exchanges often occur between presidents and senators (particularly those in leadership positions) both behind closed doors and in public over the appropriate people to nominate to certain high-profile, influential positions as well as after formal nominations have been made to those offices. These exchanges or differences of opinion have included increased opposition to, forced withdrawals of, and rejections of many presidential nominations to offices involving many policy areas of keen concern both to the voting public and to the best-organized and -financed interest groups. The latter areas include national security, the environment, economics, and civil rights. Not insignificantly, the increasing number of disputes over nominees to positions in these areas has coincided with some abdication of authority by senators in Supreme Court confirmation hearings. Moreover, the House and the Senate each have other means to check presidential appointees, regardless of whether the latter are subject to the Senate's confirmation authority. Particularly important among these are Congress's oversight and appropriations authorities, which have been extended to virtually every aspect of the executive branch.

One could argue, however, that the president has maintained the upper hand in the federal appointments process because the number of confirmable posts has increased multifold while the Senate's capacity to defeat some portion of the nominees during a given legislative session has remained relatively static. Although this supposition could be challenged on the ground that the Senate does not need many chances to thwart or embarrass the president on appointments matters to hurt him or to help themselves politically (and that individual senators have numerous prerogatives, such as holds and filibusters, to thwart particular nominations), it is clear that at least with respect to federal appointments, if not separation of powers generally, the presidency and not Congress has become potentially the most dangerous and accountable branch.[46] It is the most dangerous branch because it has unparalleled ability to energize and shape the national government's performance (and agenda) through its formal powers, not the least of which is its nominating authority. It is the most accountable because the president as a single figure is watched more closely by the public and the media (and is prone to leaks to a much greater degree) than any other government officials or institutions.

Evolution of the Senate

The Senate's role in the federal appointments process has evolved along with the president's. From the beginning of the republic to the present, the Senate has taken its advise-and-consent power seriously. The Senate has invariably refused to grant a president unchecked discretion generally in the choices of certain important kinds of personnel, though it has historically deferred more to a president's choices of executive personnel than to judicial appointments. Presidents have received such deference because (1) many if not most senators acknowledge that the president is entitled to have his own people in place to assist him in the execution or implementation of the laws, (2) executive officials remain much more accountable than judges after confirmation because of presidential removal power and congressional oversight, and (3) senators are much more wary of what federal judges will do once they are confirmed than they are about executive officials because the former wield enormous power under circumstances in which they are largely immune to political retaliation once they are in office.

Nevertheless, the Senate has never abdicated its advise-and-consent power to a president's choices for executive personnel. Indeed, the Senate's rejection of President Washington's nomination of John Rutledge to become Chief Justice in 1795 was not the first time that the Senate had asserted its authority in the federal appointments process. Barely three months into its first session the Senate rejected President Washington's nomination of Benjamin Fishbourn to the post of naval officer of the Port of Savannah. The Senate rejected Fishbourn because Georgia's two senators preferred another candidate for the position.[47] Two weeks later, Georgia's senators objected to Washington's appointment of one of the commissioners responsible for negotiating with Indians in Georgia because they again preferred another candidate, and the Senate voted to postpone confirmation.[48] These actions were the first instances of the now well established practice known as senatorial courtesy, in which senators from the president's party propose candidates for certain federal positions in their respective states.

At first glance, the practice of senatorial courtesy might seem to turn the Appointments Clause on its head by enabling senators to make recommendations on positions that it is the president's prerogative to fill. Yet, senatorial courtesy is consistent with the framers' expectation that senators would be well suited to determine the fitness of nominees or candidates from their respective constituencies.[49] Moreover, senators are obliged to give their "advice and consent" to nominations and could reasonably construe senatorial courtesy as a function or exercise of their authority to give "advice" to presidents on nominations. Also, it is obviously in each senator's interest to recognize and support the entitlements of his or her colleagues to senatorial courtesy in order to protect his or her own claim to it. Consequently, senatorial courtesy has grown beyond any narrow or formal dimensions, with senators in every period claiming the entitlement to be consulted by the president on nominations to federal office of any candidates from their states or in their respective areas of responsibility or expertise within the Senate. For instance, in spite of the fact that the Democrats held a majority of seats in the Senate, Senator David B. Hill from New York successfully organized most senators in 1893 to block Democratic president Grover Cleveland's nominations to the Supreme Court of two New York attorneys of whom Hill did not approve.[50] After failing to persuade a third New Yorker to accept the nomination to the Court and face Hill's likely opposition, President Cleveland refused to nominate another New Yorker to the Court, even though at that time different seats were generally viewed as belonging to certain regions. Instead, President Cleveland in 1894 successfully nominated Edward Douglas White, a senator from Louisiana, who was popular with his colleagues and thus entitled to the courtesy customarily (but not always) extended by the Senate to one of its own.

Much more recently, by mid-1999, Senator Jesse Helms of North Carolina had bottled up 493 of President Clinton's ambassadorial and other foreign relations nominations. As the powerful chair of the Senate's Foreign Relations Committee, Helms controlled the scheduling of confirmation hearings for these nominations and refused to schedule any hearings because of foreign policy and other disagreements with the administration. This was by no means the first time that Senator Helms had exercised his authority as committee chair in such a manner. In 1995, shortly after he became the chair of the Foreign Relations Committee, Helms delayed the confirmations of more than a dozen ambassadorial nominations as a means of forcing the administration to agree to some major reorganizations within foreign policy agencies. In the first year of the Clinton administration, Senator Helms joined with Senator Lauch Faircloth, also of North Carolina, to delay the president's nomination of Walter Dellinger, then a professor of law at Duke University, to become the assistant attorney general in charge of the Justice Department's prestigious Office of Legal Counsel. They claimed that as North Carolina's senators they were entitled to be consulted by the president before he nominated anyone from their state to a confirmable office. The delay was thus justified in their view as a retaliation against the president's breach of senatorial courtesy (even apart from their differences with the nominee over various social and civil rights issues). Similarly, in 1980, Senator Helms exercised his prerogative to put holds on four of President Reagan's nominees for key regional bureau jobs in the State Department in the hope of ensuring the Reagan administration's adherence to certain conservative values in its foreign policy.

The evolution of the Senate's role in the federal appointments process has come about through structural changes in both the election of its members and its operations. The Seventeenth Amendment,[51] ratified in 1913, changed the way senators were selected, taking the power of election away from state legislatures and giving it to the people. The amendment was the product of the Progressive Era in American politics, a period in which the Supreme Court was widely condemned for being out of touch with American life and the Senate for being out of touch with the electorate. The amendment was widely viewed at the time as endorsing the importance of the popular will to lawmaking.

One obvious effect of the Seventeenth Amendment has been to make the Senate's constitutionally imposed duties, such as the confirmation of presidential nominees, subject to electoral review, comment, and reprisal.[52] There is no hard evidence establishing precisely how just much the Seventeenth Amendment has influenced the kinds of people elected to the Senate or the nature of the Senate's proceedings or activities. Prior to the Seventeenth Amendment's adoption it was not unusual for conflicts to arise between the president and the Senate in confirmation proceedings. These conflicts were complicated on a few occasions (such as with President Andrew Jackson's ill-fated nomination of Attorney General Roger Taney to be secretary of the treasury—the first cabinet nominee ever rejected by the Senate)[53] by the practice of instruction (the passing of resolutions by a state legislature directing a senator how to vote on a particular matter) or by political parties. The Seventeenth Amendment's passage coincided with the increasing tendency of senators to take positions on legislative matters, including federal appointments, commensurate with their reelection chances, popular or political support, and relationship with the president.[54] Consequently, the friction between presidents and senators over nominations did not subside after the Seventeenth Amendment's passage.

For instance, the adoption of the Seventeenth Amendment did not preclude President Woodrow Wilson from having more than a dozen confirmation conflicts with the Senate,[55] including one of the most contentious battles over a Supreme Court nomination in the first half of the twentieth century—the hotly contested but ultimately successful nomination of Louis Brandeis in 1916. The number of confirmation contests increased with each subsequent presidential term, along with the potential for Senate interference with presidential nominations (in keeping with the increase in offices requiring such activity).

In addition, the Senate has made several important changes in its internal operations and procedures. These innovations have helped to change the Senate from a collegial body to one dominated by individuals with separate agendas and characterized by delegation of substantial authority (such as on agenda setting or scheduling) to smaller units, including committees (and subcommittees), powerful committee chairs, and individual senators. These developments are crucial for explaining or evaluating the Senate's efforts to maintain a roughly equal footing with the president regarding appointments while at the same time trying to increase its efficiency and to handle increased media coverage of its operations.

For example, since 1929 the Senate has operated under the rule that its sessions would be open to the public unless ordered closed by a majority vote. Prior to that, the Senate, with very few exceptions, considered all nominations in closed executive session.[56] Two notable exceptions during this period were the contentious confirmation hearings for Louis Brandeis in 1916 and the Senate floor debate on the nomination of Harlan Fiske Stone to the Supreme Court in 1925. The move to public hearings was prompted by uncontrollable press leaks about Senate business (made mostly by members interested in applying public and other pressure to open them) and the desire of many senators to conduct their business in the open so that the public would be more aware of their actions. To paraphrase Justice Brandeis, openness operates as a disinfectant; it exposes a process to the light of day (i.e., public scrutiny). It allows more media coverage, but it also allows interest groups to exert more influence on senators and outcomes. The reason in part is that public hearings have raised the stakes for all concerned in confirmation hearings. Interest groups can use the occasion to gain greater attention for their agendas. The more attention they receive, the more they can signal (and perhaps mobilize) their membership to put pressure on senators to comply with their demands.

Another major procedural change in Senate operations relates to the practice of having nominees appear personally before members of appropriate committees or subcommittees, first seen in 1925 in the confirmation hearings on President Coolidge's nomination of his attorney general, Harlan Fiske Stone, to the Supreme Court. On his own initiative, Stone appeared before the Senate Judiciary Committee to answer questions about his refusal as attorney general to dismiss an indictment brought by his department against a sitting senator.[57]

Subsequent Supreme Court nominees have had to make increasingly lengthy appearances before the Senate Judiciary Committee. Prior to his own appointment as a circuit judge in 1999, Robert Katzmann suggested that Supreme Court confirmation hearings had gone through four periods: 1925–55, "when senators infrequently questioned nominees; 1955–67, the Warren Court era, when the nominee's appearance before the Senate Judiciary Committee became a regular feature of the confirmation hearings; 1968–97, the transition from the Warren Court through the Burger era; and 1987 to the present, in which the hearing has become a venue of conflict and consensus."[58] Today's Supreme Court nominees face intensive questioning about their past records (particularly potentially controversial lower-court decisions or political activity) and views on the contentious constitutional issues of the day.

In contrast, nominees to cabinet-level positions have a longer history of testifying or appearing personally before Senate committees, while the intensity of their questioning has differed from hearing to hearing depending on the office being sought, the familiarity of the committee with the nominee, and the controversial issues on which the nominee would likely be working if confirmed. Lower-court or subcabinet nominees have testified sporadically over the years depending on a wide variety of factors, including but not limited to their reputations, prior experiences in government or with the Senate, relationship to the president, and the relative influence of their sponsor(s) within the Senate.

The aggrandizement of Senate committees has made it easier for small(er) blocs of senators, their powerful chairs, or individual senators to thwart nominations.[59] Moreover, numerous procedural mechanisms and Senate rules allow committees and their chairs (or other powerful and crafty senators) to impede nominations. The first signs of opposition to a nomination usually (but not always) come from senators with a serious or vested interest in the nomination because it involves their state or a subject matter of concern to them. In many cases, the senators likeliest to express initial concern (or support) are on the committees responsible for holding hearings, but this is not an absolute rule — certain offices have salience for some senators because of the policymaking or other authorities of the positions and corresponding constituencies involved.

An especially prestigious and powerful committee is the Senate Judiciary Committee, which is composed mostly of senior senators with safe seats.[60] Its members aspire to seem more independent and less partisan than their colleagues on other committees, and this has often been thought to work to their political advantage. They try to appear as independent judges of the characters of the nominees and guardians of judicial independence, rather than just party hacks. This nonpartisan stance has elevated the status of the Judiciary Committee and is bolstered by the popular conception of an independent federal judiciary.

The Rise and Transformation of Interest Groups

Organized interest groups are largely a twentieth-century phenomenon. One of the first times that concerted effort by groups organized to promote or protect special interests made a difference to the outcome of the confirmation process was in 1881, when the National Grange and other populist groups representing farmers successfully lobbied against President Rutherford B. Hayes's nomination of Stanley Matthews to the Supreme Court based on Matthews's long-standing close ties to the interests of big business. The populists' success in defeating Matthews was, however, short-lived. Not long after Matthews was rejected, Hayes's successor, fellow Republican James Garfield, renominated him, and the Senate confirmed him by the margin of a single vote after two months of acrimonious debate that included intense lobbying on his behalf by controversial financier Jay Gould and his associates.

The Supreme Court's subsequent invalidation of various state and federal social welfare statutes at the turn of the century angered trade unionists and Progressives. Labor groups upset by these decisions organized opposition to, but ultimately failed to block, two of President William Howard Taft's Supreme Court nominees, Horace Lurton in 1909 and Mahlon Pitney in 1912.

The watershed event signaling the importance of interest groups in influencing federal appointments was, however, the four-month-long confirmation contest over President Woodrow Wilson's nomination of Louis Brandeis to the Supreme Court in 1916. The main opposition came from big business, along with a number of prominent Bostonians and the current and six past presidents of the American Bar Association (ABA). The opposition questioned Brandeis's character and judicial temperament, sometimes openly exhibited anti-Semitism, and generally stressed the radicalism of his social and economic views. Labor and consumer groups (and some religious organizations) were influential in convincing both the Judiciary Committee and the full Senate to confirm Brandeis. A little more than two decades later, in 1930, labor and civil rights groups joined forces to ensure the Senate's rejection of President Hoover's nomination of Judge John Parker to the Supreme Court.

In the ensuing years, interest groups have grown in number, political strength, and influence over federal appointments. Their influence has largely been exerted through campaign donations, lobbying (both publicly and privately), advertising, media campaigns, and other actions for the purposes of persuading executive branch officials, including the president, or members of Congress to support the policies and nominees they favor or to oppose the programs or nominees they do not support. Hence, the pressure these groups have exerted on presidential and senatorial decisions about appointments derives from the expectations among all of the parties concerned that presidents will bestow some favors, including nominations, or that members of Congress will exchange some votes for the support of certain groups.[61] Moreover, interest groups have frequently supplied useful information regarding potential or actual nominees to sympathetic senators or presidential advisers, including drafting questions or statements for senators and otherwise assisting members of Congress or the president with rhetoric or data to clothe their partisan positions. Interest group activity has also signaled to presidents and senators the likely costs of not supporting the groups' favored candidates. High levels of interest group activity have proven to help cultivate substantial public sentiment to ensure the making or breaking of various nominations. Ultimately, the degree of interest groups' influence over the appointments process has turned on how successfully they have signaled to the powers that be the costs of noncompliance with their objectives and succeeded in exchanging their support for or against nominations with the objectives of the decision-making authorities. In short, the higher the rate of congruence, the greater is the influence of such groups over particular appointments.

A critical question is, Why do interest groups become involved in opposing particular nominations, particularly to federal judgeships? With respect to the latter, it is clear that many groups are aware that particular issues important to their core members will inevitably come before courts for decision. It is also clear that many groups or organizations use confirmation proceedings as events in which they will try to focus on or bring attention to issues that are especially salient for their members or major contributors. In the latter case, the groups are seeking to shape their agenda by creating a catalyzing event.[62] The support of particular interest groups can serve as a signal to legislators and the public about the ideology of a candidate. Indeed, because political parties' positions are so similar on so many issues, interest group support may be a more credible signal of a nominee's ideology than his or her party affiliation. Moreover, public choice theorists argue that smaller groups may be able to organize collectively and combine their resources, with less of a free-rider problem. For large groups, each potential individual member has less incentive to participate in the group, because the individual can still benefit from the group's actions ("free ride") without participating.[63] Public choice theory further suggests that legislatures will be more prone to capture by narrow private interests, sometimes called factions. Broader public interests will be unable to counteract this influence, because they will find it difficult to organize. Elections will not necessarily counteract this influence. Interest group politics is thus, according to public choice theory, biased in favor of narrow economic interests. Consequently, legislation will typically favor narrow interests at the expense of the general public.[64]

No case better illustrates the impact of interest groups on a nomination's fate than that of President Reagan's nomination of Robert Bork as an associate justice in 1987.[65] The Bork nomination faced the early, united, and vigorous opposition of the interest groups traditionally allied to the Democratic party—labor and civil rights. The Bork nomination arose in the midst of a decade in which many interest groups, particularly liberal ones, had begun to recognize the importance of the federal judiciary to the achievement or success of their respective causes. Up until the battle over Bork's confirmation, feminist and pro-choice forces had functioned largely as single-issue interest groups that cut across partisan party alignments;[66] however, these groups formed an alliance with civil rights organizations to block Bork from being confirmed and thus tipped the ideological orientation of the Court against the groups' joint concerns. Democrats saw the participation of these interest groups as an occasion for attacking the Republican party (for having taken the Court in a wrong direction). Moreover, the groups also got the support of some moderate Republicans (such as Senator Arlen Specter of Pennsylvania) whose re-election depended on critical support from voters intensely interested in the groups' causes.

Ironically, liberal interest groups battling Bork's nomination used tactics borrowed from the campaigns that some conservative groups had waged earlier in the 1980s to defeat state judges subject to election or retention votes. Conservative groups in the aftermath of Bork's defeat formed their own organizations (such as the Judicial Election Monitoring Group headed by Thomas J. Jipping and the Free Congress Research and Education Fund led by Paul M. Weyrich) to lobby and use the media and other means to counteract the influence of liberal interest groups closely aligned to the Democratic party.[67]

The Expansion of Media Coverage

Up until the twentieth century there was limited media coverage of and means for publicizing the federal appointments process. The period of limited coverage coincided with the Senate's policy of keeping its doors closed during confirmation deliberations. Hence, the appraisals of nominees were furnished largely, as the late Paul Freund noted, "by a politically polarized press and intimate correspondence among influential figures in legal and political circles."[68] Neither was an infallible source. In the twentieth century, the development of new media outlets, including radio, network television, cable, and the Internet, has expanded news coverage about federal appointments and helped to subject the political process generally and the appointments process in particular to increasing public scrutiny.[69] The increased coverage of the appointments process has had several consequences. First, it has raised the stakes for nominees and other political actors involved in the process by making it much harder to downplay missteps. For example, President Clinton withdrew his nomination of Henry Foster as surgeon general when a majority of senators refused to allow a final vote on the Senate floor in part because of the lingering negative effects of a White House aide's mistake in miscalculating the number of abortions Foster had performed.[70] Second, increased coverage of the appointments process has pressured some presidents to move too quickly in announcing certain nominees in the hope of avoiding leaks or catching the opposition unprepared, as illustrated by President Reagan's hasty nomination of Judge Douglas Ginsburg to the Supreme Court after Bork's defeat, before Ginsburg's background could be thoroughly vetted. Third, increased media coverage has induced some presidents to take too much time (and thus to appear indecisive in the course of trying) to name someone in order to ensure the nominee's confirmability. This was likely the problem with both of President Clinton's searches for Supreme Court nominees. Fourth, increased media coverage has impelled some presidents to choose nominees with the fewest apparent liabilities rather than those with the strongest records, and thus to select so-called stealth nominees who make difficult targets in confirmation proceedings because of the absence of anything apparently controversial in their records (such was the case, presumably, with President Bush's nomination of David Souter to the Supreme Court). Moreover, increased media coverage has probably facilitated mobilization for or against nominations by disseminating information useful to supporters or opponents. Additional consequences of expanded media coverage of the federal appointments process have included dissuading some well-qualified people from taking public office to avoid losing their personal privacy and inducing senators or interest groups to prolong hearings or take other actions in such proceedings to get coverage for themselves and their agendas. The competition for news (and for viewers or listeners, particularly in an age with so many news outlets and limited attention spans) has produced a voracious appetite within the media for conflict, scandal, and speculation or commentary (rather than just the simple reporting of verified information).[71] This trend was widely apparent in the media's coverage of President Clinton's impeachment proceedings, and it is likely to be a concern in the coverage of any high-profile nomination or confirmation skirmish.

Last but by no means least, the expansion of new information technologies has helped to strengthen the media's and other groups' control of and ability to shape the news (or the flow of information) and thus the public's perception or understanding of appointments.[72] New information technologies, including the Internet, have also allowed for more significant—and quicker—participation by organized groups in political processes. These technologies provide various organizations with the means to communicate more effectively and quickly with lawmakers and voters.

Historical Changes and Patterns

Thus, the expansion of information technologies has helped, along with the other historical, social, and political developments mentioned, to create a complex set of internal and external pressures that presidents, senators, and others routinely involved in the federal appointments process must cultivate or master to achieve their desired outcomes.

CONFIRMATION PATTERNS

In spite of the impact that various social and political developments have had on the operation of the federal appointments process, some aspects of the process have remained relatively unchanged. Most notably, presidents from all historical periods have tended to have similar objectives in making Supreme Court and cabinet nominations. Senators, on the other hand, have differed in the kinds and sequence of considerations they have taken into account in supporting or opposing various kinds of nominations.[73] These patterns of presidential and senatorial decision making provide useful bases for making comparisons and holding public officials accountable.

Presidents and senators have tended to base their decisions regarding certain executive (particularly cabinet) and Supreme Court nominations on their respective calculations of various long-term and short-term considerations—or what the framers regarded as grand and petty political concerns, respectively. The long-term concerns have included a nominee's philosophy about the role of the national government in U.S. society and the relationship among the different branches of the federal government, while the short-term concerns have included a nominee's political party (which can also be a proxy for a very long-term concern—the nominee's ideology and policy views),[74] chances for confirmation, domicile, age, and benefactors or supporters. Both long- and short-term concerns have depended on political circumstances, the state of presidential-Senate relations, and presidents' and senators' other priorities and ambitions for the federal office being filled. For instance, the relevant political philosophy for high-ranking nonjudicial nominees has usually pertained to the nominee's viewpoint on the appropriate functions or duties of the office to which he or she has been nominated and on the office's significance to the president's agenda.[75] For Supreme Court nominees, the relevant ideology would relate to their basic attitudes about interpreting the Constitution generally and, increasingly, regarding contentious areas such as property or economics, federalism, race, privacy, or gender.[76]

Moreover, presidents and senators have differed in how they have ranked these different factors and the sequence in which they have taken them into account in their decision making on Supreme Court appointments. Presidents have been disposed to be guided by grander rather than baser political concerns, such as objective merit, commitment to a particular constitutional philosophy or vision, or the long-term relations between the federal and state governments or between federal institutions. In choosing nominees from within this set of candidates, however, presidents have largely been guided by pragmatic concerns such as ease of confirmation, the ramifications for their popularity, personal knowledge or acquaintance, party loyalty, geographic balance, or the need to appease certain constituencies. Hence, the long-term, or grand, political considerations function as concerns of the first order (because they function as criteria for identifying or designating the universe of possible candidates), while the short-term or pragmatic considerations function as secondary or second-order concerns (because they function as criteria for prioritizing the candidates who have met the first-order criterion).

Compare, for example, the criteria and sequence of considerations taken into account in Presidents Jefferson's, Harding's, and Clinton's Supreme Court nominations.[77] President Jefferson nominated three men to the Supreme Court: William Johnson, Henry Livingston, and Thomas Todd. Jefferson's first-order criterion was fidelity to his constitutional and programmatic vision, a criterion on which he was not disposed to compromise. Once satisfied that he had candidates who met this first criterion, Jefferson chose nominees whom he believed could give the Court geographic balance (and thus win the strong advocacy of the senators from the regions selected). Hence, in making his third nomination to the Supreme Court, Jefferson chose Thomas Todd rather than George Campbell, a congressman who had been the choice of most members of Congress. Jefferson chose Todd over Campbell because he believed Campbell did not fully satisfy his second-order criteria. Jefferson doubted

Campbell's skills as a lawyer (and also the constitutionality of appointing a sitting member of Congress to an office created during his incumbency), while he had no doubts that Todd fully satisfied both orders of concern.[78]

Though one might not expect President Harding to have cared as much as other presidents about the constitutional philosophy of his Supreme Court nominees, he did. President Harding appointed four men to the Supreme Court—William Howard Taft, Pierce Butler, George Sutherland, and Edward Sanford—and each nominee met Harding's general criteria for candidacy. Like Taft before him (and, indeed, with Taft's input), Harding assembled the names of possible Supreme Court nominees based on their disposition to protect economic liberties and to oppose progressive social and economic legislation.[79] Once satisfied that a candidate (or set of candidates) met his general criteria, Harding chose nominees because they were friends whom he trusted (such as William Howard Taft and George Sutherland) and men who could be expected to win relatively quick confirmation.

In nominating Ruth Bader Ginsburg and Stephen Breyer to the Supreme Court, President Clinton followed a similar sequence of reasoning. For each of the two vacancies he filled, President Clinton instructed his staff to assemble a list of prospective candidates for the Court based on their capacity for taking a leadership role on the Court and their having a "progressive" judicial ideology, including a commitment to constitutional stability, an energetic national government, and a sensitive reading of the individual rights provisions of the Constitution.[80] He chose, however, from among the names assembled on the grounds of their appeal to certain constituencies, age and health, and likelihood for confirmation.

The sequence of considerations taken into account seems to be the converse once a nomination reaches the Senate. In the Senate, opposition to a nomination initially has developed for partisan or even personal reasons (though sometimes it quite clearly has developed because of philosophical or ideological differences). The opposition generally has succeeded, however, only if it has been framed in terms of some grander or seemingly neutral or nonpersonal factors, including the preservation of certain constitutional ideals such as federalism.[81]

Consider, for example, reactions in the Senate to President Reagan's nomination of Robert Bork to the Supreme Court and President Clinton's nomination of Zoë Baird as attorney general. Initially, the opposition to Bork followed partisan lines.[82] Democratic senators were eager to block any additional Republican nominees to the Court. They could not block Bork, however, unless they found a way to frame their opposition in nonpartisan terms that would hold a majority of the Senate, including some Republicans, to vote against Bork (while keeping their constituents and interest group supporters largely happy). In the aftermath of Bork's defeat, Republican senators eagerly sought a chance to get even with Democrats; President Clinton's election gave them their first meaningful opportunity.[83] The challenge was to find an appropriate nominee to oppose. They chose Zoë Baird, successfully grounding their opposition on seemingly nonpartisan bases. They argued that her failure to pay Social Security taxes for a domestic couple working for her and her husband deprived her of the moral authority she would need as attorney general to oversee enforcement of the law. Such arguments reflect how senators can make different calculations than presidents on particular appointments—differences that are quite relevant for evaluating the performances of senators and presidents in the appointments process.

Part Two

EVALUATING THE ROLES OF
THE MAJOR PLAYERS IN THE FEDERAL
APPOINTMENTS PROCESS

Chapter Four

THE PRESIDENT'S ROLE IN

THE FEDERAL APPOINTMENTS PROCESS

OF ALL OF THE ACTORS routinely involved in the federal appointments
process, the one with the greatest potential to influence events or outcomes is the president of the United States. This is not to say that presidents will get all of the appointments they want, or that they can count
on unlimited control of the appointments process; it simply means that a
president occupies a unique position, by virtue of his nominating power,
to set the terms of debate on any given appointment.

This chapter attempts in four ways to put presidential efforts to influence the appointments process into perspective. First, it explores the
limited utility of the conventional means of personalizing the presidency
for assessing presidential performance in the appointments process. Second, it examines how different presidents have managed to expand the
powers of their office, particularly their unique nominating authority, to
control or ensure dominance in the federal appointments process. Third,
this chapter identifies the factors that can enhance or impede certain outcomes in the federal appointments process. Finally, we will briefly review
the criteria that presidents have adopted for selecting judicial and nonjudicial nominees. Obviously, such criteria reflect to some extent presidents' priorities in office.

THE LIMITATIONS OF A PERSONALIZED EVALUATION

Legal scholars are still developing useful criteria for evaluating presidential performance in the federal appointments process. This exercise is

primarily a normative one; it aims to develop standards for evaluating presidential contributions and performances in the appointments process rather than just to define context or explain some past events. This exercise is a crucial precursor for making comparative judgments about presidential performances.

Legal scholars have a tendency to personalize the confirmation process. This approach is quite natural, for the dominant focus of the appointments process is usually on the fate of a single person—the nominee. Moreover, the often dramatic conflicts that arise between presidents and senators over nominations shed considerable light on the respective priorities, temperaments, political skills, allegiances, and personal values of these political leaders. In our federal system, the choices a president makes in the people he nominates to critical positions provide significant insights into his personal priorities, including the persons on whose advancement he prefers to spend political coinage.[1] Similarly, senators reveal a great deal about themselves in intensely contested confirmation proceedings.[2]

The temptation is intense to draw on personal angles to explain particular incidents in the federal appointments process. It makes sense, for instance, to use such an approach in evaluating President Polk's nominations, including his negotiations with members of Congress regarding appointments, because he insisted on doing the work in this area by himself. Polk did not wish to share his nominating authority with anyone else in his administration, including the members of his cabinet. Indeed, Polk did not trust his cabinet in selecting subordinates, for he believed its members would be inclined to appoint underlings who would be more loyal to them than to him. Consequently, Polk obliged each cabinet member to renounce presidential aspirations as Polk had done at the outset of his presidency when he announced he would not seek a second term. (Interestingly, the only cabinet member who refused to be pinned down in such a manner was Polk's secretary of state, James Buchanan, whom Polk appointed nevertheless because of Buchanan's experience in foreign affairs and much-needed representation of Pennsylvania in Polk's cabinet. Ironically, it was Buchanan whom Polk had to watch more closely than any other cabinet member in order to ensure compliance with his policy objectives.) Polk's secretary of war, George Bancroft, observed many years after the end of Polk's term of office that Polk always exercised enormous oversight and control over his secretaries, thereby ensuring that they adhered to his wishes and acted in unison.[3]

Moreover, some appointments, such as President John Kennedy's selection of his brother Robert as his attorney general, seem to make sense in terms of the close personal ties and trust shared by the two.[4] When such a nomination fails, the president is made to seem singularly responsible for the outcome. For instance, the failure of Robert Bork's Supreme Court nomination is frequently blamed in part on President Reagan's delay in coming to the defense of his embattled nominee.[5] Similarly, President Clinton took the blame personally for having nominated Lani Guinier, a law school friend, as head of the Justice Department's Civil Rights Division without having read, much less considered the implications of, her legal scholarship.[6] In still other cases, a president's support for a nominee in spite of the damage it causes the president is often explained in terms of stubbornness, as with President Nixon's sticking to his Supreme Court nominee Harrold Carswell in spite of widespread condemnation; or loyalty to his allies, as with President George Bush's willingness to stand by his embattled nominees Robert Gates (as CIA director), John Tower (as secretary of defense), and Clarence Thomas (as associate justice).[7] Similarly, senators' actions in confirmation hearings are sometimes depicted as based on personal feelings, as with the portrayals of many Republican senators as being vicious, ignorant, or sexist based on their ardent defense of Clarence Thomas or aggressive questioning of Anita Hill.[8]

Characterizing the appointments process in personal terms clearly has implications for the appropriate criteria to be employed for evaluating the performance of presidents or senators in the federal appointments process. Under this approach, presidents are made personally responsible for every action or decision made in their name or on behalf of those (such as the nominees) aligned with them. Moreover, performance is measured in terms of the president's personal traits or qualities, such as intelligence, popularity, charisma, strength of character or conviction, loyalty, stubbornness, ambition, or political acuity.[9] Hence, in evaluating presidential performance in the appointments process, many people ask how well presidents knew the people they were nominating, whether presidents made intelligent choices on which people to nominate or whose advice to follow, to whom a president felt indebted, whether a president had strong convictions (and, if so, regarding what), what benefits a president received from making a particular appointment, what price(s) a president paid for certain successful or failed nominations, whether presidents were sufficiently or perhaps too loyal, to what extent a president's stubbornness or anger influenced his actions in the appointments process, and how well a president understood or handled the state of his relations with the Senate.

Perhaps the most sophisticated version of personalizing the federal appointments process is game theory, which assesses performance as strategic behavior. At the risk of some oversimplification, one could describe the federal appointments process as a multi-iteration game of chicken with multiple players (as opposed to its normal form with two players).[10] A good illustration of the confirmation process as a game of chicken is President Bush's nomination of Clarence Thomas to replace Justice Thurgood Marshall on the Supreme Court. President Bush dared Democrats, who at the time had been criticizing his opposition to affirmative action, to reject a conservative African American nominee. Bush gambled that the southern Democrats, at least, would be unable to oppose the nomination, regardless of the nominee's views. Justice Thomas also played chicken with the Senate, daring it to ignore his moving life story and to reject him on the basis of his weak and sometimes inconsistent testimony before the Senate Judiciary Committee. Later, he played the race card by denouncing the second phase of his hearings (investigating Anita Hill's charge of sexual harassment) as a "high-tech lynching" and thereby forcing his critics to prove that their opposition was not racist.[11] The nomination and hearings damaged President Bush because his forays into some blind alleys harmed his credibility. Many senators were similarly damaged because they charged into the same blind alleys, seemingly oblivious to the risk that they would look cowardly rather than statesmanlike by deferring to the president's choice of a weak but sympathetic nominee.

Another example of a confirmation contest as a game of chicken is the process leading up to President Clinton's two Supreme Court nominations. In both cases, each side engaged in extensive maneuvering to influence the choice of a nominee and engineer a confirmation hearing that would help its image and agenda.[12] Along the way, both sides strategically leaked information to the press to influence the choice of the nominee and the ultimate confirmation decision.[13] Sometimes the leaks came from the same camp, as with the many rumors from within the Clinton administration regarding likely nominees. These rumors were designed to keep senators off guard, to test the public and interest group reaction to possible nominees, to pressure the president to support or oppose certain possible nominees, or to gain momentum or build support within the administration for or against a particular nomination. In the end, both sides got something but neither got the biggest payoff possible. As game theory suggests, the biggest payoff occurs when survival depends on one side's choosing not to flinch in the face of confrontation with the other and the former does not falter; when both parties flinch and prefer to avoid damage, neither gets the biggest payoff possible.

A confirmation skirmish could also be described as a game of tit-for-tat.[14] Tit-for-tat is an "infinitely repeated game," with cooperation as its ultimate goal. It is played in a potentially unending series of periods in each of which one player tries to cooperate while the other is retaliating for wrong done in a previous period.[15] Examples of such interaction in the appointments process abound. Just a small sample from this century might include the forced withdrawal of Abe Fortas (compelled by some Republican and southern Democratic senators in retaliation against the liberalism of the Warren Court), the Senate's rejections of Clement Haynsworth and Harrold Carswell (led by Senate Democrats out to get revenge for the forced withdrawal of Fortas), the Senate's rejection of Robert Bork (engineered by the Democrats and liberal interest groups to punish President Reagan for Iran-contra and for his successful appointments of strongly conservative ideologues to the lower courts and to the Supreme Court in his first six years in office), and the forced withdrawals of Zoë Baird and Lani Guinier (led by Republican senators retaliating against the Democrats' scuttling of the Bork nomination and near-fatal opposition to Clarence Thomas's nomination).[16]

A dramatic example of senatorial tit-for-tat (or a game of chicken in which both parties blinked) is the failure of President Clinton and senators from both parties to agree on nominations for the U.S. Sentencing Commission throughout 1997 and 1998. By law, the Sentencing Commission consists of seven commissioners who are supposed to be appointed to staggered six-year terms. Federal law further requires that at least three of the commissioners be federal judges, and that no more than four commissioners may be registered members of the same political party. In order to meet these requirements when selecting nominees, presidents must work closely with senators from both parties. In 1997–98, however, this process broke down completely. The commission had three vacancies as of the beginning of 1998, and by the end of the year all seven slots were unfilled. The problem was that President Clinton could not find any candidates who satisfied key senators. Many of the leading or senior senators from both parties on the Judiciary Committee have long had a proprietary interest in the commission's composition; they view the commission to some extent as an extension of their domain or prerogatives. Though Chief Justice Rehnquist chided President Clinton for the failure to make nominations in his end-of-the-year report on the federal judiciary in 1997, he condemned both sides in his 1998 report, referring to the matter as a "political impasse . . . of stunning proportions."[17] The public condemnations apparently helped to break the deadlock. By November 1999, both sides had worked out an agreeable slate of nominees, including five sitting federal judges. The final deal allowed the commission to recommence its business, but not without a substantial backlog and not before Congress had to cut its budget to avoid the embarrassment of fully funding a comission without any members.

Of course, game theory can do much more than personalize the interaction among players. It is possible, for instance, to explain or predict presidential nominations or the outcomes of confirmation skirmishes on the basis of more than just personal interaction.[18] For example, using more complex formulas one could juxtapose the vertically oriented decision-making structure of the executive branch (reflecting the pathways by which information flows to and from the president and other actors or groups within as well as outside the office of the presidency and the executive branch) against (or with) the horizontally oriented decision-making structure of the Senate (reflecting staffs and external groups, who of course also lobby the president or his advisers, and other interested parties who pressure senators in multifaceted ways). Any major problem with the development of such complex game theories would arise not because they personalize the process but rather because of the uncertainty over the timing and magnitude of impact of major events (both external and internal) that might send shock waves through the appointments process. (To be sure, some events are much more predictable than others. Midterm or presidential elections, for example, typically produce slow-downs within the appointments process, while catastrophic events such as impeachment or assassination, which occur unpredictably, can completely paralyze the appointments process for substantial periods.)

The development of increasingly sophisticated games to reflect the environment or institutional context in which appointments decisions are made or controversies arise derives from the recognition that presidents and senators are more than merely people who occupy certain federal offices; they are also the leaders of powerful governmental institutions, and they act as such when they operate within the federal appointments process. Moreover, they do not try to manage these institutions in a vacuum; presidents operate in particular social, economic, historical, and political contexts. They must react to various developments or movements within both government and society at large. The presidency is not static; its responsibilities and structure have evolved over the course of U.S. history. Consequently, no study of presidential performance within the federal appointments process would be complete without assessing the relationship between such performance and changes within the office or powers of the presidency.

THE SIGNIFICANCE OF INSTITUTIONAL ANALYSIS

Leading or managing the institution of the presidency, including clarifying and coordinating its various powers, presents challenges that require a different set of criteria for evaluating performance than those suggested by an approach grounded in personal traits or character. This other set of criteria constitutes the second means—that is, historical institutionalism—for assessing presidential performance in the federal appointments process. Historical institutionalism suggests that every president faces a peculiar combination of external and internal challenges in the course of trying to put his individual stamp on the office of the presidency if not also on the Constitution and the nation's course in history. Among the external challenges that have been faced by presidents are major military conflicts, including world wars; assassination; governmental corruption; the need to appease certain constituencies pivotal to a president's initial election, legislative successes, or reelection; civil war; the institution of slavery; the depression; and the civil rights, labor, states' rights, equal rights, progressive, and popular sovereignty movements. The internal challenges have included the desire among powerful constituencies or supporters within an administration to control its appointments, agendas, or policies; senatorial courtesy; ideological, policy, or personality disputes among a president's advisers; and the pressure to negotiate with Senate leaders or to trade some choices for certain appointments for critical support on other appointments or particular legislative matters (reaching, of course, crisis proportions on the brink of and in the midst of impeachment).

The measure of a president's performance in terms of institutional analysis is largely based on how well he has managed—or has marshaled the powers of his office to control—the particular challenges confronting him in the course of trying to achieve certain long- and short-range objectives.[19] In the course of managing these challenges and pursuing their legislative and other objectives, presidents are called on to develop or exercise a variety of different management skills, including cultivating and maintaining a good working relationship with the Senate (particularly with a majority of the Senate, including its leaders), organizing or deploying judiciously and effectively the resources and personnel of their office and administration, appreciating the full range of executive powers and presidential authority, articulating and implementing a clear constitutional vision or program, and keenly understanding or defining their time and place in history.[20]

The point of institutional analysis is to measure presidents in terms of the clarity of their articulation of and the significance of their objectives and their relative mastery of the skills necessary for achieving them. Clearly, a president's nominating authority is one of his most significant powers, and a successful or effective president must use his authority in ways that facilitate his achievement of the larger objectives that are crucial for distinguishing presidential leadership.[21]

The latter measure of success does not necessarily turn on a normative evaluation of a president's agenda. Meaningful success depends a great deal on the kinds of challenges a president must overcome in order to achieve his preferred goals. The more ambitious the goals, the greater the challenges for achieving them are likelier to be. For example, it is possible to conceive of President Lincoln as having done nothing more than preserve the original Union, but this understates the nature and significance of his achievement. First, even if Lincoln had been trying to do nothing more than preserve the status quo, he faced challenges of unprecedented scope. Preserving meaningful constitutional order under those conditions required extraordinary management skills. Lincoln, however, did more than that. He also "shatter[ed] existing power arrangements" by ending slavery.[22] Under any credible system of evaluation, that accomplishment, coupled with the preservation of the Union, has to be considered a truly remarkable feat.

To be sure, preserving an existing constitutional order under difficult circumstances is a significant and potentially monumental presidential accomplishment in its own right. For instance, one could argue that one of President Clinton's primary objectives has been to protect the cores of the New Deal and the Great Society from being dismantled or weakened by the Republican Congress that came into office during the midterm elections of 1994.[23] He could be scored well for having accomplished that objective, but helping to preserve the basic features of these programs from attack is a different kind of achievement from the accomplishments of the presidents who first put them into effect. Moreover, President Clinton has preserved these programs in part by not turning some areas into battlegrounds. Such has been the case with his judicial appointments, which have consistently been designed both to avoid controversy and to achieve consensus.[24] He has also sometimes articulated a purposely vague or ambiguous constitutional vision, leaving himself maneuvering room for reelection and compromise. The merits of this strategy have been confirmed at least in part by his reelection to the presidency in 1996 and his high public approval ratings throughout his second term, including during his impeachment proceedings in the House and the Senate.

By the same token, the broader the vision implemented, the greater the degree of presidential success. Of course, very few presidents have implemented such visions, and those who have are relatively easy to predict: Andrew Jackson and Abraham Lincoln in the nineteenth century and

Teddy Roosevelt, Woodrow Wilson, and Franklin Roosevelt in the twentieth century. All five of these presidents used and expanded the means available to them, including federal appointments, to implement their respective constitutional visions.

To some, predicating a president's success or effectiveness on how much constitutional change he was able to effectuate might be too demanding a test because it requires a president to have demanded a lot more from his nominations than just relatively easy confirmations or post-confirmation loyalty. Yet, that is precisely the point. Success is not difficult to achieve if one merely lowers one's sights. Such, for example, was the case with President Calvin Coolidge, who succeeded in appointing many distinguished people to his cabinet as well as to the Supreme Court, but he also sought to implement few — and intended to avoid if at all possible any — constitutional or policy initiatives through his appointments and other actions.

If success were measured strictly in terms of the percentage of a president's confirmed nominations, the figures would be misleading, partly because the Constitution generally establishes a presumption of confirmation by putting "a political burden on the Senate [that] makes it difficult to successfully oppose a president of ordinary political strength for narrow or partisan reasons."[25] Moreover, a high percentage of successful confirmations could be explained as much by the lack as by the presence of a clearly articulated, well-executed presidential vision. The statistics could conceivably reflect a president without any ability or desire to withstand even the threat of opposition.

In effect, this means that the more weighted a president's calculations of his objectives for his appointments are in the direction of long-range governmental or constitutional change, the greater are his chances for scoring well in this area in terms of institutional analysis. This does not necessarily mean that a president must make bold appointment decisions, but rather that his nominating authority be coordinated with his exercise of his other powers to achieve something significant in office. The more successful a president is in implementing his vision through his appointments, the more obstacles through which he will have to maneuver the institution of the presidency to realize his vision. Consequently, presidential performance can be assessed in terms of the institutional objectives sought, the obstacles confronting them, the strategy adopted or skills employed for achieving the objectives or bypassing the obstacles, and the goals actually achieved.

Andrew Jackson's record on federal appointments as president provides a good illustration of how such an assessment would work. Jackson came into office riding the crest of a wave of democratic fervor among the voting public. He dedicated his presidency in large part to democratizing the national government—that is, to making it more responsive and thus more accountable to the common citizen.[26] He also came into office at a time when Congress claimed to be the preeminent and most truly representative national institution; the movement, particularly in the South, in favor of states' rights was gaining momentum; the national government, especially the executive branch, was suffering from unprecedented corruption; and his political party was new and not yet fully stabilized. Jackson served as president against this backdrop for two terms, from 1829 to 1837, during which he repeatedly vied with Congress to establish the president as the preeminent national policymaker and leader based on his status as the only federal official elected by all of the American electorate. A significant portion of the contest was played out in the appointments process. Indeed, Jackson confronted an unprecedented number of confirmation contests. In his first year in office the Senate rejected ten of his nominations, and in his first term it rejected Roger Taney twice—once as secretary of the treasury and later as an associate justice. Yet, by the end of his presidency Jackson had won far more contests than he had lost. More important, he left the presidency enhanced in terms of its scope of authority and stature vis-à-vis Congress—as a result of his tenacity and repeated efforts to expand the president's prerogative in filling key offices with his preferred choices, and his willingness to test the resolve of a majority of senators to remain organized in opposition to a string of well-qualified nominees, and to go to the public to test the popularity of his actions (and his nominees and policies) against those of opposing senators.

Moreover, President Jackson had to control factions within his administration competing for control of his appointments. No sooner had he announced his initial cabinet selections than Vice President John Calhoun and Secretary of State Martin Van Buren, who had worked together to forge the victorious Jackson coalition, began vying with each other to control key federal appointments and to win Jackson's support in naming a successor. Jackson's initial cabinet appointments had been made on the basis of such diverse factors as close personal friendships and political expediency; consequently, the appointees confirmed during his first administration differed widely in terms of quality and loyalty to him. Increasingly bitter and open conflicts between Jackson and Calhoun (and Calhoun's allies within the administration) led Jackson eventually to purge his cabinet of Calhoun supporters. Jackson's second cabinet was a marked improvement in terms of quality and loyalty to him and his policies. Nevertheless, the struggle did not end with Jackson's announcement of his reconfigured cabinet, for the Senate still had to confirm the new members, and in it Jackson faced some of his most bitter political foes, including Henry Clay, Vice President Calhoun (acting as president of the Senate and later, after his resignation from the Jackson administration, as a senator from South Carolina), and Daniel Webster.

Jackson's foes wasted little time in trying to thwart key appointments, including rejecting his nomination of Martin Van Buren to become the minister to Great Britain. The Senate had confirmed Van Buren as secretary of state only three months before the latter nomination, but that was before Jackson's open break with Calhoun (and his supporters) and designation of Van Buren as his heir apparent. Exercising one of his prerogatives as vice president, Calhoun retaliated by casting the decisive vote against Van Buren's nomination as the minister to Great Britain. Jackson turned defeat into victory by publicly extolling Van Buren's virtues and blaming his defeat on Jackson's own political enemies. Never doubtful of his popularity with a majority of the electorate, Jackson decided to use the Senate's blatant partisanship against it in the next presidential election. Ironically, it was Calhoun who gave Jackson his chance. On December 28, 1832, Calhoun resigned the vice presidency to protest Jackson's denunciation of states' rights to nullify federal laws. Immediately thereafter, Calhoun was elected to represent South Carolina in the U.S. Senate. Jackson responded to these developments by naming Van Buren as his running mate to illustrate both his disdain for the Senate's action and his faith in Van Buren's merit. Jackson's victory was not just a personal triumph; it reinforced his claim that the presidency rather than Congress was the branch most truly representative of the will of the American people, and it signaled widespread support for his efforts to reform the national government and preserve the Union.

The presence of many confirmation contests in the course of a president's term of office thus does not alone necessarily indicate something problematic about a president's performance in the federal appointments process. Indeed, the presence of such conflicts could be a sign of significant presidential accomplishment. Compare, for example, the relevance of such conflicts for measuring the performances of Presidents Andrew Jackson and Ronald Reagan in office with the significance of the absence of such conflicts (for the most part) in the presidencies of their respective successors, Martin Van Buren and George Bush. Both Jackson and Reagan came into office as successful opposition candidates; that is, they were not invested heavily in the status quo but rather were positioned with significant electoral victories to implement initiatives in opposition to the constitutional views or policies of their predecessors. Both Jackson and Reagan took advantage of their popularity and status as opposition candidates to implement, by any means available (and in Jackson's case to expand the means available), significant aspects of their constitutional visions for lasting change. For these two presidents, confirmation contests offered significant opportunities to define themselves and their opposition, and Jackson throughout his presidency and Reagan for at least six years in office used such opportunities in precisely that endeavor. (The same, of course, could be said for at least two other opposition presidents—Woodrow Wilson and Franklin Roosevelt.)

As Jackson's and Reagan's respective successors demonstrated, the absence of many confirmation contests in a president's term of office does not necessarily mean that a president has skillfully employed his nominating power to implement lasting constitutional vision or policy initiatives. For instance, as president, Martin Van Buren rarely quarreled with the Senate over appointments. His challenge was to perpetuate if not extend Jackson's legacy, and his appointments were designed to maintain party unity by reflecting the diversity of viewpoints in the Democratic party. As a result, Van Buren did not have an administration unified in purpose or outlook, and he failed to find ways to unite the diverse viewpoints of his most important political appointees.

The President

93

In dealing with appointments (as well as in his administrative style), George Bush resembled Van Buren much more than Reagan. It is perhaps fitting that this should be so, given that Bush was the first sitting vice president since Van Buren elected to the presidency. As president, Bush won far more contests than he lost in the federal appointments process, but his victories had little enduring value because they were made largely on the basis of his perceived need to obtain a short-term political advantage rather than to implement a clearly conceived, articulated, and popular constitutional or political vision.[27] Although Bush's effort to reflect the diversity of the views in the Republican party within his administration made sense as a means of solidifying his support within the party, it also reflected his lack of a strong constitutional vision. In all likelihood, the absence of such a vision (particularly one that could easily be identified as a unifying theme for his presidency) spelled doom for the Bush presidency in the minds of both the voters and the historians.

Nor do serious differences of opinion with the Senate or presidential concessions in the confirmation process necessarily signal a failed presidency or poor institutional leadership. The critical thing is to examine how a president's handling of confirmation contests or concessions figured into his overall agenda, including his attempt to achieve some lasting change in the constitutional order. For instance, President James Madison's appointments difficulties undoubtedly impeded the effectiveness of his administration. In an effort to achieve regional balance and appease a faction of Republican senators who held the balance of power in the Senate (and who wanted, among other things, to preclude the appointment of Jefferson's treasury secretary Albert Gallatin as Madison's secretary of state), Madison settled on an initial cabinet consisting of people who, with the exception of Gallatin, were undistinguished, disloyal, or both. Madison endured the disloyalty and, in the case of his initial appointee as secretary of state, Robert Smith, did much of the work of the office himself for at least two years. This circumstance helped to produce a significant degree of inefficiency in the decision making and implementation of policy in the Madison administration. During his two terms as president, Madison reshuffled his cabinet several times. His repeated difficulties in getting the people he wanted confirmed by the Senate and linking his appointments to the implementation of policy reflected his basic failures to keep Republican senators unified in support of key nominations and his policies; to match available talent with the responsibilities of the offices being filled; to articulate his evolving constitutional vision with sufficient clarity; to build sufficient political and public support for his vision; to devise and implement long-term strategies for the direction and composition of his administration; to calculate the appropriate amount of time for making nominations as well as the costs and benefits of certain nominations; and to reconcile various policies (and the people who were charged with implementing them), including his administration's support of certain Republican beliefs (such as the need for greater state autonomy), maintenance of the national bank, and consolidation of national power to combat foreign threats.

Like Madison, President Jackson had heated confirmation battles with the Senate each year he was in office. Jackson's contests often entailed thinly veiled tugs-of-war between himself and his Senate rivals over dismantling the national bank, reforming and democratizing the national government, and establishing presidential supremacy in formulating national policy. Unlike Madison, however, Jackson repeatedly tested the Senate's resolve to thwart his appointments. Also unlike Madison, President Lincoln had no serious confirmation skirmishes because he used his nominating power to secure the unity of the Republican party and popular and Senate support for his most important policies, including preserving the Union and setting the stage for Reconstruction.

As Jackson's and Lincoln's performances in office demonstrate, the management or leadership skills a president uses (or does not use) in the appointments process reflect and draw on the same skills or judgment a president employs (or fails to employ) generally to achieve the objectives of greatest importance to him. For instance, it is fair to say that President John Quincy Adams's appointments signaled the doom of his administration. First, Adams's appointment of Henry Clay as secretary of state backfired. Although Andrew Jackson received the most votes for president in 1824, he failed to get a majority, and the election had then to be decided in the House of Representatives, whose Speaker, Clay, gave Adams his votes. Adams's subsequent appointment of Clay as secretary of state (a position then regarded as the steppingstone to the presidency) appeared to have been the culmination of, in Jackson's famous phrase, "a

The President

corrupt bargain" in which Clay received a key appointment in exchange for his support of Adams. Further, in an effort to demonstrate that parties had ceased to exist, Adams assembled a cabinet most of whose members had opposed his candidacy. This placed Adams in a position in which he could not readily count on his cabinet to support his bold initiatives. Nor did Adams try to keep his cabinet officers in line by putting constraints on their use of patronage. Instead, he allowed them to appoint his political enemies, including many of Clay's Republican followers and Jacksonian Democrats. Adams's strategy did not produce a harmonious administration, nor did it help to bring greater harmony to the nation. It also was based on a serious miscalculation, for parties still mattered. Adams's appointments alienated, in the estimation of one contemporary, "hundreds of his former friends," who thereafter refused "to promote his reelection." [28] The leadership Adams failed to provide in building support within his own administration and party for his policies and his reelection was symptomatic of his presidency.

Similarly, the Senate's dramatic rejection of President Bush's secretary of defense nominee John Tower and near rejection of his Supreme Court nominee Clarence Thomas overshadowed many of his successes in the confirmation process. The Tower and Thomas episodes underscored some of Bush's weaknesses as a leader by reflecting his failures to map out beforehand a successful confirmation (or legislative) strategy (including developing consensus within the country or the Senate for his agenda beforehand) and to articulate (or command public respect for) the vision underlying the nominations. In contrast, President Clinton assiduously avoided controversy and looked for common ground in the appointments process after having made a few missteps early in his presidency. President Clinton's willingness to compromise in making appointments, to devise a confirmation strategy before making a nomination, to reorganize his office or staff more than once to maximize its quality of performance, and to ensure to the extent possible public support for his most important nominees (such as those to the Supreme Court) paralleled his general efforts in office to look for common ground with congressional leaders, to stand firm on select issues, and to compromise for the sake of keeping the federal government energized and moving generally in a direction of his liking.

Major Players in the Appointments Process

To be sure, merely securing the appointments of people of high quality and like mind (i.e., people who largely agree with or support his constitutional and programmatic visions) has been no guarantee of a president's achievement of his preferred short- and long-term institutional objectives. Generally, some relationship between a president's use of his nominating power and his exercise of other executive powers is inevitable; the problem is to determine the extent to which this has been constructive insofar as the presidency and the nation's welfare are concerned, including the seriousness of any missteps and the nature and ramifications of the objectives sought. For example, President Teddy Roosevelt, who saw himself initially as a president operating within the "Jackson-Lincoln tradition" of presidential leadership (i.e., of trying to reform the constitutional order and understanding of the powers of the presidency within the framework of the national government),[29] had enormous success in the appointments process. Indeed, Roosevelt expanded the domain of presidential power, particularly by transforming it into a "bully pulpit" from which he fought the power of private corporations.[30] Moreover, reforming the appointments process was one of Roosevelt's highest priorities. Before becoming president, Roosevelt had campaigned vigorously for Benjamin Harrison in the 1888 presidential campaign partly because Harrison supported civil service reform. Harrison subsequently appointed Roosevelt as one of three members of the U.S. Civil Service Commission, a position that Roosevelt occupied through the first three years of President Cleveland's second term. Both as a member of the Civil Service Commission and later as president, Roosevelt crusaded for civil service reform. The incessant campaign provoked tension in the Republican party, for Roosevelt's ability to maintain and wield power as president depended on his balancing the need to cultivate party support with the advancement of his initiatives. Moreover, Roosevelt expected all of his federal appointees (including his three appointments to the Supreme Court) to have outstanding qualifications and to share his constitutional and programmatic vision, and he refused to accept the recommendations of people who failed to meet his standards, even from senators of his party. In spite of this rather aggressive stance, Roosevelt had few contested nominations largely because of the intimidating zeal with which he promoted his nominations and his resolve to draw, seemingly at the drop of a hat, on his extraordinary

The President

popularity to test the will of any opposition. Nevertheless, Teddy Roosevelt, by his own admission and the apparent judgment of history, failed to anticipate or to deal adequately as president with the political fallout from the very governmental and party reforms he had initially championed and set into motion.[31] In the end, it was one of his appointments that symbolized Teddy Roosevelt's partial failure as a leader, for in choosing William Howard Taft as his successor, Roosevelt made a fatal mistake. In promoting this choice, Roosevelt not only terminated his own institutional leadership but also selected a successor who failed to endorse many of the reforms preferred by Roosevelt or to exercise the kind of progressive institutional leadership Roosevelt had proven himself capable of exercising.[32]

Ironically, Roosevelt's subsequent split from the Republican party and its leader (and his successor), Taft, paved the way for the election of another committed reformer, Woodrow Wilson. Wilson became the advocate for and personification of the New Freedom's quest for social and political justice. Unlike Teddy Roosevelt, Wilson preferred to work behind the scenes in the appointments process and experienced only a few seriously contested nominations, including most notoriously the first of his three Supreme Court appointments, Louis Brandeis. At the time of his nomination, Brandeis was closely associated with the boldness of Wilson's presidential vision and was a controversial lawyer in his own right; thus, he became the center of one of the most protracted, vicious, and bitter confirmation contests in the twentieth century.

In contrast, Wilson studiously avoided controversy in his nonjudicial appointments. This strategy made sense for Wilson because he had initially been elected as a plurality president who was expected to use patronage appointments to unify party loyalty and support. When Wilson became president in 1913, the Democrats had been out of office for sixteen years, and there was a substantial rush of aspiring appointees. Rather than take on the responsibility himself for handling the pressure from this rush, Wilson took the advice of his closest advisers and turned over to the departments the primary responsibility for handling most of the appointments within them. Wilson assumed the responsibility for picking his cabinet. Since he felt few debts to party leaders, his aim in choosing a cabinet was to keep the party relatively unified behind him while at the same time finding individuals whom he believed were firmly committed to and capable of implementing his progressive policies.[33] When Wilson met significant opposition within his party, he tended to defer to its demands. In dealing with the Senate on appointments, Wilson, like Lincoln, rarely permitted patronage disputes to deflect him from trying to coordinate his powers for the purpose of achieving certain broader objectives and avoiding the alienation of members of his party whose support he needed to ensure the success of his legislative program and efforts in the international arena.

Of course, appointing someone is one thing, and the work that appointee does with others, including a president, is quite another. Even in the latter case, it is asking a lot to attribute significant constitutional change to the action(s) of a single appointee, especially a judge. The problem is that individuals acting alone can accomplish very little in the national government. This difficulty is compounded when a president does not have the means to control directly his appointee's exercise of power, as is the case with judicial appointments and the heads of independent or quasi-independent agencies. Significant change is much more likely to be achieved through the combined or coordinated efforts of a team; hence, a string of appointments and the consequent activities of those people as coordinated or managed by a president provides a much more extensive record for assessing presidential management. For example, President Jackson succeeded, in spite of considerable resistance from the Senate during his eight years in office, in reforming the national government and thus "providing the American people with one of the most honest and least corrupt administrations in the early history of the nation."[34] Moreover, in making six, five, and nine appointments to the Supreme Court, Presidents Jackson, Lincoln, and Franklin Roosevelt, respectively, succeeded in changing its ideological composition.

Although the appointment of an able, well-qualified individual is a significant short-term accomplishment, it does not say much about a president's management of his office or branch to achieve long-term goals such as influencing the direction of the Supreme Court. A president usually achieves that only by appointing several justices. In other words, one should be careful not to read too much into a single success. President John Adams, for instance, undoubtedly regarded his appointment of John

Marshall as a great achievement, but Marshall accomplished all that he did on the Supreme Court without Adams's help. Otherwise, Adams's appointments, which included keeping Washington's entire cabinet, reflected his lack of appreciation of the importance of maintaining a unified administration to ensure the achievement of his desired objectives.

Finally, it is extremely important to understand that different presidents have had different objectives in making different kinds of appointments (particularly in making judicial nominations as opposed to nominations to executive offices), and different appointments have sometimes figured differently into different presidents' agendas. Compare, for instance, the presidencies of Dwight Eisenhower and William Howard Taft. The former proved to be, in Stephen Skowronek's estimation, "a master" at not doing more than he could realistically accomplish; hence, he "was content to prune the radical edge off New Deal liberalism."[35] He achieved a relatively well defined, modest goal, but his achievement "faded quickly as a national political alternative upon his departure [from office]."[36] Moreover, Eisenhower did not include within his agenda a radical overhauling of the federal judiciary. Whereas he preferred for his nonjudicial nominees to share his political commitments, he did not link his choice of judicial nominees to a strict ideological litmus test. Consequently, Eisenhower's overall performance in the appointments process was not neatly linked to a general policy agenda. He deliberately chose not to pursue a full-scale assault on the constitutional foundations of the New Deal, an assault that would have required significantly different kinds of judicial appointments.

Whereas President Eisenhower generally succeeded (at least for a short time) in constraining legislative expansions of the New Deal but not in reshaping the federal judiciary, William Howard Taft was relatively passive on legislative and policy matters and took a much more active interest in judicial appointments. Both as president and later as Chief Justice, Taft selected judges based primarily on their adherence to judicial enforcement of property rights (also known as economic due process) and antipathy toward progressive legislation. Through the six Supreme Court appointments he made in his single term as president and the influence he wielded over lower-court nominations for almost three decades on the Court, Taft was instrumental in putting into place a federal judiciary that

Major Players in the Appointments Process

refused to embrace unconditionally progressive economic legislation until Franklin Roosevelt's second term in office.

The previous section suggests that the management of the federal appointments process, at least insofar as the president is concerned, requires the cultivation and exercise of various political skills, including effective and timely use of the presidency as a bully pulpit, manipulation of the media, building and maintaining support from important interest groups or constituencies, developing and maintaining strong support within the president's party (particularly with its leadership in the Senate), cultivating and maintaining good working relations with the Senate and the media, developing and articulating clearly policy priorities and objectives, making intelligent delegation decisions, and campaigning (particularly, knowing how much should be done on behalf of certain nominees). This section examines some lessons that presidents have drawn from their own and their predecessors' experiences (including successes and mistakes) about the factors or conditions they must control in order to achieve desired outcomes in the federal appointments process.

One of the most important lessons derives from positive political theory, which suggests that political actors try to achieve the policies closest to their preference, taking account of the future actions of other political players who will have subsequent roles in policy formation.[37] For example, one would imagine that the requirement of Senate confirmation affects a president's initial nomination decision profoundly. The fact that the Senate can reject (or that individual senators can use parliamentary maneuvers to frustrate) a nominee may alter a president's behavior or strategy so that we might see very few, if any, such rejections in practice. How can we ever know the extent of that effect when we are trying to measure a president's failure to act in a particular way?

A related issue has to do with the possibility that presidents might respond to their concerns about the need for Senate confirmation by shifting responsibilities from certain confirmable offices to officials who do not need confirmation. In the modern era, for example, certain White House officials, such as the chief of staff or the chief White House counsel, often wield greater power than many cabinet officials. Indeed, some such offices have expanded considerably over the years (as reflected, for example, by the White House counsel's office, which had only one person throughout the Nixon administration, and today has nineteen full-time attorneys and more than a dozen other lawyers rotating through the office from other agencies). The conventional wisdom is that such officials are largely beyond the control of Congress, which in all likelihood would not be able constitutionally to require their confirmation because such a requirement would probably be viewed as an illegitimate intrusion on a president's right to structure his office in accordance with his official needs.

The difficulty is that most of the people who have benefited from such shifting and wield such power in shaping policy do so behind closed doors. Consequently, it is hard to document or to say with much confidence just how much shifting there has been. Nevertheless, not all such bypassing is cost-free; it raises the ire of many members of Congress, particularly senators, who regard it as an illegitimate attempt by the president to escape the constitutional requirement of advise and consent. (Such, for instance, was the widespread reaction in Congress to President Clinton's unusually high number of acting appointees.)

In the absence of concrete data on these issues, the critical thing is to identify the other factors (besides the knowledge of possible Senate rejection) that presidents have learned to take into account in developing strategies generally for securing confirmation or for ensuring the confirmation of particular nominations. One can then begin to measure a president's performance by how well or poorly he adjusted (or was able to develop strategies or take actions that account for the likelihood that certain factors or conditions would influence outcomes). These other conditions or factors (which to varying degrees can be planned for or taken into consideration, if not manipulated) include presidential popularity; the relative strength of a president's party (or the opposing party) in the Senate; timing; and the quality of a president's staffing, organization, or strategy in making appointments generally or on any given appointment. Presidents have had mixed results in trying to deal with more than one of these conditions or factors at a time. As presidents (and others) have all learned, some combination of these conditions or factors is almost always at work in the federal appointments process. Thus, presidents (as well as senators) have had to learn how (and can be measured by how well they have been able) to control these factors for the sake of achieving their desired outcomes.

Presidential Popularity

It seems axiomatic that a president's unpopularity or the unpopularity of his policies might incline some if not many senators to oppose nominees who can be closely associated with the president personally or with his unpopular policies. The difficulty is to find empirical support for the connection between the opposition of some senators and the unpopularity of the president or his policies, because senators generally do not characterize their opposition in terms of a president's personal unpopularity. Instead, they tend to couch their rhetoric in terms of something a nominee has done or might be understood to stand for. By the same token, a president's popularity or the popularity of his programs (and therefore of a pledge to maintain such programs) provides important leverage on behalf of a nomination. Though it is not always easy to draw a direct connection between a president's popularity and a nomination's success (because the connection is not explicitly made by the key decision makers), one can often infer from the circumstances under which some confirmations occurred that just as a president's unpopularity or the unpopularity of some of his programs can weaken support for some nominations, a president's popularity or the popularity of some programs can insulate a nomination from fatal attack. For instance, Lawrence Summers, President Clinton's nominee to replace his friend Robert Rubin as secretary of the treasury, had rubbed some Republican senators the wrong way with his arrogant manner and his opposition to reforming estate tax laws. Moreover, Summer's confirmation hearings and the final committee and floor votes on his nomination were temporarily delayed because the confirmation process was held hostage by a few senators in retaliation against some recess appointments made by President Clinton without the proper notification. Yet, the strength of the nation's economy and the widespread perception that then–Deputy Secretary of the Treasury Summers would continue the widely popular economic policies of his predecessor gave his nomination irreversible momentum. On July 1, 1999, the Senate confirmed him ninety-seven to two.

The absence of empirical support should not preclude an inquiry into the relevance of presidential popularity (or the absence thereof) to outcomes in the federal appointments process. There is substantial anecdotal evidence, not to mention reasonable inferences and common sense, to suggest that such popularity (or, again, its absence) was a factor in the mobilization of support or opposition to certain nominations. It was a factor in the sense that it existed at least in the form of senators' (if not voters') general perceptions of a president's relative political support (among important constituencies) and access to the means to punish or retaliate against senators who opposed certain nominations. In other words, a president's popularity is potentially a powerful weapon, for it signals to anyone or any institution bent on crossing the president the possibility of a serious backlash not just from him but also from the American people.

Presidents who have succeeded in cultivating or maintaining their popularity have learned that the challenge in the appointments process has been to take advantage of their popularity judiciously—to use it when it can benefit them and their administrative goals the most and to avoid squandering it on unimportant things. Ironically, presidential popularity can be crucial for triggering political support for important nominations or related causes.

Conversely, presidents who have squandered or lost their popularity, or perhaps never developed much to start with (such as Presidents Tyler, Fillmore, and Pierce in the nineteenth century and Presidents Truman and Carter in the twentieth century), have learned that their unpopularity can come back to haunt them in confirmation proceedings. Nominees of unpopular presidents have sometimes been viewed by some senators, media, or factions as the embodiments of unpopular programs, policies, or aspects of presidents. In other words, certain nominees have become political casualties because of serious grievances one or more senators have had with a president. Opposing a nominee because of a desire to punish a president has proven to have two advantages insofar as the Senate is concerned. The first is that presidents have little or no way to prevent it.

Second, presidents have learned that their unpopularity or the unpopularity of some of their policies (with some or many senators) may be a problem whenever the Senate considers a nomination. The difficulty lies in predicting or anticipating when that unpopularity will provoke opposition to a nominee. Presidents, that is, understand that such opposition might arise, but they have not perfected a means by which to anticipate the particular nominations in which it will occur.

The federal appointments process is a popular forum for senators who disapprove of or dislike a president or some of his policies to test the popularity of the president or his policies. The unpopularity of a president can signal his weakness as a manager or leader or perhaps the absence or loss of the resources necessary for him to withstand substantial or serious opposition to his policies or important nominees. The more unpopular a president or the more controversial one of his policies, the likelier it is that a confirmation contest will arise regarding a nominee closely associated with the sources of the unpopularity or controversy.

History is replete with examples of this phenomenon. One of the first instances occurred at the end of Thomas Jefferson's administration. By that point, Jefferson's popularity and influence had declined, in large part because of the economic hardships felt throughout the country as a result of Jefferson's successful efforts to get Congress to enact legislation designed to restrain U.S. trade with belligerent nations. Consequently, the Senate unanimously rejected Jefferson's last nomination—that of his close friend William Short to be the minister to Russia. At the request of the Russian emperor, President Jefferson had agreed to exchange ministers and had dispatched Short to St. Petersburg. Nevertheless, the Senate disapproved Short based on the prevailing opposition in the Senate to the establishment of permanent diplomatic posts at the courts of other countries rather than because of any personal objection to Short. Knowing that the nomination would face opposition, Jefferson delayed sending it to the Senate until the end of the session. The nomination failed because Jefferson was not able in the meantime to regain sufficiently good relations with the Senate to change the outcome of the vote on Short's confirmation.

A more dramatic example of unpopular presidential policies affecting nominations is the Senate's rejection of Roger Taney as President Jack-

The President

son's second secretary of the treasury. Although the Senate had confirmed Taney as President Jackson's second attorney general in 1831, it rejected his nomination three years later as secretary of the treasury because a majority of senators disapproved of Taney's conduct in the interim as acting treasury secretary in overseeing the dismantling of the national bank in response to what President Jackson had regarded as its mismanagement. No one questioned Taney's ability, but Taney's nomination as treasury secretary, and not long thereafter as an associate justice, provided perfect opportunities for those in the Senate opposed to the president's national bank policies to debate the propriety of these policies and Taney's actions to facilitate them.

Surely President Tyler's unpopularity emboldened senators to oppose more than half of his nominees. Besides his difficulties in filling the two Supreme Court vacancies that arose while he was president, Tyler had to make twenty nominations to fill his six cabinet posts. The Senate confirmed thirteen of his cabinet nominations and rejected seven — the most cabinet nominations rejected in American history. Three of the Senate's seven rejections of cabinet nominees were of Tyler's nomination of Caleb Cushing to be secretary of the treasury, a nomination he made three times in a failed contest of wills with the Senate.

A more recent example of the tendency of some senators to thwart important presidential nominations because of nominees' real or potential association with unpopular presidential policies or traits is President Clinton's unsuccessful nomination of then-National Security Adviser Anthony Lake in 1997 to head the CIA. No one questioned Lake's qualifications. Nevertheless, Lake ultimately withdrew his nomination when it became apparent that some powerful Republican senators were delaying the final Senate vote indefinitely because of unresolved questions about his managerial skills and possible involvement in inappropriate fund-raising activities undertaken by his staff.[38] Even though the latter might not have been illegal, Lake, like Taney before him in dealing with the national bank, was associated with and had allegedly engaged in or allowed some activity to occur that the president's political foes in the Senate viewed as inappropriate.

Presidents' unpopularity has at times been so widespread or extreme as to create a predisposition among some senators to resist important nominees with the aim of undercutting the president. For example, the steady opposition in the Senate to President Tyler's nominees for the Supreme Court and for his cabinet derived not from any flaws in the nominees' qualifications but rather from widespread contempt in the Senate for Tyler, particularly for his abandonment of the Democratic party and rejection of Whig policies. Another example is the forced withdrawal of President Lyndon Johnson's nomination of then-Associate Justice Abe Fortas to become Chief Justice. Justice Fortas undoubtedly had the requisite skills to be Chief Justice, but his nomination failed for several reasons, one of which was the inability of his Democratic supporters to stop a Republican filibuster against the nomination based in part on the president's growing unpopularity and the expectation among Senate Republicans that Johnson would be replaced by Richard Nixon, whom Fortas's opponents preferred to be the one to name Warren's successor.[39]

Of course, as President Jackson's experience with the federal appointments process demonstrates, popularity does not necessarily insulate presidential nominees from criticism or opposition in the confirmation process. Presidents have learned that senators will oppose some nominees to maintain their own popularity or support from some critical constituencies. For instance, President Franklin Roosevelt experienced more problems with nominations in his second and third terms than during his first, though these hardly signaled any serious diminution in his popularity. The only major presidential nomination that met with strong opposition in the Senate during Roosevelt's first term was that of Rexford Tugwell, whom the Senate confirmed as undersecretary of agriculture by a vote of fifty-three to twenty-four. After the 1938 election, President Roosevelt's nominations of people who were widely viewed as politically liberal were consistently opposed by Republicans and conservative Democrats in the Senate, and several were defeated in spite of the fact that the Democrats held a substantial majority of seats at the time (and continued to do so for the remainder of his presidency). Just as political liberals in the Senate during the Coolidge and Hoover administrations had opposed the appointments of conservatives to high federal offices, the conservatives in the Senate during Roosevelt's terms in office tried to turn the tables and oppose the appointments of liberals. Although in most cases conservative forces were unable to defeat the liberals nominated by Roosevelt, their opposition sent warnings to top civil service employees and prominent people outside the government of the hazards (and sometimes the humiliation) involved in undergoing Senate confirmation proceedings. Moreover, President Roosevelt assiduously looked for ways either to distance himself from troubled nominees or to turn their troubles to his advantage by reminding voters that the policies or programs for which Roosevelt was responsible and to which he owed at least some of his popularity were at stake.

Franklin Roosevelt's confirmation contests with the Senate pale in comparison with those encountered by his successor, Harry Truman. President Truman, who had served for a decade as a senator, knew and tried (sometimes vainly) throughout his presidency to maintain relatively good personal relationships with key Republican leaders in Congress, particularly Joe Martin in the House of Representatives and Arthur Vandenberg in the Senate. These relations took a downturn after the Republicans took control of both houses of Congress in 1946. Between the midterm election of 1946 and the presidential election set for 1948, the Republican-controlled Senate held up most of Truman's important nominations, subjecting them to virtually endless scrutiny in the hope that many or all of the vacancies could be filled by the person expected to be the next president—Thomas Dewey. During this period the Republican Senate did not formally reject any of Truman's nominations, but it did force Truman to withdraw 153 nominations and did not act on another 11,692 (the latter were mostly postmasters and other minor officials). After the 1946 midterm election and before the 1948 presidential election (in which Truman staked his reelection on the public's agreement with his condemnation of the "do-nothing Congress"), President Truman sought to avoid unnecessary controversies by nominating to important posts persons who were acceptable to the Republican Senate—including career civil servants or people who had never been active in politics (the most prominent having been General George Marshall as secretary of state).

President Truman understood, as have all other presidents, that in order to win confirmation contests with the Senate a president sometimes must draw precious political coinage from other legislative priorities. The compounding problem is that presidents whose popularity has declined (or perhaps never fully took root) might have limited political coinage to expend on appointments.

Compare, for example, President Reagan's success in getting his political and judicial nominees confirmed prior to 1986 and his difficulties in getting many key nominations approved after 1986. For the first six years of his presidency, virtually all of President Reagan's major nominations were approved by the Senate, with a couple of notable exceptions (e.g., Brad Reynolds's failed nomination as associate attorney general). After 1986, the Democrats regained a majority of seats in the Senate, and President Reagan became embroiled in the Iran-contra scandal. The latter clearly detracted from his popularity and required expending political coinage that he might have otherwise been able to use on important nominations. Consequently, several of his nominees ran into difficulties. The Senate rejected Robert Bork's nomination to the Supreme Court; opposition from senators in Reagan's own party forced the withdrawal of Douglas Ginsburg's nomination to the Supreme Court; the Senate Judiciary Committee refused to forward the nomination of Bernard Siegan to the U.S. Court of Appeals for the Ninth Circuit, forced the withdrawal of another nominee to the Fifth Circuit Court of Appeals, and failed to take final action on six other nominees to the federal courts of appeal and nine nominees for district judgeships in Reagan's last two years in office.[40]

A different scandal paralyzed the Senate's processing of President Clinton's judicial nominees from the fall of 1998 through the first half of 1999. By the fall of 1998, the president was already being threatened with possible impeachment by the House for false or misleading testimony and other actions that he had undertaken to conceal (from both the press and the Office of Independent Counsel) an illicit relationship with a former White House intern. As the impeachment proceedings unfolded, they had an increasingly devastating effect on the processing of the president's judicial nominations. Thus, as of the fall 1998, the Senate had confirmed only twenty-two of President Clinton's judicial nominations made that year and had not taken final action on forty-one others (twelve to the district court and twenty-nine to the federal circuit courts of appeals).[41] Moreover, there were also (as of that date) thirty-one judicial vacancies (five for the district court and twenty-six for the circuit court) to which President Clinton had not yet made any nominations.

During the period from mid-December 1998 (when the House impeached Clinton for perjury and obstruction of justice) through mid-February 1999 (when the Senate acquitted him), nothing happened with respect to any of the president's nominees, in spite of his steady popularity in opinion polls. Almost four months after his acquittal, the Senate had confirmed only two of President Clinton's judicial nominations and had not taken final action on forty-two others. Moreover, by the end of the first session of the 106th Congress, there were twenty-nine other judicial vacancies for which President Clinton had not yet nominated replacements.

The fact that associating a nominee with some potential danger to the public or some problem associated with the president constitutes the strongest trigger for mobilizing public support for or opposition to a nomination has serious consequences for constitutional law. The utilization of such factors suggests that the president and the Senate have tended to treat judicial and nonjudicial nominations in some strikingly similar ways. For instance, the potential for demonizing a nominee treats the person's philosophy about government as a potentially disqualifying concern. The policy could be related to the judiciary (such as its role within the constitutional order) but does not have to be. Consequently, nominees will be rejected for their political philosophies regardless of the positions they are seeking. To be sure, judicial and nonjudicial nominees do receive somewhat different treatment (the significant reasons for which I will explore at greater length in the next section). For instance, the former are often scanned more closely by both the president and the Senate because they will have life tenure. Even so, the lower the profile of the nominee, the more outrageous the person's philosophy has to be in order to create a plausible case for public concern about the person's appointment. As the nominee's chances for elevation to more powerful positions rise, so too do the costs of a president's—or, for that matter, a senator's—support or opposition.

Divided Government

Presidents have learned that divided government—the circumstance in which different political parties control the White House and the Congress, particularly the Senate—poses a potentially serious problem for the achievement of their objectives in the federal appointments process, regardless of their popular support or stature. Operating successfully in a divided government requires leadership and administrative skills, including management and communication skills; the ability to cultivate and take advantage of good relations with key Senate leaders or forces; and abilities to mobilize public support and opinion.

The fact that divided government makes a difference to the dynamics of the appointments process is indisputable. Indeed, confirmation contests occur much more frequently in periods of divided government than at other times. For instance, the correlation between party membership and Supreme Court confirmation votes has remained quite strong throughout U.S. history.[42] In 1971, Robert Scigliano found that the confirmation rate for Supreme Court justices was 91 percent when the president's party controlled the Senate and 42 percent when the president's party did not control the Senate.[43] Subsequently, there have been thirteen nominations to the Supreme Court. Seven of these nominations were made under circumstances in which the opposition party controlled the Senate, and two of them—Robert Bork and Douglas Ginsburg—failed. Hence, over the past twenty-seven years the confirmation rate for justices has been 100 percent when the president's party has controlled the Senate and approximately 66 percent when the president's party did not control the Senate.

Generally, the political realities of divided government have proven to be a significant challenge for presidents (and senators) in the federal appointments process. Whenever the presidency and the Senate are controlled by different parties, presidents have felt much greater pressure from the Senate to compromise in making their most important appointments, including sometimes appointing people from the opposition party. For instance, Republican presidents Warren Harding and Dwight Eisenhower nominated Democrats Pierce Butler and William Brennan, respectively, in part to demonstrate their own ability to rise above partisan politics in making Supreme Court appointments and in part to curry favor with senators and voters from the other party. President Harding nominated Butler shortly after the midterm elections of 1922, in which the Republicans lost seven seats, cutting their majority in the Senate from twenty-four seats to ten. President Eisenhower nominated Brennan after the Democrats had taken control of the Senate and Eisenhower had promised in his reelection campaign to consider putting a Democrat on the Court.

Divided government is an especially difficult problem for presidents who are eager for significant governmental or constitutional reform. For example, President Andrew Jackson's newly organized Democratic party barely controlled a majority of the Senate for most of his presidency. Jackson understood the magnitude of this dilemma, particularly after the Senate, with Democrats controlling only half of the seats, blocked Roger Taney's nomination as an associate justice within six months of rejecting his nomination as treasury secretary. In the next cycle of congressional elections, Jackson stumped for Democratic candidates. His campaigning succeeded, so that in his last two years in office Democrats regained a majority of seats by a slim margin of twenty-seven to twenty-five. This thin margin helped to ensure Taney's subsequent confirmation as Chief Justice in 1837. Jackson had won.[44] In the end, Jackson succeeded in filling a number of important offices with his preferred choices, expanding the grounds for exercising presidential veto authority, implementing his program of weakening the national bank, and invigorating states' rights but without acceding to nullification or succession.[45]

Subsequent presidents have discovered, however, that their own party's control of the Senate does not guarantee the success of their nominations. For example, only two of the five cabinet nominations rejected or forced to be withdrawn in this century occurred while the opposition party controlled the Senate: the Democrat-controlled Senate rejected Republican president Eisenhower's nomination of Lewis Strauss as secretary of commerce in 1959, and a Democrat-controlled Senate subsequently rejected Republican president Bush's nomination of former senator John Tower in 1989. On three other occasions the Senate rejected or forced the withdrawal of cabinet nominations made by a president from the same political party: a Republican-controlled Senate twice rejected Presi-

Major Players in the Appointments Process

dent Coolidge's nomination of Charles Warren as attorney general, and a Democrat-controlled Senate forced President Clinton to withdraw his nomination of Zoë Baird as attorney general in 1993. These failed nominations turned on a combination of factors that included payback for some previously rejected nomination of consequence (Baird), the nominee's failure to establish (or the president's failure to establish on behalf of the nominee) credibility and support from some of the powerful or influential constituencies responsible for the president's election (true for both Warren and Baird), the nominee's failure to maintain popularity or credibility with a majority of senators (true for both Warren and Baird), and the nominee's past error of judgment on some matter arguably relevant to the position being sought (Baird).

When his own party controls the Senate, certain things become possible for a president regarding appointments and other related matters. For instance, when Martin Van Buren became president, he inherited a Democratic Senate, and all of his most important nominations (such as to the cabinet and the Supreme Court) were confirmed. The most difficulty he encountered came near the end of his presidency after he had been defeated in his reelection bid by Whig William Henry Harrison. A vacancy arose on the Supreme Court because of the sudden death of Justice Philip Barbour, and Van Buren nominated his long-term friend and political adviser Peter Daniel to the post. Though the Whigs tried to block Daniel's nomination in the hope of preserving the vacancy for Harrison to fill, the Democrats, who were in control of a majority of the seats in the Senate until Harrison's inauguration, succeeded in bringing the matter to a vote and confirmed Daniel's nomination by an overwhelming margin.

Van Buren made sure not to antagonize his Democratic allies in the Senate by trying to appoint men to his cabinet who represented the different factions or views of the Democratic party. While he avoided having to spend excessive political capital on his appointments, however, Van Buren was largely unable to take further advantage of the Democratic majority in the Congress to fashion clear or popular solutions to the critical political, social, and economic issues of the day. Jackson was able to pass on to his successor a Democratic Congress, but his successor lacked Jackson's popular appeal, rhetorical skills, tenacity, and clarity and boldness of vision to make constructive use of it.

The President

In contrast, Bill Clinton experienced difficulties in the appointments process regardless of which party controlled the Senate. In his first two years in office, the Democrats controlled the Senate, but several nominations met high-profile resistance that culminated in embarrassing forced withdrawals. After the Republicans took charge of the Senate in early 1995, Clinton took great pains to consult with the Republican leadership about certain nominations and to avoid making judicial or other nominations that would provoke serious opposition in the Senate. Nevertheless, the Republican leadership slowed down the confirmation process for the next four years. First, it brought judicial confirmation hearings to a virtual standstill throughout the year of Clinton's reelection in 1996 (confirming a total of only seventeen judgeships) and again for most of 1997 (confirming thirty-six in all); and in 1998 and 1999 it confirmed a smaller percentage of Clinton's judicial nominees than it did in the corresponding years in the Reagan and Bush administrations.

Moreover, as the next two chapters discuss, Clinton's consultation with Senate leaders about his nominations might have produced fewer casualties in the appointments process, but it also produced longer delays in Clinton's announcing his nominations and in the Senate's scheduling confirmation hearings or votes. Perhaps most important, Clinton's consultations, undertaken for the sake of preserving political capital for other legislative initiatives, came at the further price of compromising some of his selection criteria for certain posts and thus partially abandoning some of his appointment prerogatives.

The Quality of Presidential Organization and Staffing

The relative quality of the president's staff and how he allocates authority for decision making on nominations can have a significant effect on the appointments process. To be sure, inefficient or poor organization has not necessarily precluded finding well-qualified nominees who have met presidential criteria for selection and confirmation. In the nineteenth century, for instance, every president, including the few who tried to delegate to their cabinet secretaries the responsibility of making subcabinet nominations, felt the need to spend a significant portion of his time in office (often hours on end) personally interviewing prospective officeholders and making major decisions about appointments. The primary challenges posed by this practice were to ensure that the nominees chosen fit presidential criteria for selection and that the time spent on appointments matters did not unduly impede or interfere with other presidential responsibilities.

The most dramatic example of a nineteenth-century president who failed to meet these challenges was Ulysses Grant. As Grant's biographer William S. McFeely observes, President Grant "had no sense of statecraft. He spent an inordinate amount of time on appointments to petty offices, in an endless attempt to balance state representation and placate party factions."[46] The excessive attention spent on inferior appointments failed to pay off, for Grant proved to be "capricious and fitfully personal in his appointments."[47] He appointed so many old friends to office that his chief critic in the Senate, Charles Sumner, was led to observe on the Senate floor that the country was suffering from "a dropsical nepotism swollen to elephantiasis."[48]

President Grant's appointments to cabinet posts and to the Supreme Court were equally if not more problematic. Too often Grant failed to match talent or experience with the responsibilities of the office being filled. These appointments also reflected Grant's desire to avoid conflict rather than to implement any particular constitutional or political philosophy. Consequently, Grant's administration experienced an unusual amount of turnover at the top. In all, twenty-five men served in seven cabinet posts, and the frequency of changes increased as the administration reached its conclusion: there were five new department heads in Grant's last year in office, 1876.

Moreover, Grant lost a chance to reconstruct the Supreme Court in spite of making four appointments to it. He had no plan or goal in trying to appoint justices other than, it seems, to secure their confirmation by the Senate. Nor did Grant have any strategy about whom to turn to for sound guidance on Court appointments. His difficulty in filling the Chief Justiceship is illustrative. With no apparent strategy in mind other than filling the post as quickly as possible, Grant offered the position to seven people. Four (all senators) turned it down; two—George Williams and Caleb Cushing—agreed to be nominated but were forced subsequently to withdraw their nominations; and the last nominee—Morrison Waite— was confirmed in spite of being generally unknown outside his native

The President

Ohio. (If Grant had had experienced, knowledgeable advisers, it is conceivable, for example, that they might have been able to save him from the embarrassment he endured in trying to find a suitable Chief Justice.) As one observer of Grant's efforts to settle on a nominee to become Chief Justice lamented, "The President needs advisers badly and if he does not get them soon, Heaven only knows how this session will end."[49]

Grant's failure to appreciate both the need to delegate subordinate appointments to his department heads and the relative importance of various appointments became a huge liability for his administration. Although Grant was reelected largely because of the nation's gratitude for his military successes and leadership that brought an end to the Civil War, his second term was marred by charges of corruption against many of his administration's highest-ranking officers, including his chief of staff, secretary of war, minister to Great Britain, and secretary of the navy.

Grant's approach to making important nominations stands in marked contrast to that of most other nineteenth-century presidents. Andrew Jackson, for instance, was the first chief executive to employ a so-called kitchen cabinet for advice on critical matters, including important appointments.[50] (It was not uncommon, however, for Jackson to ignore his advisers altogether and trust his own judgment and instincts.) A critical element of Jackson's success in reshaping and energizing the U.S. government was his choice of advisers who were experienced in government, had good political judgment, and were committed to Jackson and his political agenda.

The norm for subsequent nineteenth-century presidents was to heed the advice of party leaders, close personal acquaintances or advisers, or members of Congress in deciding how to exercise their nominating authority. Presidents had little staff in those years and thus had to rely a great deal on the opinions of the political sources most familiar to them. The end result was that oftentimes "[a]ppointment decisions vibrated to the rhythms of political exigency; administrative considerations rarely intervened."[51]

With the advent of Franklin Roosevelt, the dynamics shifted significantly. In large part to control the direction and energy of the national government, Roosevelt consolidated White House control over most of the influential appointments. Subsequent presidents have delegated to subordinates many of the important tasks of gathering, evaluating, and making recommendations—if not the actual selection—of important federal appointments. Modern presidents have coordinated the challenges of assembling and overseeing substantially larger administrations (larger than those needed or used by their nineteenth-century counterparts) with their personal obligations as chief executives to interact with many other political leaders and constituents and to manage their other administrative, policymaking, and public obligations.

The challenges confronted by modern presidents include ensuring that in exercising delegated responsibility to choose their subordinates cabinet secretaries and other high-ranking officials comply with presidential criteria for selection. The president's staff must determine whether it desires every political and judicial appointee to meet certain presidential criteria (particularly in terms of ideology) and, if so, how closely it should supervise cabinet secretaries and other high-ranking officials to ensure fidelity throughout an administration to the president's political and ideological agenda. In short, each administration has had to decide how much control the White House should exercise over nominations for positions throughout the federal government and how much the White House should defer to the judgments and needs of the cabinet heads.

There is little doubt that Presidents Nixon and Reagan exercised very tight control of the nomination process. In contrast, much of the disorder associated with President Carter's administration has been attributed to his insistence on giving his cabinet secretaries free rein in choosing their subordinates and managing their departments. Each cabinet department became the fiefdom of its secretary, and many of Carter's policy initiatives were frustrated because they did not enjoy sufficient support from the people in key positions in his administration. Despite his good intentions and best efforts, President Carter was never able to (re)gain tight control over federal appointments below the cabinet level.

The challenge to determine the proper allocation of authority within an administration for making determinations about the fitness of lower-level nominations extends to political and judicial nominations. Some presidents (e.g., Nixon and Reagan) placed the primary locus of decision-making authority for all significant appointments primarily in the White House; others (e.g., Gerald Ford, Carter, and Clinton) charged the Justice

The President

Department with some responsibility to identify and evaluate the credentials of possible judicial candidates while certain White House personnel retained the responsibility for assessing the political ramifications of every possible nomination. A president's choice of which of these systems to use for making a Supreme Court appointment largely has turned on the location of the advisers he knows best or whose judgment he trusts the most on this issue.

To be sure, all presidents have relied rather heavily on senatorial input for district court appointments (except for those in the District of Columbia). The first assertions of senatorial courtesy were made early in President Washington's term of office; the practice began to decline in importance during the latter quarter of the nineteenth century. In the twentieth century, it has by and large retained its influence over a president's choices of federal district judgeships and U.S. attorneys and marshals and, to a lesser extent, on circuit court nominations. This trend has paralleled the decline in the strict control exercised by political parties over appointments and the fact that as the country became larger, presidents have had as a practical matter to rely more on senators from their own party (or suitable substitutes in their absence) to name potential candidates for lower-court judgeships. Rather than increasing their staffs to deal with the increasing number of federal judgeships they must fill, more recent presidents have instead looked for assistance from senators and their staffs.

In several post–World War II administrations (including the presidencies of Eisenhower, Ford, and Carter), the Office of the Deputy Attorney General handled most of the work regarding lower-court nominations. Usually, the staff of the deputy's office obtains information on prospective candidates and makes lists of possible nominees in conjunction with or after negotiations with other powerful interests, including party officials, bar leaders, and especially senators from the state in which the vacancy exists. The cooperation or support of the appropriate senators is essential for most district court appointments, while the Justice Department has more leeway in processing positions on the federal courts of appeals and the District of Columbia courts. Concerning vacancies on the federal appellate courts, Sheldon Goldman has noted that "the first reality is that the president's [people] in the Justice Department, i.e., the Attorney General and the Deputy Attorney General and [the latter's] assistants, are primarily responsible for judicial selection. . . . These officials use their vast network of friends, acquaintances, and friends of friends as a source of possible appointees."[52] Judge Harold Tyler reports that when he served as deputy attorney general in the Ford administration, he (and his staff) handled roughly 95–97 percent of the work on judicial appointments, while by the mid-1990s there were "some sixty people in the White House and the Justice Department involved in this process."[53]

Even when the administration relies on Justice Department input to make judicial nominations, the process usually is not completed once the Justice Department has made its recommendations to the president. Instead, the recommendations are reviewed by White House officials who are responsible for assessing the political ramifications of suggested nominees and maintaining communication with the Justice Department to ensure that the president's criteria have been fulfilled. The White House staff's congressional liaison team sometimes verifies the Justice Department's understanding about senatorial preferences. In many cases, the liaison team has played a vital role in gaining and maintaining support for the administration's nominees in close confirmation votes.

President Carter tried to change the system for judicial selection dramatically. In moving away from the governing norms in this field, he encountered difficulties in his administration and particularly the Senate. President Carter and his attorney general, Griffin Bell, sought to ensure "merit selection" of federal judges by establishing nominating commissions for district courts and courts of appeals.[54] This plan quickly met opposition from James Eastland, then the powerful chair of the Senate Judiciary Committee, and others, and no legislation was ever passed requiring the commissions. Instead, Carter's executive order of February 1977 established nominating commissions only for the courts of appeals. However, Carter urged senators to set up nominating commissions for district court judge selection, and they were established in some thirty states. Some Democratic senators continued to resist the commissions, straining the president's relationship with many of them throughout his term in office. Although the establishment and use of commissions did not completely remove the nominating power for judgeships from senators, the commissions produced more diverse candidates who also received relatively high marks from the legal academy and the legal profession on their temperament, legal acumen, and general skills to serve as judges. For instance, 57 percent of President Carter's judicial appointees were rated either "exceptionally well qualified" or "well qualified" by the American Bar Association. The only president to have a higher percentage of his judicial nominees with higher ratings from the ABA is President Clinton; 59.5 percent of his judicial nominees as of the end of June 1999 had been rated "well qualified," and 39.9 percent "qualified." (During the Carter administration the ABA had "exceptionally well qualified" and "well qualified" as separate categories, but it combined them by the time President Clinton entered office.)[55]

President Reagan fashioned a system for making judicial nominations that fit both his desire to ensure the ideological orientation of his judicial nominees and conventional modes of judicial nominating.[56] While in previous administrations the deputy attorney general's office had been primarily responsible for judicial selection, Reagan shifted the selection focus in the Justice Department to the Office of Legal Policy and created the post of special counsel for judicial selection. (President Clinton also placed primary responsibility within the Justice Department for judicial selection in the same office, which is now known as the Office of Policy Development.) In addition, the Reagan administration ordered the dismantling of judicial nominating commissions (though some senators continued to use their assistance in suggesting three names for each district court vacancy within their respective states) and created the President's Committee on Federal Judicial Selection, a nine-member group that institutionalized and formalized an active White House role in judicial selection.[57] The committee's weekly meetings brought together some of the president's most trusted advisers—close adviser and later attorney general Edwin Meese, the White House chief of staff, political adviser Ed Rollins, and White House Counsel Fred Fielding, who served as chairman—as well as the president's assistants for personnel and legislative affairs, the head of the Justice Department's Office of Legal Policy, and three other top Justice officials. The committee recommended candidates (drawn in part from the recommendations of Republican senators) and discussed the department's recommendations. The White House further centralized the selection power by conducting investigations of potential nominees that were independent of the Justice Department investigation.

President Bush retained some but not all of the features of President Reagan's system for judicial selection. He downgraded the status (and thus the influence) of the Office of Legal Policy; it became the Office of Policy Development, and its head was no longer subject to Senate confirmation. Bush moved the principal responsibility for judicial nominations into the White House counsel's office. Under President Bush, the White House became primarily responsible for evaluating prospective judicial nominees' ideological credentials. This approach sometimes created friction with Justice Department personnel, whose background work and verification of nominees' qualifications were closely reviewed to the point of being almost completely redone—and sometimes undone—by White House officials. This duplication cost Bush precious time in processing potential judicial nominations.[58]

A contrast to Bush's inefficient system for judicial selection is the one adopted by President Ford when he needed to nominate someone to replace Justice Douglas on the Court.[59] Ford divided the responsibility for counseling him between his attorney general, Edward Levi, and his White House counsel, Phil Buchen; he charged Levi with assembling a list of potential candidates based largely on professional ability and a moderate judicial ideology, while he asked Buchen to assess the political ramifications of different potential nominees. Levi's and Buchen's offices interacted like clockwork, and once a nominee was chosen the Senate moved quickly to approve him unanimously.

President Clinton's system for judicial selection has consisted of at least three phases. Initially, he planned to vest primary authority for vetting judicial nominees in the Office of Policy Development, whose chief would regain the status held during the Reagan administration. The problem was, however, that President Clinton was not able to get an attorney general nominated and confirmed by the Senate until six months into his administration. Thereafter, several nominees to assistant attorney general positions had some trouble getting confirmed based, variously, on their failure to pay certain Social Security taxes on their domestic help, their academic writings, their personal activities, or some combination of these.

Consequently, the White House counsel's office, initially under the direction of Chief Counsel Bernard Nussbaum, occupied the vacuum left by the understaffed Justice Department and took control of judicial nominations. The counsel's office felt pressured to move quickly, but there was a limit to how fast it could proceed given its size, the quantity of work involved, and the administration's desire to avoid mistakes like those committed in the nominations process during the first year of Bill Clinton's presidency. Hence, by the time the Office of Policy Development was up and running (in the latter half of 1993), the Clinton administration was well behind schedule in filling judicial vacancies.

The second phase of President Clinton's system for judicial selection began once his administration was fully staffed to handle nominations. Not surprisingly, a turf war developed between the Justice Department (which had thought it would be primarily responsible for handling judicial nominations) and the White House counsel's office, which was reluctant to give up the authority it had gained over judicial nominations. Eventually, the administration settled on a trio of officials—the assistant attorney general in charge of the Office of Policy Development, the deputy White House counsel, and an associate White House counsel—who would have the primary responsibility for judicial nominations.

The third phase of President Clinton's approach to judicial selection took shape after the Republicans gained control of the Senate in the midterm elections of 1994 and held onto it through the presidential election of 1996 and the midterm elections of 1998. With a Republican majority in the Senate, the Clinton administration became more seriously committed to avoiding controversial judicial appointments and preserving precious political coinage for other important legislative initiatives.

The Clinton administration consulted widely on appointments with people outside the administration, including senators, representatives, state and party officials, and civil rights leaders and certain other interest group leaders. By frequently floating various names before the media or the Senate in the hope of determining which had the likeliest chance to win confirmation or make the largest number of people happy, the Clinton administration effectively transformed consultation into a preview of or substitute for the confirmation process. Used in this manner, consultation can lay the groundwork for a relatively smooth confirmation. The problem is that frequent or ongoing consultation can protract the nomination process, and precious time can be lost. Moreover, it can make a president look weak or indecisive or reinforce the public's image of him as one or the other. If accompanied by leaks, consultation can also hurt the reputations of and embarrass prospective nominees who are not in the position of being able to properly defend themselves given the circumstances and timing.

Timing

Presidents have learned that the timing of a nomination can make a big difference to its success. For example, lame duck presidents or presidents with dubious or unclear reelection prospects have faced the stiffest opposition to their nominations (particularly judicial ones) from their political foes in the Senate during presidential election years. Indeed, one study found that the confirmation rate for Supreme Court justices is 90 percent in the first three years of a president's term but drops to less than 67 percent in the fourth year.[60]

Generally, nineteenth-century presidents John Tyler, Millard Fillmore, Franklin Pierce, James Buchanan, Andrew Johnson, Rutherford B. Hayes, and Chester Arthur experienced delays in Senate confirmation of their nominations in their last two years in office. The first dramatic instance of this practice in the first quarter of the twentieth century occurred in the closing days of the Taft administration when progressive Republicans joined with the Democrats to prevent the Senate from going into executive session to confirm thirteen hundred nominations that Taft had submitted for its consideration.[61] In subsequent administrations, the opposition party has generally slowed down or stalled a president's nominations, particularly his judicial nominations, as the date of a presidential election has drawn nearer.[62]

For example, the Democratic majority in the Senate effectively stopped holding confirmation hearings for President Bush's judicial nominees in the summer preceding the 1992 presidential election.[63] Consequently, President Clinton inherited more than two dozen unfilled judicial vacancies.[64] In 1994, just before the Republicans took control of both houses of Congress in January 1995 as a result of the midterm elections of 1994, the Senate confirmed 101 judicial nominations. No sooner did the Republicans retake control of the Senate in 1994 than Republican leaders began to slow down the processing of President Clinton's judicial appointments, precipitating one of the longest periods of paralysis of judicial appointments in American history.[65]

In 1997 (a year in which scandals within the White House began increasingly to dominate both the news and Congress's attention), the Republican-controlled Senate confirmed thirty-six of President Clinton's judicial nominees but had not taken action on forty-two others (including thirteen to the federal courts of appeal).[66] By the end of 1997, the average number of days from nomination to confirmation or final vote in the Senate was 212, the longest such average for any administration in American history.[67] This figure contrasts with the average delay in 1996 of 183 days and even more dramatically with the average delays of 86 and 87 days in 1994 and 1995, respectively. From 1993 to 1998 the average number of days between nomination and final action for all judicial nominations was 144. In contrast, the corresponding figures for Reagan and Bush were 65 and 120, respectively. In Goldman's opinion, the Senate's delays in considering President Clinton's judicial nominations in 1996 and 1997 were "unprecedented. . . . [Such delays constituted] a congressional analogue of President Franklin Roosevelt's court-packing plan of 1937. Both Roosevelt's court-packing and the Republicans' court-blocking plans had their genesis in displeasure with court opinions."[68]

By mid-July 2000, the Senate had confirmed a total of thirty judicial nominations for the year. By this same date, there were seventy-five vacancies in the federal judiciary, for only thirty-seven of which President Clinton had made nominations. The prospects for any of the pending nominations, much less for any made later in the year, looked dismal, because Republicans in the Senate were already preparing to bring the judicial confirmation process to a halt, pending the outcome of the 2000 presidential election.

No doubt President Clinton's failure to make nominations relatively quickly was a contributing factor to the unusually high number of judicial vacancies. Indeed, the average number of days from the occurrence of a judicial vacancy to President Clinton's formal nomination to fill it was 536 days in 1998–99, 690 in 1994, and 753 in 1993, the latter two constituting the longest such delays for any president in the twentieth century.

The only other president with similar delays was President Bush in his first year of office, during which the average number of days from vacancy to nomination was 682. (Also, the average number of days between nomination opportunity and nomination by the president was 315 and 296 for Clinton and Bush, respectively.)

The Republicans' strategy of slowing down the confirmation of President Clinton's judicial nominations succeeded in part because they took advantage of the president's preference to maintain the public spotlight on the other legislative priorities on which his administration intended to expend its capital. In October 1997 the president changed his tactics; he began to use the presidency as a bully pulpit to denounce publicly the Republican efforts, which, he claimed, were driven solely by partisan political considerations and were hurting the administration of justice. Attorney General Janet Reno also heightened her own public denunciations of the Republicans' strategy regarding the Clinton judicial appointments. These public outcries, followed by several prominent newspapers' editorials decrying the Republicans' pettiness in blocking or stalling perfectly sound judicial nominations, had an effect (perhaps confirming the value of public shaming as a check on senators' abuse of power). The Republican leadership in the Senate announced that it would begin to break the logjam and promised to bring many, if not most, pending judicial nominations to final resolution.[69] But shortly after this promise was made, the sex scandal that led to the president's impeachment broke. The scandal clearly drew the president's and senators' attentions away from judicial selection and thus helped the Republican leadership to bring the judicial confirmation process to a virtual standstill. No sooner did the scandal die down than many Republican senators intensified their efforts to stall judicial confirmations, pending the results of the next presidential election.

Timing can be a problem for presidential nominees in another way as well. Sometimes presidents have moved too slowly (waiting until too late in the term, as was the problem with more than a dozen of President Bush's judicial nominees) in coming to the defense of an embattled nominee or in organizing support for a nominee. For instance, President Reagan nominated Robert Bork to the Supreme Court on July 1, 1987, but allowed the Democrats in control of the Senate to postpone Bork's confirmation hearings until after Labor Day.[70] Bork's opposition used the summer to organize and to attack the nomination publicly. By the time President Reagan rallied to Bork's defense, the hearings had begun and the nominee was already seriously wounded. A similar problem arose with President Clinton's nomination of Lani Guinier to head the Civil Rights Division of the Justice Department. The nomination quickly drew fire from conservatives in Congress and the media, but neither President Clinton nor any of his top political appointees came to Guinier's defense. She was forced to withdraw her nomination before she had had a hearing and without ever receiving the president's public support.

There are, of course, other ways that timing can affect the appointments process. As the examples from the first few months of President Clinton's first term demonstrate, a president might be mistaken in thinking that he will enjoy a honeymoon period in the appointments process. Just the opposite. His inexperience — or the inexperience of his advisers — might be a liability. At the very least, the time a president consumes learning the ropes might be turned against him. He might find, as President Clinton did, that his political opponents or the interest groups unsure about him (or steadfastly against him) will use his inexperience against him by resisting or delaying his nominations. Moreover, the appointments process can come grinding to a halt (as I have indicated) when the president becomes embroiled in a pitched battle with Congress, such as the four months in which Andrew Johnson and the six months in which Bill Clinton faced possible forced removal in 1868 and 1998–99, respectively.

Strategy

A badly conceived defensive strategy can hurt a nomination just as much as a belated or nonexistent defense. Such was the case with President Jackson's nominations of his political ally Roger Taney to become secretary of the treasury and associate justice, for Jackson had no response to the predictable resistance to Taney's nominations based on his records as attorney general and acting secretary of the treasury.

Consider further the example of President Lyndon Johnson's nomination of his old friend Justice Abe Fortas to succeed Earl Warren as Chief Justice. No doubt a major reason for the ultimate failure and forced withdrawal of the nomination was President Johnson's failure to develop a strategy to offset the awkwardness of the timing (it occurred after he had indicated that he would not run for reelection) and the perception that it was part of a sordid deal both to reward a political crony (for Fortas had long been a close adviser to the president, even after his appointment to the Court) and to appease Chief Justice Earl Warren (who, it became publicly known, had agreed to step down before the 1968 presidential election to allow President Johnson to name a replacement acceptable to both the president and Warren). The perception of Fortas's nomination as an act of cronyism was reinforced by President Johnson's nomination of another old friend, Fifth Circuit Judge Homer Thornberry, to the Supreme Court vacancy that would have arisen had Fortas been confirmed as Chief Justice. The double nomination of Fortas and Thornberry probably constituted yet another impetus for Fortas's withdrawal of his nomination as Chief Justice because the two nominations could have been perceived as a reflection of President Johnson's overconfidence, which surely would have attracted the attention and ire of his political foes in the Senate.

Richard Nixon's first two attempts to fill Abe Fortas's seat on the Supreme Court provide further examples of poorly conceived confirmation strategy. In both cases Nixon failed to devise and employ effective operations within his administration for evaluating nominees' backgrounds, to develop intelligent strategies for securing confirmation, and to provide the means for overseeing and maintaining a good working relationship with the Senate.[71]

An effective strategy also includes characterizing nominees in terms or ways that at the very least do not raise unreasonably high expectations regarding their qualifications, background, or integrity. For example, President Bush's announcement of Clarence Thomas as the "best qualified" person in the country to replace Justice Thurgood Marshall raised public expectations for the nominee, who, as Stephen Carter suggests, "might, in time, have acquired [the] experience needed for service on the high court, [but] did not have it at the time of his nomination."[72] Similarly, one factor that hurt Zoë Baird's chances as President Clinton's initial nominee for attorney general was Clinton's prior public promise that he would hold his cabinet nominees to the highest ethical standards and that the appointments process would proceed without "politics as usual."[73]

Baird's (and her husband's) lapse of judgment in failing to pay certain Social Security taxes for domestic help in spite of her awareness of the legal obligation to do so was made to seem all the more egregious because the public had heightened expectations regarding the ethics of President Clinton's cabinet appointments.

The previous sections in this chapter have drawn some parallels and mentioned some differences in presidents' (and senators') approaches to the selection of judges, executive personnel, and agency officials. This section initially considers the criteria presidents have used in choosing nominees for these positions and then examines how the differences between them are a function of the different degrees to which presidents can control these different officials after their confirmation.

Selection Criteria

The criteria adopted by different presidents have reflected essential aspects of their agendas, including but not limited to influencing or energizing the implementation of national policy, rewarding political allies, and influencing the direction of the federal judiciary. Although presidents (and their administrations) have varied in their selection criteria for confirmable positions, the single most commonly used criterion for federal appointments is demonstrated personal commitment to a president's agenda. Virtually all presidents have placed close personal allies or people with whom they have worked closely for substantial periods in key administrative positions, including judgeships. (Of course, while Dwight D. Eisenhower initially brought almost none of his close personal friends or political allies into his administration, he turned increasingly for counsel throughout his presidency to people with whom he had worked closely.)

A related concern among presidents has been the extent to which prospective nominees' party activities are an appropriate proxy for or measure of their political beliefs. In practice, past political appointees have largely been people with whom the president has worked closely prior to coming into office, people who have helped the president in some significant way to win or remain in office, party leaders, and others who have had close ties to one or more of these groups.

For Supreme Court nominations, presidents have varied in their use of one or more of the following criteria: (1) objective merit, (2) personal friendship with or proven loyalty or long-standing service to the president or his party, (3) diversity (usually encompassing geographic, racial, gender, or political), and (4) agreement with the president's basic political and constitutional philosophy.[74] Presidents have differed in their respective priorities in ordering these criteria. For example, James K. Polk, Theodore Roosevelt, Franklin Roosevelt, and Ronald Reagan placed a premium on the fourth factor (though Polk and the two Roosevelts paid serious attention to the second factor as well). Gerald Ford and Bill Clinton, on the other hand, picked justices with relatively quick confirmation and consensus in mind (with President Ford focusing on the first and fourth factors to do so and President Clinton in making his two choices focusing on the first, third, and fourth factors).

The selection criteria for lower-court judges have often included one or more of the same four standards. For instance, William Howard Taft, Warren Harding, Calvin Coolidge, Franklin Roosevelt, Ronald Reagan, and George Bush stressed a dominant criterion (usually ideology) in guiding their choices of federal district and especially circuit court nominees. Moreover, modern presidents have stressed the relevance of prior judicial experience in choosing circuit court nominees. Indeed, at least 53 percent of the circuit nominations made by every president since Herbert Hoover have been of people with prior judicial experience.[75] Modern presidents' district court nominations have also tended to include people with prior judicial or prosecutorial experience, or both.

Moreover, the importance of party affiliation (as a proxy for or demonstration of fundamental agreement with a president's objectives) is reflected in the fact that the percentage of federal district and circuit court appointees from the same party as the appointing president has been above 80 percent for president from Grover Cleveland through the present. From the latter quarter of the nineteenth century through the present, the lowest percentages of federal district court appointments

The President

to come from a president's political party were made by Presidents Taft (81.2 percent) and Bush (88.5 percent), while the highest percentages were made by Presidents Cleveland (100 percent), McKinley (100 percent), Teddy Roosevelt (100 percent), Wilson (98.2 percent), and Franklin Roosevelt (98.5 percent). The lowest percentages of federal circuit court of appeals appointments to come from a president's party during the same period were made by Presidents Cleveland (50 percent), McKinley (60 percent), Harrison (66.7 percent), and Teddy Roosevelt (70 percent), while the highest percentages were made by Presidents Harding (100 percent), Franklin Roosevelt (96.0 percent), and Reagan (96.2 percent).[76]

To be sure, all presidents have expected their judicial nominees to share many of their political and policy views, and all presidents have claimed a desire to appoint "outstanding," "well qualified," or the "best" individuals. (Consequently, for some people these terms have become relatively meaningless, while to those in the know they might be viewed as signaling compliance with a president's objectives or selection criteria.) It is not surprising to find that presidents have differed in their assessments of the appropriate qualifications. For instance, President Eisenhower wanted experienced judges and gave great weight (following Truman's example) to the ratings of the American Bar Association. President Kennedy wanted nominees of "incorruptible character" who would be able to "temper justice with mercy" and had "respected professional skill," "unquestioned ability," "firm judicial temperament," and the "intellectual capacity to protect and illuminate the Constitution and our historic values."[77] President Nixon candidly acknowledged that he wanted "men who shared my legal philosophy."[78] Nixon was determined to appoint "competent, experienced men . . . sensitive to the [proper] role of the judiciary."[79] In his campaign speeches Nixon promised to appoint federal judges who would favor "strict construction" of the Constitution and the "police forces" against the "criminal forces."[80]

President Carter tried to create an "independent" federal judiciary by advocating "merit selection" and affirmative action in the selection of federal judges.[81] In a single term, he appointed more minorities and women to federal judgeships than any previous president; 35 percent of his judicial appointments included women and minorities.[82] (Indeed, the Carter administration succeeded in placing twenty-eight African Americans on the federal district courts in nineteen states and the District of Columbia. In fourteen states, President Carter named the first African American ever to serve; and three of the nine appellate circuits to which he appointed African Americans were racially integrated for the first time.)[83] In contrast to President Carter, Presidents Reagan and Bush emphasized ideology—particularly a strong fidelity to the original understanding of the Constitution and to widespread deference to democratic decision making—almost to the exclusion of any other criterion in picking judicial nominees. Whereas 27 percent of President Bush's judicial nominees were women and minorities and 14 percent of President Reagan's were women and minorities, their nominees generally shared a conservative judicial ideology (including greater judicial deference to the elected branches and narrow readings of the individual liberties guarantees of the Constitution).[84]

For his part, President Clinton vowed even before he took office that he would appoint judges (and other officials) who "looked like America." Consequently, his administration gave serious consideration to ethnicity and gender in making judicial nominations. Of 373 judicial appointments made by mid-July 2000, 112 were women, 6 were Asian Americans, 25 were Hispanics, and 62 were African Americans. These appointments undoubtedly reflect the fault lines of contemporary America. Whereas geography was a key issue in the appointment of judges, particularly justices, in the nineteenth century, the balance today is driven much more by ethnicity and gender. (Interestingly, throughout the Clinton administration, some senators and interest groups viewed ethnicity and gender to some extent as rough proxies of nominees' ideology under the theory that minorities and women who are Democrats are likelier to be politically liberal and oriented to support judicial activism on behalf of minority or women's rights and interests. Whether because of concerns about their ideology or for some other reason, women or minorities nominated for judgeships by President Clinton experienced longer delays and a higher percentage of successful opposition than the white males he nominated faced.) Nevertheless, the one constant in Clinton's appointments (including to federal judgeships) was relatively strong confidence in the nominee's fidelity to the president's agenda. Hence, almost all of President Clinton's judicial nominees were Democrats.

The President

The Possible Relationship between a
President's Nominating and Removal Powers

It is clear that presidents use different criteria selecting different kinds of officials. One obvious reason is that presidents view the responsibilities or duties of different offices (and perhaps respectively their symbolic significance to society) differently. The conventional wisdom posits further that presidents employ different selection criteria for different offices because of the different degrees to which officials are subject to presidential control after confirmation. Thus, given the differences between a president's postconfirmation relationship with his executive branch agents and federal judges—and the long-term effects that judges can have on the political or social order—the considerations of presidents and senators have differed in the two contexts. For example, the prospect that once confirmed a federal judge is virtually immune to a president's entreaties, pressure, or revenge (except for the ambitious judges who harbor hopes of elevation) puts enormous pressure on the president to pick the right people as judges, people he is confident will perform as he would like in the absence of monitoring or threats. Thus, it is not surprising to find that over the past few decades, as federal judges (particularly justices) have become widely viewed as an important part of a president's legacy (for they will serve long after he has left office, during which time they will continue to reflect his constitutional vision and values), each president has looked for the people likeliest to ensure the achievement or preservation of his desired legacy. Precisely because of the prospects that a president's judicial nominations are likely to be inclined to embody or implement his legacy and because of their immunity to the usual means of political retaliation, senators from an opposing party (and thus as signaled by such membership likely to have opposing views) are unlikely to approve of the legacy and thus will not be disposed to give the president a blank check in this realm. In fact, they are likely, as chapter 5 indicates, to do whatever they can to impede the president's legacy.

Executive officials, on the other hand, largely serve at the president's discretion. He has the authority to remove them at will, and thus throughout their service they remain amenable to the president's influence and direction. Moreover, the recognition that a president is effectively disabled from doing his job if he does not have people whom he trusts serving as his agents leads many senators to defer to a president's choice of executive personnel. Members of Congress understand as well that they can pressure the president to discipline these people and, if he fails to do so, subject them to congressional oversight. The presumption that a president has the right to select his own employees effectively means in a confirmation hearing that the burden of persuasion lies with the senators challenging the nominee's fitness.

There is also an important distinction between appointments to independent agencies and appointments to other executive branch departments and entities. The important difference here lies yet again in the president's ability to remove the official, which is limited with respect to independent agency heads. Given this legal limitation in his ability to control such appointees, it follows that a president would probably want to exercise more control over their appointment—to be even more sure that each official shares his views on policy.[85] Indeed, because many independent agency officials serve terms of office that do not coincide with the presidential election cycle, the president can influence policy past his term through his appointments to such agencies. Thus, one would expect the president to show a greater concern with the ideology of his appointments in this realm and to be more willing to take on Congress to put trusted agents in these offices. A countervailing consideration is that Congress thinks of the independent agencies as more closely associated with the legislative branch. Thus, some senators might claim a more active role for themselves here than with executive branch officials who are more firmly under the legal control of the president.

Finally, the respective roles of the president and the Senate may differ in the appointments process for different kinds of executive branch officers not serving in independent agencies. For example, since the early 1970s, the Senate has played a role in the appointment of the director of the Office of Management and Budget. Before that, the head of the Bureau of Budget was an official closely aligned with the president and the White House. Congress required confirmation as part of the 1974 Budget Act to support a general effort to reassert its control over the budget process.[86]

Congress's efforts to require confirmation for certain offices, in addition to its funding and oversight responsibilities, are just some of the ways in which it attempts to constrain a president's exercise of his appointment powers. The next chapter explores in greater depth how the Senate addresses and tries to influence a president's appointment and related powers.

Chapter Five

THE ADVICE AND

CONSENT OF THE SENATE

NO OTHER ACTOR routinely involved in the federal appointments process receives more attention or criticism than the Senate. The reasons for
this attention are multifold. First, the Senate's formal authority in the
appointments process has never been as clear as that of the president.
While the Appointments Clause clearly vests in the president the power
to identify the individuals he wishes to place in confirmable offices, the
Senate's official functions or duties in the appointments process are not
so clear. Commentators have long disagreed about the Senate's role in the
process. They disagree, for instance, about whether the Senate is more
sensitive to the national mood than the president (and therefore more entitled to make pronouncements in the name of the public) because of its
diversity (in terms of party, age, viewpoints, geography, and life experience) and because one-third of its membership stands for reelection every
two years. Commentators disagree about whether senators have the expertise or competence to measure the requisite qualifications for certain
confirmable offices and about the extent to which senators are able generally to make sound judgments in the confirmation process. They also
disagree about whether it is a good thing for small states to be represented
equally with larger states in the Senate, so that representatives from the
former have the means to exert tremendous (and disproportionate, given
the percentage of the population they represent) influence over Senate
votes.[1] Moreover, given (as public choice theory suggests) that the Senate
is institutionally incapable of engaging in coherent collective action, it is
unclear, even apart from questions about senators' competence to partici-

pate in the appointments process, by what measure the Senate's actions should be evaluated.

In an attempt to clarify and analyze the Senate's performance in the federal appointments process, this chapter first considers the means for evaluating such performance and then examines how senators have tried to expand their authority in and to check presidential efforts to direct the federal appointments process. Each of these efforts may be assessed in terms of its legitimacy, utility, fairness or equity, and outcome.

EVALUATING SENATE PERFORMANCE GENERALLY

The Senate needs to be assessed in different institutional terms than those used to evaluate the presidency. Unlike the presidency, the Senate's powers are not unified in a single person; the Senate operates primarily but not exclusively through a combination of individual, small group, and other collective action. With the decline of political parties as an organizing construct for Senate action, it has become increasingly misleading to conceive of the Senate as having an agenda separate from the individual or aggregate interests of its members.

Public choice theory is useful for clarifying the Senate's operations, for it helps to explain the apparent ad hoc nature of Senate decision making.[2] Public choice theory suggests that when institutions make decisions by a majority vote, the majority will generate logically inconsistent results unless the voters have very similar preferences. In fact, Senate confirmation deliberations and sometimes even presidential nominations are group decision-making efforts, and the individual participants in these decisions bring different values and preferences to the task that need to be identified in order to understand fully how the process has worked in any given case. Senators, for example, each have their own orderings of preference with respect to the long- and short-term political objectives at stake in a particular confirmation proceeding.[3] Given that the Senate's final action on a nomination is an aggregate of many different (in all likelihood as many as one hundred distinct) orderings of preference, the outcome is not likely to provide much insight into the dynamics giving rise to it.

Moreover, public choice theory suggests that the most effective means by which to change the order of preferences of the individuals participating in a group decision-making process is through structural alterations to the system. For instance, the Senate has attempted to check the growth of presidential appointment authority through exercising senatorial courtesy and by delegating decisive authority (such as agenda setting) to committees, subcommittees, or their chairs, which are potentially subject to domination by a single person or faction.

In order to assess the limits of applying public choice theory to the federal appointments process, it might be useful to consider the ways in which the Senate's decision making on legislation is similar to or different from its decision making on federal appointments. In legislation, logrolling—that is, the building of support for a bill (or parts of a bill) by agreeing to support other legislation (or pieces of other legislation)—is popular. Such trading is certainly possible in the federal appointments process (though it is likely to be difficult to document because senators are unlikely to advertise the practice in an age when they are popularly elected and concerned that some voters might be turned off by it). As long as a position is not unique or a president is trying to fill several fungible positions (such as federal district judgeships), a senator can probably build support for a nominee he wants by agreeing to support a nominee sponsored by some other senator for a similar position or perhaps related legislation sponsored by another senator or the president. Moreover, senators can and do exchange support or opposition for certain nominees for other legislative favors. Similarly, the president might be able to get support for one nominee about whom he feels strongly in exchange for abandoning another about whom he is lukewarm or honoring a senator's objections to or preferences for a particular nominee or legislation on a related subject. Such trading is more difficult with respect to a unique position such as a cabinet secretary or Supreme Court justice. In such cases, presidents (or, for that matter, senators) have fewer, if any, similar positions they can trade for support. Consequently, a trade is likely to depend on the president finding (or a senator's making known) the project(s) near and dear to the senator's heart that will serve as the functional equivalent of a unique appointment for purposes of effecting a trade.

The full extent to which logrolling involving appointments has occurred is difficult to confirm because a good deal of the interactions among senators and between presidents and senators occur behind closed doors.

The Senate

Nevertheless, the interaction sometimes becomes so intense that it spills over into public disputes. Such was the case when Senator David B. Hill of New York rallied a majority of his colleagues to oppose two of President Cleveland's nominations to the Supreme Court because Cleveland failed to consult with Hill prior to making them.[4] (The fact that Hill had also been an in-state rival with Cleveland for control of New York Democratic politics as well as an unsuccessful rival for the Democratic party's presidential nomination in 1892 undoubtedly added to the enmity between the two.)

The Senate's rejection of President Eisenhower's nomination of Lewis Strauss as secretary of commerce—at the time it occurred (1959) only the second instance in the century a nominee to a cabinet position had been rejected by the Senate—also turned to some extent on logrolling. As President Eisenhower's biographer Stephen E. Ambrose explains, President Eisenhower put a lot of the blame for the rejection on then-Senate majority leader Lyndon Johnson, who had "instructed the Democrats [in the Senate] to vote against confirmation. Johnson . . . had nothing against Strauss personally, but he owed [a favor to Senator Clinton] Anderson [of New Mexico, a member of the congressional watchdog committee for the Atomic Energy Commission, and an ardent critic of Strauss's performance as commissioner on it] and Anderson had asked to have it paid off by opposing Strauss."[5] In 1969, Democratic Senator Richard Russell of Georgia, in retaliation against President Johnson's indecision and delay over nominating Russell's preferred candidate to a federal district judgeship in southern Georgia, refused to support—and even helped to organize opposition to—Johnson's nomination of Abe Fortas as Chief Justice.[6]

More recently, in response to the resistance of Senator Jesse Helms, chair of the Foreign Relations Committee, to schedule hearings to consider President Clinton's nomination of Governor William Weld as ambassador to Mexico, Senator Richard Lugar publicly declared that if Helms did not change his mind about scheduling Weld's hearings, Lugar would try to delay or otherwise hinder Senate action regarding agricultural and other interests of concern to Helms.[7] In spite of Lugar's status as the next most senior Republican member of the Senate Foreign Relations Committee after Helms, the committee's other Republican senators did not support Lugar's gambit. Instead, they supported Helms's refusal to schedule hearings in part to demonstrate their support for Helms's authority as chair to make such decisions unilaterally. Moreover, they feared possible retaliation from Helms on appointments and other matters of concern to them. Weld asked President Clinton to withdraw his nomination after it became clear that the public was not going to rally to his side. Nor did the president want to alienate Helms unduly because Clinton needed Helms's support on other foreign relations matters.

President Clinton's struggle to appoint William Fletcher, a professor of law at the University of California at Berkeley, to the federal court of appeals provides an even more intricate example of logrolling. In 1995, President Clinton nominated Fletcher to the Ninth Circuit. There was little or no doubt about Fletcher's qualifications: he was widely regarded as one of the nation's leading scholars in the field of federal jurisdiction; he had graduated at the top of his law school class at Yale; he had been a Rhodes Scholar (at the same time Bill Clinton was); and he had served as law clerk to Justice William Brennan. The opposition to Fletcher was not based on his writings, speeches, or even his clerkship with Justice Brennan, the embodiment of the kind of liberal judicial activist most disliked by conservative Republicans in the Senate. Instead, the opposition against Fletcher's nomination was based on some Republican senators' construction of a virtually abandoned antinepotism statute passed by Congress in 1877, which they construed as barring the appointment of a person to a federal court on which a relative already sits.[8] Under this construction, President Clinton was prohibited from appointing Fletcher because he is the son of Betty Fletcher, a Ninth Circuit judge appointed by President Carter. President Clinton's legal counsel responded that if this construction of the statute were accurate, then it should also have barred—though in fact it did not preclude—several other notable judicial appointments, including those of Augustus Hand to the Second Circuit to which his cousin, Learned, had previously been appointed; and President Bush's nomination of federal district judge Morris Arnold to the Eighth Circuit, to which his brother Richard had previously been appointed by President Carter. President Clinton's lawyers suggested that a more reasonable reading of the 1877 statute is that it bars only a judge's relatives from being hired as employees of the courts on which the judge sits. Just before the 1996 presidential election, Senator Orrin Hatch suggested that the Fletcher nomination might move forward if Fletcher's mother took senior status. Fletcher, however, refused to allow his nomination to be made at his mother's expense.

Fletcher's nomination languished until May 1998,[9] when the president reached a deal with Republican senator Slade Gorton, from Washington, that included his nominating a prominent conservative candidate selected by Gorton (Chief Justice Barbara Durham of the Washington State Supreme Court) and Judge Betty Fletcher's agreement to take senior status once her son was confirmed by the Senate.[10] The exchange arranged between President Clinton and Senator Gorton was highly unusual for three reasons. First, the apparent coercion of a sitting judge to take senior status in exchange for the appointment of a family member (or anyone else, for that matter) was completely unprecedented. Second, the president never would have nominated Senator Gorton's choice for another vacancy on the Ninth Circuit but for his eagerness to get the younger Fletcher confirmed. Third, for two decades Democratic and Republican presidents alike had maintained that they would not share their authority to nominate federal appellate judges with senators.

As it happened, the deal was never fully consummated. William Fletcher was finally confirmed on October 8, 1998, but Chief Justice Durham withdrew her nomination for personal reasons just before his confirmation.[11] On November 4, 1998, Judge Fletcher's mother, Betty, took senior status.

The prerogative of senators to put any nomination on indefinite hold has also given them leverage to negotiate for such trades or to retaliate against the president or other senators for any reason. Examples of senators' aggressive exercise of their prerogative abound. For instance, in 1997, then-Senator Carol Moseley-Braun, a Democrat, put a hold on President Clinton's nomination of Joe Dial for another term on the Commodity Futures Trading Commission (CFTC), precluding the nomination from being voted on before the end of the congressional session and thereby killing the nomination for good. In retaliation, Republican senator Phil Gramm, a friend of Dial's, maintained as of the spring of 1998 a hold on two judicial nominees for the state of Illinois.[12] In retaliation against Gramm's hold, Illinois's other Democratic senator, Richard Durbin, blocked the Senate's consideration of a Republican education bill pending final Senate action on the two judicial nominees from Illinois.[13] The logjam ended, however, at the end of March 1998, when President Clinton agreed to nominate a Republican to the CFTC seat to which Dial had not been appointed. Almost immediately thereafter, Senator Gramm released his hold on the two Illinois judicial nominees, who were easily confirmed in early April 1998.

A more monumental logjam arose in 1999. Senate Judiciary Committee chair Orrin Hatch had put a hold on all of President Clinton's pending judicial nominations throughout the first half of 1999 to pressure President Clinton to nominate Hatch's preferred candidate, Ted Stewart (then-chief of staff to the governor of Utah), for a federal district judgeship in Utah. Hatch's hold marked the first time that a senator had halted all pending nominations in exchange for a single candidate since 1959, when Senate majority leader Lyndon Johnson stalled all of President Eisenhower's pending nominations in exchange for the nomination of Johnson's friend Joe Fisher a federal district judge. Johnson's ploy succeeded; the Senate confirmed Fisher three days after he was nominated, and the deadlock was broken.[14] Eventually, Senator Hatch and President Clinton also choreographed an exchange. On June 16, Senator Hatch agreed to hold confirmation hearings on eight of the president's judicial nominees — the first hearings, in fact, to have been held by the 106th Congress.[15] In exchange, President Clinton submitted Stewart's name to the ABA for rating and to the FBI for a background check. Senator Hatch indicated that he would keep other pending judicial nominations moving through the remaining stages of the confirmation process as long as the president kept Stewart's name moving through the nomination process. Although the Senate confirmed Stewart on October 5, 1999, other pending judicial nominations stalled. Most dramatically, the Senate rejected (on a strictly party-line vote) Missouri Supreme Court Justice Ronnie White for a federal district judgeship—the first district court nominee to be rejected by the Senate in twelve years. Ostensibly, White was rejected because he was against the death penalty and not tough enough on criminals, although his voting in criminal appeals was virtually identical to Republican justices on the Missouri Supreme Court.[16]

Senatorial exercise of the prerogative to put nominations on hold generated considerable controversy again in the aftermath of President Clinton's recess appointment of James Hormel as ambassador to Luxemborg on June 4, 1999. The president had initially nominated Hormel for the position in October 1997, but several influential Republicans (including Senator Hatch) blocked a final vote on the nomination (approved by the Senate Foreign Relations Committee sixteen to two) because Hormel was openly homosexual and had provided financial support for several gay-rights activist groups. On June 8, Senator James Inhofe (R.-Oklahoma) asserted his privilege to put all of President Clinton's then-pending nominations on hold in retaliation against President Clinton's breach of the custom of notifying the Senate of his intended recess appointments. Senate majority leader Trent Lott recognized Senator Inhofe's right to block all nominations, but only temporarily. Senator Inhofe demanded that President Clinton pledge to the Senate that any future recess appointments made by him would be in compliance with the customary practice, which, he claimed, originated in an agreement between Democratic senator Robert Byrd and President Reagan (reached after Byrd had put a hold on more than a thousand of Reagan's nominees in 1985 to retaliate against Reagan making some recess appointments without having announced them prior to the recess). In a letter to Senator Lott dated June 15, President Clinton promised not to make any more recess appointments in violation of Senate customs. Shortly thereafter, Senator Inhofe withdrew his holds.

The controversy, however, did not end there. In November 1999, President Clinton notified the Senate of thirteen people whom he intended to grant recess appointments. Senator Inhofe objected to five names on the list and threatened again to block all of the president's judicial nominees for the remainder of his term. In December, President Clinton made nine recess appointments. Senator Inhofe responded by claiming that there were two recess appointees (Sara Fox to the NLRB and Stuart Weisberg to the Occupational Safety and Health Review Commission) about which the Senate had not been previously informed. Again Senator Inhofe vowed to block all of the president's judicial nominations for the remainder of his term. The block held until early February 2000, when Senator Lott allowed the Senate to confirm two judicial nominees. Lott also adhered to a deal reached earlier with the White House to allow a final Senate vote on the two judicial nominations pending for the longest time — Richard Paez (for over four years) and Marsha Berzon (for two years) to the U.S. Court of Appeals for the Ninth Circuit. Both were eventually confirmed.

Beyond senators' prerogative to put nominations on hold, there is, as Senator Dennis DeConcini of Arizona has noted, a "long-existing tradition that permits any [Judiciary] Committee member, for any reason, to request that a vote on a [judicial] nominee be delayed for one week from its scheduled date."[17] The filibuster is another time-honored practice that allows any senator who opposes legislation or a nomination to delay or prevent a vote by extending debate on the matter through lengthy speeches. Filibusters end only by the invocation of cloture, a special procedure in which sixteen senators sign a motion to end the debate and three-fifths of the Senate vote in favor of the motion. After that, any further debate is limited to thirty hours.[18] The combination of the means available to individual senators to delay nominations, including but not limited to indefinite holds, filibusters, and special procedures described below, provides individual senators with substantial means to impede a president's nominating authority.

ANALYZING SENATORIAL POWERS
TO INFLUENCE FEDERAL APPOINTMENTS

Senators have developed numerous procedures that allow them to influence the outcome of confirmation proceedings. This part examines each of these ways as well as some lessons that senators have learned about their individual and collective power in the federal appointments process.

Senatorial Courtesy

Traditionally, the term *senatorial courtesy* has referred to the deference the president owes to the recommendations of senators from his own political party on the particular people whom he should nominate to federal offices in the senators' respective states. A second form of senatorial courtesy is the deference a member of Congress, particularly a senator, expects to get from his or her Senate colleagues (or, in the case of a representative, from his Senate counterparts) with respect to his or her own nomination to a confirmable post. Yet another form of senatorial courtesy is the expectation that senators (usually from the president's political party) will confer or consult with the president prior to his nominating people to fill confirmable posts in their fields of expertise (such as foreign affairs) or people from their respective states to fill national offices.

Each of these three forms of senatorial courtesy has been in effect to varying degrees throughout U.S. history. The reasons for the durability of these practices are easy to understand. First, it is plainly in the interest of each senator to protect a colleague's request for senatorial courtesy as a means of ensuring his or her own chance to take advantage of it. Second, senators use their influence over certain appointments to reward party loyalists (and thereby ensure continued support for themselves from the party).

It is difficult but not impossible to document the full range of instances in which senators have demanded that the president defer to their recommendations for certain federal offices in their respective states. These demands are rarely made publicly, but no one doubts that they are routinely made. Indeed, as I have already suggested, the first instances occurred in the early days of the Washington administration. In 1789, Washington responded to the first demands of courtesy by suggesting to the Senate in writing that prior to voting down a presidential nominee it should initially determine the nominee's qualifications and the president's reasons for nominating him.[19] Nevertheless, senators persisted in trying to advise Washington and other early presidents about whom to nominate to federal offices in their respective states.

One dramatic instance in which senators took an unusually aggressive role in asserting their authority to control presidential nominations occurred in the aftermath of a struggle for control between President Madison and various senators over certain diplomatic appointments. In an effort to bring the conflict to an end, the Senate in 1813 adopted a resolution designating a special committee to confer with the president on the nomination of the minister to Sweden.[20] President Madison declined to meet with the committee on the ground that the Constitution permitted the Senate only limited options in attempting to advise the president on matters entrusted to both the president's and the Senate's discretion (such as treaties and appointments)—such as requesting information from the president or designating a committee to communicate with the department head. According to Madison, the appointment of the committee "to confer immediately with the Executive himself appears to lose sight of the coordinate relation between the Executive and the Senate which the Constitution has established, and which ought therefore to be maintained."[21] When the committee called on Madison, he gave them a chilly reception. The Senate subsequently confirmed Madison's choice for the office, Albert Gallatin, only after Gallatin had agreed first to step down as Madison's secretary of the treasury.

Every president after Madison has paid at least lip service to senatorial courtesy. In the nineteenth century, for example, Presidents Jackson and Lincoln acceded to the practice but only in exchange for the senators' support of certain legislative initiatives. Early in the twentieth century, President Teddy Roosevelt made clear that he would defer to senators' choices only if their recommendations satisfied the professional and ideological standards that he had set for the offices in question. In contrast, President Warren Harding repaid many of the friends who had helped him to become the compromise Republican candidate for president in 1920 by nominating them (or their friends) to important governmental offices. Otherwise, President Harding, as was expected by those who had helped to get him elected, deferred widely to Republican senators' choices of the people to be appointed to federal offices in their respective states. Ironically, many of Harding's appointments backfired: three members of his cabinet withdrew in disgrace (including Attorney General Harry Daugherty) for misdeeds committed while in office; his veterans administrator was ousted and subsequently convicted of fraud and sentenced to prison; and several other officials were charged with misconduct, two of whom committed suicide. Several decades later, President Reagan took a different approach. Though Harding and Reagan both wanted to appoint federal judges who shared a certain approach to constitutional interpretation, President Reagan put his popularity and mandate on the line by insisting that for every judicial vacancy in their respective states Republican senators had to recommend at least three people who met certain criteria or standards (especially including ideological compatibility).[22]

Much more often than not, presidents have paid dearly for ignoring or failing to give adequate respect to senatorial courtesy. (Of course, the critical judgment call for presidents has always been just how much respect is "adequate.") For instance, in 1845 the Senate rejected Democratic president James K. Polk's nomination of George W. Woodward of Pennsylvania to the Supreme Court. The major force behind the rejection was Senator Simon Cameron, an Independent and a major force in Pennsylvania politics. Not only had Polk failed to consult Cameron about Woodward's nomination, but Cameron regarded the nomination as a personal affront because Cameron had won a controversial victory over Woodward in the most recent Senate election. Cameron persuaded five Democratic and several Whig senators to join him in getting the necessary votes to defeat Woodward's nomination.[23]

In spite of his widespread popularity, President Franklin D. Roosevelt encountered serious opposition in the Senate when he attempted to curtail the patronage of the Democratic senators who opposed his legislative agenda. For instance, Roosevelt failed to take federal patronage away from Senator Pat McCarran of Nevada (over a U.S. attorney post in 1939), both Virginia senators (in 1939, over nominations to federal district judgeships in their state), and Senator W. Lee O'Daniel (who blocked Roosevelt's 1943 attempt to nominate to a judgeship in his state someone who had run against the senator the previous year).[24]

The resilience of senatorial courtesy is reflected by the fact that only two twentieth-century presidents have made significant efforts to abandon the practice. One failed altogether, and the other met with only limited success. The first was President Herbert Hoover, who on entering office declared that he intended to end the practice of awarding judicial appointments strictly on the grounds of patronage and instead planned to raise the standards and requisite qualifications for lower-court nominees.[25] He met swift opposition from Republican senators who did not want to relinquish their chance to dispense favors to important constituents and supporters. President Hoover had little or no sway over the liberal Republican or Progressive senators who commanded the pivotal votes on key nominations in the Senate. The resistance to Hoover's reforms and choices only intensified over time. Eventually, he abandoned his objective.

The second president who tried to buck the system of senatorial courtesy for judicial appointments was Jimmy Carter. Both as a candidate and shortly after he entered office, President Carter expressed his desire to have senators use merit selection panels to assist them in recommending highly qualified and more diverse nominees for district court judgeships. Many Democratic senators resisted. Among other things, they refused to support legislation proposed by Carter to create merit selection panels for circuit court judgeships. Consequently, by executive order, Carter established his own nominating commissions for circuit court appointments. Although President Carter generally succeeded in increasing the diversity and quality of the federal judiciary, his efforts to do so strained his relationships with many of the senators from his own party in ways that came back to haunt him repeatedly throughout the last two years of his one-term presidency.

The endurance of senatorial courtesy (at least with respect to judicial nominations) is further reflected by the institutionalization of the practice in the judicial confirmation process in the form of "blue slips." During the past few decades, whenever the Judiciary Committee has considered a judicial nomination, it has sent a blue slip to the senators from the nominee's home state. If a senator, regardless of his party, returns the slip marked "objection," the custom has been that no hearing will be scheduled. The nomination dies at the end of the congressional session.[26]

Senatorial courtesy in the form of deference to presidential nominations of other senators (or representatives) to confirmable posts has proven to be at least as enduring as the more traditional form. Presidents have nominated more than seventy senators and representatives to cabinet posts, Supreme Court posts, ambassadorships, and other high-ranking offices; only seven failed. The reasons for such nominations are fairly obvious. Among other things, they help to build bridges with members of Congress, particularly in areas of critical concern. In addition, such appointments can bring expertise in the ways of the nation's Capitol and familiar faces to an administration, particularly in circumstances in which the chief executive has not spent much time there before becoming president.

Every president has engaged in this practice. Some of the more notable nominations include the following: President Monroe's nomination of former senator John Quincy Adams as secretary of state; President John Quincy Adams's controversial nomination of House Speaker Henry Clay as secretary of state; President Jackson's nominations of Senator Levi Woodbury of New Hampshire first as secretary of the navy and later as secretary of the treasury, and of former senator William Smith of South Carolina to the Supreme Court (he declined to serve after having been confirmed for the post by the Senate in 1837); President Lincoln's nomination of Senator Salmon P. Chase of Ohio as his initial secretary of the treasury and subsequently as Chief Justice in 1864; President Rutherford B. Hayes's nominations of three senators to his cabinet;[27] Grover Cleveland's nomination of Senate majority leader Edwin Douglass White of Louisiana as his third choice for the Supreme Court; President Warren Harding's nomination of Senator George Sutherland of Utah to the Supreme Court in 1922; President Franklin D. Roosevelt's nomination of Senator Hugo L. Black of Alabama to the Supreme Court in 1937; President Truman's nomination of Senator Harold Burton from Ohio to the Supreme Court in 1945;[28] President Nixon's nomination of Senator William Saxbe from Ohio to become attorney general (to replace Elliot Richardson, whom the president fired after he had refused to dismiss Archibald Cox, then the special Watergate prosecutor); and President Jimmy Carter's nomination of Senator Edmund Muskie of Maine to be his secretary of state. More recently, President Clinton in his first term successfully appointed six members of Congress to his cabinet and other important positions: Democratic senator Lloyd Bentsen of Texas as secretary of the treasury, former senator and vice president Walter Mondale as ambassador to Japan, former Mississippi congressman Mike Espy as secretary of agriculture, former Tennessee senator Jim Sasser as ambassador to China, former Colorado senator Tim Wirth as undersecretary of state for global affairs, and former congressmen Leon Panetta and Les Aspin as head of OMB and defense secretary, respectively.[29] In his second term, President Clinton successfully appointed three other members of Congress to his cabinet (or cabinet-level offices): former senator William Cohen of Maine as secretary of defense, former Kansas congressman Dan Glickman as secretary of agriculture, and former congressman Bill Richardson first as ambassador to the United Nations and subsequently as secretary of energy.

Moreover, in late November 1999, Carol Moseley-Braun, a former senator from Illinois, was confirmed ninety-six to two as President Clinton's ambassador to New Zealand, in spite of the efforts of Senate Foreign Relations Committee chair Jesse Helms to delay hearings on her nomination. He opposed the nomination because of concerns about her possible financial and other misconduct as a senator and her success in blocking his efforts to have the Senate renew a design patent on an emblem for the United Daughters of the Confederacy that included the Confederate flag. In hearings before the Senate Foreign Relations Committee, Moseley-Braun vehemently denied having committed any financial improprieties as a senator. In the end, Helms cast the only negative vote against her nomination in committee and one of the two negative votes against her nomination once it reached the floor (the other negative vote came from Peter Fitzgerald, the Republican who took her seat after defeating her in a bid for reelection). No doubt, such appointments were partly intended to provide Clinton, a Washington outsider, with the counsel and assistance of veteran Washington insiders who presumably had, among other things, good relations with Congress.

Of the members of Congress nominated to the cabinet and the Supreme Court, only four failed to be confirmed, only one of them in this century. The Jacksonian Democrats, who became a majority in the Senate for the first time during the last couple of years of John Quincy Adams's administration, decided in February 1829 to postpone indefinitely President Adams's nomination of former senator John Crittenden of Kentucky. Senate Democrats made this decision because Adams was a lame duck when he made the nomination in December 1828 and the Democrats wanted to preserve the vacancy for their leader, incoming president Andrew Jackson, to fill. Not long thereafter, in spite of the Democratic majority in the Senate, the Senate rejected former New York senator Martin Van Buren as President Jackson's minister to Great Britain (shortly after it had confirmed Van Buren as Jackson's secretary of state).

In 1852, President Fillmore nominated former North Carolina senator George Badger as his second choice to fill a vacancy on the Supreme Court. The timing proved to be disastrous for Badger, a well-known Whig who had served prior to his election to the Senate as secretary of the navy under Presidents Harrison and Tyler. By the time his nomination arose, Franklin Pierce had been elected president. The Democrat-controlled Senate voted twenty-six to twenty-five to postpone Badger's nomination indefinitely. Aware that the Senate wanted to preserve the vacancy for the newly elected Democrat Pierce to fill, Badger withdrew his nomination. Fillmore next nominated Judah Benjamin, who had just been elected to the Senate from Louisiana, but Benjamin turned down the nomination.

The next senator whose nomination to the Supreme Court or a cabinet post ran into insurmountable trouble was George Williams, whom President Grant unsuccessfully tried to appoint as Chief Justice in 1873. A year earlier, President Grant had successfully nominated Williams, a senator from Ohio, as his attorney general. Williams was forced to withdraw his nomination as Chief Justice after widespread charges that he lacked the integrity and legal skills to serve in that position with distinction.

Subsequently, the Senate in 1989 rejected President George Bush's first choice for his secretary of defense, former Texas senator John Tower. Tower's nomination failed for several reasons, including his unpopularity with many Democratic colleagues (who by the time of his nomination controlled the Senate by a ten-seat margin) and his history of drinking and womanizing.

The Senate has also, in a few instances, rejected senators' nominations to high-ranking positions other than the Supreme Court and the cabinet. In the first such rejection, the Senate, with Vice President John Calhoun casting the deciding vote, rejected President Jackson's nomination of former New York senator Martin Van Buren to become minister to Great Britain. A little more than a century later, President Truman, in February 1949, nominated his friend and former Senate colleague Mon Wallgren as chairman of the National Security Resources Board, an agency charged with the important task of planning the industrial mobilization of the country for national defense. Though most senators liked Wallgren personally, several questioned his qualifications for this post, and Wallgren withdrew his nomination after the Armed Services Committee voted seven to six to reject the nomination. (Except for one Democratic member's vote to reject the nomination, the vote followed party lines.) In October 1949, President Truman successfully nominated Wallgren to the Federal Power Commission.

Nor has the Senate always accepted the nominations of other senators without some difficulty. For instance, President Franklin D. Roosevelt decided not to nominate Justice Black to become Chief Justice in 1941 because he feared that the nomination would encounter serious opposition in the Senate, in spite of its Democratic majority, because of Black's admission shortly after becoming a justice that he had been a member of the KKK in his youth.[30] Similar concerns precluded President Truman from nominating Black (with whom he had served in the Senate) when Truman had the chance to fill the Chief Justiceship in 1946.[31] Instead, Truman nominated his friend and former seven-term congressman Fred Vinson, who had previously been confirmed as Truman's secretary of the treasury.

There is a rich history of individual senators who have been successful, either by manipulating Senate rules or by building coalitions, at thwarting or delaying nominations in situations in which the nominating president failed to consult them before making nominations (or failed to accept their recommendations) for offices in the senators' fields of interest or home states. A colorful example is Roscoe Conkling, who served from 1866 through 1881 as a senator from New York and the influential leader of the so-called Republican Stalwarts (composed of the radicals in the party). Conkling dominated the patronage in New York for most of his time in the Senate. His successes—and the obvious price any president who failed to heed his desires would have to pay—made him a force to be reckoned with during those years. He achieved such prominence that President Grant offered to nominate him to be Chief Justice of the United States in 1873. Conkling refused,[32] preferring to remain in the Senate in order to control the federal patronage in New York and to pursue his own presidential ambitions. Conkling failed to become the Republican nominee for president in 1876, and in 1881 he resigned from office after it became clear that he was going to lose a pitched battle to defeat President James Garfield's nominee for the office of collector of the Port of New York.[33] That confirmation turned out to be Garfield's only legislative achievement as president. He rallied a majority of Republicans in the Senate to overcome the protests of both Conkling and New York's other senator, Thomas Platt, in order to appease the other major faction in New York Republican politics, to implement his disdain for senatorial courtesy, and to secure the prerogative of the president to make nominations as he saw fit. To Conkling's surprise, the New York state legislature failed to reelect him to the Senate, something on which he had counted to send a signal to Garfield of the political support for his control of patronage in his state. After Garfield's assassination, Chester Arthur, a close political associate of Conkling's, ascended to the presidency. President Arthur offered Conkling a seat on the Supreme Court in 1882, an appointment that Conkling initially accepted but rejected five days after his former colleagues in the Senate confirmed him for the post.[34] Conkling's bravado in rejecting the appointment because its pay was insufficient, along with the scandal ensuing from his affair with another senator's wife, effectively brought his colorful political career to an end.

Perhaps no senator in recent years has invoked senatorial courtesy more effectively or aggressively than Jesse Helms from North Carolina. In 1993, for example, Senator Helms successfully resisted a cloture vote to end his filibuster in opposition to President Clinton's nomination of Walter Dellinger to become assistant attorney general of the Office of Legal Counsel in the Justice Department. Helms opposed the nomination on the grounds that the president had failed to consult him before naming Dellinger, a highly respected professor of constitutional law from Duke University in Helms's home state. Senator Helms also opposed the nomination both because he regarded Dellinger as too liberal (particularly because of his support for the constitutionally protected right of a woman to choose to have an abortion) and because he was a key strategist who helped to orchestrate the Democratic-controlled Senate's rejection of Robert Bork's nomination to the Supreme Court in 1987.[35] Helms failed to stop a second cloture vote made possible by the defection of nine Republican senators (later described by Helms as the "Dellinger nine") who joined the Democratic majority after having supported the filibuster through one round of voting as a demonstration of their solidarity with Senator Helms. After that, they felt it was no longer in their interest to oppose the president's nomination.

After the midterm elections of 1994, Senator Helms became the chair of the Foreign Relations Committee. In his first year in that post Senator Helms successfully stalled nineteen ambassadorial appointments.[36] In 1997, he nixed President Clinton's nomination of former Massachusetts governor William Weld to be ambassador to Mexico by refusing in his capacity as chair of the Foreign Relations Committee to schedule confirmation hearings to consider the nomination. Senator Helms did not believe that Weld would be a good representative of American values and policies because of his support for legalizing marijuana for medicinal purposes. As of mid-June 1999, Senator Helms had successfully stalled more than four hundred ambassadorial and other foreign relations nominations based on policy disagreements with the president.

Moreover, Senator Helms has successfully blocked all of President Clinton's efforts to fill any of North Carolina's seats on the U.S. Court of Appeals for the Fourth Circuit. As of mid-July 2000, there were three vacant seats on the Fourth Circuit Court, one of which had been open since 1990 (the longest vacancy in the federal judiciary), while another had not been filled since 1994 (the fourth most protracted vacancy on the federal courts). President Clinton nominated four different people, three of them African Americans, for these slots, all of whom Helms opposed. The senator has explained that his opposition is based on his belief that the caseload of the Fourth Circuit does not merit having any more judges added to the court. Moreover, he has argued that few people in North Carolina have heard about the composition of the Fourth Circuit, much less care about it.[37] Consequently, Senator Helms introduced a bill in 1999 to eliminate two of North Carolina's seats on the Fourth Circuit Court. As the next section explains, such bills have been commonplace in our history as measures by the political branches to check judicial authority.

Abolishing or Establishing the Criteria for Confirmable Offices

Working in conjunction with the House of Representatives, the Senate has also tried to influence the federal appointments process by abolishing certain federal offices (including federal judgeships or the number of seats required to be filled on the Supreme Court) or trying to establish (by means of legislation) criteria for the occupants of certain federal offices. The Appointments Clause empowers Congress to create (and, by implication, to eliminate) confirmable positions, and U.S. history is replete with examples of congressional attempts to use this power to facilitate the legislative branch's control over the federal appointments process.

The events culminating in *Marbury v. Madison*[38] were among the first attempts made by Congress to use its power to create (or abolish)

Article III courts or to limit (or create) seats on the Supreme Court as a means of maximizing its (and correspondingly decreasing the president's) control generally, and particularly over the federal judiciary. The attempt made by the outgoing Federalist Congress on the eve of Thomas Jefferson's inauguration to create sixteen circuit judgeships and more than forty justices of the peace for the District of Columbia was clearly designed to stack the federal judiciary "deck" against the newly elected Republican regime.[39] Moreover, in an effort to postpone the day when President Jefferson would be able to nominate a Republican sympathizer to the Supreme Court, the Federalist Congress provided that when the next vacancy occurred it should not be filled, thus reducing the Court from six justices (the number originally allocated to it by the First Congress) to five.[40] The Republicans' reaction—to abolish the newly created judgeships by means of an act repealing them and eliminating any planned reduction in the Supreme Court's size in 1802—proved to be an effective response, but only after the Republican Congress (elected along with President Jefferson) abolished the entire 1802 term to preclude (or at least to delay) the Court from hearing challenges to both President Jefferson's refusal to honor the commissions issued by the Adams administration and the Republican Congress's 1802 repeal bill.[41]

Congress made four other successful attempts in the nineteenth century to change the Court's size in an effort to control presidential influence over it. In 1807, the Republican Congress created a seventh seat on the Supreme Court to give President Jefferson a third opportunity to appoint a justice.[42] (Jefferson had filled two other vacancies on the Court—one in 1804 and another in 1806.) In 1835, the Senate, with many powerful senators enraged by President Jackson's efforts to weaken the national bank and with its forty seats evenly divided between Jacksonian Democrats and Republicans, postponed President Jackson's nomination of Roger Taney to fill a vacancy on the Court, but only by voting to eliminate the seat to which Taney had been nominated.[43] The proposal to eliminate the seat failed, however, to pass the House. Two years later, after intensive campaigning by Jackson to get more Democrats elected to Congress, the House and the Senate were each back under the control of the Democrats. Consequently, they joined together to expand the number of associate justices on the Court from six to eight, thereby increasing the

Court's size to nine—and, of course, also increasing President Jackson's influence over it.[44] Briefly during the Civil War, the Republican Congress expanded the Court to ten, giving President Lincoln a fourth opportunity to nominate a Supreme Court justice in just his first term. In 1867, however, Congress contracted the Court to seven to prevent the unpopular Andrew Johnson from having any opportunity to nominate someone to the Supreme Court (there had been a vacancy that year) and to preserve the influence of Lincoln's five appointees.[45] Within a month after Johnson left office in 1869, Congress restored the Court's membership to nine. Although the Senate re-created the ninth seat as a "gift" to President Grant, he squandered it by unsuccessfully nominating his attorney general, Ebenezer Hoar, who was highly qualified but had earned the enmity of many Republican senators by generally opposing senatorial courtesy with respect to federal appointments.[46]

The most notorious legislative attempt in the twentieth century to regulate the Court's size as a means of expanding a president's influence was President Franklin D. Roosevelt's infamous Court-packing plan, under which Congress had been asked to pass legislation authorizing the president to appoint one new justice for every sitting justice who had reached the age of seventy, up to a maximum of six new justices. Congress resisted the initiative, forcing the president to wait for vacancies to arise through natural attrition. Although he had to wait until the beginning of his second term for his first opportunity to make a Supreme Court appointment, President Roosevelt took delight (after his first choice, Senate majority leader Joseph Robinson, had died) in nominating Hugo Black based in part on Black's enthusiastic support as a senator for the president's Court-packing plan.[47] Roosevelt predicted correctly that Black's Senate colleagues would not have the temerity to thwart his nomination in spite of their disagreements with him about policy and constitutional matters.

More recent organized efforts within the Senate to delay or thwart several nominations made by President Clinton were based on concerns (or disagreement) about the need to preserve or maintain the offices to which they were made. For example, the offices of associate attorney general and surgeon general were both left vacant throughout the election year of 1996 because several senators had expressed skepticism about their neces-

The Senate

sity.[48] For his part, President Clinton promised to carry the debate about the necessity of maintaining a surgeon general into his reelection campaign. Another example is the initiative taken for more than a year preceding the presidential election by Republican senator Charles Grassley, a member of the Senate Judiciary Committee, with the support of then-Senate majority leader Robert Dole, to determine which vacant circuit judgeships should be abolished because they were superfluous.[49] Senator Grassley successfully stalled the nomination of Merrick Garland to the U.S. Court of Appeals for the District of Columbia for more than two years because of his doubt about the need to fill the seat to which Garland had been nominated.[50] First nominated in 1994, Garland was finally confirmed by the Republican Senate in 1997 (subsequent to President Clinton's reelection).

Moreover, several senators stalled consideration of nominations to the Ninth Circuit for well over a year beginning in January 1996 because they thought consideration of legislation to split the Ninth Circuit should take precedence. The Senate began to consider some but not all nominations to the appellate court in late fall 1997 after a compromise had been reached to study whether the boundaries of the nation's regional courts of appeal should be changed.[51] Republican senator Conrad Burns had begun the movement to delay nominations because he supported legislation that would split the Ninth Circuit to ensure Montana's representation on equal footing with other states in the circuit, which is presently dominated by several bigger states with many more seats.[52]

Besides trying to control the federal appointments process by means of eliminating or varying the number of confirmable positions within certain offices, Congress has frequently considered or experimented with legislatively mandating qualifications for or placing limits on the kinds of people suitable to fill particular offices. The constitutionality of such efforts and proposals depends initially on the approach one takes to separation-of-powers issues. Formalist analysis would likely lead a court to view as unconstitutional a law restricting the discretion of either the president to nominate or the Senate to confirm. A formalist would likely reason that the absence of any explicit standard in the Constitution to guide a president in making nominations or the Senate in approving or disapproving nominations means that there is no such standard and Congress lacks authority to construct one. Presidents and senators have complete, un-fettered discretion to exercise their respective authority over federal appointments as they see fit.

In contrast, functionalist analysis might lead a court to uphold qualifications required for certain officers as long as those qualifications do not unduly interfere with the president's basic ability to discharge his duties, including his nominating authority (at least with respect to officers of the United States), or the Senate's ability to discharge its functions, including its advice and consent on presidential nominations. For a functionalist, it is likely that a great deal will depend on the particular officers involved, including their relationship to the president. In other words, the more integral a job is to the functioning of the president, the less likely or the lesser extent to which Congress may restrict a president's calculation of the pertinent factors in making a nomination for the position.

Of course, there will be some cases in which functional and formalist analyses would lead to similar results, particularly with respect to offices deemed critical or indispensable to the functioning of the president. For example, there is no doubt that a congressionally mandated requirement that certain high-level White House staff, such as the White House Counsel, should be subject to Senate confirmation is unconstitutional, regardless of the kind of analysis used. Under a formal separation-of-powers analysis, such a proposal would plainly fail because it would directly interfere with and undermine the president's authority to organize the office of the chief executive as he sees fit *and* allow the Congress (by means of having made the law) and the Senate (by means of having been empowered legislatively to offer its advice) to interfere with the internal, day-to-day decision making and the organization of the executive branch as its apex—the presidency. Under a functional separation-of-powers analysis, such a proposal would undoubtedly aggrandize the Congress at the expense of weakening the chief executive and allow for undue congressional interference with the president's discretion to choose his closest advisers.

The same could be said for a recent proposal in Congress to establish a special inspector general in the White House to be nominated by the president and confirmed by the Senate.[53] Again, a formal separation-of-powers analysis would suggest that such a law would impermissibly allow congressional interference with the basic authority of the president

The Senate

to organize his office as he sees fit (by placing the Senate in the position of trying to pressure his choices or to frustrate his exercise of his authority by delaying or failing to schedule confirmation hearings). Functional separation-of-powers analysis would suggest that the law is unconstitutional because it allows Congress by creating the position and the Senate by having the power to disapprove the official to interfere unduly with the president's ability to organize his office as he sees fit and to assemble a staff of his own choosing in a timely fashion.

A critical concern arising whenever the Congress has attempted either to require Senate confirmation for a particular office or to limit or eliminate presidential authority to nominate is whether the position involves "an officer of the United States." Some early Supreme Court decisions attempted to define this central phrase in the Appointments Clause. For example, the Court defined an office as "a public station, or employment, conferred by the appointment of government. The term [*officer of the United States*] embraces the ideas of tenure, duration, emolument, and duties. [The duties of an officer are] continuing and permanent, not occasional or temporary."[54] According to the Court, mere agents, not officers, discharge occasional or intermittent duties.[55] Unless a person holds his or her position by virtue of a presidential appointment or by an appointment from the courts or department heads as authorized by the law, that person is not an officer of the United States.[56]

Perhaps the most significant Supreme Court decision construing which officers the president is entitled to nominate is *Buckley v. Valeo*.[57] The case involved the constitutionality of a congressional law empowering Congress to appoint four of the six members of the Federal Election Commission. The law required that all six members (two of whom the president was empowered to nominate) be subject to confirmation by the majority of both houses of Congress. The Supreme Court struck down the law, determining that while the "Necessary and Proper" Clause of the Constitution empowers Congress to create the Commission it does not empower Congress to appoint its members. The Court emphasized that the "Necessary and Proper" Clause must be read consistently with other constitutional provisions. For instance, Congress could not, merely by concluding that a measure was "necessary and proper," pass a bill of attainder or an ex post facto law. Nor could it violate other portions of the

Constitution, such as the Appointments Clause, especially when Congress was attempting to create a commission designed to exercise more than legislative functions. The members of the Federal Election Commission exercised "substantial authority,"[58] and this could be exercised only by "officers of the United States" appointed pursuant to the Appointments Clause. According to the Court, the latter clause gives Congress only two options when creating a position to be filled by an "officer of the United States": nomination by the president, subject to the advice and consent of the Senate; or vesting the appointment power in the president alone, in the courts of law, or in department heads. Congress chose the first option when it rewrote the act in 1976.[59]

In *Buckley v. Valeo,* the Court noted that if an agency's powers are "essentially of an investigative and informative nature," Congress may appoint the agency's officials.[60] Subsequently, in reauthorizing the Civil Rights Commission in 1983, Congress enacted legislation that vested it with the authority to appoint four of the eight members of the commission and allowed the president to appoint the other four members.[61] In signing the bill, President Reagan acknowledged that it was constitutional, in his view, because the essential functions of the commission were investigative (and thus within Congress's authority to assign to people at least some of whom it appointed).

Subsequently, in *Bowsher v. Synar,*[62] the Court held that Congress may not vest certain officials subject to its direction or removal with executive functions. Two years later, in *Morrison v. Olson,*[63] the Court upheld congressional legislation empowering a federal court to appoint a special or independent prosecutor responsible for investigating possible criminal conduct by, and if necessary bringing criminal charges against, certain high-level executive officials, including the president of the United States. When read together, the two decisions clearly prohibit Congress from appointing (or vesting) an officer who exercises executive functions. Moreover, in *Morrison v. Olson,* the Court attempted to clarify the line between "inferior officers" and principal officers or "officers of the United States." Acknowledging that the line is not clear, the Court concluded that the independent counsel is an inferior officer for several reasons: it may be removed from the office by the attorney general under certain specified conditions for certain proscribed misconduct (implying that the independent counsel is inferior in rank and authority to an officer who clearly qualifies as an "officer of the United States"); it has statutory authority to perform only particularized, limited duties (such as undertaking criminal investigations and prosecutions); and it has limited tenure and jurisdiction (constrained by statute and the appointing authority).

Since *Morrison*, the Court has rejected three additional constitutional challenges to nonpresidential appointments. In *Freytag v. Commissioner of Internal Revenue*,[64] the Court held that the appointment of special tax judges by the chief judge of the Tax Court as authorized by the Tax Reform Act of 1984 to conduct certain hearings does not violate the Appointments Clause. The Court found that the special tax judges created by the act have sufficient discretion and importance to be "inferior officers" to whom the Appointments Clause applies.[65] The Court found further that their appointment by the chief judge of the Tax Court is permissible because the Tax Court qualifies as a "Court of Law" within the meaning of the Appointments Clause.[66] The Court reasoned that even though it was not created by Congress pursuant to Article III, the Tax Court exercises the judicial power of the United States, and its "exclusively judicial role distinguishes it from other non–Article III tribunals that perform multiple functions and provides the limit on the diffusion of appointment power that the Constitution demands."[67]

Three years later, the Court in *Weiss v. United States*[68] rejected a constitutional challenge to the appointments of military judges by the judge advocate general to serve on special and general courts-martial. The Court noted that although the officers in question had received judicial assignments from the judge advocate general rather than the president, they had already been appointed as commissioned officers by the president.[69] Hence, there was no ground for "suspicion that Congress was trying to both create an office and also select a particular individual to fill the office. . . . Although military judges obviously perform certain unique and important functions," the Court said, "all military officers consistent with long tradition play a role in the operation of the military justice system."[70]

Three years after *Weiss*, the Court in *Edmond v. United States*[71] upheld the authority of the secretary of transportation to appoint civilian members of the Coast Guard Court of Appeals, an intermediate court that hears appeals from courts-martial. The Court explained: "Generally speaking, the term 'inferior officer' connotes a relationship with some higher ranking officer or officers below the President: Whether one is an 'inferior' officer depends upon whether he has a superior. ['Inferior] officers' are officers whose work is directed and supervised at some level by others who were appointed by presidential nomination with the advise and consent of the Senate."[72] The Court held that civilian judges on the Coast Guard Court of Appeals are inferior officers who can be appointed by a head of department because they are supervised by the judge advocate general, who engages in administrative oversight and can remove judges from the court without cause, and by the Court of Appeals for the Armed Forces, which has appellate jurisdiction over the Coast Guard Court of Appeals.

The Ineligibility and Incompatibility Clauses of the Constitution further limit congressional authority (and presidential discretion, for that matter) with respect to federal appointments. The former clause prohibits members of Congress from being appointed to any federal office created—or to any federal office whose salary has been increased—during their term of office.[73] The latter clause provides that no officer of the United States "shall be a member of either House during his Continuance in Office."[74] These provisions reflect the framers' concerns about the corruption that would result from allowing the members of one branch to assume offices in or exercise the authority of another branch.

Nevertheless, Congress has tried to work around these clauses to facilitate certain appointments. For example, in some instances in which a president has nominated a senator for a position to which Congress has granted a pay increase during the senator's tenure in Congress, Congress has tried to avoid violating the Ineligibility Clause by reducing the salary of the position to the level it had before the pay raise at issue was enacted.[75] Examples of such maneuvering include the following: Congress's agreeing to reduce the salary of the secretary of state to allow President Taft to appoint Senator Philander Knox to the position; Congress's enacting legislation in 1973 to keep the compensation of the attorney general at its previous level so that President Nixon could nominate Senator William Saxbe to the position; Congress's passage of special legislation in 1980 to permit Senator Edmund Muskie to become secretary of state; and Congress's enactment of special legislation in 1993 to allow President Clinton to nominate Senator Lloyd Bentsen to become secretary of the treasury.

A strict or formalist reading of the Ineligibility Clause (sometimes called the Emoluments Clause), such as the one given by Michael Stokes Paulsen,[76] construes violation of the so-described clause as unconstitutional. The strict view is that the clause does not explicitly provide any exceptions. Consequently, it means what it says and therefore does not allow Congress any discretion or authority to disregard its directive by passing legislation trying to undo a violation of the clause that has occurred beforehand (because a member of Congress has been nominated or appointed to an office whose salary he or she has previously voted to increase). If such legislation is constitutional, it must be as the result of different constitutional analysis. Such legislation might be construed as constitutional if the critical inquiry is not whether the letter of the law has been broken (it has) but rather whether the problem that the clause exists to preclude—conflicts of interest in nominating a member of Congress who has been able to vote himself or herself a raise—has been avoided. The corrective legislation conceivably achieves this end.

OTHER SIGNIFICANT PATTERNS AND PRACTICES

During the course of U.S. history, senators have engaged in several significant practices in the federal appointments process besides those already canvassed. These practices further reflect the compromises and other efforts that have been made by senators in their never-ending quest to preserve and sometimes to expand their prerogatives.

Senatorial Practices Regarding Presidential
Nominations of Executive Officials and Judges

Generally, the Senate defers far more to a president's nominees to executive offices than to his nominees to judicial offices, particularly to the Supreme Court.[77] There are many reasons for such deference. Many if not most senators, for example, support a president's need to have his own agents assist him in trying to implement his agenda, because they want to be president (and thus would like to have that privilege someday), they have previously served in high-level executive offices, or they can curry favor with a president by doing so.

Twenty-seven Supreme Court nominations, however—nearly one in six—have not secured Senate confirmation, including those whose names were withdrawn before a floor vote. Invariably, senators have insisted on closely scrutinizing Supreme Court nominees because justices, once confirmed, enjoy life tenure and will wield enormous power in reviewing the constitutionality of federal and state laws. Consequently, it should not be surprising that political factors, including a judicial nominee's political or constitutional views or other indications of how he or she would perform as a judge or justice (and thus his or her fitness to serve on the Court), are the most important reason for failed Supreme Court nominations (and, for that matter, failed nominations to other Article III courts). Nominees whose political or constitutional views had an important effect on their confirmation to the Supreme Court include the following: John Rutledge (rejected in part for opposing the Jay treaty), Alexander Wolcott (rejected for vigorously enforcing the Embargo and Nonintercourse Acts as the federal customs collector for Connecticut), George Woodward (rejected for supporting restricted immigration and discrimination against ethnic groups), Ebenezer Hoar (rejected for opposing senators' control of political patronage and the impeachment of Andrew Johnson), Caleb Cushing (rejected for shifting political allegiances too often throughout his political lifetime), John Parker (rejected in part for uttering racist sentiments as a gubernatorial candidate in North Carolina and for upholding yellow-dog contracts), Abe Fortas (rejected in part for being too closely linked to the liberalism of the Warren Court and the troubled presidency of his close friend, Lyndon Johnson); Clement Haynsworth (rejected because of his allegedly antiunion attitudes and racism), Harrold Carswell (rejected in part for racist statements and activities), and Robert Bork (rejected in part for opposing the 1964 Civil Rights Act and for firing the first special Watergate prosecutor).

Even some justices who have been confirmed have faced stiff opposition because of senators' concerns about their political and constitutional views. Such justices include Nathan Clifford (barely confirmed after bitter debate over his support for slavery), Louis Brandeis (attacked for being too liberal), Charles Evans Hughes (opposed by a significant minority for being too closely aligned with the nation's wealthiest corporations), Thurgood Marshall (harshly questioned about his views on civil rights issues and his support for certain Warren Court decisions), and Clarence Thomas (criticized for some of his actions as the chair of the Equal Employment Opportunity Commission and for allegedly harboring ultra-conservative views).

In contrast to its close scrutiny and frequent interference with judicial nominations, the Senate has rejected only nine cabinet-level appointees in floor votes while confirming over seven hundred such nominations—obviously a far smaller percentage of rejections than the percentage of rejected Supreme Court nominees. Alexander Hamilton anticipated the Senate's reluctance to interfere with a president's nominees for high-level executive offices. In Federalist Number 76, Hamilton explained his belief that "[a]s [senators'] dissent might cast a kind of stigma upon the individual rejected, and might have the appearance of a reflection upon the judgment of the Chief magistrate, it is not likely that their sanction would often be refused, where there were not special and strong reasons for the refusal."[78] Justice Joseph Story, in his *Commentaries on the Constitution*, also predicted that senatorial interference with appointments to executive offices would be rare: "The more common error, (if there shall be any) will be too great a facility to yield to the executive wishes, as a means of personal, or popular favor."[79]

The relative rarity of rejected cabinet (or cabinet-level or important subcabinet) nominations has ensured great embarrassment to both the nominating presidents and the nominees when they have occurred. The first cabinet nominee to be rejected was Roger Taney, President Jackson's nominee for secretary of the treasury in 1836. Subsequent cabinet nominees who have been rejected include Caleb Cushing (rejected by the Senate three times as President Tyler's secretary of the treasury), Henry Stansberry (rejected when renominated as Johnson's attorney general after serving as counsel in his impeachment trial), Charles Beecher Warren (turned down twice in 1925 as President Coolidge's nominee for attorney general), Lewis Strauss (rejected by the Senate in 1959 as President Eisenhower's secretary of commerce), and John Tower (rejected by his former colleagues in the Senate in 1989 as President Bush's secretary of defense). The reasons for these particular rejections were largely personal. For instance, Cushing's rejections were due in part to the Senate's contempt for President Tyler, while both Strauss and Tower were disliked by many senators who eagerly used their opportunity to frustrate the nominees' confirmation chances. More often than not, however, the Senate's rejections of cabinet nominations have been based on other factors. For instance, the rejection of Taney as secretary of the treasury occurred as part of the struggle between the Senate and President Jackson over the fate of the national bank, which Taney had played a major role in dismantling by withdrawing its funds at President Jackson's instructions. In 1925, Charles Beecher Warren proved to be the perfect target for Democrats and Progressive Republicans in the Senate. Warren had been closely associated in private practice with some of the big businesses with which he would have had to deal as attorney general, including a long term as a representative of the sugar trust. Democrats and progressive Republicans doubted that Warren, with this kind of background, would be able to avoid the conflicts of interest and corruption in which so many high-ranking officials in the Harding administration had engaged. After the Senate rejected Warren (the first time since 1868 that a cabinet nominee had failed to be confirmed), President Coolidge renominated him and the Senate again rejected him. When President Coolidge offered Warren a recess appointment, Warren declined. The Senate's rejections of Warren signaled to Coolidge, who had just been elected president in his own right after having ascended to the office after President Harding's death in 1923, that he should be more cautious in making important nominations in the future. Although Coolidge took heed (and appointed many people who went on to have distinguished careers in government),[80] the Warren rejections foreshadowed the difficulties Coolidge generally would have in trying to work with the Senate, in which a pivotal coalition was dedicated to opposing his conservative policies.

Moreover, the statistics on nonjudicial nominations rejected or forced to be withdrawn by the Senate are somewhat misleading. Formal rejections of cabinet nominees tell only a small part of the story of presidential-senatorial relations in any given period. For example, as already noted, the Republican-controlled Senate during the period 1947–49 did not formally reject any of President Truman's nonjudicial nominees, but it did force him to withdraw more than two hundred such nominations and to compromise on many others.

Similarly, President Clinton, at least as of mid-March of the last year of his presidency, had had only two nominations formally rejected by the Senate, and over sixty judicial nominations returned to him without final action (and therefore forced to be withdrawn). Moreover, he had been forced to withdraw even more high-profile nominations, including some to cabinet-level offices. The forced withdrawals included, among others, Zoë Baird for attorney general, Bobby Inman as secretary of defense, and Anthony Lake and Michael Carns to head the CIA. In addition, on October 24, 1997, President Clinton withdrew his nomination of Hershel Gober, the deputy secretary of veterans affairs, to be the department's secretary after it became clear the nomination was going to be delayed indefinitely while the Veterans Affairs Committee conducted an investigation into a potential conflict of interest that arose when Gober had been cleared by the department's Office of General Counsel of sexual harassment charges made against him as deputy.[81]

Moreover, some of the forced withdrawals included nominees to ambassadorships and mid-level administrative posts (e.g., Lani Guinier as assistant attorney general of the Civil Rights Division and Gerald Torres as assistant attorney general of the Lands Division). Other forced withdrawals, perhaps less notable but still embarassing, include Kenneth Kizer as an undersecretary in the Veterans Affairs Administration (withdrawn after his nomination was delayed because of complaints from various veterans' organizations about his effectiveness), James Wetzler (withdrew his nomination to serve on the IRS Oversight Board after all eleven Republican senators on the Finance Committee opposed him based on his opposition to the creation of the oversight board), J. Brian Atwood (withdrew his nomination as ambassador to Brazil after it had been blocked indefinitely by Senator Helms because of the nominee's efforts as the head of the U.S. Agency for International Development [AID] to withstand Helms's attempt to bring AID under the control of the State Department), and Daryl Jones (withdrew his nomination after it had been stalled subsequent to the Armed Services Committee's split over whether to recommend his nomination as secretary of the air force to the full Senate because of questions raised about his record and integrity).

As I have previously suggested, many of President Clinton's nominations were also delayed, oftentimes for reasons that had little to do with their merits. For example, in the middle of June 1997, Senate majority leader Trent Lott announced that he would block Senate action on *all* of President Clinton's nonmilitary nominations (including several top-level Justice Department positions) unless the president agreed to fill four seats on the six-member Federal Election Commission (FEC) (two of which belonged to Republicans). Shortly thereafter, the president agreed to nominate Senator Lott's two candidates for the two empty Republican seats on the commission.

Almost two years later, another Republican seat opened on the FEC. When the Republican Senate leadership asked President Clinton to consider nominating Brad Smith, an outspoken critic of campaign finance regulations and reform, the president balked. In response, Republican Senate leaders threatened, among other things, to continue delaying a final confirmation vote on Richard Holbrooke's nomination as U.S. ambassador to the United Nations unless the president agreed to nominate Smith. After the president showed signs of relenting, Holbrooke was confirmed on August 5, 1999. The president finally decided to nominate Smith on February 10, 2000.

And, as I have also indicated, President Clinton's federal district and appellate court nominees have confronted historic delays. For instance, 1999 was a historic year for the Clinton presidency not only because of the president's acquittal in his impeachment trial but also because by midyear the Clinton administration had had only two judges confirmed—the lowest number ever confirmed midway through a nonelection year. Moreover, the statistics for some other years are quite striking. For instance, the percentage of President Clinton's judicial nominations confirmed in 1997 —47 percent—is significantly lower than the percentage of judicial confirmations for any president (except for Clinton's own record the previous year) over the past four decades. In 1998, the percentage of judicial nominees confirmed climbed well back into the respectable range at 79.5 percent. Though 101 judges were confirmed in 1998, the numbers of confirmed judicial nominees in 1997 and 1999 were each lower than the number of President Reagan's judicial nominees confirmed in 1988 (41) and the number of President Bush's judicial nominees confirmed in 1992 (66), both of which were election years.

President Clinton's confirmation troubles clearly reflect seriously strained relations with the Senate. Indeed, they parallel a disturbing trend over the past fourteen years. From 1985 until 1993 (the year in which Bill Clinton took office), the highest percentage of party-line votes in a given year was 13 percent in 1991. After Clinton became president, the percentages of party-line votes increased dramatically—30 percent in 1993, 28 percent in 1996, 26 percent in 1998, and 40 percent in 1999. A full explication of the reasons for this trend is beyond the scope of this book, though plausible possibilities include fallout from the ongoing culture wars over the past two decades; paybacks for the Senate's rejection of Robert Bork and the badgering of Clarence Thomas; the Republican Revolution (and the Contract with America) in 1994; and the dwindling numbers of moderate Republicans in the Senate. Although the reasons for increased party-line votes in Congress may not be clear or settled, they have certainly driven debates over federal appointments. The conflicted relationship between the president and the Senate has thus posed significant challenges in making decisions about federal appointments and other related legislative matters.

Moreover, President Clinton's record on federal appointments is the most recent manifestation of a modern trend (dating back to at least the 1970s) in which senators have significantly increased the proportion of high-level political nominations they have opposed. Only four of Presidents Eisenhower's, Kennedy's, and Johnson's nonjudicial nominees were rejected, forced to be withdrawn, or faced substantial opposition in the Senate. Every president subsequent to President Johnson has had at least one in ten of his cabinet-level nominations seriously opposed. With a Democratic Senate throughout his presidency, Jimmy Carter fared best among recent chief executives with only 10 percent of his high-level political nominations opposed to any significant degree.

The increasing potential for significant senatorial resistance to a president's nonjudicial nominees is attributable to several factors, including changes in the Senate itself. The Senate has evolved from a collegial body populated mostly by specialists to a group in which individual senators tend to fend for themselves, work to secure their own reelections or other ambitions (such as laying the groundwork for presidential campaigns), are somewhat less beholden to political parties than their predecessors, and must interact with a growing number of interest groups and factions with vested interests in or serious concerns about increasingly divergent kinds of legislation.

The fact that some political offices deal with or are responsible for issues or areas that are of great concern to certain interest groups or segments of society is another basis for increased scrutiny of and opposition to certain nonjudicial nominations. According to one survey, not a single nominee to eleven of twenty-one nonjudicial or political offices faced significant opposition during the period 1945–89.[82] Yet during the same period three-fifths of the nominations that did face serious opposition were to three offices: attorney general, secretary of the interior, and director of the CIA. The nominees to these offices generate more concern among senators because the offices deal with some of the political, social, and constitutional issues of greatest concern to the American electorate.

For instance, Presidents Carter, Reagan, Bush, and Clinton each had their nominations to sensitive national security posts meet with considerable resistance and opposition in the Senate. In 1977, Theodore Sorensen withdrew his nomination by President Carter to head the Central Intelligence Agency "in the wake of assertions that he lacked experience, was a pacifist, and had used secret documents in writing about the Kennedy administration."[83] In 1987, the Senate rejected President Reagan's nomination of Robert Gates, then acting director of the CIA, to become the full-time director because of unanswered questions involving Gates's involvement in some of the events leading up to the so-called Iran-contra scandal.[84] In 1989, the Senate rejected President Bush's nomination of John Tower to become secretary of defense. Bush countered this rejection nicely by nominating former congressman Dick Cheney as secretary of defense and Colin Powell as the first African American to be the chair of the Joint Chiefs of Staff, both of whom were easily confirmed. Two years later, the Senate confirmed President Bush's nomination of former acting director Gates to head the CIA, but only after a highly contentious confirmation hearing that left Gates politically damaged.[85]

In 1994, President Clinton's choice as his second secretary of defense, Bobby Ray Inman, withdrew his nomination after "accus[ing] a syndicated columnist of conspiring with Senate Republicans to sabotage his candidacy."[86] In 1997, George Tenet became the fifth person nominated by President Clinton to head the CIA in four years.[87] Tenet received the nomination in the wake of Anthony Lake's withdrawal after influential Republican senators had delayed the Senate vote on his confirmation indefinitely. The senators were concerned about Lake's management record as President Clinton's national security adviser and his failure to prevent inappropriate fund-raising activities by some people under his supervision.[88] Lake would have succeeded John Deutsch, who was confirmed as the head of the agency after Michael Carns withdrew his nomination in 1995 because of reports that he had violated immigration laws to hire a Filipino servant.[89] In addition, two of President Clinton's nominees as secretary of the air force withdrew their nominations, one because of concerns about his integrity and the other because of his belated response to some senators' expressed concerns about lax security in some Energy Department nuclear labs.

Moreover, offices with responsibility over civil rights matters draw considerable attention from presidents, senators, interest groups, the public, and the media. The machinations in the Senate involving President Clinton's nomination of Bill Lann Lee in the fall of 1997 to head the Justice Department's Civil Rights Division illustrate both the intensity of feelings such nominations trigger and the lengths to which the contending sides seem prepared to go to secure victory. Shortly before the Senate Judiciary Committee was scheduled to vote on the nomination in early November 1997, Senator Hatch, the committee's chair, declared his opposition to Lee based on Hatch's perception of him as a proponent of affirmative action and a liberal construction and enforcement of the nation's civil rights laws. The prospects for the nomination's chances looked dismal given Hatch's declared opposition and the fact that if Hatch got (as he predicted he would) at least eight of the committee's nine Republican members to join his opposition, the ensuing tie vote would be sufficient to defeat the nomination because the committee's rules provide that a nomination requires the support of a majority of the committee to get to the floor of the Senate for a final vote. Although Democrats on the committee succeeded in blocking a committee vote before Congress adjourned for the year a couple of weeks later, they failed to prevent nine Republican members of the committee, including Senator Hatch, from refusing to add the nomination to its list of nominations to be held over for consideration the next year. The split vote on the nomination precluded it from reaching the floor of the Senate or otherwise going forward.[90] Consequently, the nomination's only chance for revival depended on the president's willingness to resubmit it for consideration by the Senate the next year. (Lee was by no means the first nominee to have trouble being confirmed as the head of the Civil Rights Division. President Bush's nomination of William Lucas and President Clinton's nomination of Lani Guinier to the same post failed to win confirmation because of negative inferences drawn from the nominees' records in dealing with civil rights issues.)

It is, however, important to recognize that the fact that an office involves very sensitive or divisive political issues or the potential for straining relations with the Senate might lead a president to hesitate but not necessarily to avoid exercising his prerogative to have his preferred choice occupy an especially high level or influential office. It is fair to say that the more important a position is to a president's agenda or long-range political or constitutional plans, the likelier it is that senators will meet resistance or staunch opposition in trying to make deals with him on appointments. From the perspective of senators (particularly those from the opposing party or with conflicting political views), the problem is that presidents have viewed the naming of cabinet officials, Supreme Court justices, and the like as indisputable prerogatives of their office. In the latter quarter of the nineteenth century, Presidents Rutherford B. Hayes, Chester Arthur, Benjamin Harrison (who appointed Teddy Roosevelt as one of three members of the U.S. Civil Service Commission), and Grover Cleveland set the stage for the establishment of this mindset. Much to the dismay of many of their political supporters and party leaders, these presidents championed civil service reform, granted senators from their political parties only limited control of the patronage in their respective states, and made some critical appointments primarily on the basis of merit.[91] Early in the twentieth century, Presidents Teddy Roosevelt and Woodrow Wilson helped to establish this prerogative even more firmly by standing their ground successfully to put the people of their choice in important offices — including the Supreme Court — influencing the direction, substance, and implementation of national policy.

To some extent, the tendency of senators to question or oppose nominations depending on the importance of the offices to which they are made helps to explain the differences in how senators deal with Supreme Court as contrasted with lower-court nominations. Obviously, the stakes in Supreme Court confirmation hearings tend to be higher because the justices wield unique power that can have long-lasting impacts on the political and constitutional order. Moreover, senators typically assume a more active role in recommending lower-court nominees. Because the source of many lower-court nominations is senatorial courtesy, senators have a vested interest in not interfering too much with another senator's choices lest their own preferences be given little respect by their colleagues. In addition, because there are relatively large numbers of judicial vacancies that have to be filled during any given presidential term of office, senators may be inclined not to care about many of them as long as they are able to get the particular judgeships about which they care the most filled to their satisfaction. This is not to suggest that some senators might be willing to give an administration carte blanche with respect to its judicial nominees generally. Indeed, as the impasses in the Senate regarding many of President Clinton's judicial nominations demonstrate, there are certainly senators prepared to examine, and block, every nominee. Rather, the point is that judicial selection may be an issue of great salience for only a few senators, which is more than enough to impede the process. In contrast, the dynamics tend to differ in the rare circumstances in which a Supreme Court vacancy arises. The unique authority of that office ensures that every senator will have an interest and indeed a stake in whom the president chooses to fill it. The heightened interest and stakes ensure, among other things, that much of the debate — and any trading — are likely to attract considerable attention.

In spite of the eagerness with which many senators have tried to block presidential appointments to offices involving sensitive subjects, senators have had far less success in directing presidents' choices for such offices. Some of this difficulty is no doubt owed to the fact that senators are formally placed in a negative or defensive posture in the appointments process. Moreover, it has proven to be difficult for senators to get and remain sufficiently organized to direct a president's choice for an important confirmable office. For instance, only twice has the Senate been able to direct a president to forgo his preference for a Supreme Court appointment and nominate its preferred candidate instead. The first instance involved President Ulysses S. Grant.[92] In the midst of the Senate's deliberations over President Grant's nomination of his attorney general, Ebenezer Hoar, to the Court, another seat opened when Justice Robert Grier resigned in 1870 after twenty-three years of service on the Court. Thinking that he might be able to boost Hoar's chances by reaching a compromise with Hoar's opponents in the Senate, Grant agreed to follow the dictates of a petition signed by a large majority of both the House and the Senate that he nominate Edwin Stanton to the seat vacated by Justice Grier. The deal fell through, however, when Stanton died four days after the Senate had confirmed his appointment.[93]

The second president who acquiesced to the Senate's choice of a nominee to the Court was Herbert Hoover. Chastened by his failure to get Judge John Parker confirmed by the Senate in 1930 and increasingly aware of his dwindling political strength both inside and outside the Senate, Hoover was not in a position to push hard for his preferred choice when Justice Holmes announced his resignation in 1932. With the Republican party then controlling the Senate by only a single seat and his own popularity plummeting, Hoover was eager to avoid a fight. Initially, his preference had been to nominate a noncontroversial western Republican to replace Holmes.[94] In response, the chair of the Senate Judiciary Committee, George Norris, explained to the president that he and his fellow committee members, most of whom were Democrats and progressive Republicans, preferred Judge Benjamin Cardozo of the New York Court of Appeals.[95] (Norris had established himself as a strong, progressive Republican voice in previously opposing President Harding's nomination of Pierce Butler as an associate justice, President Coolidge's nomination of Harlan Fiske Stone to the Supreme Court, and President Hoover's nominations of John Parker as associate justice and Charles Evans Hughes as Chief Justice.) Cardozo received further backing from prominent business and labor leaders and academicians, but Hoover still resisted because he did not want to appoint a second Jew (Justice Brandeis, the first, was still on the Court) and a third New Yorker (in addition to Chief Justice Hughes and then-Justice Stone). Nevertheless, needing bipartisan support to get an appointment through the Senate and urged insistently by Senator William Borah to make merit the prime consideration in nominating a justice, Hoover relented and nominated Cardozo in early 1932.[96] Borah's intercession was especially noteworthy, given that he had sacrificed his own self-interest as a western Republican in having someone from his region put on the Court in favor of what he had believed was a purely meritorious appointment. The kind of approach undertaken by Senator Borah regarding Cardozo's appointment to the Supreme Court, combined with the willingness of a majority of senators, beginning at or near the turn of the century, to approve justices from different regions than those from which the retiring justices had come, helped to end the dominant practice in the nineteenth century for presidents and senators to regard seats on the Court as belonging to different regions of the country.

Congressional Oversight of Presidential Bypass
of the Advice and Consent of the Senate

Of course, the Senate's interest (and success) in influencing or directing federal appointments is not confined just to high-level offices — or, for that matter, only to confirmable ones. When presidents have used temporary or recess appointments and other means (such as placing people on their staffs) to bypass the confirmation process, senators have invariably used their other powers, particularly oversight and appropriations, to put pressure on those choices. A dramatic example of this occurred in the nineteenth century with President Lincoln's naming of four different generals to head the Union Army.[97] No doubt, the pressures of winning the Civil War, public anxiety, and trying to maintain civilian control of the military exacerbated the situation. In addition, the House established a special oversight committee that put constant pressure on President Lincoln to take certain actions in dealing with the military and trying to resolve the Civil War in accordance with its wishes and priorities.[98]

Much more recently, President Clinton's record number of chief White House counsels — six in eight years — is clearly attributable at least in part to Congress's intense (and certainly frequently unpleasant) scrutiny of these officials. Similarly, President Clinton has had four chiefs of staff, another record number. No doubt, as the movement of influence toward nonconfirmed figures such as the chief of staff or chief counsel has become more widely known, it has attracted intensified attention from Congress, the media, and interest groups.

Confirmation Contests as Extensions of Policy Disputes

One theme running throughout the history of the federal appointments process is that confirmation hearings are just one more mechanism — along with the appropriations process, legislation, and oversight and investigation — by which senators have tried to influence the direction and substance of national policy. In other words, the confirmation process has always been a forum for extending policy struggles between the president and Congress. The confirmation process has provided excellent opportunities for senators to sensitize nominees about particular issues or values that the latter are likely to confront if confirmed and to extract promises (in public hearings or private meetings) from nominees to nonjudicial offices in exchange for their confirmation. (Concerns about judicial independence seem to have led some senators to avoid exacting precise promises about prospective rulings from judicial nominees, who fend them off in any event by declaring the need to maintain a credible appearance of impartiality in deciding cases.)

The use of confirmation hearings to extend policy disputes between senators and presidents has taken several forms. Two are especially noteworthy — the first is the degree to which such disputes follow the pattern of war, and the second is the hearing as a forum for postelectoral politics.

Confirmation contests as war. Two classics — Carl von Clausewitz's *On War* and Sun Tzu's *The Art of War* — provide a background against which one can identify several features or aspects of war in the appointments process.[99] Some of Sun Tzu's advice — such as learning that anger is a fundamental cause of defeat and the importance to victory of building viable organizations, maintaining discipline within one's troops, and planning ahead — have previously been discussed as some of the lessons presidents have learned from their or their predecessors' experiences in the federal appointments process. Moreover, Sun Tzu's most famous dictum — "To

The Senate

win without fighting is best" — is no doubt appreciated by all major parties involved in the process.[100] For they have all learned one way or another that conflict imposes heavy costs, and they thus prefer to avoid it most of the time by negotiated settlement.

Clausewitz suggested that conflict that produces war arises when intense uncertainty (over likely outcomes) and emotionality (because of the high stakes that each contestant identifies in the outcome) converge. There was, for example, uncertainty over the confirmability of Robert Bork and Clarence Thomas even before they were nominated, because they did not have the luxury that President Reagan's Supreme Court nominees from 1982 through 1986 had of being considered for confirmation by a Republican-controlled Senate. There was also uncertainty about which, if any, Clinton nominees would face stiff confirmation bids in the aftermath of the contests over Bork and Thomas, not to mention those involving several lower-court judges in the last years, respectively, of Reagan's and Bush's presidencies. Moreover, no one doubts that interest groups, party leaders, presidents, and many senators have strong stakes in the outcomes of certain nominations, including those for the Supreme Court or offices responsible for civil rights, environment, and national security.

Once war breaks out, it tends, as Clausewitz suggested, to unfold in certain ways, featuring escalation, dangerous overconfidence, and blunders that can work to the advantage of the blunderer. Again, these aspects of confirmation struggles as war are apparent. The Bork and Thomas hearings are classic illustrations of the escalation involved in such contests; indeed, they escalated to a point at which many observers of the political process claim they are still producing ramifications in the halls of Congress and the White House.

The danger of overconfidence is well illustrated by President Reagan's hasty nomination of Douglas Ginsburg to the Supreme Court and President Clinton's boasts shortly after being elected in 1992 that he would have his cabinet fully appointed by well before Christmas of that year (he didn't) and that his administration would be the most ethically distinguished administration in American history (a claim subject to widespread dispute, particularly after the president's impeachment by the House and acquittal by the Senate for behavior that almost everyone condemned). Another good illustration of dangerous overconfidence is Vice President Calhoun's casting of the decisive vote against Martin Van Buren's nomination to become minister to Great Britain, thinking it would ruin Van Buren and shift administration or popular support to his candidacy for president (he was wrong on both counts). A more recent example is the celebration that Clinton's initial slate of Department of Justice nominees held before the assembled masses of the department on the day of their nomination.

There are many examples of blunders working to the advantage of the blunderer (there are also many counterexamples). For instance, President Clinton's staff missed the fact (and thus the significance) of a surgeon general nominee's having performed abortions as part of his residency and practice. Though the nomination failed, the failure worked to the advantage of the president, who used it against Republicans in his reelection campaign. President Nixon's nomination of Harrold Carswell to the Court illustrates a counterexample of the problems that can arise when a president yields to his anger.

Confirmation contests as illustrations of postelectoral politics. If, as Clausewitz suggested, war is a continuation of politics by other means,[101] it is by no means the only such continuation. According to Benjamin Ginsberg and Martin Shefter, there is "a new technique of political combat — revelation, investigation, and prosecution,"[102] that has coincided, in their view, with the declining importance of presidential elections. Though it is uncertain that the latter have declined nearly to the extent as the two political scientists claim, it is clear that the phenomenon of investigations as political tools has flourished and that a variation of it has extended (along with the proliferation over the last few decades of ethics laws) to the confirmation process. Indeed, senators have always used the confirmation process to continue disputes that began in presidential elections. The inordinate delays in the confirmation process for many of President Clinton's judicial nominations, for example, are attributable at least in part to the suspicion of many interest group leaders and senators that President Clinton is really interested in appointing liberal judges rather than the moderates that he promised as a candidate (and again as president) to appoint. Consequently, some interest groups and many senators (or their staffs) examine judicial candidates' speeches, articles, and activities at least as closely as they look at the nominees' tax records to uncover problematic attitudes or behavior (in terms of the likelihood of how these nominees would perform on the bench).

Many confirmation hearings reflect the extension of disputes begun in presidential campaigns. For example, Senator Jesse Helms's opposition to President Clinton's nomination of Duke law professor Walter Dellinger to become assistant attorney general in charge of the Office of Legal Counsel was based in part on Dellinger's well-known support for *Roe v. Wade*, reflecting a dispute that dated back to the 1992 election in which candidate Clinton vowed to pursue policies and nominate people who supported the right to have an abortion while the party platform of his major opponent, then-President Bush, endorsed the appointment of judges and other officials who favored pro-life policies.

The prolonged investigation and consequent delay of a final Senate vote on President Clinton's nomination of Richard Holbrooke to become the U.S. ambassador to the United Nations is an excellent example of the extension of "postelectoral politics" into the confirmation process as Ginsburg and Shefter have conceived it. In June 1998, the president selected Holbrooke to succeed Bill Richardson as the United Nations ambassador, but the nomination was not forwarded to the Senate until February 1999 to allow the State and Justice Departments to investigate an anonymous tip that Holbrooke might have accepted speaking fees in violation of certain conflict-of-interest rules during the short period between his departure from his post as undersecretary of state for European and Canadian affairs and his nomination to become the U.S. ambassador to the United Nations. On April 30, 1999, the State Department cleared Holbrooke of any wrongdoing. Nevertheless, Senator Helms refused to hold confirmation hearings for Holbrooke until the Foreign Relations Committee had had a chance to review the records of the Justice Department's probe of Holbrooke (who in the interim had been accused of other conflict-of-interest violations). In June 1999, the Foreign Relations Committee finally held confirmation hearings for Holbrooke during which he acknowledged paying a small fine imposed by the Justice Department for his ethical violations and profusely apologized for any mistakes in judgment that he had made. He promised to conduct himself in the future in full compliance with all ethics laws and also agreed to work with Helms, if confirmed, to implement several recommendations that Helms's committee had made (and the administration had agreed in 1998 to implement) to overhaul the United Nations. The Foreign Relations Committee eventually voted to recommend Holbrooke's nomination to the full Senate. While some Republican senators urged a rapid confirmation so that Holbrooke could help to resolve the crisis in the Balkans, opposition to Holbrooke's confirmation persisted throughout most of the summer of 1999 as Republican leaders continued to oppose the nomination based on the president's Balkans policy, concerns about Holbrooke's compliance with ethics laws, and disagreement over the administration's support for Planned Parenthood funding. In one way or another, these issues can all be traced back to complaints made during the 1992 and 1996 presidential elections about the president's foreign policy, his character, and his support for some liberal interest groups. Though the Senate eventually confirmed Holbrooke eighty-one to sixteen on August 5, 1999, he is typical of the numerous presidential nominees who have become targets or proxies in disputes between the president and senators. The ways in which nominees can be treated as such targets are explored further in the next chapter.

Chapter Six

THE NOMINEE'S FUNCTIONS

THE CONSTITUTION EXPLICITLY recognizes only three actors as being formally involved in the federal appointments process: the president ("who shall nominate officers of the United States"); the Senate (which shall provide its "advice and consent" on such nominations); and those nominated by the president, subject to Senate confirmation, as "officers of the United States."[1] Lacking formal authority over the fate of their appointments, nominees generally have received the least amount of attention in studies of the major actors in the federal appointments process. Moreover, the Constitution specifies nothing about the qualifications nominees must or should have in order to be nominated or confirmed, leaving the responsibility to the president and the Senate to work out between themselves the requisite qualifications for various offices. Although the Constitution also says nothing explicitly about what, if any, functions nominees should perform in the appointments process (other than the obvious ones of being nominated and being eligible after nomination for consideration by the Senate for confirmation), the Constitution clearly allows the Senate to require nominees to participate in some fashion in confirmation hearings pursuant to the Constitution's grant of authority to the Senate to develop and adopt rules for its own proceedings.

Perhaps the most vexing question involving the nominee's role in the federal appointments process is the extent of the nominee's influence over his or her nomination or confirmation. Personal and institutional analyses can answer this question by explaining and evaluating the functions that nominees may perform in the federal appointments process. It makes sense to analyze nominees in personal terms because they have personal stakes in their own appointments and because a basic purpose of the process is for senators, the public, and the media to get to know nominees personally. Moreover, support for or opposition to nominees often turns on their personal characteristics or accomplishments.

Yet, it is also important to understand that analyzing nominees in personal terms provides only a limited glimpse into the functions they may perform in the federal appointments process. Whether they are seeking to get nominated or to be confirmed, the people who become nominees, like presidents and senators, do not operate in a vacuum. To wend their way through the system nominees need to marshal certain institutional powers. It is difficult, if not impossible, to understand fully the fates, functions, and roles of nominees in the appointments process without analyzing what they have done to get appointed and what has been done for and to them within the larger framework in which confirmation disputes arise.

Figuring out this larger framework, including evaluating how nominees have been able to influence or control their own appointments, requires clarifying the primary functions nominees have performed in the federal appointments process. The first section of this chapter examines each of these functions, including the lessons nominees have learned from their own and others' experiences. The second section examines the kinds of people who have been nominated and confirmed. The kinds of people who become nominees, particularly successful ones, illustrate the dynamics of the federal appointments process.

THE ROLES OF NOMINEES

Nominees have tended to perform one of two primary functions in the federal appointments process: they have either functioned passively as objects or targets around or against which different groups, people, or institutions have rallied; or they have functioned actively as actors lobbying or testifying on their own behalf and organizing support for their nominations or confirmations. Below I examine the nature, implications, and limitations of each of these functions.

The Nominee as Object

Once a presidential nomination has been made, the presumption of confirmation—the likelihood or propensity of senatorial deference—generally provides a structural public impediment to its undoing. The presumption is not easily or lightly overcome, particularly in the case of high-profile offices or nominees, especially if the nomination can get to the floor of the Senate. The outcomes of past confirmation proceedings suggest that the more distinguished a nominee or the higher the profile of the office being filled, the bigger or more numerous are the kinds of problems necessary to weaken or defeat the nominee's confirmation. History further suggests that the more accomplished a nominee is, the bigger the target he or she will be in a confirmation hearing; that is, the more substantial a nominee's public record of activities, the greater the likelihood that he or she has done things that will merit support or trigger opposition in the Senate. In practice, this means that by the time a nomination of a person with a substantial record of accomplishments reaches the floor of the Senate, the nomination will rarely fail for a single reason, unless it is a very compelling one.

A single disqualifying factor is much more likely to undo someone's chances to be nominated (or to get past a committee and reach the Senate floor) than it is to cause the nominee's formal rejection by the Senate. The reason is that until the formal announcement of a nomination, a prospective nominee primarily has to convince only one person—the president—to make the nomination; and the president, who has not yet invested political capital in the nominee, can decide for any reason he deems appropriate to change his mind and nominate a different candidate.

The presumption of confirmation embodied in the Constitution generally puts the onus on those interested in impeding a nomination to mobilize opposition to it. With respect to high-profile nominees or offices, such mobilization requires objections with broad enough appeal to attract a critical mass of senators to stand (often publicly) in opposition to the president's formal exercise of his nominating authority. With respect to lower-profile nominees or lower-ranking offices (such as the federal district courts), less mobilization is required because it is less likely that the public generally will be aware of, much less care about, any dangers or problems with delaying the nomination. Consequently, lower-profile nominations can be frustrated much earlier in the process than those of higher-profile people in the higher-profile offices.

For example, it took several problems to force Justice Abe Fortas to withdraw his nomination as Chief Justice. Fortas was a formidable nominee. He graduated at the top of his class at Yale Law School, became a name partner in one of the country's most prestigious law firms and a distinguished Supreme Court advocate, and served with distinction in government in several positions, including as an associate justice on the Supreme Court.[2] When Fortas's nomination to become Chief Justice failed, it failed for several reasons: the timing was bad (he had been nominated by President Johnson, who was an unpopular lame duck at the time); Fortas's nomination was widely perceived as political payback rather than a merit appointment, a perception reinforced by the fact that at the same time he nominated Fortas President Johnson nominated another old friend, Judge Homer Thornberry, for the Supreme Court vacancy that would arise if Fortas were confirmed as Chief Justice; and Fortas had taken (but later returned) a consulting fee from an indicted financier.[3]

Almost two decades later, the Senate rejected Robert Bork's nomination as an associate justice by the largest margin of any Supreme Court nominee in U.S. history. The rejection occurred in spite of Judge Bork's distinguished record. He was a Yale Law School professor and one of the nation's leading antitrust and constitutional law scholars; solicitor general in the Nixon administration; partner in a leading Washington, D.C., law firm; and a federal court of appeals judge.[4] The nomination failed because, as Stephen Carter observes, Bork "had much to answer for,"[5] including his opposition to desegregation; his firing of Watergate Special Prosecutor Archibald Cox; his claim that a number of historic precedents not grounded in original intent, such as *Brown v. Board of Education*, lacked "legitimacy"; and his inconsistent testimony during his confirmation hearing.[6]

What kinds of problems are likely to impede or obstruct nominations? The most potent factor is the nominee's record. That this should be so is hardly a surprise, for the basic issue in a confirmation hearing is the suitability of a particular nominee to assume a specific post. To the extent that a nominee exemplifies very appealing or enviable traits or can make a positive impression on a critical mass of senators, he or she has a greater chance for successful confirmation. The more appealing the public image, the greater the chance for confirmation. For instance, Justice Scalia's status as the first Italian American nominated to the Supreme Court clearly worked in favor of his confirmation. Moreover, a significant factor in Clarence Thomas's confirmation was the so-called Pin Point strategy, which required Thomas to remind the senators on the Judiciary Committee whenever possible about his difficult childhood and upbringing in Pin Point, Georgia, in order to keep them from focusing the hearings on his public record.[7] More recently, President Clinton's characterization of Ruth Bader Ginsburg as the "Thurgood Marshall of the feminist movement" helped to build support for her at the outset of her hearings by portraying her as a progressive lawyer and jurist who had paid her dues.[8]

Conversely, demonizing a nominee is the most common way to frustrate his or her chances for confirmation. Making the case that something personal about a nominee ought to be of substantial concern or poses a serious danger to the public is the surest way to weaken support for or to organize opposition to a nomination. The critical safeguard insofar as the president is concerned is that he makes the ultimate decision regarding whom to nominate. He has the power to set the initial terms of debate or discussion in a confirmation hearing. The challenge for the opposition is to tear apart or find some glaring flaw in the portrait that the president has constructed of his nominee.

Consequently, the institutional and other actors working for or against confirmation (including interest groups and political parties) have found that linking some personal or private flaw of a nominee to some public concern, especially a heated issue of the moment, provides a crucial basis for mobilizing opposition. The more easily articulable or more immediate the danger that a particular appointment poses to some public interest because of some private lapse, the more potent is the attack. For instance, John Rutledge's strident criticism of the Jay treaty, which had become, in the words of Charles Warren, "a touchstone of Federalism,"[9] naturally provoked—indeed, it virtually invited—considerable opposition to his nomination from the treaty's supporters in the Senate; and Rutledge's opponents went further to characterize Rutledge's stridency as reflecting a mental instability that disqualified him for the Court.

Similarly, no sooner had President Reagan's nomination of Robert Bork to the Supreme Court been made official than Senator Ted Kennedy pronounced the dangers of living in "Robert Bork's America."[10] This warning became the rallying cry for widespread opposition to the nomination. In 1993, Lani Guinier's nomination as assistant attorney general for the Civil Rights Division was scuttled in part because of the threat she posed to white America as one of the president's "quota queens."[11]

Less than a year after President Clinton was reelected, General John Ralston was forced to withdraw his nomination as the chair of the Joint Chiefs of Staff because he was viewed as a hypocrite. Ralston had failed to show how his participation in an extramarital affair (while he was separated from a woman whom he ultimately divorced) differed from a well-publicized case in which a female pilot had been forced to leave the U.S. Air Force because she had engaged in an affair with another air force officer who had been married at the time.[12] Ralston's perceived hypocrisy reinforced the appearance of a double standard in the armed forces because Secretary of Defense William Cohen had both recommended Ralston for the promotion in spite of Ralston's misconduct and approved the decisions to oust the female pilot from the air force and to deny her an honorable discharge on the basis of what seemed to many to be misconduct exactly like Ralston's. Similarly, in 1999 Charles Curtis stopped his nomination to become secretary of the air force from going forward after it became apparent that the nomination would face stiff opposition because as a Department of Energy (DOE) official Curtis had responded with seeming indifference to some Republican senators' concerns about the lax security at some DOE nuclear labs. Subsequent revelations of Chinese thefts of national security secrets from some of these labs turned Curtis's seeming indifference from an honest mistake into a fatal problem for his confirmation.

In fact, as judicial and other kinds of nominees have discovered, their personal backgrounds, traits, or records can be exploited in at least four different ways. First, a nominee's unethical conduct may either exhibit a lack of judgment or deprive the nominee of the moral authority necessary to exercise the power of office. For instance, Justice Fortas's lapse in accepting a substantial fee raised by dubious means for teaching a seminar clearly undermined his support.[13] Two other relevant examples here are Clement Haynsworth's failures to divest himself of all corporate directorships on first being confirmed for a federal appellate judgeship and to recuse himself from all cases in which he had a direct financial interest in the business of one of the litigants,[14] and Douglas Ginsburg's smoking marijuana as a tenured Harvard Law School professor. Moreover, charges of philandering and excessive drinking led the Senate to reject one of its own, Senator John Tower, as President Bush's secretary of defense.

Several of the Clinton administration's nominations were complicated or undone by charges of personal misconduct by the nominees. For instance, President Clinton's nominee to head the CIA, Michael Carns, withdrew his nomination after he admitted that he had provided false information to the U.S. embassy in the Philippines and to the Immigration and Naturalization Service in order to secure a visa to allow a Filipino citizen to come to the United States to live with Carns's family.[15] Even more recently, federal district judge James Ware withdrew his nomination by President Clinton to the Ninth Circuit after admitting that he had lied for some years about his connection to the fatal shooting of a young African American boy in 1963 by white racists in Alabama. Judge Ware had said that the shooting victim was his brother and that he had witnessed the shooting; neither claim was true.[16] President Clinton agreed to withdraw his nomination of Hassan Nemazee as ambassador to Brazil after press inquiries produced indications that Nemazee had engaged in suspicious business dealings.[17] In addition, charges of ethical lapses made against President Clinton's nominee for U.S. ambassador to the United Nations, Richard Holbrooke, stalled the nomination for more than a year. Holbrooke's profuse apologies for these lapses ultimately proved sufficient to ensure his final confirmation by the Senate. With the exception of Holbrooke (whose nomination enjoyed relatively widespread bipartisan support based on his prior service in the State Department), support for the nominees began to weaken once the charges were made and to crumble once the charges were confirmed.

Second, nominees' political views or records can be used either to bolster or to defeat their nominations. The political views of a nonjudicial nominee can become a target because they provide an easy way to retaliate against the president for holding the same views or because they are controversial in their own right. For instance, President Carter was forced to withdraw his nomination of Ted Sorensen to head the Central Intelligence Agency partly because of widespread doubt about the compatibility of Sorensen's self-declared pacifism with the official duties of the CIA director. Similarly, the Senate Judiciary Committee rejected President Reagan's nomination of Brad Reynolds as associate attorney general because it disapproved of the ideological direction in which Reynolds had been trying to take the Justice Department's Civil Rights Division.[18] The subsequent nominations of William Lucas by President Bush and Lani Guinier and Bill Lann Lee by President Clinton to head that division failed because some senators had problems with the nominees' views on and records in dealing with civil rights issues.

The political views of a judicial nominee frequently generate opposition because they are controversial in their own right or because they signal a controversial judicial ideology. At least ten of the twenty-nine Supreme Court nominations thus far rejected or forced to be withdrawn failed in part for this reason.[19]

An example of this phenomenon involving a lower-court judicial nominee is James Beatty, a federal district judge in North Carolina whom President Clinton nominated to the Fourth Circuit in 1995. If confirmed, Beatty would have been the first African American to serve on the Fourth Circuit. Beatty's potential as a historic appointment made it appealing to some senators and constituencies, but for more than two years the nomination stalled because Senator Helms (in whose state and circuit Beatty serves) had concerns that Beatty was too soft on crime based on Beatty's vote to overrule a murder conviction while sitting by designation on a Fourth Circuit panel, a vote that was later overturned by the Fourth Circuit en banc. Another of Senator Helms's objections to Beatty's nomination was Helms's belief that the Fourth Circuit had more seats than its caseload warranted, including the vacancy to which Beatty had been nominated. Moreover, Helms objected to the nomination in retaliation against President Clinton's failure to nominate another federal district judge in North Carolina who Helms believed was deserving of a seat on the Fourth Circuit. Though Beatty's nomination was resubmitted to

The Nominee

Congress in 1997, the president did not resubmit it in either 1998 or 1999, effectively nullifying it.

Another example of a judicial nominee's personal beliefs or political record undoing his nomination involves Michael Schattman, a former state judge nominated by President Clinton in 1995 to a federal district judgeship in Dallas. Schattman had been a state court trial judge from 1979 until 1996, when he resigned his position in anticipation of his confirmation as a federal trial judge. Schattman had attended Georgetown University as an undergraduate with President Clinton and went to the 1992 Democratic convention as a delegate pledged to Clinton. The opposition to Judge Schattman was not, however, based on his judicial record or his long-standing friendship with the president; it was based on Schattman's heavy involvement in state Democratic politics (even though he had to be involved because he was an elected judge) and his having been a conscientious objector during the Vietnam War. The latter was regarded as problematic by Schattman's opponents, including Texas's two senators, both Republicans, who construed it as signifying that Schattman would not be impartial in cases involving defense contractors or their employees in the Dallas federal courts. Lawyers who represented defense contractors in Judge Schattman's court rejected the assertion that Judge Schattman could not be impartial in cases involving their clients, calling it "preposterous."[20] Nevertheless, Schattman withdrew his nomination in mid-1998 when it became apparent that those opposing his nomination would not allow it to come to a final vote in the Senate.[21]

The third attribute that can be used to weaken or defeat nominations is one over which nominees have least control: opposition as payback. Seniority among senators and longtime staffers, in addition to the employment of a full-time parliamentarian, ensure that the Senate has developed a strong institutional memory when it comes to past incidents within the confirmation process. Consequently, it is not uncommon for senators (sometimes comprising a critical mass) to mobilize against a nomination as payback for some earlier injustice. While it is difficult to document the full extent to which such paybacks have occurred (because many senators have not wanted to disclose that as the real reason for their opposition), it is possible to find some public acknowledgments of this practice. For instance, at least thirteen Democratic senators claimed that their opposition to President Nixon's nomination of Clement Haynsworth was payback for the forced withdrawal of President Johnson's nomination of Abe Fortas not long before. These senators believed that Fortas had been forced to withdraw in part because of ethical lapses that were far less serious in their estimation than those they believed Haynsworth had committed.[22]

The absence of any desire for payback helps to explain to some degree why the Senate, in contrast to its decision with respect to Judge Haynsworth's nomination, confirmed Justice Stephen Breyer. Shortly after Breyer was nominated to the Court, some senators and reporters raised questions about whether he had committed ethical lapses as a judge: he had failed to pay Social Security taxes on his domestic help, and he had made rulings in eight cases involving environmental cleanup costs that could have conceivably helped his investment in Lloyd's of London.[23] However, Breyer weathered the storm: he was popular with senators from both parties (based in part on his work as chief counsel to the Senate Judiciary Committee and as a member of the U.S. Sentencing Commission), and his distinguished credentials as a Harvard law professor, leading administrative law scholar, and well-regarded federal judge outweighed any doubts about his character, integrity, or qualifications.[24]

Senator Jesse Helms stalled President Clinton's nomination of Walter Dellinger as assistant attorney general for a few months in 1993 because Helms believed that, among other things, Dellinger had helped Democrats on the Senate Judiciary Committee to build a case against the confirmation of Robert Bork. Similarly, Senator Charles Grassley stalled the nomination of Merrick Garland to the U.S. Court of Appeals for the District of Columbia for well over two years in part because of Grassley's desire for revenge on Democratic colleagues who had blocked final Senate action on President Bush's nomination of John Roberts to the same court.[25]

Payback is also, of course, a problem for nominees to executive or administrative offices. For instance, J. Brian Atwood withdrew his nomination by President Clinton as ambassador to Brazil after Senator Helms declared steadfast opposition to it because Atwood had resisted Helms's measures to bring the U.S. Agency for International Development (which Atwood had headed at the time) into the State Department.[26]

The Nominee

The final factor that can be used to mobilize support for or against nominations is a nominee's level of skill. In many respects this is the most difficult ground on which to object to a nomination, because no consensus exists on the appropriate qualifications for most confirmable positions. Moreover, a credible case can be made for the competence of almost any nominee. Even so, establishing a nominee's lack of appropriate qualifications for the position to which he or she has been nominated is potentially fatal. For instance, the Senate rejected President Nixon's nomination of Harrold Carswell partly on the ground that Carswell simply was not qualified to sit on the Supreme Court.[27] Serious doubts about Ted Sorensen's qualifications were another factor leading President Carter to withdraw his nomination to become director of the CIA.[28] Serious questions about Zoë Baird's qualifications to be attorney general weakened her chances for confirmation.[29] A similar argument hurt but did not ultimately lead to the rejection of Clarence Thomas's nomination to the Supreme Court.[30] In 1998, the Senate Judiciary Committee favorably reported on the nomination of Frederica Massiah-Jackson, a state court judge, to be a U.S. district court judge in Philadelphia, but she was subsequently forced to withdraw her nomination after it had been placed on indefinite hold because many Republican senators persistently charged that her judicial record reflected "bias against police, [bias in favor of giving] excessive leniency for criminals, and [too many instances of] profanity on the bench."[31]

Attacks on a nominee sometimes backfire to the president's or nominee's advantage. Attacking a nominee because of public problems posed by his or her alleged personal shortcomings can help to turn the nominee into a martyr. The martyr syndrome is a phenomenon that occurs when a nominee is attacked publicly on the basis of some personal trait, such as political philosophy, that it is in the president's interest or advantage to defend. A loss can sometimes be turned into a victory when it builds sympathy for both the defeated nominee and the disappointed president. Perhaps the most dramatic example of this phenomenon is the fallout from the Senate's rejection of President Jackson's nomination of Martin Van Buren to become minister to Great Britain. No sooner had Van Buren been defeated than many observers of the American political scene predicted that his political career was made.[32] Jackson turned defeat into victory by publicly extolling Van Buren's virtues and blaming his defeat on Jackson's political enemies. By naming Van Buren as his running mate in 1832, Jackson guaranteed Van Buren's status as his successor.

President Jackson similarly turned defeat into victory after the Senate rejected his nomination of Attorney General Roger Taney as secretary of the treasury. Roughly a year later, Jackson repaid Taney by nominating him to become Chief Justice, and Jackson's Democrats, who held a slim majority in the Senate, rewarded Taney for his loyal service by confirming the nomination.[33]

A more recent example of the martyr syndrome is President Clinton's nomination of Henry Foster as surgeon general. Opposition to Foster initially formed within the Senate because he had performed abortions and had misstated the number of abortions he had done as an obstetrician.[34] Defending Foster on the ground that the abortions he had performed had been both necessary and constitutional worked to the president's political advantage; thus, he supported the nomination in spite of the fact that it was doomed almost from the start. The loss helped to confirm for the public President Clinton's resolve not to compromise in a case involving abortion rights.

An even more recent instance of the martyr syndrome (or at least of an attempt to cultivate it) involves President Clinton's nomination of Republican governor William Weld of Massachusetts as ambassador to Mexico in July 1997. Well before the nomination was formally announced, Senator Jesse Helms had declared his opposition to it. Helms (and other conservative Republicans) opposed the nomination because he believed that Weld's support for legalizing the medicinal use of marijuana and needle exchanges for addicts undercut the credibility Weld would need to have in order to work effectively with the Mexican government to stop the flow of illegal drugs into the United States.[35] Helms also believed that Weld's support for abortion and gay rights did not make him an appropriate representative of American values. In Helms's view, Weld's politics simply did not make him "ambassador quality."[36] In a surprising response to Senator Helms's threatened opposition, Weld publicly accused the senator of "ideological extortion" and declared that he was not nor did he want to be "Senator Helms' kind of Republican."[37] Shortly after making this announcement, Weld resigned the Massachusetts governorship to fight full time for his nomination as ambassador to Mexico. By

The Nominee

all accounts, Weld's public statements seemed to have ensured that his nomination was dead on arrival.

There was, however, good reason for Weld's apparent madness in resigning his governorship and publicly chastising Senator Helms. Weld's aides explained that the resignation was "part of a campaign to win himself the posting in Mexico City or highlight his longheld belief that the Republican Party must be more inclusive if it hopes to regain the White House."[38] They calculated that if Weld were somehow to win the nomination, he would look as if he were rising above partisan politics to be of service to an administration led by a member of the opposition party. If Weld were to lose the nomination, they believed he still could look as if he had won, because he might have been able to put a spotlight on some critical political differences between himself and Helms—differences that would reflect a larger divide between conservative Republicans (as represented by Helms) and moderate or liberal Republicans (as represented by Weld). In other words, Weld and his aides figured that he could help his own cause by trying to position himself as—and look as if he had paid a price for being—a leader of the moderate wing of the Republican party. (Nor was this the first time Weld had put himself in such a position. In 1988, he resigned as associate attorney general in the Reagan Justice Department to protest then–Attorney General Edwin Meese's decision to remain in office while being investigated by an independent counsel.[39] In 1992 and 1996, Weld made waves during the Republican national conventions by calling for a plank supporting abortion rights.)

In the end, Weld miscalculated. He failed to become a martyr for several reasons. First, the public showed little concern or interest in the fate of his nomination. The position at stake was not one about which Americans apparently had much concern. Moreover, Republicans mostly avoided making public displays of divisions within their party. In addition, Weld's attitude that he could take or leave the Massachusetts governorship did not endear him to the public. Nor did the president rally publicly to Weld's defense, thereby leaving Weld almost largely on his own in his quixotic quest. Weld also was not aided by the first lady, a friend of his since their service together as staffers on the House Judiciary Committee in 1974.

An example of someone who has in all likelihood successfully become a martyr is James Hormel, whom President Clinton nominated as ambassador to Luxemberg. Hormel's nomination was put indefinitely on hold by a few Republican senators who objected to Hormel's open homosexuality. On other grounds, the Senate Foreign Relations Committee had found Hormel suitable, as reflected by its sixteen-to-two vote to approve him as ambassador and by the Luxemborg government's signal to the Clinton administration that it would welcome Hormel in that post. The intransigence of the opposition led President Clinton to make Hormel the ambassador to Luxemborg by means of a recess appointment. At Hormel's swearing-in ceremony, Secretary of State Madeleine Albright used the occasion to emphasize, "Today, we do send a message that neither race nor creed nor gender nor sexual orientation is relevant to the selection of an ambassador of the United States."[40] There is little doubt that the Democrats will resurrect the controversy over the appointment as an issue in the presidential election of 2000.

A nomination is sometimes undone not because of the nominee's personal shortcomings, but because it is turned into a fight over some unpopular policy or program of the president's. The more closely the nominee is linked to the unpopular program or policy, the easier it is to mobilize or organize opposition to the nomination. Moreover, the more unpopular a president or program, the likelier it is that a nominee closely associated with one or the other will be challenged to pay the price for that unpopularity. Opposing a nominee because of a desire to punish the president has two advantages insofar as the Senate is concerned: the president can do little or nothing to prevent it, and it can arise whenever the Senate considers a nomination and thus is difficult for the president to plan for.

Numerous nominees have run into trouble because of this problem. A small sample from the nineteenth century includes the Senate's rejections of Roger Taney's nominations by President Jackson to become secretary of the treasury and subsequently associate justice, the Senate's rejections of four of President Jackson's nominees to become directors of the Bank of the United States in 1833,[41] the Senate's rejection of Caleb Cushing's nomination to become secretary of the treasury each of the three times it was made by President Tyler in a single day in 1843,[42] the Senate's rejections of five of President Tyler's nominations to the Supreme Court, the Senate's rejections of three nominations made by President Millard

Fillmore to fill a single vacancy on the Supreme Court in 1852, and the Senate's rejection of President James Buchanan's nomination of Jeremiah Black to the Supreme Court in 1860.

Nominees as Active Agents on Their Own Behalf

Nominees have taken action on their own behalf in every phase of the federal appointments process, but especially so with respect to getting nominated in the first place. Nominees are rarely passive figures in the selection process. It is quite common for potential nominees to wage campaigns to get themselves nominated or to have others wage such campaigns on their behalf. Unfortunately, a good deal of the negotiating or maneuvering that culminates in a nomination tends to occur behind closed doors (except to the extent that the media reports leaks or makes guesses about nominations likely to be made by an administration), and it is often left to historians to enlighten subsequent generations on the precise reasons for certain presidential choices. Nevertheless, an excellent illustration of a successful campaign is the one waged by Martin Ginsburg, a prominent and well-connected tax professor at Georgetown University, to secure President Clinton's nomination of Ginsburg's wife, Judge Ruth Bader Ginsburg, to the Supreme Court.[43] Working with influential senators from both parties, including Senator Moynihan, the influential chair of the Senate Finance Committee (critical to the success of President Clinton's first-term budget-cutting and health reform plans), Professor Ginsburg worked to keep his wife's candidacy alive until she was the only prominent choice acceptable to all sides at the end of the president's unusually long search for a successor to replace Justice Byron White.[44]

A notable example of an unsuccessful campaign is the intense letter writing and personal lobbying through which Justice Felix Frankfurter in 1942 tried to persuade President Roosevelt to nominate Judge Learned Hand to the Supreme Court. Although Justice Frankfurter's tactics had been effective in securing a variety of different nominations for his friends and ideological allies in the past, his campaign on behalf of Hand was virtually doomed from the start for several reasons: Justice Frankfurter no longer wielded significant influence with the president; Judge Hand was seventy-two, and thus his appointment would have made Roosevelt look like a hypocrite for having lobbied Congress in 1937 to adopt his own Court-packing plan, which opposed septuagenarian justices;[45] Judge Hand's age made him unlikely to serve for long on the Court; Hand's appointment would likely have strengthened, insofar as Roosevelt was concerned, the wrong wing—that is, Frankfurter's wing—of the Court, which was resistant to judicial enforcement of noneconomic liberty claims; and Judge Hand had never been the kind of party loyalist the president preferred to nominate to the Court.[46] Instead, President Roosevelt chose to nominate Wiley Rutledge, then forty-eight, to the Court. Ironically, Justice Rutledge died six years after his appointment, and Hand outlived him by twelve years.

People who have worked closely with a president, have made significant contributions to a campaign, or have accomplished something noteworthy in an administration are well positioned to wage campaigns on their own (or their friends') behalf for important appointments. Although insiders in an administration sometimes find themselves at a disadvantage because they are already known commodities (and thus their liabilities are well known to other administration officials or senators from either party), such appointments have been legion throughout U.S. history. This is especially true at times—such as a presidential election year in which the sitting president is up for reelection—when an administration wants to get positions filled quickly or to avoid wasting precious political coinage.

Nominees have learned, however, that politicking on their own behalf (or against others interested in the same position) can backfire unless it is done with delicacy and tact. Some aspiring nominees have hurt, if not effectively killed, their chances for appointment by appearing to be too interested in self-promotion (as opposed to public service) or too covetous of the position (and the power that goes with it). Some prospective nominees have inflicted damage on their chances to be nominated by mishandling questions or misrepresenting themselves in the interview phase or background check.

For example, after Zoë Baird's forced withdrawal, President Clinton had narrowed his choice for attorney general to Judge Kimba Wood. Judge Wood did not get the nomination, however, because she lost the president's confidence when she failed to give a frank answer to an inquiry

The Nominee

195

about whether she had a "Zoë Baird problem." Even though she, unlike Baird, had legally hired an illegal alien, the president and his advisers felt that Wood should not be nominated for two reasons: first, they believed the public would oppose the nomination because illegal aliens were increasingly entering the country at that time and taking jobs away from legal residents; and, second, they thought Judge Wood either should have had sufficient political acumen to know this or should have been disposed to confide as much information as possible to White House personnel so that they could assess the political ramifications of her nomination.[47]

An even more striking example of lack of candor undoing a nomination involves Judge Douglas Ginsburg, whom President Reagan nominated to the Supreme Court in 1987 shortly after the Senate rejected Robert Bork. Judge Ginsburg, who had received his appointment to the U.S. Court of Appeals for the District of Columbia after having served in two other confirmable offices in the Reagan administration, had been through several background checks prior to his nomination to the Court.[48] Nevertheless, he had failed to make two important disclosures during these examinations. First, in spite of direct questioning on the subject, he failed to disclose that he had used marijuana as a tenured law professor at Harvard Law School.[49] Once this failure was made public, Republican senators who had wanted the president to appoint, and were determined to support, only a tough law-and-order judge for the Supreme Court withdrew their support for Judge Ginsburg.[50] Moreover, Judge Ginsburg's failure to disclose the fact that his wife had performed abortions during her residency further alienated some Republican senators, who did not want to vote for a Supreme Court nominee who had explicitly or implicitly approved the performance of abortions.[51] Only nine days after he had been nominated to the Court, Judge Ginsburg was forced to withdraw.

Politicking or campaigning for appointive office sometimes produces statements or activities that can become fodder for one side or another in a confirmation hearing. A prominent example of this phenomenon is Robert Bork, who as a federal court of appeals judge on the D.C. circuit frequently courted conservative political figures or interest groups who wielded influence with those responsible in the Reagan administration for making recommendations on possible Supreme Court nominees.[52] More than once during his confirmation hearings Judge Bork was confronted

with statements he had made in speeches or before conservative political groups declaring what he would or would not do if appointed to the
Supreme Court.[53] Bork's comments posed a problem for him in the confirmation process because he was forced either to embrace them (and thus
alienate completely much of the Democratic majority of the Senate) or
distance himself from them (and thus put his credibility in doubt). In opting largely to do the latter, Bork helped to create the image of what some
of his critics began to refer in the hearings as Bork's "confirmation con-
version," that is, his abandonment of previously stated views for the sake
of securing final approval by the Senate.[54] In his quest to be nominated to
the Supreme Court, Judge Bork created a record that came back to haunt
him in his confirmation hearings.

In a more complicated sequence of events, Lani Guinier, President
Clinton's initial nominee to head the Justice Department's Civil Rights
Division in 1993, did several things after her nomination that undermined
her confirmation. For instance, her behavior on the day of her nomination undoubtedly provoked hostility among conservative Republicans and
interest groups. She treated her first public appearance as a nominee as
a kind of pep rally by proclaiming to loud cheers from the audience her
plans to take aggressive action to vindicate civil rights and to reverse the
Reagan and Bush records on civil rights enforcement.[55] This challenge
echoed throughout the halls of the Senate in subsequent months as Guinier tried to defend herself against charges that she had a radical civil
rights agenda. Although Guinier was hurt in the course of defending herself by the president's silence, she hurt herself further by her inadequate
defense of her own views. For example, she often suggested that her position on voting rights was similar to her four-year-old son Nikolas's suggestion about how to resolve a situation in which six children disagreed
over which game to play, with four wanting to play tag and two wishing
to play hide-and-seek. As Guinier later explained in her book, "Nikolas . . . replied, 'They will play both. First they will play tag. Then they
will play hide-and-seek.' [He] was right. To children, it's natural to take
turns. The winner may get to play first or more often, but even the 'loser'
gets something. His was a positive-sum solution that many adult rule-
makers ignore."[56] The problem with this story was that it suggested that
it was permissible to guarantee the losers in a popular election a substan-

The Nominee

tive outcome regardless of the reason for their preference or loss. Even if the story could somehow have been fairly construed to make a point about the need to redraw voting districts with a history of past discrimination to ensure minority voters a fairer process rather than a substantive outcome, it is hard to see why people concerned about Guinier's voting rights stance should have found the tale reassuring.

Once a nomination has formally reached the Senate, nominees can still help their own cause. It is quite common, for example, for nominees to work behind the scenes putting together a strategy for countering criticisms or otherwise keeping opposition to a minimum and mobilizing sufficient support within the Senate. Even nominees who do not make personal appearances on their own behalf are rarely passive observers of the confirmation phase. For instance, even though Louis Brandeis did not testify or make any public statements on his own behalf during his Supreme Court confirmation proceedings, he nevertheless worked behind the scenes (with the help of many friends as well as the personal involvement of President Wilson and the daily oversight of Attorney General T. W. Gregory) to ensure his confirmation. Among other things, Brandeis fed useful information to friendly senators, helped to cultivate good press, and prepared his law partner to testify in response to some of the charges made against Brandeis.[57]

Along with the expectation that they will be required to make personal appearances before the Senate comes a challenge for nominees to avoid doing or saying something that will make it easier for those disposed to oppose a nomination to overcome the presumption of confirmation with which nominations are usually cloaked. Generally, nominees have fared better in confirmation hearings by making themselves into the smallest targets possible. The most effective strategy has usually been for nominees to say less publicly rather than more, or at least to avoid expressing controversial opinions. For instance, Justice Scalia avoided making any waves in his confirmation hearings by saying as little as possible about his likely judicial ideology. Although this tactic frustrated the Senate Judiciary Committee, it also deprived them of a target. (Justice Scalia was already an elusive target because he was nominated at the same time that President Reagan nominated William Rehnquist to become Chief Justice, and Justice Rehnquist had drawn so much political fire in his hearings that little, if any, was left for the Scalia hearings afterward. Moreover, Justice Scalia enjoyed bipartisan support as the first Italian American ever nominated to the Supreme Court. Virtually no one was prepared to take a shot at a nominee whose major vice seemed to be reticence.) Besides trying to take a low profile in the confirmation phase, nominees often meet privately with senators, administration officials responsible for assisting or guiding them through the process, or representatives from influential interest groups interested in their nominations. Many nominees also have off-the-record conversations or meetings with the media.

Adopting a low profile even in high-profile hearings is an effective strategy if circumstances have reached the point at which the nominee's testimony has become a significant means by which to save his or her nomination. Personally appearing before a Senate committee has a much greater potential to hurt than to help a nomination. For one thing, such appearances give opponents a chance to take further shots at the already weakened nominee.

Nevertheless, in relatively rare situations, nominees have used their personal appearances before the Senate to help themselves. Four instances are especially noteworthy. The first, previously mentioned in chapter 3, involved Harlan Fiske Stone, the first Supreme Court nominee ever asked to testify personally before the Senate Judiciary Committee. After Stone had restored integrity to the Justice Department in the aftermath of the corrupt Harding administration, President Coolidge nominated him to the Supreme Court. Stone quickly encountered stiff opposition from Montana's two Democratic senators: Burton Wheeler, whom the Senate had cleared of wrongdoing in a land fraud case and who had succeeded in having one indictment against him dropped but who was still being targeted by the Justice Department for an indictment in the District of Columbia; and Thomas Walsh, an influential Judiciary Committee member who had himself been considered more than once as a possible nominee to the Court. On Wheeler's behalf, Walsh had arranged to delay the Senate's consideration of Stone's nomination pending his questioning of Stone's involvement with and support for the Justice Department's investigations of Wheeler. Stone responded to Walsh's intensive interrogation calmly and thoroughly, and his appearance before the Senate Judiciary Committee convinced the majority of members both of the emptiness of Walsh's charges and of Stone's integrity and professionalism.

A second nominee who helped to salvage his nomination through a personal appearance before the Senate was David Lilienthal. Shortly before his death in 1944, President Franklin Roosevelt decided not to renominate Lilienthal to a third term as a member of the Board of Directors of the Tennessee Valley Authority. The opposition to Lilienthal's reappointment had been led by Senator Kenneth McKellar of Tennessee, who at the time was the longest-serving member of the Senate. McKellar had been fighting with Lilienthal for years over the privilege to control appointments to the TVA. When President Truman later nominated Lilienthal to a third term on the TVA, McKellar decided against pressing a personal objection to it even though he made it clear at the time that he regarded Lilienthal as "personally and politically obnoxious to him."[58]

When President Truman decided to nominate Lilienthal to the chairmanship of the Atomic Energy Commission in 1947, Senator McKellar strenuously objected on numerous grounds, the most damaging of which was his claim that Lilienthal had communist leanings and employed Communists on his staff.[59] It was against this backdrop that Lilienthal testified before the Senate Committee on Atomic Energy in defense of his nomination. In response to a question from Senator McKellar about whether he had "very leftist" political sympathies, Lilienthal gave an impassioned defense of his support for the Constitution and American values and his opposition to communism.[60] The testimony won praise for Lilienthal in the press, from the public, and from many senators on both sides of the aisle; and it helped, along with the growing perception among senators that McKellar's objections were becoming increasingly distasteful, to turn the tide in favor of the nomination. In the end, the Senate confirmed Lilienthal by a margin of fourteen votes (including a handful of Republicans and several southern Democrats).

A more recent example of someone who helped to clinch his nomination through his testimony is Justice David Souter. Prior to testifying before the Senate Judiciary Committee, Souter was an enigma because few people outside his home state of New Hampshire knew anything about him. His testimony proved, however, to be remarkably articulate, poised, refreshing, candid, and witty; indeed, it set the standard for all subsequent Supreme Court nominees.[61]

Even more dramatic was Justice Thomas's testimony before the Senate Judiciary Committee, which salvaged his appointment. His repeated emphasis on his impoverished youth and the distance he had come, and especially his characterization of the second phase of his confirmation hearings as a "high-tech lynching," put opposing Democrats on the defensive, forcing them to prove that their opposition was not racist.

WHAT KINDS OF PEOPLE QUALIFY AS NOMINEES?

Of course, figuring out how nominees become nominees requires more than examining the means by which they secured their nominations. While it is true that anyone may become involved in politics and try to pursue his or her political ambitions or apply to be nominated to a confirmable post, the appointments process is not democratic. Some people, for reasons already discussed above, are better positioned than others to get nominated. The kinds of people who become successful nominees reveal a lot about the nature of the appointments process.

Most nominees have a close personal or professional relationship with the president or those responsible for advising the president on the nominations he should make. The latter have included high-level White House staffers, high-ranking department or agency officials, influential interest groups, and close personal friends of the president.

Moreover, nominees to important policymaking positions or administrative or judicial offices must satisfy certain criteria. Such criteria are crucial for ensuring the appointment of people who are likely to repay political debts, yield political dividends to the president who selected them, or implement the constitutional and political ideals of greatest importance to the president. In addition, because nominees are almost invariably chosen pursuant to these criteria, members of the Senate, the media, and the general public tend to regard nominees as embodiments of the selection criteria. Such was the case with almost all of Presidents Reagan's and Bush's judicial nominees, who were chosen largely because of their antipathy for the Warren Court's record of liberal judicial activism and their proven agreement with and support for rigid interpretation of the Constitution pursuant to its original understanding.[62] Even in the relatively rare situations in which Reagan's and Bush's judicial nominees lacked a substantial record of having an ideology in conformity with the preferred criteria, they still received support from many Republican senators and conservative interest groups who had confidence in the infallibility of the respective administrations' systems to nominate as federal judges people with certain ideological views. By the same token, many Reagan and Bush judicial nominees faced opposition or skepticism from Democratic senators and liberal interest groups who shared their Republican counterparts' conviction of the thoroughness and precision of the Reagan and Bush administrations. In some cases, judicial nominees, regardless of their protestations to the contrary, were generally perceived to share the ideological views or orientations of their sponsors. Among the latter are David Souter to the Supreme Court (backed strongly by Senator Warren Rudman and White House Chief of Staff John Sununu, both of whom were, like Souter, from New Hampshire), Daniel Manion to the U.S. Court of Appeals for the Seventh Circuit (pushed by Senator Dan Quayle and supported by Vice President George Bush), and James Edmondson to the U.S. Court of Appeals for the Eleventh Circuit (his chief sponsor being Assistant Attorney General Richard Willard).

Although all presidents have criteria for selecting nominees for confirmable positions, they differ with respect to the rigidity with which they insist on compliance and the substance of the standards preferred. In general, the more powerful the position, the more refined the selection criteria and the more closely potential nominees are scrutinized to ensure compliance with the chosen criteria. This is especially true for Supreme Court nominees. For example, Henry J. Abraham has noted that President Washington picked justices based on their "(1) support and advocacy of the Constitution; (2) distinguished service in the Revolution; (3) active participation in the political life of state or nation; (4) prior judicial experience on lower tribunals; (5) either a 'favorable reputation with his fellows' or personal ties with Washington himself; (6) geographic suitability; [and] (7) love of country."[63] Each of the next five presidents chose Supreme Court nominees primarily on the basis of their party loyalty or compatibility with the president's constitutional ideology, their public service, and their geographic suitability.[64] President Jackson emphasized party loyalty, service to his administration, and assistance to and support for his election or reelection.[65] And while President Polk's criteria consisted of party loyalty, geographic suitability, and compatibility with the president's ideology, President Fillmore emphasized a nominee's antislavery views, political experience, and character.[66] President Lincoln preferred to pick nominees based on their service to him or his administration or the Republican party as well as their likelihood for being a "partner in the nation's preservation."[67] Presidents Cleveland, Harrison, and McKinley emphasized support for economic conservatism when picking their respective Supreme Court nominees.[68]

In the course of considering whether to nominate Oliver Wendell Holmes Jr. to the Supreme Court in 1902, President Teddy Roosevelt told his friend Senator Henry Cabot Lodge of Massachusetts, "I should hold myself as guilty of an irreparable wrong to the nation if I should put [on the Court] any man who was not absolutely sane and sound on the national policies for which we stand in public life."[69] In explaining to Lodge some of his doubts about Holmes's political reliability, President Roosevelt explained further:

> In the ordinary and low sense which we attach to the words "partisan" and "politician," a judge of the Supreme Court should be neither. But in the higher sense he is not in my judgment fitted for the position unless he is a party man, a constructive statesman, keeping in mind his relations with his fellow statesmen in other branches of the Government. The Supreme Court of the [eighteen-]sixties was good exactly insofar as its members fitly represented the spirit of Lincoln. This is true of the present day. Now I should like to know that Judge Holmes was in entire sympathy with our views, that is with your views and mine before I feel justified in appointing him.[70]

Near the end of his presidency, after he had appointed three justices (Holmes, William R. Day, and William H. Moody), Teddy Roosevelt confessed to Senator Lodge that in contemplating judicial nominations, he had considered that "the *nominal* politics of the man has nothing to do with his actions on the bench. His *real* politics are all important."[71]

Most twentieth-century presidents have openly campaigned on the kinds of judicial appointments they would make (thereby increasing the potential for members of the Senate and the public to expect the nominees chosen to fulfill or embody the criteria announced).[72] After being elected, each president has sought information about likely nominees' approach to constitutional issues in the hope of covering specific areas of concern to the president (and his advisers) and other issues likely to arise in the future.[73]

By and large, presidents have used less rigid criteria in choosing political appointees than in selecting judges or justices, largely because the president retains so many more ways to keep the former under his control than he does with respect to judicial appointees. In his study of the federal courts of appeals, J. Woodford Howard found that his interviews with certain circuit judges during the late 1960s and early 1970s revealed that their appointments had been based on four major factors: "political participation, professional competence, personal ambition, plus an oft-mentioned pinch of luck. . . . Judgeships normally are rewards for political service. . . . To the politically active as well as to the party faithful go the prizes."[74]

Howard's study revealed further that most nominees had been active in party politics, particularly on the president's behalf, and had the reputation of being competent or distinguished attorneys. Sheldon Goldman confirmed this finding in a more recent study; for instance, he determined that 53.9 percent of President Clinton's first-term judicial appointees had a history of party activism, while 60.8 percent of President Bush's, 59 percent of President Reagan's, and 60.9 percent of President Carter's judicial nominees had been party activists.[75]

Background (including party activity) can make a difference not just to getting appointed but also to the kind or substance of judicial decision making those appointed are disposed to make. In an exhaustive study conducted on this issue that included surveying 27,772 opinions by one thousand federal district judges during a forty-four-year period, political scientists Robert A. Carp and Claude Rowland concluded that in "those cases for which the precedents and evidence are strong, for new areas of the law where innovative decision making is required, for issues about which the precedents and evidence are ambiguous or contradictory, [factors] such as the judges' basic philosophy, the mores and traditions of their particular circuit or state, and the attitudes and values reflected in their own political backgrounds do indeed measurably affect their judicial decision making."[76] Carp and Rowland's analyses illustrate dramatically why presidents and senators care a great deal about the backgrounds and dispositions of judicial appointees. Carp and Rowland found, for instance, "that between 1933 and 1977, Democrats were on the whole about 7 percentage points more liberal than their Republican colleagues."[77] This divergence was consistent with the agendas or aims of the presidents who appointed the federal district judges studied by Carp and Rowland. "The sharpest cleavage between the appointees of two presidents," the authors found,

> has been between those selected by Lyndon Johnson and those by Richard Nixon. Politically powerful presidents and/or those who placed an inordinate emphasis on the ideological purity of their judicial nominees (e.g., Wilson, Johnson, and Nixon) appear to have had a greater impact on subsequent judicial decisions than chief executives who lacked the desire or the clout to fill the judiciary with ideologically similar persons (e.g., Hoover, Truman, and Ford). Subsequent analysis also revealed that most of the political party variation among the judges could be accounted for by these differences among appointing presidents.[78]

Based on a comparison of federal district court judges in terms of their circuits, domiciles, and cases (especially those involving labor and economic regulations, criminal justice, and civil rights and liberties), Carp and Rowland determined that "it is possible to predict district court policy decisions from aggregate estimates of their environment and judges' political background under controls for legal factors" (i.e., the relative strength and weakness of the contents of the cases, circuits, and timing involved).[79]

The point is that a nominee's professional and personal background, party allegiance and political activities, education, and region can affect not just the person's selection but also the person's performance in cases in which the result is not strictly dictated by governing precedent or the weight of evidence. This apparent link is consistent with the general practice of most presidents to inquire beyond a nominee's assurances and

The Nominee

into the particulars of the nominee's activities and accomplishments. The latter provide insights into the nominee's qualifications, chances for confirmation, and likely job performance.

Of course, this perspective raises questions about the degree to which the appointments process has achieved the framers' aim to avoid the appointment of presidential cronies or buddies. That presidents have been allowed to make these kinds of nominations (and that senators have been frequently willing to allow them to do so) is beyond question. Two examples—one involving Harry Truman and the other Bill Clinton—should suffice to illustrate the commonality of this practice.

In spite of the fact that the Democrats controlled the Senate when Truman first became president, his attempt shortly thereafter to appoint many of his close friends and political allies to confirmable offices drew widespread criticism. Two such nominations that overcame stiff opposition were of George Allen, a former Democratic party secretary, to be a member of the Reconstruction Finance Corporation, and of James Vardaman first as Truman's naval aide and subsequently to the Federal Reserve Board in 1946 (a position in which he later embarrassed Truman by giving speeches on banking and economic subjects that displayed his lack of qualifications and varied from the policies of the Federal Reserve Board). Truman also succeeded in getting the Senate to confirm his friend Mon Wallgren, a former senator from Washington, to a seat on the Federal Power Commission, where he later voted with a majority of commissioners against federal regulation of natural gas in direct violation of Truman's preferred policy as president.

Bill Clinton also appointed many close friends to key positions in his administration, particularly during his first term. In fact, President Clinton brought more than 175 friends from Arkansas to join his administration. While the vast majority of these people discharged their official duties with great skill and professionalism and without any hint of scandal, some of the Arkansans closest to him in the administration (or at least most closely identified with him) ran into trouble. The latter include Joycelyn Elders (confirmed but later fired as surgeon general because she made embarrassing remarks to the press), Webster Hubbell (confirmed but later resigned from his post as associate attorney general amid rumors—later confirmed by his guilty plea—that he had defrauded his former law partners and some former clients), William Kennedy III (eventually resigned from the White House counsel's office after having been demoted from its number three position subsequent to his disclosure that he had failed to pay Social Security taxes for a family nanny), Thomas F. "Mack" McLarty (demoted from presidential chief of staff to presidential adviser), and David Watkins (fired as White House aide for taking a presidential helicopter on a golf outing).

Such examples—and the many others that could be cited—are not an indication that the system is broken or has failed. The fact that someone has been a close friend or associate of a president does not mean that the person is unqualified for important public service. The framers designed a system that was meant to discourage presidents from appointing political cronies; they empowered the Senate to check presidential abuse of discretion. Indeed, when one examines more closely the appointments made by Presidents Truman and Clinton, it becomes clear that the Senate has closely scrutinized many of their most important nominations, and that in relatively few instances did people with dubious credentials get through.

Nor are Presidents Truman and Clinton unique among chief executives in appointing close friends or allies. Every president has done it. For instance, President Lincoln appointed his old friend and campaign manager David Davis to the Supreme Court in 1862. By almost any standard, Davis's tenure was undistinguished. He not only sought the Liberal-Republican nomination for president while sitting on the Court but also resigned from the Court only after the Illinois legislature had elected him to the U.S. Senate and he had taken the Senate oath. Davis's decision to leave the Court is also sometimes explained as an effort to avoid serving on the electoral commission Congress had created to resolve the dispute over the 1876 presidential election.

In 1920, President Harding appointed his campaign manager and old friend, Harry Daugherty, as attorney general in spite of his meager credentials and dubious reputation as a political operative. Daugherty resigned from office two years after President Harding's death in order to stand trial on charges that he had been involved in various scams perpetrated by old Ohio friends brought to Washington by Harding and Daugherty. Daugherty went through two trials in 1926–27; the first ended in a hung jury and the second declared him not guilty because of insufficient evidence.

Similarly, President Nixon made his old friend and campaign manager John Mitchell his attorney general. Nixon later ordered Mitchell to resign in disgrace after it was revealed that he had approved both the illegal entry by White House operatives into the Democratic campaign headquarters in 1972 and the subsequent cover-up of the break-in.

Although there are many instances of presidents appointing cronies with dubious credentials to high federal office, virtually every president has, like Truman and Clinton, appointed an even greater number of friends or allies who have proven to be more than up to the tasks they were appointed to handle. For instance, Louis Brandeis was a close political adviser to President Wilson both before and after his appointment to the Court, but Brandeis proved not to be the radical his critics expected. Rather, he demonstrated great learning, careful and precise reasoning, and high regard for institutional values such as judicial restraint and federalism. President Coolidge had known Harlan Fiske Stone from their days together as students at Amherst College, and Stone had been a political and legal adviser to Coolidge for years before Coolidge ascended to the presidency. Nevertheless, as dean of Columbia Law School for thirteen years and a highly respected Wall Street lawyer, Stone was more than qualified to serve as attorney general. After he helped to restore integrity to the Justice Department in the aftermath of the scandal-ridden administration of President Harding, Stone's appointment made eminent sense. Indeed, Senator William Borah, who later championed Benjamin Cardozo as a Supreme Court nominee in 1932, supported Stone's nomination even though he had "the deepest regret" that Stone was leaving the attorney general's office, where he had done "splendid work."[80] President Franklin D. Roosevelt brought many close friends into his administration and appointed some of them to the Court, including William O. Douglas and Felix Frankfurter, both of whom continued to advise the president after their appointments. Nevertheless, Douglas and Frankfurter had achieved unusual levels of professional accomplishments prior to their appointments to the Court, and each was widely perceived as more than qualified to serve. Surely President Kennedy appointed more than a few so-called cronies, including his brother Robert as attorney general and his friend Byron White (whom he had known since they met while both were studying abroad after college and while they were fellow PT boat officers in the navy) as deputy attorney general. Both men helped to energize the Justice Department, particularly in the sensitive area of civil rights. Although Robert Kennedy could be hailed for his courage as attorney general in many respects, he could also be criticized as a partisan attorney general bent on protecting his brother the president at all costs. In 1962, President Kennedy appointed White to the Supreme Court, where White became known for his independence, sharp questioning, and careful reasoning until he retired in 1993. Similarly, Abe Fortas qualified as a crony of President Lyndon Johnson in light of the fact that they had known each other for decades prior to Fortas's appointment to the Court; however, Fortas's record in public service and private practice and his stature as a distinguished Supreme Court advocate and founder of one of Washington's most prestigious law firms clearly qualified him to be an associate justice.

The critical question is not whether presidents have been able to appoint political hacks or cronies to high public offices. Such appointments have been commonplace. The critical questions are: What are the possible harms resulting from such appointments? Do the constitutional safeguards adequately protect against these? One problem in answering these questions is the fact that absence of any consensus on the credentials required for certain offices makes it easy for many of these appointees to fill them. Nevertheless, Congress and the media tend to scrutinize close friends or allies appointed by a president, either because they have been placed in highly visible posts, because of suspicions about cronyism, or both. Consequently, a president's efforts to put his so-called cronies into office have often been penalized. Take, for example, the appointments of Presidents Jackson and Grant. By helping to establish the spoils system at the federal level, Jackson increased substantially the chances for future presidents to appoint cronies. Jackson himself appointed more than a few, perhaps the most notable being his old friend John Eaton as secretary of war. Jackson wanted Eaton in his cabinet in order to have a close friend in his inner circle; ironically, however, it was Eaton's young wife, Peggy, who was the major reason behind Jackson's first reorganization of his cabinet, many of whom angered Jackson by snubbing Eaton and his wife. Although Jackson also implemented reforms to improve the integrity of those appointed to federal offices, he nevertheless appointed (over Martin Van Buren's objections) an early supporter, Samuel Swartwout, as collector for the Port of New York, a position from which Swartwout stole more money than all of the felons in the previous administration together.

Ulysses S. Grant appointed more than a few cronies who committed felonious acts in office. Many of his appointments lacked merit, alienated senators, or both. The few exceptions sent the right signals, though Grant, ironically, failed to heed them. For instance, in 1874 Grant appointed his solicitor general, Benjamin Bristow, as secretary of the treasury. Unfortunately for Grant, Bristow was scrupulously honest (and had presidential ambitions of his own), and he uncovered and pursued the trail of fraud wherever it led in the Grant administration. In addition, even though Congress had given Grant nine circuit judgeships to fill, he did not defer to senators on their choices for these judgeships. Instead, Grant deferred to Attorney General Ebenezer Hoar's recommendations, which were based on merit rather than senatorial courtesy. Senators remembered these slights in dealing with Grant's other nominations (including rejecting Hoar's own nomination to the Supreme Court) and legislative preferences. Moreover, by the end of Grant's presidency, the charges of extensive corruption in his administration—made most loudly by Treasury Secretary Bristow—led to widespread demand for civil service reform. The appeal attracted increasing public support in the last quarter of the nineteenth century, during which every president took some steps to implement civil service reform.

Those instances in which presidents have appointed close friends to important federal offices, particularly friends who lacked professional distinction, do raise concerns about whether a president's close friends should be barred altogether from public service or at least should be precluded from holding certain appointments, particularly to positions with life tenure. A major problem with such rules, of course, is that many such friends may have very credible credentials. Such rules would bar many qualified people from public service *and* rob presidents of a natural constituency from which to choose trusted advisers. Moreover, many people with close ties to the presidents who nominated them have served in government with great distinction. In addition, the vast majority of problems that have led many so-called cronies to leave office in disgrace arose subsequent to their confirmation.

Perhaps an even more vexing problem than avoiding or regulating the appointment of presidential cronies has been ensuring that presidents nominate and senators confirm people who are among the best qualified to do the jobs entrusted to them. Meeting this challenge depends on developing a measure for determining the quality of presidential appointments and designing a set of professional qualifications or credentials for service (as predictors or measurements of performance). At present, no such standards exist. In part 3, I will examine possible reforms of the federal appointments process that may lead to solutions for these problems.

Chapter Seven

PUBLIC AND INTEREST

GROUP PARTICIPATION IN THE

APPOINTMENTS PROCESS

THE EXTENT TO WHICH and the manner in which the public and other interested parties and organizations have been involved in the federal appointments process have evolved over the years. Since the late eighteenth century, select citizens, based on their political connections, past government service, or personal wealth, have exercised occasional influence over the outcome of the federal appointments process. Among the earliest of these powerful citizens and political bosses were Thurlow Weed of New York, Mark Hannah of Ohio (who became a senator after helping to finance the successful presidential bids of his friend William McKinley in 1896 and 1900), and Jay Gould and J. P. Morgan of New York. In the early twentieth century, C. C. Burlingham, a politically well connected leader of the New York bar, wielded enormous influence, particularly regarding judicial appointments, with the Republican leadership in Washington, D.C. For instance, it was Burlingham who persuaded President William Howard Taft's attorney general, George Wickersham, to push the nomination of Learned Hand as a federal district judge through both the administration and the Senate in 1907.[1]

Before the adoption of the Seventeenth Amendment in 1917, members of the general public were rarely directly involved in and wielded little influence over the federal appointments process. They were kept informed by newspapers and word of mouth and had the opportunity, of which only a small number took advantage, to write letters to or visit their senators. The degree to which such letters or visits made any real difference is unclear, given that prior to the amendment's adoption senators were beholden more to state legislatures than to the citizens of their states, and that Senate confirmation hearings were held behind closed doors and thus the records on many proceedings are sparse. Perhaps the most significant impact the public had on the appointments process before the adoption of the Seventeenth Amendment occurred with respect to civil service reform. Undoubtedly, civil service reform—that is, the requirement of some demonstration of objective merit or accomplishment for certain jobs in the federal government below the policymaking level—would not have happened without widespread popular support. Much of the public supported civil service reform as a solution to prevent a recurrence of the widespread corruption uncovered in the Grant administration and the fervent rush for patronage that led to the assassination of President Garfield. The willingness of some presidents, particularly Rutherford B. Hayes and Chester Arthur, to risk significant unpopularity with their own party's leaders and hierarchy for the sake of addressing the public clamor for civil service reform made such reform possible.

THE PUBLIC'S PARTICIPATION
IN THE FEDERAL APPOINTMENTS PROCESS

In the twentieth century, members of the general public have been able to participate in the federal appointments process in several ways. The first is by contacting members of Congress directly through a variety of different means (which have developed and become increasingly sophisticated with the passage of time). Through at least the first half of the century, these means included letter writing, phoning, submitting petitions, and telegraphing. In the 1990s they expanded to include faxing and e-mailing. Since the enactment of the Seventeenth Amendment, senators have paid close attention to the views of their constituents, and it has been commonplace for some time for senators to instruct their staffs to keep running tallies on the numbers of phone calls, faxes, and e-mails directed to their offices on behalf of or against particular nominations.

The fallout from the Thomas-Hill hearings illustrates the public's potential to influence the federal appointments process. When the Senate Judiciary Committee initially learned about Anita Hill's charge that Clarence Thomas had sexually harassed her while she was an employee in his office, it refused to hear her testimony or hold any special hearings, even behind closed doors. When the public learned (by means of the media) about this refusal, a flood of calls, faxes, and telegrams to the Judiciary Committee led the Senate (and the nominee and his sponsor, Senator Jack Danforth) in less than a day to agree to a public hearing on Hill's charge.

The second means by which the public has participated in the federal appointments process is through polling data (beyond senators' informal tabulations of communications for and against nominations). In the latter quarter of the twentieth century it became standard procedure for senators and presidents to engage professional pollsters to measure the public's support for or opposition to a wide range of public policy questions, including particular nominations. That both presidents and senators have taken the data gathered by such means quite seriously is beyond any doubt. For example, much of the initial opposition to Zoë Baird's nomination as attorney general came from the middle class, which resented her failure to comply with the law even though she had the financial means to provide her hired help with all of the mandated benefits and thus to avoid breaching the Social Security laws.[2] President Clinton's withdrawal of Zoë Baird's nomination was partly motivated by his recognition of the key role that the middle class had played in his election in 1992 and the necessity of retaining that group's support for ensuring his reelection and the success of his legislative agenda.

Some commentators on the federal appointments process have taken issue with political leaders' practice of basing their decisions about supporting or opposing certain nominations on polling data, particularly in Supreme Court confirmation hearings. Their complaint is that senators effectively turn to the public (by means of polling data) to determine the popularity of Supreme Court nominees, which in turn depends on how the prospective justices would vote in cases involving major constitutional issues. Focusing on the popularity of a prospective justice arguably poses a threat to judicial independence because it transforms such hearings into popular elections in which the majority will approve only those nominees who express agreement with its preferences regarding constitutional interpretation.[3]

The concern that senators rely on polling data to drive Supreme Court confirmation proceedings is misplaced for several reasons. First, the Constitution does not protect judicial independence as an absolute; that is, it does not require the Senate to back off whenever anything it does might influence the staffing or functioning of the federal judiciary. In fact, just the opposite is true. One of the critical ways in which the Constitution *limits* judicial independence is by empowering two elected branches of the federal government — the president and the Senate — to make the critical decisions on the direction and composition of the federal judiciary. The president's nominating power and the Senate's confirmation authority serve as countermajoritarian checks on the judiciary. Once a federal judge is confirmed, he or she is immune to political reprisals except for impeachment, but the Constitution clearly allows a judicial nominee to account to the political branches for how he or she has performed or intends to perform as a judge at the confirmation stage of his or her appointment.

It is also beyond question that throughout U.S. history presidents and senators have been concerned about the social or political ramifications of judicial nominations.[4] Every president has made Supreme Court nominations with certain criteria in mind, including his nominee's likely judicial ideology, and senators have often evaluated Supreme Court nominees on the basis of their likely impact on the Court's direction or disposition. In this century, coinciding roughly with the practice of having a Supreme Court nominee testify, the concern has focused more openly, but not solely, on a judicial nominee's ideology. Consequently, three Supreme Court nominees have been rejected in significant part because of their judicial ideologies, and many other nominees have been confirmed only after close scrutiny of their ideologies.[5]

Yet another problem with the argument that the confirmation process poses a threat to judicial independence rests on the mistaken premise that confirmation hearings operate in the same way as popular judicial elections in which a majority of those empowered to vote dictate who is chosen. In fact, Senate confirmation proceedings do not function in the manner of a popular election; rather, they are similar to a public referendum in which those empowered to vote have the authority to strike down a nominee but still must allow some other authority—the president—to choose another. A popular election allows citizens to choose the person they prefer most from among the available candidates. In contrast, a referendum—or confirmation proceeding—allows the decision makers to decide only if they accept the nominee. In other words, the Senate in a confirmation proceeding decides whether a Supreme Court nominee is acceptable to it, not whether the nominee is the top choice of most senators for the Court. Thus, once a nomination has reached the Senate, the public's—and the Senate's—powers to shape the outcome are limited.

Nor, for that matter, has any Supreme Court nominee ever explicitly made a promise in his or her confirmation hearings about how he or she would vote in a case likely to come before the Court. In fact, no nominee to the Court has ever been rejected for saying too little in a confirmation hearing. Thus, the most serious part of the threat to judicial independence—the coercion of a vote—has not been documented.

The third means by which the public may participate in the federal appointments process is through intermediaries such as interest groups. As previously indicated, interest groups have learned techniques that enable them to influence, or to try to influence, the federal appointments process, such as by signaling the norms that they would like key decision makers to adopt or follow in making certain nominations or voting in confirmation proceedings. Their signaling also conveys their willingness to exchange their support (financial and otherwise) for certain kinds of outcomes, votes, or nominations. Special interest groups approach the appointments process with particular goals in mind, including representing the special interests of a segment or portion of the public, educating the public and policymakers generally about the organizations' concerns and agendas, trying to shape or inform policy and public opinion, trying to sensitize the public or policymakers to certain concerns, and attempting to ensure the nominations of people who are sympathetic to their views and, ideally, have a history of support for their organizations. Interest groups have used increasingly sophisticated means for achieving these objectives. As I explain in greater detail in the next section, these means include using their resources and connections to entice or pressure officials to do their bidding and to use available technologies to coordinate their membership and to spread awareness of their influence and message.

Evaluating the participation of or contributions made by interest groups in the federal appointments process requires resolving several questions. One set of questions is definitional,[6] that is, it involves figuring out who qualifies as an interest group for analytical purposes. For example, by what criteria or tools are interest groups defined? They could be defined broadly to include private organizations with diverse elements unified relatively loosely for some overarching or general purposes (e.g., political parties or even the American Bar Association) or quite narrowly as private groups organized for the special purpose of protecting or promoting a single concern or relatively small set of issues (e.g., protecting wetlands or un-born babies). Recent scholarship on interest groups further suggests that a group's willingness to devote resources to collective action depends not only on its size and average intensity but also on the distribution of in-tensity throughout the group.[7] A related topic has to do with the relation-ship between certain social or political developments, such as the rise of identity politics or the partial decline in power or status of political party membership, and the tactics employed by interest groups.

Moreover, critical normative questions raised by interest groups' efforts to apply pressure in the federal appointments process in exchange for certain outcomes consistent with their agendas include the propriety of the ends for which and the means by which interest groups apply such pressure. (Of course, answering these questions will help to answer the more basic issue of whether such exchanges are desirable at all.) The ends pursued by interest groups in the federal appointments process are multi-fold. Obviously, they include securing the appointments of nominees viewed as sympathetic to or supportive of their agendas and defeating nominees perceived as hostile or unsympathetic. Other objectives include influencing the quality of discourse or debate in the process; controlling the media's or public's perceptions of the issue(s) at stake in a given confirmation contest; and educating legislators, presidents (or their staffs or key advisers in their administrations), nominees, or members of the general public about the groups' primary areas of concern. These groups also try to sensitize or acclimate presidents or senators to the norms that their members or sponsors share in order to increase the chances that these leaders will incorporate or follow these norms in their decision making.[8] No doubt, signaling to presidents or senators the likely costs of noncompliance with the group's norms is a major objective. Yet, it is possible that the purpose of such signaling goes beyond influencing or ensuring a particular outcome in the confirmation process. It might also be designed to move presidents or senators closer to or farther away from certain kinds of candidates, depending on the degree to which the latter are willing to conform to the group's norms. The effectiveness of such signaling raises serious questions about the efficiency of social norms,[9] a subject to which legal scholars have been devoting increasing attention (and to which I will return later in the chapter in a discussion about the potential for interest groups to cancel each other's messages).

Moreover, it is conceivable that interest group participation in the federal appointments process may be assessed in terms of the degree to which it has enhanced or impeded direct citizen participation in the process. The means developed by interest groups for influencing the federal appointments process are as varied as the groups' objectives, including feeding questions or certain information to the media, senators (or their staffs), or presidents; advertising (or media campaigns); lobbying presidents or senators; staging or sponsoring newsworthy events or public appearances or issuing public statements; and encouraging or mobilizing their membership to fax, e-mail, or call members of Congress.

That the degree of participation by interest groups in the federal appointments process has risen enormously in the twentieth century is beyond question.[10] Whether or not this expansion has been a good thing is open to debate. Answering the latter question requires identifying and assessing the consequences or ramifications that the proliferation of interest groups has posed for the federal appointments process.

First, the infusion of interest groups into every phase of the federal appointments process arguably has left less room for and helped to decrease the opportunities for citizens without special connections or resources to wield a significant influence over the system.[11] It stands to reason that interest groups with their greater resources are in a much better position than private citizens to mobilize support for or against nominees and to be heard, particularly at critical moments, in the federal appointments process. Consequently, an effective option for individual citizens who intensely want to be heard on some issue(s) is to align themselves with an organized group whose position on the issue(s) in question most closely approximates their own.

Robert Katzmann has used dramatic statistics to illustrate the rise in interest group participation and the corresponding decline in the participation of individual, unaligned citizens in the appointments process.[12] According to Katzmann, no interest groups participated in Justice Brennan's confirmation hearings in 1957, and only one interest group representative testified in Justice Thurgood Marshall's confirmation hearings twelve years later.[13] In contrast, eighty-six people representing interest groups testified in the Bork hearings in 1987, ninety-six such witnesses appeared in the Thomas confirmation proceedings in 1991, thirty-nine testified in the Souter hearings in 1990, and twenty people appeared as witnesses in the Ginsburg hearings in 1993.[14] Only a small fraction of the witnesses who testified in these hearings was not formally associated or aligned in some way with an interest group. The few people not formally associated in some way with an interest group but allowed to testify in confirmation hearings have usually been either prominent academicians (and thus have come from elite institutions) or community or bar association leaders (and thus have had close ties to other organizations that, in the opinion of some, are tantamount to interest groups).

It is important to remember, however, that individual citizens have rarely wielded direct influence over the process. Moreover, some might argue that the system is better off without the public's (direct) participation because critical decisions should be made by authorities better versed in or informed about the matters being decided. In any event, interest groups have brought a greater diversity of viewpoints and opinions into almost every phase of the appointments process. The critical question is how these viewpoints or opinions are distilled in the process.

The Public and Interest Groups

Although presidents wield enormous power to set the initial terms of debate in the confirmation process, interest groups have developed increasingly sophisticated techniques for signaling contrary messages (if they disagree) or reinforcing the same signals (if they agree with the agenda the nominee is perceived as being disposed to try to implement). This is especially evident in Supreme Court confirmation hearings. In the modern era in which Supreme Court justices (as well as most lower-court judges) have not been constrained by the original understanding or other determinate methodologies of judicial review, interest groups (working frequently in concert with political forces with whose agendas their own causes overlap) have increasingly injected into Supreme Court confirmation proceedings the modern techniques of political campaigns, complete with grassroots lobbying (by political parties, interest groups, administration liaisons, and members of Congress and their staffs or supporters) and leaks.[15] These campaigns are designed to grab the attention of senators and particularly to move targeted senators from seemingly neutral or disinterested postures into postures consistent with the targeting groups' agendas.

Take, for example, Clement Haynsworth's nomination to the Supreme Court. Haynsworth's stances on economic and civil rights issues made him a prime target for labor unions and civil rights organizations. Signaling through their mobilization against the nomination and dramatizing the significance of a conflict-of-interest problem (involving Haynsworth's sitting on a case in which one of the parties was a company in which his wife owned stock), labor unions and civil rights groups succeeded in shifting some Democratic senators into a partisan or sympathetic posture and convincing others that a vote against Haynsworth on character would be good for the Democratic party and would create a useful bond with the interest groups' constituencies.

The Supreme Court confirmation hearings for Robert Bork and Abe Fortas illustrate how quickly interest groups can help senators opposed to nominations for reasons based solely on suspected ideology or party differences to find more credible justifications to oppose them in arguably more neutral, grander terms. The opposition to Bork's nomination organized around the likely negative impact Bork's appointment would have on the Court's direction, particularly in the areas of concern to many of the nation's best-organized interest groups—civil rights, women's rights, and labor.[16] Similarly, Fortas's nomination was contested in part in terms of the impropriety of a lame duck president's exercise of a presidential prerogative rightfully belonging to the next elected president.[17]

In the 1980s, liberal interest groups for the first time waged national campaigns against two lower-court judicial nominees. The first nominee was Jeff Sessions, whom President Reagan nominated to the federal district court in southern Alabama in 1985.[18] At the time of his nomination Sessions was serving as the U.S. attorney for that district, a position for which he had been nominated by President Reagan and confirmed by the Senate in 1985. The ABA committee reviewing Sessions's qualifications split, with a majority rating him as "qualified." The split was not fatal to Sessions's nomination because he was backed strongly by Alabama's senator, Jeremiah Denton, a Republican. A bigger problem for Sessions was that several civil rights organizations, including the NAACP and People for the American Way, strenuously objected to his nomination based on his racial insensitivity, as reflected in several tasteless remarks and his unsuccessful prosecution of three black civil rights leaders for voting fraud. Sessions was forced to testify more than once to explain his remarks. He denied that he was racially insensitive, and the Reagan administration claimed that the opposition to Sessions's nomination was really based on objections to his conservative ideology and partisan politics. On June 5, 1986, the Senate Judiciary Committee voted ten to eight against recommending Sessions's nomination to the full Senate, thereby effectively killing it. In the fall after the defeat of the nomination, Senator Denton was defeated for reelection, largely as a result of a large turnout of African American voters. A decade later, the voters of Alabama elected Sessions to the seat of retiring senator Howell Heflin, who had voted against Sessions's nomination while he was a member of the Senate Judiciary Committee.

The second national campaign waged against a lower-court nominee was conducted against Daniel Manion, whom President Reagan nominated in 1986 to the U.S. Court of Appeals for the Seventh Circuit.[19] Manion's opponents (including the Chicago Council of Lawyers) argued in advertisements and mailings to the committee that he lacked the record of distinction and achievement expected of nominees to the courts of ap-

The Public and Interest Groups

peals and questioned his legal competence on the basis of the briefs he had submitted to the Judiciary Committee as representing his legal ability. Manion's supporters claimed that he was being targeted for his conservative views and for the activities of his late father, Clarence, a founder of the John Birch Society, a right-wing fringe group. Manion, like Sessions, had received a split vote from the ABA, with a substantial majority voting "qualified" and a minority voting "unqualified." On May 9, 1986, the Senate Judiciary Committee was evenly divided on the vote to approve the nomination. A second vote produced a majority in favor of sending the nomination to the floor of the Senate without a recommendation. At this point, President Reagan entered the contest and worked hard to mobilize Republican senators to support Manion. He made deals with at least two Republican senators, Slade Gorton and David Durenberger, to nominate their suggested nominees to federal judgeships in their respective states in exchange for their support of Manion. The Senate had to take two votes before Manion was confirmed (in a bare majority vote against a motion to reconsider his nomination).

Besides influencing senators' positions on judicial nominees, interest groups have also mobilized pressure to force presidents to nominate people other than those they might have been initially disposed to nominate to federal judgeships, including the Supreme Court. For instance, civil rights groups, to whom President Nixon did not listen in nominating William Rehnquist, Clement Haynsworth, and Harrold Carswell to the Supreme Court, helped to persuade him to nominate Harry Blackmun and Lewis Powell (a registered Democrat). In 1994, President Clinton was disposed to nominate his friend and Secretary of the Interior Bruce Babbitt to the Supreme Court. Babbitt fit Clinton's campaign pledge to place on the Court people with vast political experience. But conservative interest groups and environmentalist groups persuaded Clinton not to nominate Babbitt.[20] Instead, he nominated Stephen Breyer, a candidate for whom he felt little passion and whom he had bypassed in 1993 to nominate Ruth Bader Ginsburg to the Court.

To be sure, interest groups' efforts to pressure presidents or senators to understand a contested nomination in terms of a single issue are sometimes cited as an illustration of how these groups distort the appointment process.[21] No doubt, this influence was apparent in the mobilization of pro-choice forces against Robert Bork's nomination to the Supreme Court. The groups threatened to shift money and votes on the basis of a senator's vote on the Bork nomination no matter what the senator's party affiliation or ideological stance. Because Powell was considered to have had the swing vote on the Court in abortion cases, such groups also claimed that a senator's vote on Bork was so important that it would be the only Senate vote that mattered to them in deciding whether to support that particular senator in the future. A similar phenomenon occurred with respect to the opposition of civil rights and women's groups to Clarence Thomas's nomination to the Supreme Court. Those groups let it be known that voting for Thomas would be counted as a vote against their interests and that the groups would therefore work to defeat members who voted for Thomas. After the hearings had ended and the Senate had confirmed Thomas, the groups made good on their threats. In the very next congressional elections after the Thomas hearings, a few senators who had voted to confirm Justice Thomas either lost their seats in their reelection bids or prevailed over very stiff opposition.[22] For instance, John Seymour, a Republican incumbent from California, and Alan Dixon, a Democrat from Illinois, both rejected Hill's testimony as lacking credibility and voted to confirm Thomas, and both eventually lost their seats to female opponents — Diane Feinstein and Carol Moseley-Braun, respectively — who had argued, among other things, that neither senator merited reelection because each had demonstrated his insensitivity to women's issues.[23] Representative Barbara Boxer also rode a wave of anti-Thomas sentiment to victory in her contest for a Senate seat in California. In addition, Senator Arlen Specter of Pennsylvania, who gained notoriety for his especially sharp cross-examinations of Anita Hill and her defenders, barely won reelection over a woman opponent, Lynn Yaeckel. In short, when a single issue cuts across party lines, when the issue is extremely important to those engaged in it, and when a particular nomination seems likely to have a serious impact on this issue, an interest group identified with that issue may plausibly claim that it will deliver or withhold support on the basis of a senator's confirmation vote.

Not surprisingly, the signaling done by interest groups is sometimes reinforced or supplemented by strongly partisan messages emanating from a president's political foes. Such seems to have been the case with the

Fortas nomination. The fight over Fortas's nomination was clearly generated initially by partisan differences. The fight occurred on the eve of the 1968 presidential election very late in the term of an unpopular Democratic president who had announced that he would not run for reelection. The election of a Republican president seemed likely. Although there was a Democratic majority in the Senate, there was also a clear chance of forming a sufficiently strong Republican–southern Democrat coalition to defeat cloture and delay any action on the nomination until after the next election. The very terms of Chief Justice Warren's retirement—namely, that he would retire only if and when a nominee of President Johnson was confirmed—further underscored the partisanship potential of this end-of-term appointment.[24] Although the old-line Senate Republican leadership was willing to maintain a seemingly neutral posture in exchange for certain presidential favors, younger Republican senators shifted quickly to the partisan mode by challenging the prerogative of President Johnson rather than the next person duly elected by the American people to make the critical choice of Chief Justice.[25]

The rather quick shift from apparent neutrality to outright partisanship that occurred in the contest over the Fortas nomination was facilitated by the fact that Fortas, who had argued *Gideon v. Wainwright*,[26] was closely identified with the Warren Court's expansion of criminal defendants' rights, which occurred at the expense of the states' ability to maintain tough law and order. (The fact that as a justice Fortas had had virtually no involvement in this movement was not enough to counterbalance this popular impression.) The manner of Warren's projected departure left the impression that he and President Johnson had hand-picked Fortas to carry on the Warren Court's legacy. Fortas's proposed nomination thus not only set the stage for a Senate referendum on the Warren Court's decisions, but also created the conditions for the establishment of a coalition of Republicans and southern Democrats that had the potential (which it realized) of stopping the nomination by filibustering and holding off cloture.[27] Fortas's apparent support for finding ways of letting guilty people go free resonated against him with northern senators and their constituents, while his sympathy for desegregation obviously did not sit well with southern Democrats.

The increased participation of interest groups and their increased interest in the appointments process is one reason why nominations to certain offices generate more attention or opposition than others. For example, conflicts over nominations to head the Interior Department (or other high-level positions within the department) are part of an ongoing struggle for dominance of the department (or its agenda) by its two principal constituencies: conservationists wanting to preserve federal lands in their present conditions and resource developers wishing to tap the highly restricted mineral and forest resources on federal lands. Each challenged nomination to head the Interior Department (including President Nixon's nomination of Walter Hickel, President Ford's nomination of Stanley Hathaway, and President Clinton's nomination of Bruce Babbitt) featured conservationists testifying in opposition to the nominee on the ground that he or she was not sufficiently sensitive to environmental concerns.[28] Few other departments deal with areas of concern in ways that provoke such extreme reactions or easily lend themselves to concerted efforts for or against particular nominees.

The high-profile campaigns waged by various interest groups over the past few decades raise the possibility that the appointments process has fallen into a vicious cycle in which interest groups reflecting different ideological orientations ceaselessly contend with each other to raise money and to pressure elected public leaders to do their bidding. There are, however, several indications that the appointments process might not be mired in a cycle as vicious or as permanent as some commentators have suggested. First, one possible consequence of increased interest group participation in the federal appointments process is that interest groups' messages might cancel each other. No doubt, some citizens and senators tune out entirely because they have already made up their minds, because the threats of some groups do not faze them, or because the support of others has already secured their positions. Moreover, some citizens and senators gravitate toward the messages that reflect the norms they already endorse or comport with other values or positions they hold.

Undoubtedly, the competing signaling of interest groups increases the chances for polarization in confirmation contests. For instance, in the battle over Clarence Thomas's confirmation, conservative interest groups echoed the strategy of the Bush White House to dramatize Thomas's extraordinary journey from abject poverty to a position on the highest court in the land. To these groups, Thomas's story reflected the fulfillment of the American dream. The norms entrepreneurs among the liberal interest groups who were worried that this message might undermine support for affirmative action or a woman's right to choose to have an abortion (both of which Thomas reputedly opposed) developed a contrary message: that Thomas was, among other things, a hypocrite for seemingly opposing the very affirmative action programs that had helped him to make that extraordinary journey. There was no middle ground between these two messages. Once Anita Hill testified, norms entrepreneurs on both sides changed their messages. The groups that supported Thomas claimed (as Thomas himself dramatically charged) that Hill's accusations were a variation on a classic form of racism—the use of sexual stereotypes of African American men to destroy them. Thus, for these groups, the contest had become one about sex and race, particularly about the use of the former to mask an attack really based on the latter. Liberal interest groups countered that Hill's charges were not racist but rather reflected a norm (that would become an important issue in subsequent political campaigns) that had to change—the failure of government officials to take seriously charges of sexual harassment. This debate too left no middle ground.

Yet, in rare cases, norms entrepreneurs effectuate meaningful convergence rather than polarization. Such was the case with both Zoë Baird and Lani Guinier. Baird's failure to comply with Social Security tax laws regarding domestic help implicated a norm that conservative and liberal interest groups alike could support—the critical symbolic and moral importance of a high government official's compliance with the laws she is charged with administering. In the face of that convergence, President Clinton accepted the defeat of the nomination. Similarly, the charge that as a law professor Lani Guinier had expressed some support for quotas resonated not only with Republicans and southern and moderate Democrats but also with some administration officials, particularly the president. Since the administration had no interest in being perceived as supporting quotas or in alienating its foes in Congress, the president quickly abandoned his support for Guinier.

One of the questions raised in the aftermath of successful signaling by norms entrepreneurs in contested confirmation hearings is whether or not such signaling has a lasting effect on an administration or senators. The abandonment or rejection of a nominee does not necessarily mean that an administration or senator has fully embraced the norms that helped to produce the outcome of the confirmation contest. In the aftermath of Zoë Baird's forced withdrawal, the Clinton administration openly agreed that it would either forgo nominating individuals who had not complied with Social Security tax laws for compensating domestic help or ensure that future nominees would at least by the time of their nominations have done all that they could to comply with the obligations imposed by such laws. Yet, the Clinton administration also construed Baird's failed nomination as signifying the norm that hiring illegal aliens when domestic workers were available was impolitic. Thus, it refused to go forward with the nomination of Judge Kimba Wood as attorney general because, among other problems, she had hired as a nanny an illegal alien rather than a legal resident of the country.

Another question raised by the Baird and Guinier nominations and others is whether or not it is possible to predict the norms that are likeliest to prevail in the appointments process. In the parlance of the growing literature on the relationship between social norms and the law, are there any efficient norms operating in the appointments process? In the absence of empirical evidence on the role of social norms in the appointments process, one is left to speculate about their existence or absence. One possibility is that most presidents strive to avoid having the momentum or direction of their administrations (or at least of some of their policies) lost or frustrated by tie-ups in the confirmation process. This is, of course, a process-oriented rather than a substantive norm. As such, it might be adapted or relinquished by presidents, depending on the degree to which they calculate that there are substantive principles that justify deviation from the optimal norm of a relatively efficient process. Moreover, some senators (perhaps best symbolized in the nineteenth century by Henry Clay and in the twentieth century by Jesse Helms) might be interested in using all means at their disposal to keep presidents from achieving a point of equilibrium in the appointments process or to tie up the latter system in order to compromise at least some presidential initiatives. Other senators might be inclined to do what they can to help presidents achieve their optimal positioning in the process, while many others might not have any disposition or orientation.

Yet another norm that seems to have become accepted in the appointments process, at least since the mid-1980s is the belief that elected politicians are not likely to make good justices. As a candidate and as president, Bill Clinton expressed a preference to appoint as justices elected officials with substantial experience and accomplishments in public service such as governors or senators. The political figures he favored (as a candidate he expressed favor for Governor Mario Cuomo of New York and as president for Bruce Babbitt) were quickly assailed by some interest groups as lacking the requisite judicial temperaments. Thus, on his two opportunities to make Supreme Court appointments, President Clinton was persuaded to appoint veteran judges rather than experienced political leaders. (The last person nominated to the Court who served in elected office was Sandra Day O'Connor, appointed to the Court in 1982.) No one else campaigning to become president has expressed a preference to appoint someone with substantial experience as an elected official.

A second reason why the appointments process has not fallen hopelessly into a vicious cycle of endless interest group competition is that the conventional wisdom that interest groups have become too active in judicial confirmation proceedings, particularly since the Senate's rejection of Robert Bork, is wrong. A recent study by Lauren M. Cohen indicates that from 1979 to 1997 interest groups appeared in support of or opposition to judicial nominees in at least 20 percent of the judicial confirmation hearings held in the 96th Congress (1979–80), the 100th Congress (1987–88), and the 101st Congress (1989–90); however, it fell to single digits in every other congress in the covered period except for the 99th Congress (for which the figure was 11 percent).[29] The significance of the statistics, Cohen concludes, is that the important thing is not how often interest groups try to inject themselves into the confirmation process but rather what they do once they are there. It is clear that once interest groups become involved in the process, "the likelihood of confirmation is significantly decreased."[30]

Third, some legal scholars maintain that interest group participation in the political process actually facilitates rather than impedes citizen participation in government (presumably because they offer a pathway for such activity).[31] These claims are difficult, however, to reconcile with the outcome of a recent poll that indicates that most Americans believe that special interests have corrupted the political process and are a major reason for the alienation most people feel toward government.[32] This latter poll could be read to suggest that interest group participation either does not democratize the process or is not fully harmful. Indeed, the latter reading is consistent with political psychologists' finding that the public has become adept at wading through the morass of information thrown at them by the media and competing interest groups to identify those things that it needs to know.[33]

THE DILEMMA OF THE AMERICAN BAR ASSOCIATION

One thing potentially at risk in any campaign is a group's credibility or perceived legitimacy to speak on behalf of the interests it claims to represent. Once a campaign is in full swing, as in the impeachment proceedings against President Clinton, it might become very difficult for a group or organization to maintain such credibility or legitimacy, particularly against attacks claiming partisanship or lack of neutrality. Perhaps there is no better example of this dilemma than the history of the American Bar Association's participation in the federal appointments process. Purporting to act on behalf of concerns about the quality of the legal profession and judicial system, the ABA has been formally involved with evaluating prospective judicial nominees since 1952 and with evaluating both prospective and actual judicial nominees since Jimmy Carter's presidency.[34] To be sure, though it has claimed to be acting on behalf of the best interests of the legal profession, the ABA has consistently rejected the label of interest group. It is rather unique in its claim to represent impartial, special expertise about judicial qualifications rather than the interests of its members. The ABA has neither money nor votes to exchange for its participation in the evaluation of actual or prospective judicial nominees. Precisely because it neither claims to nor has any means to effect any exchange for its participation, the ABA does not signal the political interests of voters or senators in confirmation proceedings. It is best seen as a special conduit through which potentially partisan considerations can be camouflaged as "professional qualifications" concerns, both by its members' actions in the federal appointments process and by whichever senators find its formal recommendations useful.

The ABA's influence over judicial selection has ebbed and flowed. Perhaps its lowest point was reached with the decision of Senate Judiciary Committee chair Orrin Hatch in 1997 to exclude the ABA from a privileged position in testifying on judges. This decision is attributable in no small measure to another low point in the aftermath of the Senate Judiciary Committee's divided vote on Robert Bork's qualifications as a Supreme Court nominee. A substantial majority of the committee found Bork "well qualified," but a minority voted that Bork was "not qualified" because (one gathers from indirect sources) it felt he lacked the requisite judicial temperament to serve on the Court.[35] The ABA's claim of neutrality further lost credibility when its House of Delegates voted to put its support for reproductive choice on record. Given that this vote coincided with the increased intensity with which the Senate Judiciary Committee questioned judicial nominees about their views on abortion rights, it gave the appearance that the ABA was taking sides in a public debate about reproductive choice. Subsequently, the committee agreed (at least formally) not to take ideology into account in rating judicial nominees.

The ABA has not expressed any opinions about nonjudicial nominees, including the attorney general. Indeed, the participation of interest groups as a whole in confirmation hearings on nonjudicial nominees has tended to be less well established and organized than it has become for judicial nominations, which receive more attention because the federal judiciary occupies a rather insulated position in influencing policy. This is not to say that interest groups have not seriously tried to influence particular nominations or confirmation hearings that affect policy matters of concern to them. Some groups, such as the Sierra Club, tend to target nominees with policymaking responsibilities in areas of particular interest to them, such as posts in the Interior Department, the Environmental Protection Agency, and even the Department of Agriculture. Other groups, such as the NAACP, tend to monitor nominations generally to determine the propriety of their racial composition or diversity.

The absence of interest group support for a nomination sometimes has proven to be as important as its presence. A good illustration of this is Zoë

Baird's nomination to become attorney general. Prior to formally nominating Baird around the middle of December 1992, President-elect Clinton was lobbied intensely by women's groups to nominate the first woman attorney general. Indeed, the president had promised as president-elect that he would fill one of the top four positions in his cabinet with a woman. By the time he got around to choosing an attorney general, President-elect Clinton had filled three of the top four positions in the cabinet with men. Consequently, the popular expectation was that he would select a woman for the post of attorney general. When President-elect Clinton named Zoë Baird, however, women's groups began to distance themselves from the nominee because she had no history with them. They had wanted someone with a past record of association or involvement with the issues of concern to them; Baird had no such history. Hence, they did not know whether or not she would prove to be sympathetic to their agenda, so they neither supported nor opposed her nomination as attorney general; instead, they warily remained silent on its merits when it was initially announced.[36] Since Baird had no track record of support for the causes of greatest concern to women's groups, the groups did virtually nothing to help her when her nomination ran into trouble. The more doubtful the nomination became, the further the groups distanced themselves. The absence of support and the distancing of what one might have initially supposed would have been either sympathetic parties or allies in the confirmation process reinforced in the public's eye and in the confirmation process the appearance of a doomed nomination. This appearance hastened the nomination's demise.

THE SIGNIFICANCE OF INFORMAL ADVISERS
IN THE APPOINTMENTS PROCESS

There is evidence that interested individuals acting alone, and sometimes in concert, have wielded significant influence on appointments matters, particularly behind the scenes. Presidents and senators routinely consult friends and other interested individuals about possible nominations and confirmations. The significance of such consultations is that they occur informally, and are thus virtually impossible to monitor and control. It is natural and inevitable that presidents and senators will contact and be contacted by people with whom they have had close relationships about matters on which those offering the advice have some insight, expertise, or information. Such consultation may be viewed as attractive because it reflects the democratization of the appointments process, that is, the broadening of input by citizens or other interested parties in the decision making on appointments. Of course, the degree to which such broadening actually occurs rests solely within the discretion of those seeking consultation.

Some observers, however, find such informal consultation problematic for several reasons. First, informal consultation could represent the opposite of the democratization of the process by reflecting the degree to which decision makers are captive to or consult only with a relatively small elite. Moreover, such informal consultation could be problematic depending on the individuals who are consulted. This is especially true for federal judges, particularly Supreme Court justices, who have been consulted throughout U.S. history about all kinds of judicial appointments and even some nonjudicial appointments.

No doubt, formalizing consultation with the federal judiciary would be unconstitutional because it would require the federal judiciary to perform a clearly nonjudicial function or would unduly interfere with its exercise of its basic authority. Yet, informally consulting federal judges (particularly Supreme Court justices) about judicial appointments does not necessarily pose a constitutional problem, because the consultation given does not bind the appointing authorities in any way and because, as one might imagine, federal judges have a vested institutional interest in the quality of judicial appointments. Such consultations have occurred largely because the judges or justices whose counsel has been sought were once confidants of or advisers to the presidents who nominated them or the senators who approved their appointments.

For instance, Justices Brandeis, Frankfurter, Douglas, and Fortas continued to advise the presidents who appointed them well after being appointed to the Supreme Court. Perhaps no Supreme Court justice has ever been more actively involved in counseling presidents and senators about judicial appointments than William Howard Taft. As Chief Justice, Taft actively offered his advice on judicial appointments and legislation concerning the judiciary to Republican presidents Harding, Coolidge, and Hoover. Justice Willis Van Devanter, whom Taft appointed to the Supreme Court in 1910, often acted as Taft's alter ego when Taft was unavailable to provide or needed assistance in providing such counsel.[37]

The significance of informal consultation is that it demonstrates the limits of the formal constitutional structure for making federal appointments. The informality is consistent with the structure precisely because it is not barred by the formal constitutional structure. Informal consultation does not invest a judge (or anyone else, for that matter) with a power that some other formal authority (such as a president or senator) must respect. To be sure, formal authorities might take informal input quite seriously; however, as long as the consultation is informal, it has no binding force.

The remaining question is whether such informal advice, even though it has no formal binding authority, injects into the process officials who for one reason or another should not be so involved. The potential danger is that while it is possible to take the judges out of politics, it may not be possible to take the politics out of the judges, for the latter came to their offices because they, or those close to them, did some significant service for the party in power that resulted in their appointment. Allowing federal judges to provide informal input on matters of concern to them such as other judicial appointments tends to foster their political impulses. One solution for anyone concerned about the injection of federal judges into the selection process would be to pass a law that would prohibit any federal judge from advising or being involved in any way with a president's or senator's consideration of a nominee to a federal court. Such a law might reduce some informal activity, but it would be difficult to enforce. Federal judges might find ways around it by sending signals by indirect, difficult-to-detect means.

No doubt, the degree to which interested parties, including organized interest groups, wield influence in the federal appointments process (or at least with respect to high-profile nominations or offices) is aided or facilitated in no small measure by the media. The next chapter considers the relationship between the press and such interested parties and several other issues relating to the media's role in the federal appointments process.

Chapter Eight

THE IMPACT OF MEDIA AND

TECHNOLOGY ON THE FEDERAL

APPOINTMENTS PROCESS

PERHAPS NO ACTOR or institution has been criticized more for its activities in the federal appointments process than the media. It has become commonplace to attack the media for their coverage of the political process (including the nominating and confirmation processes) for several reasons. First, a popular charge is that in covering political events the media are guilty of asserting or promoting their own, frequently undisclosed agenda. Some refer to this as the "liberal" bias of the press. Others claim that the media have an interest in influencing the outcomes of the stories they report. Second, the media are sometimes charged with allowing their sources (who demand to remain anonymous) to use them for often hidden agendas. Third, with the advent of the Internet and the explosion of cable networks and programming, the pressures of competition for advertising dollars and for audiences have led media outlets and organizations to become increasingly obsessed with uncovering and reporting scandal and to substitute commentary or speculation for factual reporting.[1] Indeed, in their important study of the quality of the media's coverage of (and impact on) President Clinton's impeachment proceedings, Bill Kovach and Tom Rosenstiel conclude that in "today's mixed-media climate," "a true and reliable account of the day's events" has been undermined and displaced by "the continuous news cycle, the growing power of sources over reporters, varying standards of journalism, and a fascination with inexpensive polarizing argument."[2] The mixed media in question include "a newly diversified mass media in which the cultures of entertainment, infotainment, argument, analysis, tabloid, and mainstream press not only work side by side but intermingle and merge."[3] No doubt, the emergence of the Internet (including full-time, on-line, free-lance, self-proclaimed reporters such as Matt Drudge) has helped to effectuate this transformation. It has led to, among other things, a proliferation of unfiltered information about political events that has put additional pressure on the media to monitor and often to report rumors or risk not relaying the breaking story.

These developments raise a basic question: Are the problems with the media's coverage of the impeachment proceedings similarly reflected in the media's coverage of the federal appointments process? If so (and no one questions that to a significant degree they are), another question arises as to the extent to which these problems undermine any positive or constructive functions performed by the media. A related question concerns the ramifications of new technologies, particularly the Internet, on the nature or quality of the media's coverage of the appointments process (as well as on the quality or nature of the deliberations in the appointments process). This chapter examines these questions in light of both the media's and new technologies' contributions (pro and con) to the quality and nature of deliberations in the federal appointments process.

THE MEDIA AS EDUCATOR

In evaluating the performance of the media in the appointments process, one needs to clarify first the objectives the media have tried to achieve in the federal appointments process and then the impact of the changing landscape of news coverage on the achievement of these objectives. To begin with, one of the media's most important objectives historically has been educative. Throughout U.S. history, the media have prided themselves on their efforts to inform or enlighten the American public about public affairs. Indeed, no single organization has done more than the media to inform the general public about various episodes, events, and developments in the federal appointments process. Prior to the twentieth century, newspapers and, to a much lesser extent, magazines, pamphlets, letter campaigns, and word of mouth, particularly among influential private citizens and civic organizations, helped to publicize some aspects of the federal appointments process. In the twentieth century, the emergence and growth of the newspaper industry and magazines, radio, television (including cable), and the Internet have expanded enormously the coverage of each of the different stages of the federal appointments process. The extent of the process's coverage in each of these media is aided by the Senate's modern practice of holding open hearings.

There is no question that some modern media outlets (such as C-Span) have provided excellent instruction for the public (and even for government officials) on the operations of the national government (including the federal appointments process). Moreover, new technologies, particularly the Internet, have made available extraordinary amounts of raw data and have opened windows into the operations of important governmental institutions, such as congressional committees. It has become commonplace for individual citizens to be able to access any House or Senate committee to get a schedule of its hearings and transcripts of its proceedings, and to e-mail to a committee member (if not the committee as a whole) their views on pending issues.

One critical question has to do with the impact or consequences of the rise of new technology on the media's achievement of their educative function. Some positive developments are already evident, as reflected in recent empirical work on the Internet's effect on the operations of administrative agencies.[4] For instance, the proliferation of news outlets, including the numerous Web pages that dispense information regarding governmental events or operations, ensures the dissemination of large quantities of data regarding many if not most of the stages of the appointments process. Such dissemination makes it possible for people to retrieve extraordinary amounts of information about the process(es) in which they are interested. In addition, the Internet has given individual citizens an unprecedented opportunity to interact with lawmakers and their staffs.[5] It is now the norm for a committee to have its own Web site, to dispense information on its Web site, and to provide links on its Web site to its individual members. Consequently, individual citizens can submit their opinions to lawmakers with relatively little effort or cost. Moreover, the distribution or dissemination of information (going in all directions) is generally unfiltered. Citizens can get information largely unrefined by the media and can in turn share their opinions with small groups on-line, with committees, or with individual committee members about pending events. And, quite significantly, the responses or opinions sent to law-makers are presented in searchable forms; that is, they are submitted in such a format that lawmakers can study e-mail messages en masse to de-termine areas (and the extent) of support and opposition.

These developments are not cost-free to society, the legislative process, or the media's educative function. First, as I have indicated, the Internet is largely unregulated, and the bulk of the information on it is raw. Thus, one often must rely on others to organize it. It is not clear how many individual citizens are willing (or for how long some might be inclined) to undertake the special efforts required to organize the raw material of interest to them on the Internet.

Second, the Internet invites the spread of gossip and unreliable data. Precisely because the bulk of the information on the Internet is unregu-lated and unfiltered, much of it is unsubstantiated rumor or innuendo. It is difficult to separate fact from fiction. The Drudge Report, for in-stance, frequently spreads rumors; sometimes these check out, but quite often they do not. One problem with spreading information in this fash-ion is that it puts mainstream media organizations under the pressure of having to check the information, and often to report it as having been reported elsewhere or to risk being scooped. The second problem is that serious damage is often done once the information is released, so the spread of false information (even innocently) can wreck reputations or become a monkey wrench in the wheels of governmental or public delib-erations. Unfounded or unsubstantiated rumors spread across the Inter-net are simply the most dramatic illustration of the degree to which the Internet can invade the legitimate scope of individual privacy.

Third, the sheer speed of the Internet makes it harder to keep sensitive information confidential and invites intemperate response, deliberation, or decision making. Take, for example, the House Judiciary Committee's decision almost immediately after having received the Starr Report to put virtually all of it on the Internet before any member of the House had even had a chance to read it. The problem was that it had been poorly redacted in several places, resulting in the publication of the names, identities, conversations, and actions of several innocent people who had absolutely nothing to do with the core charges alleged in the report.[6]

It seems likely that the Internet will exacerbate the problems that have led in the past to the media's excesses in covering the appointments process. In this regard, consider initially the problems that have already occurred, and then imagine how much worse they are likely to be as a result of the prominence of Internet use. First, in an effort to obtain a competitive advantage, many reporters have felt increasing pressure to engage in sensationalist reporting. Perhaps no incident better illustrates this tendency than the behavior of the press in the later stages of Robert Bork's confirmation hearings.[7] Not satisfied with reporting on Judge Bork's substantial public and academic record, the press discovered and publicized his video rentals. The press defended its actions, as the press invariably does, as the inevitable price the nation must pay for having the First Amendment, which explicitly protects the freedoms of both speech and the press.[8]

Second, the expansion of television and cable, particularly since the first televised confirmation hearings (for Sandra Day O'Connor in 1982), has made it much easier for senators to play to the galleries. With the prospect of free airtime, senators rarely give up the chance to give a speech or engage in theatrical questioning of nominees in highly publicized hearings.

Third, the media have already extensively intruded on individuals' privacy in their quest to beat the competition in covering high-profile hearings. Again, the most outlandish examples are the reports of the video rentals of Supreme Court nominees Robert Bork and Clarence Thomas. These reports served no constructive purpose. The Internet now provides even more people with greater opportunities to spread private information of no public significance about public figures.

Fourth, heated confirmation hearings are not likely to feature much thoughtful study of nominees' writings and speeches, and the Internet might reduce even further the opportunity for deliberative or careful analysis.[9] For instance, in the heat of the Senate debate about Judge Bork's nomination to the Supreme Court, some of Bork's opponents distorted or misrepresented the substance of some of his judicial decisions.[10] Similarly, the media helped to fuel the controversy over President Clinton's nomination of Lani Guinier to head the Justice Department's Civil Rights Division by spending considerably more time reporting the contending sides' representations about the content or gist of some of her academic writings than trying to determine and convey to the public an impartial assessment of the accuracy of the representations made.[11]

Fifth, the instantaneous spread of information or charges against a nominee can make virtually any response ineffective. Take, for example, President Reagan's nomination of Judge Douglas Ginsburg to the Supreme Court. The story that he had smoked marijuana as a tenured law professor sent shock waves through his supporters. Judge Ginsburg never got a chance publicly to defend himself, and his nomination quickly fell apart.

Likewise, Lani Guinier's nomination was fatally damaged by the allegation from some conservative interest groups that she was a "quota queen." She vigorously denied the accuracy of the appellation and asked that she be given a chance to respond to it in a public hearing. The problem was that the charge was coined in a catchy way, so it spread far and wide — and Guinier's nomination was thus undone — before she had a chance to defend herself in a public hearing. In Guinier's case, the charge was initially made on television and in newspaper editorials; imagine how much bigger the damage done (particularly in the eyes of the president and members of Congress) by the criticism once it is spread on the Internet.

The media's impact on events can, however, be exaggerated or misunderstood. It does not cover nominations and confirmation proceedings in a vacuum. Instead, the critical thing is to assess how the interaction among the media, interest groups, and political and party leaders influences the event itself or the public's perception or understanding of it. Clarifying the nature of this interaction is extremely important for assessing the accuracy of the myth that the media lead or shape public opinion. An examination of the apparent impacts of this interaction on the public's opinions regarding Robert Bork's confirmation, Clarence Thomas's confirmation, and President Clinton's impeachment proceedings suggests the limitated validity or accuracy of this myth.

To begin with, the anti-Bork campaign waged by various liberal and civil rights interest groups and by some liberal senators was played out in the media, and the incessant reporting of criticism about Bork's nomination clearly helped to turn the tide against it. One month after Bork's nomination, 45 percent of those polled responded affirmatively and 40 percent responded negatively when asked whether the Senate should confirm Bork.[12] On September 28, 1987, a Lou Harris poll indicated that 29 percent of those polled favored and 57 percent of those polled were against the confirmation of Robert Bork.[13] Just after the Senate rejected Bork on October 23, 1987, a Gallup poll indicated that 32 percent of those polled opposed while 51 percent supported the Senate's vote.[14] The media campaign undoubtedly played a pivotal role in increasing public opposition to the Bork nomination.

That the Bush White House and conservative interest groups learned from the Bork defeat is obvious from their efforts to secure Clarence Thomas's confirmation. Public polling data suggest the effectiveness of their efforts (and of the lessons they learned).[15] The initial strategy of the Bush White House, aided by such conservative interest groups as the Landmark Center for Civil Rights, the Christian Coalition, and the Family Research Council, was to cultivate favorable media stories about and images of Thomas (as rising from abject poverty to the highest court in the land) and thereby to build support for Thomas among African American organizations and churches, and southern Democrats. The initial polling reflected the success of this strategy: Thomas's standing among African Americans had risen from more than 60 percent having no firm opinion at the time of his nomination to more than 65 percent approval in national polls by the start of his confirmation hearings.[16] Though Thomas's approval ratings (among both people generally and African Americans) dipped immediately after Anita Hill's testimony, efforts by the Bush White House, Thomas, and conservative interest groups to destroy her credibility and to build sympathy for Thomas shifted public opinion: during the weekend before the Senate's final vote on Thomas, the polls showed public support for Thomas running twice as high as it was for Hill, and also showed that a majority of Americans believed that Hill, not Thomas, had lied during the hearings.[17]

The interest groups' media campaigns and the tenor of the media's coverage had much less—perhaps even the opposite—effect on public opinion throughout President Clinton's impeachment proceedings. Kovach and Rosensteil have demonstrated empirically that the media's coverage was "pro-prosecution," but they also found that the public stopped paying attention early in the proceedings to the media's commentary and steadily opposed the hearings and the ouster of the president for months in spite of the media's apparent bias and the vigorous media campaigns waged by conservative interest and political groups in favor of impeachment.[18]

The disconnection between the public response to media campaigns or bias in the impeachment proceedings and the public's evident susceptibility to such campaigns or bias in other situations could be explained on several conceivable bases. First, it is possible that the public is more likely to rely on press or media accounts or campaigns in some hearings than in others. This might be particularly true when the contested event turns not on whether someone did or said something but rather on a study of the person's academic or other writings. In a circumstance in which firsthand familiarity with scholarly or other kinds of writings is important to the disposition of an event, the public might be inclined to rely more on the opinions or packaging of experts. The second phase of Justice Thomas's confirmation hearings and President Clinton's impeachment proceedings largely turned on questions about the occurrence and significance of certain alleged personal misconduct. The public could listen to both Hill and Thomas and determine for itself the credibility of either person, just as it could watch the president's videotaped testimony in the *Jones* case and before the grand jury to determine its veracity and relationship to his ability to continue to function as the chief executive.

Second, the public had no vested interest in the Bork and Thomas hearings corresponding to its vested interest in the outcome of President Clinton's impeachment proceedings. Much of the public did not want Congress to make light of the fact that it had twice expressed its support for Bill Clinton by electing him president. Since the public's first impressions of Bork and Thomas were formed in the midst of their respective confirmation hearings, it stands to reason that the public might have been more susceptible to interest group or media opinion in forming those initial impressions.

Third, it is conceivable that one significant difference between the Bork and Thomas hearings, on the one hand, and the Clinton impeachment proceedings, on the other, is that the former largely occurred in the early phase of what Kovach and Rosenstiel have dubbed "the attack culture."[19] Occurring more than a decade after the Bork hearings and almost a decade after the Thomas hearings, the president's impeachment proceedings may have happened at a time when the public had grown tired of news coverage focused primarily on personal attack, scandal, and speculation. Perhaps in response to the coverage that they have grown to dislike and to the opportunity to get more unfiltered information than ever before, the public has become more adept, as some political psychologists suggest, at cutting through the "attack culture" to find the information it needs or wants to know.

THE MEDIA AS PARTICIPANT

Yet another function performed by at least some in the media has been the effort to try to shape the events that they cover or report. Kovach and Rosenstiel suggest that national leaders and the media need "the attack culture"—the former to discredit their enemies and the latter to maintain or increase audiences. As a result, a symbiotic relationship develops, one that, in Kovach and Rosenstiel's view, drove the impeachment proceedings against President Clinton.[20] A similar phenomenon is evident in the media's coverage of key stages of important confirmation contests. In considering the following examples of this phenomenon from the recent past of the federal appointments process, one should consider the impact of the Internet, which offers a forum in which just about anyone can launch an attack.

For instance, the media have increasingly put pressure on the nominating phase by trying to report the names being considered for certain key nominations. The names then become fodder for a president's political foes or media commentators. The media get these names from a variety of sources (which may have their own agendas in releasing them), including administration insiders, people with close contacts to key administration personnel (such as senators or their staffs), and the candidates themselves (or their supporters). Perhaps the most dramatic illustration of this phenomenon occurred during the first two years of the Clinton administration when the media essentially vetted publicly the names of possible candidates for various high-level offices. This de facto partnership among the administration, interest groups, and the media has helped to make or break more than a few significant nominations.

By reporting (usually with the help of interest groups) potential problems with or complaints about various nominees for certain high-profile offices, the media also effectively helped the Clinton administration to narrow its list or even in some cases to settle on a nominee. Such apparently was the case when President Clinton was looking for a nominee to replace Justice Harry Blackmun.[21] The press reported that President Clinton had narrowed his search down to three people—Judge Richard Arnold of the Eighth Circuit, Secretary of the Interior Bruce Babbitt, and Judge Stephen Breyer of the First Circuit. In 1993 the president had decided against nominating Breyer to take the seat on the Court vacated by Justice White after personally interviewing him. Nevertheless, the problem in 1995 was that press reports indicated that Arnold and Babbitt were each for different reasons less appealing nominees. Arnold's problems were, first, that he could not provide the White House with sufficient assurance that he could serve on the Court for at least fifteen years because he had been diagnosed with an indolent form of non-Hodgkin's lymphoma, and, second, that he had authored an opinion overturned by the Supreme Court that had upheld the decision of a Jaycees organization to exclude women.[22] Babbitt failed to get the nomination because of suspicions among some Republican senators that his liberal activism as a governor was a signal that he would be a liberal activist judge and because of the discontent expressed by some interest groups, particularly conservationists, about his performance as secretary of the interior.[23] In the end, Breyer proved to have the fewest negatives.[24] President Clinton nominated Breyer even though he was still not enthusiastic about him after a second interview. The scrutiny given by the media to the prospective nominees and his own desire for a quick confirmation helped to pressure President Clinton to make a nomination he might not have made under other circumstances.

The public vetting of Stephen Breyer illustrates another important impact the media have had on the federal appointments process. In particular, the fact that Justice Breyer had on two different occasions survived the close scrutiny of the press helped to build momentum for his confirmation that subsequent reporting could not derail. By the time President Clinton nominated Breyer, it was widely thought that Breyer's confirmation would be a cakewalk. Hence, when it was reported in the midst of his confirmation hearings that Breyer might have sat in judgment on cases in which his rulings might have affected his financial interests, only a few senators took serious note. The inertia against stalling the confirmation proved insurmountable. Similarly, more than a few lower-court nominees over the past few decades have met virtually no serious resistance in Senate confirmation proceedings at least partly because no one in the media paid (and no one with sufficient clout was asking the media to pay) serious attention to the fact that several of them had almost no meaningful or relevant experience to justify their appointments. Yet, even when nominations have had problems, sometimes inertia has made the media's reporting of certain potential problems virtually irrelevant.

As one might expect, the converse is true for hastily made nominations. The latter are, at least in the public's perception, like blank slates which can be filled with dirt quickly uncovered by a media interested in sensational news events. When a hasty nomination has been accompanied by a slipshod background check (and the odds are quite good that such would be the case), then the administration and the nominee have been prone to be surprised or embarrassed by the media's investigative reporting. Such was the case with Douglas Ginsburg, who withdrew his nomination to the Supreme Court in the aftermath of press reports that he had been seen smoking marijuana as a tenured professor at Harvard Law School. The Reagan administration's haste in trying to nominate Ginsburg as quickly as possible after the Senate's rejection of Robert Bork's nomination increased the odds that something would be overlooked in the nominee's background.

The Clinton administration was similarly embarrassed by several hasty nominations, such as those of Zoë Baird and Lani Guinier. Both nominations quickly ran into trouble because of problems made public by the media that the administration had either not yet found or had discounted in its haste. No sooner had Baird been nominated than her admission that she had failed to pay Social Security taxes for certain domestic help brought a maelstrom of negative reporting. Nor did it take long once Lani Guinier was nominated for her critics to publicize their disagreement with some supposedly controversial statements in her public writings. Stephen Carter, among others, has harshly criticized the media for failing to inform the public more accurately about the substance of Guinier's writings and to correct over- or misstatements about her writings propounded by her or the administration's critics or political enemies.[25] Although it may be demanding too much to expect the media to master the technical writings of various presidential nominees, there is no doubt that merely reporting the charges or representations made about someone's writings is bound to leave a negative impression that will be difficult to remove unless some effort is made to put the public criticisms in perspective and measure them against the media's own assessments of the record(s) in question.

To be sure, it is difficult to assess cause and effect when a nomination failed and there was negative media coverage of it before its demise. Regardless of whether the media are reacting or taking the initiative in digging up dirt, they do not work alone. Political parties, interest groups, senators, the president and his team, and the nominee and his or her friends and allies or foes are all trying to influence the outcome as well. Nevertheless, without media attention, coverage, or scrutiny, it is possible for a nomination rife with problems to sail through not just an administration's vetting process but also the confirmation proceedings. Of course, just the opposite could happen. It is also conceivable that in the absence of close media attention some senators, interest groups, or partisan foes could feel emboldened to raise questions—legitimate or not—about a nomination in the hope of torpedoing it precisely because they believe they can do so with almost complete anonymity.

There is little doubt that both timing and circumstance have a great deal to do with whether or when the media will take a more assertive role in some stage of the appointments process. For instance, at least some in the press seemed much more eager to investigate and publicize Robert Bork's and Clarence Thomas's video rentals than President Clinton's alleged infidelities. One possible reason for this is that in effectively admitting that he had done some wrong things in his marriage, President Clinton took the wind out of the sails of any story about his alleged infidelities. The press would have surely appeared extremely unsympathetic and muckraking had it persisted in pursuing the story in light of Clinton's admission of wrongdoing. In addition, the press has often indulged in a feeding frenzy when a problem with the potential of undoing a nomination has emerged, only to back off later after the damage has been done. For instance, several Clinton appointees, including the late Secretary of Commerce Ron Brown, sailed through the confirmation process without any attention being given to their failure to pay certain Social Security taxes on their domestic help;[26] however, once Zoë Baird admitted that she and her husband had failed to do so, the climate of subsequent confirmation proceedings changed. After Zoë Baird's forced withdrawal, all Clinton nominees were carefully vetted to ensure that they had paid Social Security taxes for their domestic help. The media's interest in the issue diminished in time. While some prospective nominees had to forgo government service because neither the administration nor they were prepared to withstand Senate or media scrutiny of their compliance with Social Security laws, others who apologized for their oversights and acted quickly to pay reparations were both nominated and confirmed. At least one critical difference between those who survived the appointments process and those who did not was the media's disparate treatment of them.

The potential of negative coverage of a nomination by the press has undoubtedly put a lot of pressure on the White House to conduct public relations campaigns to preempt possible opposition and attract public if not also senatorial support. In an earlier era, presidents tended to announce nominations through press releases or through the formal nomination document sent by the White House to the Senate. In the past few decades, presidents have announced nominations or made statements or taken actions in the confirmation stages with the understanding that virtually everything they say or do will be covered by the media. Moreover, modern presidents have felt the pressure to design a strategy for selling nominees to high-profile offices to the public, the Senate, and the press. Such strategies have included putting nominees in the best possible light in the quickest way possible; hence, presidents began to announce nominations in formal White House ceremonies with both the nominees and the press in attendance. In addition, White House staffers have increasingly undertaken the responsibility of giving the administration's version of high-profile nominees. The awareness that the media will give close scrutiny to their most important nominees has also led modern presidents to make a nominee's ability to perform well in public (including before the media) a critical criterion for his or her selection.

Other players in the process, including senators and interest groups, also recognize the significance of expressing their opinions or positions to the media. These actors are every bit as interested as the president in trying to shape or mold public opinion about their respective agendas. For instance, the objective of interest group communication with the press has been not just to communicate to the media itself but also to signal to the general public, particularly their members or natural constituents, with the help of the press. Such communication is crucial for mobilizing support for or opposition to a nomination of concern to an interest group.

One crucial question raised by the media's tendency to engage in negative or sensational reportage concerns the extent to which the media are responsible for the general decline in the civility of public discourse, a decline that has extended to the federal appointments process. Those making this assertion point, for example, to the record numbers of representatives and senators who in 1995 and 1996 declared they would not run for reelection in part because they felt that Congress had lost much of the collegial atmosphere it had enjoyed for the better part of its history. Stephen Carter, among others, condemns the media for its tendency to focus on the negative or disqualifying factors of a particular nomination rather than its general quality, and its willingness to publish salacious gossip.[27] Carter points to a number of instances in which the press has gone beyond the bounds of propriety in focusing on the negative simply for the sake of making news or attracting an audience, including in the midst of confirmation hearings publishing unconfirmed reports that Janet Reno had been stopped repeatedly for drunken driving, editorial comments on Robert Bork's beard and video rentals, and speculation about the significance of Roberta Achtenberg's homosexuality for her position as an assistant secretary in President Clinton's Department of Housing and Urban Development.[28] Perhaps an even more dramatic example was the report in the aftermath of President Clinton's decision to drop Kimba Wood as a possible attorney general nominee that Wood prior to entering law school had worked for a short time as a Playboy bunny.[29] The story was attributed to a White House aide who was disgruntled with Wood's apparent lack of candor in her conversations with the White House counsel's office about her arrangements for domestic help. Clearly, the story was a gratuitous shot by both the aide and the media and served no constructive purpose. It also reinforces the notion that the media have contributed to the decline in civil discourse about public affairs.

Nevertheless, the charges that public discourse has reached unprecedented depths of incivility are overstated.[30] To begin with, it is easy to find instances of coarse (or perhaps coarser) discourse in the nineteenth century and the first half of the twentieth century (during the famed era of "yellow" journalism).[31] The difficulty today is not so much that discourse is worse than it ever was; it is that there is more discourse than ever before—no doubt exponentially increased by the chat rooms and other opportunities for intercommunication on the Internet. Ironically, in the midst of all of this cacophony, the media are less likely than before to lead public opinion. Thus, while it was clear in the 1980s that the media's coverage of the Bork hearings shaped public opinion, the opposite happened in the 1990s when the media adopted a "pro-prosecution" orientation toward President Clinton but the public rejected it.[32] People were turned off by the media's coverage of the president's impeachment proceedings and reached their conclusions independently.

THE MEDIA AS OMBUDSMAN

Another major function performed by the media in the federal appointments process has been to check the abuse of official power. Again, as one might imagine, this function is likely to be reinforced and perhaps superseded to some extent by the Internet, which is becoming a separate forum for spreading information critical of government.

Two examples help to illustrate the impact of the media's self-appointed ombudsman function on the appointments process. First, on the eve of the Senate's consideration of President Franklin Roosevelt's nomination of Senator Hugo Black to the Supreme Court, a newspaper reporter broke a story about Black's membership in the Ku Klux Klan.[33] The story prompted some senators to question Black about the matter and even delayed the Senate's final vote on the nomination. Black publicly addressed the story immediately after his confirmation, and his public statement acknowledging membership in the KKK in his younger years put the matter largely but not completely to rest for the remainder of his career.

More recently, shortly before the Senate was scheduled to vote on Clarence Thomas's nomination to the Supreme Court, Nina Totenberg with National Public Radio and Tim Phelps of *Newsday* reported the Senate Judiciary Committee's initial refusal to schedule hearings to consider Anita Hill's charge against the nominee of sexual harassment.[34] The story helped to incite public pressure on the committee to hold a special set of hearings, whose racial and sexual politics outraged and embittered many people, including Justice Thomas. The fact that the first mention of the existence of Monica Lewinsky's semen-stained dress was on the Internet in the Drudge Report is an important sign of things to come. The Internet will likely be the place for other important revelations in the future.

Part Three

REFORMING THE

FEDERAL APPOINTMENTS PROCESS

Chapter Nine

THE NEED FOR REFORM

EVALUATING THE NEED to reform the federal appointments process requires resolving several preliminary matters. The first entails clarifying
some crucial terms and concepts—perhaps developing a refined or new
language—for analyzing the special dynamics of the federal appointments process. Among the fundamental terms and concepts that are rarely
examined systematically in the legal scholarship on the appointments
process but that undoubtedly have implications for its reform are *politics*,
ideology, and *norms*. Obviously, these terms and concepts can mean very
different things to different people or can mean different things in different contexts; and these different meanings can clearly have a bearing on
the feasibility or coherence of various reform proposals (including the fit
between proposed means and ends).

Another important preliminary question, for which the clarifications
of basic terms and concepts pose serious ramifications, relates to the need
to clarify the significance of the distinction between descriptive and normative analyses of the system. Even if one were to posit a descriptive
account of the federal appointments process (in terms, for instance, of
interest group influence or dominance), it would not resolve the necessity
for reform. Merely describing the system does not indicate whether the
system could work more efficiently or as well as it should. One still needs
to resolve at least two other issues—whether the descriptive account is
sound or comprehensive and, if so, how the system as described measures
up to or compares with other attainable alternatives. This chapter considers these preliminary questions before moving on to an examination of
some specific proposals for generally improving or fine-tuning the federal
appointments process.

It is not possible to talk responsibly or coherently about reforming the federal appointments process without initially clarifying some basic terms and concepts. In much of the legal scholarship on the federal appointments process, commentators gloss over the meanings of critical terms and concepts. Moreover, many fundamental concepts and terms have different meanings, depending on the context, or are used (often purposely) with loaded meanings. The different meanings of critical terms and concepts pose serious challenges and ramifications for reforming the system. For instance, the feasibility of certain alternatives depends a great deal on the clarity or precision of their objectives or the evils at which they have been directed.

Perhaps the concept that is most widely but indiscriminately used in discussions of the federal appointments process is *politics*. *Politics* can of course mean many different things. To many, it might refer to partisanship or acting strictly or primarily in accord with the interests or leadership of political parties. To others, *politics* might suggest "street-fighting pluralism" (in political scientist Robert Dahl's classic characterization)[1] or simply the competition between conflicting interests or values. To still others, it might have a Machiavellian meaning, that is, it might refer to unprincipled, strictly self-serving machinations. By *politics*, some might mean the disproportionate influence wielded in the political or electoral process by some factions or organizations, such as interest groups. Still other meanings include identity politics (the degree to which people support candidates, issues, or causes with which they can identify based on common or shared concerns and experiences) or issue salience (the extent to which an issue, such as abortion, is of such importance to voters that it constitutes the primary basis on which they decide how to vote, or to elected officials who give special priority to it).[2] For still others, the term *politics* refers to *ideology*, a loaded concept that can mean more than one thing. *Ideology* could allude to either a general philosophy about governing (or judicial decision making) or a deeply entrenched mode of approaching political or moral questions (including issues of constitutional interpretation). Yet another meaning of *politics* is the "politics of personal destruction" to which President Clinton attributed his impeachment (i.e., the use of the legal and political process to demonize and destroy one's political foes). Of course, commentators, interest groups, and political leaders could understand the term to have any one or combination of these possible meanings.

Norms is another concept that has not previously been discussed in the legal scholarship on the federal appointments process but is crucial for understanding the system. Norms theorists concede that the meaning of the term *norms* is elusive. Though the focus of norms theorists is usually on private orderings and relationships, one common understanding of this term is clearly applicable in the context of the federal appointments process—informal agreements or arrangements that have developed over time for governing or constraining the discretion of principal actors. Such agreements are reflected in the patterns and practices previously described in the book as characterizing the special dynamics of the federal appointments process. Presidents and senators have developed informal agreements to fill the substantial gaps within, and moderate the ample discretion allowed by, the loose framework for making federal appointments.

That such norms do operate in the federal appointments process is beyond question. Some of these norms have been memorialized (such as Senate Rule 26, which governs basic rules for committee proceedings), while others have not been reduced to writing or encapsulated in formal procedures but are based on practice and precedent. Some examples of the norms that constrain interaction between presidents and senators in the appointments process are senatorial courtesy; senatorial deference to a president's choices of high-ranking officials in the executive branch; the president's agreement to tell Senate leaders before a recess the names of the people he expects to designate as recess appointees; the prerogatives of individual senators to put nominations on temporary (as opposed to indefinite) hold; the Senate majority leader's complete discretion over which matters he will allow to come before the Senate (including the nominations for which he will allow final votes to be taken); and the implied authority of a committee chair to direct the committee's affairs, including the timing of and numbers of witnesses to testify in hearings, subject to the ability of the committee and the Senate to override his rulings.

An important need for reform might derive from the fact that some norms have begun to deteriorate. This deterioration is especially evident in the realm of judicial selection and thus will be discussed as a justification for reform in the next chapter.

The clarifications of various terms do, however, pose significant consequences for developing sound descriptive and normative analyses of the federal appointments process. For instance, recounting the norms developed by presidents and senators to facilitate their respective interests in the federal appointments process does not indicate which norms are good or desirable. Nor does recognition of the deterioration of some norms indicate whether or to what extent such deterioration is a bad thing or whether or to what extent it might be desirable to restore disintegrated (or disintegrating) norms. Moreover, describing the operations of the federal appointments process might illuminate some of the ways in which different kinds of "politics" (such as interest group or political parties' dominance) might influence the system; however, the task remains to determine whether or to what extent such influence is a good or desirable thing or can be more effectively checked or channeled.

Clarifying basic concepts such as *politics* is also important for improving the evaluation of the feasibility and coherence of various reform proposals, particularly structural alterations. Consider, for instance, the perennial calls for depoliticizing judicial selection. One obvious problem with such proclamations is that the kind of politics reformers might like to exclude from the judicial selection process is far from clear. Different solutions are required, depending on the "politics" one would like to eradicate or reduce in the confirmation process. If, for example, the problem is perceived to be that the participation of presidents and senators virtually guarantees that they will be acutely sensitive and thus the process will be dominated or driven by their reelection concerns and short-term interests, then the focus needs to be on both the accuracy of this perception and the practicality or dangers of divesting them entirely of their respective responsibilities regarding federal appointments but also radically altering the constitutional structure in order to reduce to the fullest extent possible or desirable their respective discretion in the process. If the concern is to remove or reduce interest group dominance in the appointments process, then the focus of reformers needs to be on not just excluding or removing interest group participation but also searching (perhaps in vain) for ways to reduce interest groups' informal inputs or contacts with senators or their staffs. If, however, the problem is the effect of the influx of soft money on the appointments process, then yet another solution (such as radical campaign finance reform) needs to be considered.

Moreover, even if some agreement could be reached on the kind of politics that needs to be removed from the appointments process, it would be difficult if not practically impossible to create a system in which any of these kinds of politics is wholly absent. For instance, consider the problem of the influence of political parties (or of efforts to advance parties' agendas or dominance in the appointments process). Political parties have not diminished so much as a force in the U.S. political system that major decision makers can ignore or largely discount the concerns of party leaders or partisan support. Moreover, the process for making political appointments cannot be easily cleansed of every partisan dimension. The choices of decision makers in the system will be informed to some extent by partisan concerns (or preferences for party affiliations or attachment to certain party ideals or tenets), because of the perceived opportunities to exercise control over the appointments process as a means to reward allies, punish enemies, or advance causes. Even if it were possible to find or designate some nominally independent authority to recommend or make some or all federal appointments, the person(s) who would exercise this authority must still somehow be chosen and be subject to some incentives and be held accountable. Presumably, the appointing authority would be answerable to or be a part of one of the political branches of the federal government. It is, however, unlikely that the president would be disposed to relinquish his final authority to make nominations or that senators would be willing to forgo their final discretion to approve or disapprove nominations. Consequently, the best one could hope for is probably some fine-tuning of the system, particularly reform that is likely to be viewed as being in the best interests of the institutions responsible for making appointments decisions.

One possible reform in this regard is The Century Foundation's proposal that each administration should appoint the staff for a permanent interagency branch that would be responsible for background checks on possible nominees and for steering nominees through the confirmation process.[3] Alternatively, the Miller Center has proposed that the Senate

Judiciary Committee increase the size of its staff responsible for checking or investigating the backgrounds of judicial nominees,[4] a proposal
designed to expedite senatorial decision making.

The Century Foundation and Miller Center proposals, if adopted,
would surely produce some beneficial results, though neither is likely to
depoliticize judicial selection to any appreciable degree. The Miller Center proposal, if adopted, would likely expedite background checks for judicial nominations, an especially important goal in light of the fact that
the time-consuming nature of such investigations has been an important
cause of the unusually long delays that the Clinton administration has had
in formally announcing many of its nominations. Nevertheless, this proposal does not provide any guidelines (nor does it make any recommendations) on how senators should use the information in a confirmation
hearing. The Century Foundation's proposal goes further than the Miller
Center's proposal in helping to expedite background checks generally (by
streamlining control over them and precluding factions within administrations from contesting their control). The proposal retains, however,
an arguably troublesome dimension, because it allows each administration to appoint the staff for such an agency; the people on the staff would
thus be beholden to those who appointed them. In other words, this proposal would leave intact the present constitutional scheme under which
the primary officials responsible for making nominations or confirmation
decisions are exposed to interest group pressure and partisan influences
about which critics of the federal appointments process complain. Even if
the appointing authority were not accountable to or a part of some political body or authority, the federal appointments process would still not be
completely freed from some undesirable influences (such as factionalism
or interest group dominance) because, as the experiences in the states have
demonstrated, politics in some sense (such as the classic notion of street-
fighting pluralism) is endemic to every system of appointments ever used
in this nation.[5]

However, if one were willing to accept a federal appointments process
under some degree of control by political actors, then radical reform of the
constitutional structure would be unnecessary. The rough-and-tumble of
institutional, partisan, and interest group efforts to establish dominance
over federal appointments is a natural consequence of the allocation of

power in the present system; it is the price of having a constitutional scheme for making appointments of which politically accountable authorities are in charge.

It is telling that the critics of the federal appointments process rarely suggest abandoning the basic division of authority for making federal appointments set forth in the Appointments Clause. For instance, even though The Century Foundation condemns the presidential appointments process for being too slow, abusing nominees (by leaving them vulnerable to individual senators bent on their institutional prerogatives to advance personal, partisan, interest-group-driven, or issue-related attacks), and being infused with duplicative and unnecessary paperwork, it does not recommend depriving presidents or senators of their respective constitutional authority under the Appointments Clause. Nor is it surprising that major political actors, such as presidents and senators, would act at least to some extent and in some sense sensitive to certain institutional and electoral concerns with respect to the matters entrusted to their care or discretion. As long as the president and the Senate share the primary division of labor on federal appointments, the process will remain at some fundamental level "political"—that is, it will remain subject to some basic internal and external pressures, including a contest of wills between different actors and forces within each branch for control of or influence over its internal decision making, tension between the branches for basic control of the system generally and particular nominations or confirmations, and interest groups bent on influencing the internal dynamics of each branch's basic organization and relationship with other branches. Unless the nation is prepared to change the basic structure of its federal government and adopt or move to a different kind of political system with different rules for financing the elections of its national leaders, different terms of office for elected and appointed officials, and other conditions for selection and removal, radical reform is unlikely.

Moreover, opting for a nonpolitical entity, such as a commission of experts or even an independent agency, to make recommendations, if not final judgments, on federal appointments runs into a couple of related risks. First, it runs the risk of insulating the decision making on such matters from meaningful public scrutiny and accountability. Second, the members of such commissions might be prone to many of the same pressures that political leaders must deal with, such as interest group and political party entreaties and issue salience, but no more capable (and perhaps less so) in dealing with them competently.

Retaining national political leaders as the key decision makers in the federal appointments process does not preclude constructive change. Reform of the process is still conceivable, though in relatively nonradical ways. One possible reform would be the clarification of the objectives of the federal appointments process, a change that would help to improve evaluation of the system. At present, there is no general consensus on the basic purpose of the system—people disagree, for instance, over whether the objective in appointments is to avoid bad nominations (however that is defined), to put the best people in office (however that is defined), or some combination of these goals. Moreover, it sometimes appears that no consensus on this question exists even within some administrations, much less between presidents and senators. For their part, the framers generally had only negative ambitions for the federal appointments process; that is, they hoped to avoid certain evils rather than to attain positive objectives such as appointing well-qualified political executives or federal judges, elevating the dialogue between presidents and senators about appointments or related matters, and maximizing the accountability of the officials in charge of the process.

Creating incentives for the political actors in charge of the system to clarify their objectives or to adopt different missions than those they have traditionally pursued has two advantages over the present process. First, it provides the means by which to change or elevate the terms of debate in the confirmation process generally or in any given confirmation dispute. Moreover, it provides a basis on which to hold the actors in charge of the system accountable—one could measure their actions or achievements against the goals they have posited as their or the system's objectives.[6]

Yet another fundamental question that needs to be answered in any basic evaluation of the need to reform the appointments process is whether the transformation of the U.S. system of government from one dominated by Congress to one dominated by the president requires modifying the Appointments Clause. The concern is that the Appointments Clause gave the president some advantage in a system of checks and balances for a national government most framers expected to be dominated by Congress, whereas in today's world the clause arguably reinforces or enhances presidential supremacy in a system generally dominated by the president. The question is whether or not this state of affairs reflects an imbalance between the executive and legislative branches and, if so, whether this imbalance is sufficiently problematic to require correction.

There are at least three responses to this dilemma. To begin with, the problem might not be a problem at all. One could construe the numerous ways in which senators have developed parliamentary devices to check presidential dominance in the appointments process as reflecting a balance rather than an imbalance in the prevailing dynamics of the appointments process. More fundamentally, the problem, to the extent that it does exist, is a function of the division of authority in the Appointments Clause. The expansion of the national government is inextricably linked to the president's increased opportunities to make certain federal appointments. The Appointments Clause is based on the expectation that the president would have the upper hand in the federal appointments process while the Senate would have a veto or check in the form of its discretion to reject or withhold confirmation of presidential nominees. Moreover, congressional government, as it was constituted throughout the nineteenth and early twentieth centuries, was based in part on an arguable distortion of the division of authority in the Appointments Clause: the tendency of senators to recommend candidates for certain federal offices in their respective states subject to the president's objection or veto. The latter practice is, in the view of some, more at odds with the plain text and original understanding of the Appointments Clause than the circumstance in which the prevailing or dominant appointment authority, at least for purposes of making nominations, is the president.

The concern here is whether or not the president's increased opportunities to shape the direction of the national government frustrate some of the original or fundamental values that gave rise to the initial allocation of appointment authority in the Constitution. This concern might, however, be overstated, because the more positions the president has the authority to fill, the more chances senators with grudges of one sort or another have to oppose his choices. Moreover, it does not necessarily require too many blocked or delayed nominations to grab the president's attention or to cause him personal or political damage.

A related issue concerns the ways in which Congress may condition or constrain a president's appointment authority. Whether or not the president holds the upper hand firmly within the federal appointments process is one question; how Congress or the Senate responds to such a state of affairs is another. The answer to the latter question depends partly on the kind of separation-of-powers analysis one uses. Formalists and functionalists might agree that Congress's explicit authority to create, define, and abolish offices includes implicitly the lesser authority to dictate conditions (such as qualifications) for filling offices, but they are bound to disagree on the point at which legislation frustrates a president's nominating power or constitutes a congressional reappointment to an office whose occupant should have been nominated by the president.

At one end of the spectrum are relatively uncontroversial measures such as the requirement that the solicitor general be "learned in the law" or the Anti-Nepotism Statute's prohibition of the appointments of close relatives to all federal offices.[7] Functionalists would surely view these as de minimis restrictions on a president's nominating authority, while many if not most formalists and probably all functionalists would agree that both laws only narrowly restrict the field of eligible people from which a president may choose nominees but plainly do not designate or direct the specific persons he must nominate.

At the other end of the spectrum are more difficult questions about the outer limits of each branch's efforts to assert or protect its prerogatives regarding federal appointments. For instance, formalists might argue that a president's nominating authority is complete in itself, allowing a president complete discretion over nominations, including the discretion not to make any to a particular office. Formalists might go further to suggest that since the Constitution places no time limit on the nomination process, a president can take as much time as he needs to make a nomination; indeed, he can effectively take his entire term in office before concluding that he could not find suitable persons for certain offices. Perhaps ironically, functionalists might be inclined to agree that as a practical matter a president has no time limit on making nominations, but they would probably be inclined to view the refusal of a president to make nominations as one move in a dynamic process in which senators would undoubtedly respond by holding other nominations (and perhaps some legislative initiatives) hostage in retaliation against the president's refusal to make the nomination(s) in question. The critical question, particularly for functionalists, would be whether a president's refusal to make nominations has thoroughly frustrated or destroyed programs created by Congress (which the president is charged with implementing as part of his duty to ensure that the laws are faithfully executed). Consequently, functionalists might be more comfortable with the one decision on this question, in which a court ordered President Nixon to make nominations to some offices that were part of a program he had hoped to destroy by refusing to make the nominations.[8]

An equally if not more troublesome constitutional issue arises with respect to "ripper legislation," in which Congress abolishes an office that it originally created. Congress might pass such legislation for two reasons. First, it might be part of an effort to reorganize the national government. If passed for this reason, ripper legislation does not seem to pose any constitutional difficulties, because it would appear to be nothing more than an exercise of Congress's basic constitutional authority to make appropriations and create (or abolish) offices as it sees fit.

A second reason for "ripper legislation" is to abolish an office in order to prevent its occupant from wielding the power or responsibility of that office. Though on one level such legislation seems to be a legitimate exercise of Congress's basic authority to abolish offices it has created, it might be constitutionally suspect if Congress, after passing such legislation, were to reassign the authority of the abolished office to another officer more to its liking. To be sure, the abolition of an office for this second reason and the ensuing reassignment of its power could be defended under either formal or functional separation-of-powers analysis as mere exercises of Congress's basic authorities to make appropriations and to create or reorganize federal offices as it sees fit. Nevertheless, under either formal or functional analysis, Congress's abolition of an office and particularly its subsequent reassignment of the basic duties of that office could be consti-tutionally problematic to the extent that it interferes with the president's basic authority to retain or remove major officials on whom he depends to discharge his duties.[9] If the duties newly assigned by Congress to an office are "germane" to (or consistent with) the basic duties of that office, then Congress's reassignment of authority is not unconstitutional.[10] The reassignment is legitimate because it is an exercise of Congress's basic au-thority to create or reconfigure federal offices and to reallocate duties in a manner consistent with the balance of power in existence prior to the reassignment.[11]

Other questions arise, however, over the extent of Congress's power to lengthen the tenure of an incumbent officer. To be sure, this power would seem to be incidental to Congress's general power to create, determine the duties of, and abolish duties. Yet the concern arises whether an attempt to extend the tenure of an officer with a set term potentially deprives a presi-dent of the power that he would otherwise have to reappoint the officer or select someone else. There is little or no question that neither a formalist or functionalist would have any trouble with such a law as long as the office whose tenure has been extended is one whose occupant may be remov-able at will by the president. In the latter circumstance, the lengthening has no effect on the president's nominating or removal authorities; he re-mains unencumbered to pick the person he wants to occupy that position and to exercise his removal power to reassign the office to a new person whenever he sees fit.

A different case arises with respect to an extension of the tenure of an officer whom the president may remove only for cause. If the posi-tion is one that is integral to a president's discharge of his duties, a for-malist would undoubtedly object that no condition (such as removal for cause) may be placed by Congress on either the president's nominating power (to name anyone he pleases to the office) or removal power (so that he remain singularly in charge of overseeing the exercise of executive power, including the people responsible for implementing his directives and agendas). A functionalist would have less of a problem with Con-gress's initial decision to condition the president's removal power (as long as the limitation did not unduly interfere with his ability to discharge the responsibilities of his office). Functionalists would, however, probably disagree over the legitimacy of Congress's extension of the tenure of an office whose occupant is removable for cause by a president. Some functionalists might argue that the initial condition placed by Congress on the president's removal power has now been burdened or impeded to the point at which the lengthening of tenure has unduly interfered with the president's nominating or removal power.[12] Other functionalists might maintain that the extent to which legislation extending the tenure of an office (even one whose occupant is only removable for cause) further burdens a president's nominating or removal powers is negligible.[13] Obviously, the disagreement among functionalists that this statute is likely to generate highlights one difficulty with functionalism—its failure to posit a clear, immutable standard by which to measure the point at which impediments on a branch's prerogatives move from the point of being negligible to the point at which they become impermissible.

Another thorny constitutional issue arises with respect to whether it would be permissible for Congress to eliminate the requirement of Senate confirmation for certain officers whose nominations it currently possesses the authority to approve or disapprove. Answering this question requires determining the identity of the "officers of the United States" whose appointments require presidential nomination and Senate confirmation. Neither the original understanding of the phrase nor the structure of the Constitution points to any definitive answer to this question. The case law, though far from clear,[14] suggests that while cabinet members and other "heads of departments" are clearly not "inferior" officers of the United States (and thus must be nominated by the president and confirmed by the Senate in order to be appointed), the Constitution leaves to Congress the task of deciding which other officers to deem "inferior" for purposes of the allocation of appointment authority. Hence, some positions presently filled by presidential nominees subject to confirmation by the Senate, such as assistant attorneys general and assistant or undersecretaries, could be filled in a different manner. Such officers could be appointed by department heads pursuant to the Appointments Clause because the former are inferior "officers of the United States" who are subject to the control of several superiors in their respective departments.

The same line of analysis seems to guide The Century Foundation's proposal that

> the president should bear direct responsibility for the appointment of only those officials who have a reasonable likelihood of interacting with him or of working directly on presidential business. [Similarly,] the Senate should not be burdened with confirmation responsibilities for appointments or promotions that almost never rise to the level of senators' attention. [Hence,] both branches should be relieved of the antiquated practice of treating routine military, foreign service, and public health promotions and appointments as presidential appointments requiring Senate confirmation.[15]

The problem is that while presidents and senators might agree that many of the latter positions in the proposal are inferior offices not requiring presidential nominations or Senate confirmations, both actors would likely defend their present inclusion in the process on the grounds that it gives them some legitimate control over the exercise of certain powers, provides them with an important check against overreaching by another branch, and is important for preserving their authority within the Constitution's system of checks and balances.

Another alternative might be for Congress to eliminate or reduce the number of confirmable posts. For instance, The Century Foundation has proposed that a relatively significant number of the offices to which presidents now make appointments should be converted into civil service positions and thus removed from the cauldron of the appointments process.[16] If certain offices were made part of the civil service, presidents presumably would be spared the pain and anguish of trying to fill them and senators might have more time or resources to devote to other legislative matters (including the consideration of other nominations).

This proposal might, however, run into several difficulties. First, eliminating one office, particularly the sort that sufficient support could be mustered to eliminate, is not likely to have much impact on senators' allocations of resources, given that senators do not spend time equally on nominations; they tend to focus on nominations selectively, depending on their interests and agendas. Hence, abolishing an office (or the requirement that the Senate confirm its occupant), particularly one in which only a few senators are particularly interested, will probably not affect how those senators allocate their time on appointment matters. Second, there is a limit to the consensus one can expect from the president and Congress, particularly if different parties control each institution, in resolving the question of which offices are essential or superfluous. Third, it may be easier to create an office than to abolish it.[17] Although the president might not have vetoed the initial law creating an office, he still may veto the law abolishing it, in which case a supermajority of Congress would be needed to eradicate an office established by a majority. Congress's alternative at that point would be to eliminate the office by refusing to fund it further, a decision that is not subject to presidential veto because it is not embodied in a law that could be vetoed.

Moreover, eliminating an office requiring Senate confirmation (and presumably shifting its responsibilities into a position not requiring Senate approval) changes the dynamic between the president and the Senate. As long as Congress acquiesces in the appropriations process, a president may make various appointments of administrative personnel not requiring Senate confirmation. For example, although a majority of the Senate agreed to bar the full Senate's consideration of President Clinton's nomination of Henry Foster as surgeon general, several months later President Clinton named Foster as a special assistant in charge of advising him how to resolve the national problem of teenage pregnancy. In addition, during the first year of President Clinton's second term in office, he followed the practice of many previous administrations in bypassing confirmation battles, particularly in election years, by naming acting officials to take charge of certain sensitive posts. More recently, after the Senate Judiciary Committee split its vote on and thus effectively terminated President Clinton's nomination of Bill Lann Lee to head the Justice Department's Civil Rights Division, President Clinton designated Lee the division's acting assistant attorney general during the ensuing congressional recess.

The latter appointment generated widespread criticism in Republican circles for violating the Vacancies Act.[18] Enacted in 1868, the Vacancies Act applied to temporary appointments made by the president to certain federal offices. Congress amended the act in 1994 to expand the amount of time in which acting appointments could be made and such appointees could serve as well as the range of executive offices covered. The amended Vacancies Act provided that a vacancy in the top position of a confirmable office could be temporarily filled either by the first assistant of that department, bureau, or agency or by another official designated by the president to occupy the position for no more than 120 days. The amended act provided further that this 120-day time limit could be suspended, pending the outcome of Senate proceedings regarding a formal presidential nomination to the vacant office. Critics of Lee's acting appointment charged, among other things, that the president was barred from designating Lee the acting head of the Civil Rights Division because the 120-day period had been exhausted by the 181-day tenure of Acting Assistant Attorney General Isabelle Pinzler before Lee's formal nomination and subsequent acting designation were made. Once the time period had been exhausted, the critics argued, President Clinton had only two options if he wanted Lee to serve as the head of the Civil Rights Division: either make a recess appointment[19] or renominate Lee after Congress had reconvened and await the outcome of the confirmation process while leaving the office vacant in the meantime.

In March 1998, the Senate Governmental Affairs Committee, chaired by Republican senator Fred Thompson of Tennessee, held special hearings to consider the degree to which the Clinton administration was complying with the Vacancies Act (including the propriety of Lee's acting appointment) and the need to revise the act to clarify the scope of its coverage. The concern expressed by many senators in the hearings (and in public statements at or around the same time) was that at the end of February 1998, sixty-four acting officials—roughly 20 percent of the 320 positions requiring Senate confirmation in the various departments—had been serving in offices requiring Senate confirmation in fourteen executive departments. Moreover, at least forty-three of these sixty-four officials had served beyond the 120-day limit imposed by the Vacancies Act without any formal nomination having been made.[20]

At the hearings, the Justice Department made two powerful arguments in defense of Lee's acting appointment as well as other similar designations. First, it maintained that the Vacancies Act, even after amendment, did not apply to the Justice Department. In their view, the act applied to the head of a bureau or executive agency, but the Civil

Rights Division did not qualify as either. A bureau is generally understood to be an organizationally distinct branch or office within an agency (such as the Federal Bureau of Investigation, which is technically part of the Justice Department), while an executive agency is generally understood to be a department. In other words, the Vacancies Act's references to executive "agencies" and "bureaus" did not refer, in the Justice Department's view, to subcabinet-level offices or divisions within an executive branch department, such as the Office of Legal Counsel or the Civil Rights Division in the Justice Department.

Moreover, the Justice Department argued that it is not organized like other departments or agencies because of its singular organic statute.[21] The Justice Department's organic statute also provides that "[a]ll functions of other officers of the Department of Justice and all functions of agencies and employees of the Department of Justice are vested in the Attorney General."[22] In a different section, the statute further provides that the attorney general "may from time to time make such provisions as [she] considers appropriate authorizing the performance by any other officer, employee, or agency of the Department of Justice of any function of the Attorney General."[23] According to the Justice Department, a natural inference to draw from this language is that the attorney general may temporarily delegate some of her authority to her subordinates for an indefinite period. Hence, Lee could have been named as an acting head of the Civil Rights Division because Attorney General Janet Reno had delegated some of her authority to him indefinitely. To underscore the fact that there had been such a delegation, Attorney General Reno also named Lee as a counselor to the attorney general in the area of civil rights. Thus, even if Lee's nomination were never confirmed by the Senate, he could retain, in the view of the attorney general, his acting post and counselor position because the attorney general had delegated responsibility to him in the area of civil rights.

Lee's appointment is hardly novel in the annals of the Justice Department. For instance, although the Senate rejected President Reagan's nomination of Brad Reynolds (then assistant attorney general in charge of the Justice Department's Civil Rights Division) as associate attorney general, Ed Meese nevertheless appointed Reynolds counselor to the attorney general. For those positions over which the Senate relinquishes appointment authority or for those people who fail to be confirmed but wind up in positions not requiring confirmation, the Senate and the House retain their respective oversight and appropriations powers.

Alternatively, President Clinton could have designated Lee the head of the Civil Rights Division pursuant to a recess appointment. Explicitly authorized by the Constitution, recess appointments are valid until the end of the next session of Congress. Recess appointments have been commonplace throughout U.S. history and have proven to be a popular route by which presidents have occasionally bypassed the confirmation process because they wanted to avoid a skirmish with senators or the prospect of an unfilled office or both. Recess appointments have become more difficult since Congress amended the Pay Act to preclude compensating certain recess appointments unless the latter have been confirmed.

Hence, a recess appointment posed three problems for both Lee and the president. First, a major source of contention between the branches has involved the appropriate construction of the term *recess*, with presidents maintaining that it can be as short as a three-day holiday weekend while members of Congress understand it to refer only to the periods between sessions.[24] Second, if Lee were never confirmed by the Senate, he would be ineligible to be paid for most of his services to the national government. Third, Lee could serve in a recess appointment only until the end of the next congressional session, whereas he could serve indefinitely as an acting assistant attorney general because he was delegated authority by the attorney general. In light of these problems, President Clinton chose not to make Lee a recess appointment.

Regardless of the propriety of the Justice Department's or other executive departments' arguments regarding the coverage of the Vacancies Act, Congress eventually passed the Federal Vacancies Reform Act (FVRA) to cover temporary appointments to confirmable offices in every executive agency or department.[25] There is little doubt that the new statute's effort to cover all temporary appointments to confirmable positions is constitutional. First, the Constitution plainly empowers Congress to create and fund offices. Under formal separation-of-powers analysis, this congressional power has been granted without any explicit limitations; therefore, it presumably encompasses the authority to establish the conditions for occupancy, including the length of time for an occupant to serve without Senate confirmation.

Under functional analysis, a congressional effort to broaden or clarify the reach of the Vacancies Act would have been undertaken to restore some of the Senate's advise-and-consent power lost or frustrated by virtue of an administration's efforts to make temporary appointments last indefinitely. Such broadening or clarification would not unduly interfere with a president's discretion to exercise his nominating power, for it would not direct whom he might choose to nominate. Instead, any statutory revisions would restrict only the length of time a president (or department head) could act unilaterally in filling confirmable offices temporarily.

The policy advantages of extending the coverage of the Vacancies Act are twofold. First, such an extension helps to clarify the reach of the act and thus helps to inform decision makers about their respective powers in making temporary appointments. Second, the extension provides uniformity in making temporary appointments, and such uniformity helps to improve the administration and oversight of the process for making temporary appointments.

If there were any mystery about the amendments to the Vacancies Act, it is why President Clinton did not veto them. (Indeed, at the congressional hearing on the need for new legislation, representatives from the Clinton Justice Department strongly recommended against revising the act.) At the very least, one would have expected the president to veto the legislation on the ground that Congress was acting unconstitutionally in trying to limit his inherent authority to make executive appointments so that he could fulfill his constitutional oath to "take Care that the Laws be faithfully executed" during any impasse with the Senate over appointments.[26]

Yet, there were several compelling reasons for the president to sign the amendments into law, as he in fact did. First, the new law was passed as part of the Omnibus Budget Bill of 1999, an important compromise for both Congress and the president on the eve of the fall 1998 midterm congressional elections. The president had other important legislative concerns in mind, not the least of which was to shift some of the balance of power in Congress back to the Democrats as a result of the election and to stem the movement at that time in favor of impeachment.[27] The compromise bill reflects, in other words, how appointment battles (even those with constitutional ramifications) become intertwined with other legislative matters. Second, the new law expands to 210 days the amount of time temporary appointees may serve.[28] The longer time granted reflects recognition in Congress that a president might not be singularly responsible for delays in finding permanent appointees acceptable to the Senate. Third, though the president said nothing about his understanding of this particular bill at the time he signed it into law, he might have construed it as not constituting a waiver or compromise of his inherent authority to make temporary appointments whenever necessary to ensure the discharge of his constitutional duties. Fourth, the president or his counsel might not have read the new law as overriding or abrogating some prerogatives to which they believe some cabinet secretaries are entitled by virtue of the organic statutes creating their respective departments. In other words, the failure of the new law to list all the offices covered or to specify in so many words that special offices or divisions of departments are covered by the act creates an opening for disagreement. Fifth, the president might have figured that vetoing the law would enrage many senators and encourage them further to delay his appointments.[29]

Besides considering various ways to constrain a president's appointment powers, many senators ponder how to alter the powers of those who are appointed. With respect to temporary appointees to executive offices, agencies, or commissions, members of Congress contemplate precluding them from exercising the same powers as those confirmed for the offices. Moreover, a popular technique is to reorganize confirmable offices in a manner that reduces or alters the power currently wielded by their occupants. A good example of the latter is the almost annual effort made in Congress for almost two decades to consider splitting the U.S. Court of Appeals for the Ninth Circuit into smaller units. Some senators have complained that some states' interests are diluted or undervalued,[30] while others have complained that the sheer size of the circuit (which includes judges from California, Washington, Oregon, Montana, Hawaii, and Alaska) has made it unwieldy or inefficient to sit en banc. Over the years, the debate has included, among other things, delaying the confirmation proceedings for some nominees (to force an administration to nominate people from certain states or to dilute the influence on the court of the states from which the contested nominees came) and engaging in protracted negotiations with the president over whom to nominate (to ensure the ideal balance of judges on the court in terms of geography and ideological orientation). For instance, in an effort to pressure the Clinton White House into supporting a proposal to divide the circuit, the Republican-controlled Senate did not confirm anyone to the Ninth Circuit for more than twenty months, from January 1996 through most of the next year, leaving nine positions vacant. This delay had the effect of forcing the Ninth Circuit to delay hearings in more than six hundred cases and to produce a gap of roughly fourteen months between the time of an appeal and a final ruling on it. In his annual State of the Judiciary addresses for both 1997 and 1998, the Chief Justice of the United States denounced the delays in judicial confirmations for the Ninth Circuit as hurting the quality of justice administered in that circuit.

The perennial debates over the need to divide the Ninth Circuit led Congress to create a special commission to consider the issue. In October 1998, the commission, led by retired Supreme Court justice Byron White, issued a draft seeking comments on several recommendations for improving or streamlining the Ninth Circuit as well as several other circuits and the entire federal appellate system. The final report was rendered December 18, 1998, the day before the House impeached President Clinton.[31] The commission concluded that dividing the Ninth Circuit into separate circuits would be counterproductive, impractical, and unnecessary. Instead, the commission proposed that Congress pass legislation authorizing the Ninth Circuit to reorganize itself into three regionally based, semi-autonomous divisions. Though Congress quickly adopted some of the commission's proposals for streamlining appellate procedures, its proposal regarding the Ninth Circuit has yet to be approved.

THE FEASIBILITY OF LEGISLATING MINIMAL QUALIFICATIONS

The prior section suggested a very troublesome separation-of-powers issue arising from proposals to legislate qualifications for certain offices. The perennial popularity of such proposals justifies more extensive analysis of their merits.

One suggestion, made by Stephen Carter, is that the president and the Senate should try to agree on legislation or guidelines setting forth the qualifications for different kinds of appointees.[32] At least insofar as Supreme Court precedent is concerned, the constitutionality of such legislation is in all likelihood beyond question. In fact, every justice in *Myers v. United States*[33] agreed that it was within Congress's authority to establish minimal or reasonable qualifications for all federal offices. In dissent, Justice Louis Brandeis went so far as to suggest a long list of requirements that Congress had placed on the president's selection of nominees in the past, including citizenship; being a resident of the United States, a state, a particular district, a particular territory, the District of Columbia, or a particular foreign country; specific professional attainments or occupational experience; test by examinations; requirements of age, sex, race, property, or habitual temperance in the use of intoxicating liquors; selection on a nonpartisan basis; and representation by industrial or geographic criteria.[34]

Legislated qualifications for appointed offices might help to set the terms of debate or discourse in confirmation hearings. While some formal consensus on the minimum qualifications for some or all confirmable offices would not preclude presidents, senators, interest groups, or the media from manipulating them to advance their particular agendas, it might prevent further degeneration of the level of discourse in the process by focusing the primary discussion on relatively objective standards for merit.

It is of course unlikely that such a proposal would ever be adopted unless the president and the Senate could be convinced that it would be in their respective self-interest to do so. The arguments that neither could be so persuaded are relatively easy to imagine. For one thing, reasonable people will disagree about the requisite criteria for various confirmable offices, and the criteria on which most people could agree are likely to be so vague as to be easily manipulated. One might further suppose that neither the president nor the Senate would be disposed to view the time and resources expended on such an endeavor as worthwhile. It is also unclear whether either actor would want to tie its hands before a decision on a particular nomination has been made, because the circumstances under which consideration of the nomination would occur (including the relative popularity of the president and the Senate and their respective agendas in the areas of responsibility of the office being filled) might dictate how each would proceed. Each might prefer to retain complete discretion to expend its political coinage as it sees fit on nominations on a case-by-case basis.

Nevertheless, it is not inconceivable that the president and the Senate might find that it would be in the self-interest of each to adopt minimum qualifications for certain confirmable offices. Presidents and senators frequently complain about the time and anguish they have to expend in dealing with the demands of patronage. Adopting minimum qualifications for at least some confirmable offices would provide both presidents and senators with an objective or credible basis for turning away some aspirants to office. While presidents and senators might be reluctant to acknowledge publicly that reason for their support of a formal declaration of minimum qualifications (out of fear that it would alienate some supporters), they could support the proposal on the grounds that it raises the standards for holding certain offices and reduces the demands of party and monied interests on some federal appointments.

For those who might suppose that formal agreement between the president and the Senate on the minimal qualifications for at least some confirmable offices is unrealistic, the history of the movement toward civil service reform is instructive. In the aftermath of the charges of widespread scandal in the Grant administration, the public outcry for civil service reform intensified.[35] Members of Congress, particularly senators, generally resisted because they did not want to relinquish the control over the patronage in their respective states that they had lost to some extent under Lincoln and regained under Grant. Nevertheless, the outcry persisted, and a succession of presidents took heed.[36]

The first such president was Rutherford B. Hayes. Hayes assumed the presidency beholden to his fellow Republicans in Congress because they had been instrumental in securing his victory. Hayes's opponent, Democratic governor Samuel Tilden of New York, had won most of the popular vote, but Hayes became president after a peculiar set of circumstances: no candidate had received a majority of votes of the electoral college, so the matter subsequently fell to the House to determine a winner, and a special commission appointed by a bipartisan majority of Congress declared Hayes the victor (pursuant to a strict party-line vote based on dubious and, many Democrats suspected, fraudulent calculations of Hayes's popular vote in certain swing states in the South).

Almost immediately after his inauguration, Hayes stunned many of his Republican supporters by trying to implement his campaign pledge of civil service reform. At the first meeting of his cabinet (to which he had appointed Democrats and Republicans, including Carl Schurz, a leading crusader for civil service reform, as interior secretary), he appointed a special committee to make recommendations for rules about appointments to federal offices. He later implemented several policies that the committee had recommended to curb some of the excesses of political appointments.[37] Moreover, President Hayes ordered an inquiry into the management of the New York Customshouse, the centerpiece of Republican Senator Roscoe Conkling's political machine. The resulting report described a pattern of overstaffing, incompetence, and petty bribery and sharply criticized the collector, Chester Arthur, and other officials.[38] (The fact-finding might not have been entirely justified because Arthur had actually improved overall efficiency and had implemented several recommendations made by President Grant's Civil Service Commission to upgrade the customshouse's integrity.) President Hayes did not specify that customshouse employees had to be Republicans, only that they should not be allowed to to use their official positions as a base from which to manage state and local politics. Moreover, President Hayes did not object to the collection of voluntary contributions from customshouse officials. Nevertheless, he twice proposed civil reform on a grander scale to Congress, but Congress, in spite of the fact that both parties had campaigned on platforms pledging to implement civil service reform, refused to take action.

Hayes's successor, James Garfield, was president for less than a year. In his short time as president, however, Garfield expressed disdain for presidential deference to senatorial courtesy for federal appointments. Moreover, Garfield's major act as president was to challenge Senator Conkling, the leader of the Republican Stalwarts, for control of federal patronage in New York. The challenge proved to be fatal when Charles Guiteau, who had been unsuccessfully seeking an appointment as the administration's consul in Paris, assassinated Garfield. On shooting Garfield, Guiteau exclaimed, "I am a Stalwart and Arthur is now president."[39]

Veteran political observers expected Arthur, after he had become president, to turn over control of the administration to his former benefactor, Senator Conkling and the Stalwart machine. Instead, Arthur refused to appoint Conkling to his cabinet (though he tried later, unsuccessfully, to get Conkling to accept a Supreme Court appointment), made no attempt to replace the person whom Garfield had appointed over Conkling's objection to head the New York Customshouse, and did not open up other patronage jobs for his friends by purging earlier appointees. Moreover, President Arthur recognized that the shock of Garfield's assassination had made civil service reform a proposal whose time had come. He signed into law the Pendleton Act, which established the Civil Service Commission (to which Arthur appointed well qualified men), required open competition examinations for certain classes of federal employment, and restricted the president to choose from those with the highest grades on those examinations.[40]

The Pendleton Act also empowered the president to extend the classified service by executive order. Every succeeding president except William McKinley extended that coverage, from about one-seventh in 1883 to about half of the federal jobs below policymaking level in 1901.[41] President Cleveland oversaw the repeal of the Tenure in Office Act (including its subsequent amendments), which had impeded rotation in office, a practice Cleveland believed was crucial for improving the quality of people in government service. Presidents Teddy Roosevelt and William Howard Taft extended the merit system rapidly, as did the Republican presidents in the 1920s.[42] By 1928, about 80 percent of the positions below policymaking level were covered civil service positions.

To be sure, the civil service has outlived at least some of its utility. Civil service was for many years a well-intentioned effort to control specific abuses, namely, patronage hiring and political manipulation of public employees. In most places it accomplished its goals. But, as the authors of the provocative study *Reinventing Government* suggest, "most of what civil service procedures were established to prevent has since been ruled illegal or made impossible by collective bargaining agreements. Yet the control mentality lives on, creating a gridlock that turns public management into the art of the impossible."[43] Thus, a system that began as an instrument of progressives interested in introducing and maintaining professionalism in government service became one administered by bureaucrats primarily interested in enforcing the system's rules for their own sake rather than for the sake of good government.

The critical question is not whether the civil service system still works but rather what one can learn from its passage and implementation. For one thing, its constitutionality is beyond challenge. The positions covered by civil service legislation are not offices of the United States and are thus neither the subject of nor covered by the Appointments Clause. Although civil service requirements impose some limits on the president's power to appoint or remove certain people below the policymaking level in the executive branch, these limits are not regarded as serious intrusions on the president's fundamental executive authority to nominate or remove the highest-ranking officials in this branch because positions covered by the civil service are not crucial to the functioning of his office. It is also telling that both major parties eventually accepted the virtues of reducing partisan control over the distribution of some federal jobs. No doubt, presidents in the last quarter of the nineteenth century had to balance the challenges of maintaining popular support in their party and the voting public with upgrading the quality of government service. It is likely that the support of Presidents Hayes, Arthur, and Harrison for civil service reform cost them the loyalty and support of many members of their own parties (who yearned for control of patronage) and explains to some extent the failure of each to serve more than a single term in office. Nevertheless, these presidents, along with Presidents Cleveland, Teddy Roosevelt, Taft, and Wilson, helped to secure the implementation of civil service reform while reestablishing the president's control of his nominating power as a crucial prerogative of his office. In addition, civil service reform was made possible because these presidents and many members of Congress came to accept that the expansion of the civil service helped to reduce some of the pressure on them to dispense patronage *and* acceded to the popular will to improve the quality of certain federal appointments.

Similarly, there is no doubt that congressional legislation requiring or mandating qualifications for inferior federal offices is constitutionally permissible. In *United States v. Perkins*,[44] the Supreme Court held that Congress has complete authority to impose qualifications on such federal offices.

Another practical problem with establishing minimal qualifications for certain offices of the United States is that the president and members of Congress have often differed over its necessity. And even when they have agreed, they have sometimes not lived up to their bargains. Arguably, this is one reason for senators' complaints that the Clinton administration failed to comply with the Vacancies Act, for Congress allowed the administration's practices in this area to go unchecked. Moreover, a similar problem arose after President Clinton signed into law the 1995 Lobbying Disclosure Act, which disqualified anyone who had worked as a foreign lobbyist or for any foreign government from becoming the U.S. trade representative or deputy trade representative, both of which require presidential nomination and Senate confirmation. After President Clinton nominated Charlene Barshefsky to be the U.S. trade representative, the Senate confirmed her shortly after Congress had passed a waiver exempting her from the application of the 1995 law (necessary because she had previously represented some foreign governments).[45]

When presidents and senators do not agree on the requisite qualifications for certain offices or are not disposed to live with the ones they have agreed to, less formal action is still possible. For instance, a president or some congressional leaders could develop and publicize recommendations on the qualifications for various confirmable positions. Such a move would help establish the credibility of the claim of neutrality or nonpartisanship asserted by those promoting the adoption of minimal qualifications for confirmable positions. Alternatively, the Senate committees entrusted with dealing with certain appointments, or nongovernmental, nonpartisan organizations such as the American Bar Association, could publicize their criteria for evaluating the qualifications for different kinds of nominees and challenge the president, the Senate, or both to adopt those standards. The publication or adoption of such a list created by a Senate committee would have the effect of ostensibly guiding, if not restricting or constraining, the committee's discretion in the factors it could consider in voting on certain nominees. It would also put a president on notice about the attributes his nominees should have for various posts or otherwise risk substantial opposition.

INFLUENCING THE TERMS OF DEBATE

One critical problem in the appointments process, to which I have already alluded, is the failure of commentators or participants to agree on a common language or terms for debate on federal appointments. In this section, I consider the ways in which the absence of such consensus has undermined the debates on some appointments, particularly those to the Supreme Court. The next chapter considers in more detail the significance of a common language for discussing or analyzing judicial appointments generally (though a similar objective can be undertaken with respect to nonjudicial ones) as a condition for a streamlined appointments process.

As chapter 4 suggested, presidents do have unique authority to set the terms of debate in the nomination and confirmation processes, although no administration has been able to predict infallibly which factors will undo which of its nominees. One way for a president to maximize his influence over this system is to assess formally, prior to the making of a nomination, how strongly he will support or defend it. This evaluation is obviously difficult to make because it requires forecasting with some precision—a time-consuming task, to be sure, for White House or administration officials—the political circumstances under which the Senate is likely to be considering certain nominations.

The effort to increase the sophistication of political analysis of the system must also assess the significance of the public's attitudes about the appointments process and the possibilities for serious reform. For instance, Ronald Dworkin suggests that we need to abandon the myth that judges are thoroughly nonpolitical actors and that once we have done so political leaders should find it easier to focus on the appropriate traits nominees for high judicial offices need to be confirmed.[46] More fundamentally, we should accept that political leaders face considerable pressures to act in accord with various short- and long-term interests, including party and interest group support, major contributors, media scrutiny, and issue salience. As long as presidents and senators remain involved in the federal appointments process, the system will be subject to these forces and more. Within such a system, it is difficult to mandate eloquence in discourse. Distortions and misstatements are the inevitable price we pay for open, vigorous debate about important political issues and events. A dispute that arises in a political forum, such as a Senate committee, rather than in the pristine environment of a judge's chambers or a classroom is unlikely to be pretty, polite, and linear. Yet, none of this means that the system fails to cut through to the real issues at stake, especially when presidents and senators can check each other's rhetoric and mistakes. And if presidents and senators overstep their boundaries or are thought to have abused their prerogatives, the media and the public each have some means to keep the system honest — the press by what it scrutinizes (and how it covers it) and the American people by their support (and how they vote).

Recognizing the potential political accountability of the major governmental actors in the federal appointments process leads one to consider the extent to which the public's understanding of this system may be enhanced. Several notable critics of the modern confirmation process, such as Stephen Carter, believe that the public's attitudes help explain one of the system's biggest defects: the apparently increasing "politicization" of the judicial selection process.[47] Carter, for instance, suggests that judicial confirmation hearings have become overly contentious in recent years because of the growing popular conception of the Court as a national policymaker whose authority as such can be controlled through the appointments process. Carter and others suggest that one possible solution to this dilemma is to depoliticize judicial selection by changing the attitudes of the general public or those who serve in the Senate, finding justices capable of exercising their duties more responsibly, or perhaps all of these.

The perception of the Supreme Court as an institution capable of influencing or shaping national policy is hardly new. The stakes in Supreme Court confirmation hearings have always been high. For instance, in 1857 the Senate barely confirmed Nathan Clifford as an associate justice after debating the propriety of his strong proslavery views.[48] Surely the decision a year earlier in *Dred Scott v. Sandford*[49] had taught the nation a lasting lesson about the Court's potential to shape society (particularly social relationships and the relationships between people and government) through rulings inextricably linked to its ideological composition.

The critical question is whether the perception of the Court as a national policymaker is amenable to change or is an inevitable consequence of its having judicial review over the Constitution and state and federal statutes. The answer turns in large part on the recognition that the federal judiciary has been engaged in a dialogue with political forces throughout the history of the republic. This dialogue allows every generation to formulate and, if need be, act on its opinions or attitudes about the Court's role. This is not to say that people's attitudes about the Court are impervious to change; as the next chapter explores in greater deal, people at the very least can be educated to think about the Court differently. For instance, one does not have to view the Court as a national policymaker simply because its decisions impact or influence the policymaking process. For one thing, courts arguably make policy in the course of construing or attempting to apply statutes. They do so by clarifying the language (including its gaps and ambiguities) or reach of a statute. Constructions of laws by the courts are not meant to substitute for the policymaking in which legislatures engage. They do not purport to supplant or amend statutes enacted by legislatures but rather to implement or effectuate the legislative intent embodied in statutes.

Moreover, the charge that the Court has become a national policymaker is often hyperbole rather than an accurate statement of its basic functions. Almost every effort made by the Court to construe a statute or the Constitution can be criticized as either policymaking of the sort properly made by Congress or the states or as unduly or insufficiently interfering with the policymaking authority of the political branches. Condemning a decision of the Court as inappropriate policymaking more often than not becomes a rallying cry for organizing that portion of the electorate for whom the issue of the Court's direction is especially important. The charge that the Court is a national policymaker is similar to the oft-repeated directive that a judge's job is to interpret rather than make the law. For the overwhelming majority of people in Congress (if not most citizens and academics), the idea that judges should be making policy (similar to that made by legislatures) is anathema. The more important inquiry is how the Court should interpret laws (not whether they should interpret them) or in what specific ways the Court has assumed an inappropriate policymaking function.

Moreover, the source of the contentiousness of modern-day confirmation hearings may not be grounded so much in the public's attitude about the Court's role in the constitutional system as in its growing concern that the selection of federal judges has become overwhelmingly driven by interest groups or embroiled with partisan politics and that insufficient attention has been paid to a nominee's fitness to serve. This complaint is not the same as lamenting that the Court has become a national policymaker or that, as Dworkin suggests, we should abandon as a myth our belief that law and politics are completely distinct. Nor does it imply a desire to move the Court in any particular direction. Instead, it may simply mean that many if not most Americans hope that the most experienced, even-tempered lawyers, judges, and political leaders become justices of the Supreme Court. This desire rests on the belief that law is not just politics in some other guise, that law is a discipline requiring considerable study, reading, training, and practice if it is to be done well.[50] Of course, this is not to say that law is completely separate from politics (broadly defined, for instance, as the competition between interests and values); at the very least, laws are made by political bodies, enforced by still other political bodies, and interpreted by courts staffed by judges who get their positions through a political process. Law and politics are on some level intertwined: laws are not made, enforced, or interpreted without some sensitivity to the political ramifications of these endeavors (though, of course, there can be considerable debate about how much sensitivity there should be). Nevertheless, law does have some existence separate from the political domain; it exists as a code that binds and perhaps defines a society until such time as the latter chooses to follow a different course.

It is also important to appreciate that the friction in confirmation hearings reflects the awareness that the Court will have an enormous impact on the distribution of power at the federal level and between the federal and state governments as well as on the understanding of the nation's preeminent political document—the Constitution. Moreover, politics (broadly understood) is not an unfamiliar terrain or arena for the justices themselves. For instance, no one gets to sit on the Court without being approved for that position by the political branches of the federal government; to be confirmed, one must be political at least in the sense of knowing the right people or convincing the right people of one's fitness to serve. Nor is it an indictment of any Supreme Court justice to say that he or she has demonstrated the skills of a successful politician; justices must navigate through a special political thicket in order to be nominated and confirmed. Once a justice is on the Court, "politics" still matters in how one gets along with one's colleagues (which helps to maintain or preserve coalitions), with the other branches (by testifying before appropriate congressional committees to get more funds for the Court, to modify or block efforts to modify federal jurisdiction, to provide input on federal rules of civil or criminal procedure or on sentencing guidelines, or by trying to get good law clerks or place one's friends in key governmental positions), or even with the press (in how one tries to preserve the image of the Court or one's own image through interviews or off-the-record comments).

Ultimately, it is not possible to criticize the Supreme Court selection process without developing a credible theory about the proper role of the federal judiciary in American society. The constitutional structure permits political actors to form different perspectives on or attitudes about appropriate judging, but it does not take sides on this matter. Hence, if one is content to live with a system in which each presidential election and each confirmation hearing provides yet another opportunity for contending sides to fight for control over the ability to determine or define the proper qualifications for judges, then the present process is not broken and does not require radical reform. If one were to prefer, however, that the system as a structural matter should restrict the kinds of people who select judges, then in all likelihood one would be inclined to prefer serious structural revisions to the process by which we currently appoint judges. The next chapter considers in detail some specific proposals for reforming judicial selection, while the next two sections examine proposals (beyond those previously considered by the Miller Center and The Century Foundation) for reforming the process for making nonjudicial appointments.

The extent of dissatisfaction with the process for making federal appointments has inspired more than a few proposals for reforming the system. One common proposal is to routinize consultation between the president and the Senate. Not surprisingly, presidents have consistently rejected formalizing such consultation as a violation of their nominating power. A president sometimes defers to senators in making nominations because he has calculated that there are more important nonappointments matters for which he needs corresponding deference from senators. For instance, modern studies suggest that the key to presidential reelection is the growth rate of the economy. Therefore, a president might be willing to rationally trade some appointments (or, as President Clinton's acceptance of the FVRA in exchange for a budget compromise reflected, some executive prerogatives regarding appointments) for a freer hand from the Senate on economic matters.

Yet another solution to problems in the confirmation process is for a president to use the presidential transition period to lay the basic ground rules and structure for federal appointments. One complication here is that there is no easy answer to whether an administration is better off drafting a profile of its desired appointments and then finding the people who fit them or selecting the people it wants and then justifying their selection. A sensible solution (from the standpoint of a president interested in relatively hassle-free nomination discussions and confirmation hearings) is to establish as early as possible in his campaign an official team of experienced, trusted advisers whose primary responsibility is to assemble lists of possible candidates or criteria for different offices. The idea is to create a hierarchy of decision making on federal appointments (even before the president takes office) that places him at the top with a relatively small set of competent advisers to assist him. (Indeed, Presidents Eisenhower and Reagan employed such a system.) These advisers, rather than the president, should be primarily responsible for sifting through all of the available information on prospective nominees acquired from the president himself, interest groups, and senators. (Obviously, a president cannot do this job himself, even for a Supreme Court appointment.

The Need for Reform

Hence, the talent, judgment, and reliability of the advisers is crucial. The extent to which a president distrusts their judgment and feels the need to go beyond them to outside advisers or groups is the degree to which they are failing him. The track records of presidents who relied heavily on their own personal knowledge of and acquaintance with their nominees are mixed at best.) The choice of the advisers should be relatively easy; on the evening after his election the president probably has at hand the people he is inclined to use as his close advisers in office. Hiring the right people to assist selection is at least as important as adopting the right criteria. The best criteria in the world may not make any difference if put in the hands of inexperienced neophytes, while an experienced adviser with a track record of solid political judgment is apt not to need much guidance in knowing which particular people or at least which kinds of people can best assist a president in office.

A related point is the necessity for a president to have in place throughout his time in office a relatively stable set of advisers on appointments. One reason given by some critics for the inordinate delays in the Clinton administration's designations of appointees (particularly for judgeships) is the high turnover in key staff positions responsible for processing nominations; President Clinton has had, for example, a record number of both chief White House counsel (six) and associate counsel (at least six) responsible for judicial nominations. The time required for each new counsel to get settled into his or her new position—becoming familiar with the details of the duties, the nuances of White House and Senate procedures, and all of the other players in the system—is time taken away from the actual selection and lobbying for nominees.

ENHANCING PUBLIC PARTICIPATION BY MEANS OF THE INTERNET

At present, senators, executive branch personnel, the media, interest groups, and the public use the Internet to varying degrees to trade information and interact regarding federal appointments. Every committee with confirmation responsibilities publicizes at least some of its activities regarding appointments on the Internet, and every department or agency publicizes both the confirmable offices filled (with sketches of the people who occupy such positions) and the confirmable offices not yet filled. And each committee and department or agency provides the means for public feedback on pending matters, including but not limited to those relating to appointments.

Yet, more information could be provided. For example, Senate committees could routinely list *all* nominations pending before them, including those for which no hearings have yet been scheduled. These committees could share all relevant information — or links to such information — for pending nominations. Moreover, Web sites could include the transcripts of all testimony, submissions by interest groups, and summaries of or reports on public reactions or comments (i.e., the numbers for and against, cumulated periodically).

Indeed, it is conceivable that the Internet could provide, as it has already begun to do in the realm of administrative law, the means for radical change. Some administrative agencies have already reported that the Internet has made possible unprecedented public feedback and participation in the notice-and-comment phase of anticipated rules changes or rule making.[51] One could easily imagine that within a few decades (if not sooner) the federal appointments process could be overhauled in revolutionary ways. The need for confirmation hearings could be substantially reduced because the Internet could provide the means for expediting or streamlining the process to the point at which nominations could be posted on the Web; feedback (from interest groups, individual citizens, and the media) could be collected, analyzed, and published; and senators could release preliminary statements on the Internet. If hearings become necessary, they could be broadcast on the Internet (presumably, some hearings for certain high-profile nominees or contested nominations would be simultaneously broadcast on cable), allowing for instantaneous feedback from interested parties.

There are several obvious advantages to the system described above. First, and perhaps most important, it would allow more of the public to get informed about the federal appointments process and to be heard by senators on pending nominations or confirmation hearings. Second, Senate committees could use the communications system now available to collect more meaningful feedback from the public than just the sheer numbers who approve or disapprove of particular nominations. For instance, committees could develop their own questionnaires about pending nominations to determine the public sentiment regarding particular aspects of contested nominations. Moreover, senators might be able to move more quickly or might have less credible reason (at least in the public's opinion) to delay confirmation proceedings because of the speed with which they can collect meaningful feedback from the Internet on contested nominations.

There are, however, some potential problems with the streamlined process described above. First, some senators might not want to advertise or publicize pending nominations for which they have not yet scheduled hearings. Senators might have little incentive to post on the Internet delays for which they are (or at least appear to be) responsible. One obvious check on this is for presidents to develop their own Web sites that provide detailed information (with appropriate links) on their pending nominations.

A second possible problem is that this system might promote quick rather than careful or cautious deliberation. Consequently, it could put senators into awkward positions, making those who move fast appear to be closed-minded or to have had their minds made up from the start, while those who take more time might be chastised for appearing indecisive. Moreover, the groups that move the fastest in organizing their members are likely to have a greater impact on the all-important first impressions of the public and senators on a nomination's strengths and weaknesses (including its chances for success).[52]

A related problem is that the responses might not be truly representative of public sentiment. As with other means of electronic communication (such as the telephone and faxing), public reactions are not likely to reflect careful deliberation. To begin with, the Internet is not yet designed to foster anything remotely like a real community in which individuals have the opportunities to interact with others in the course of formulating or refining their opinions on public issues.[53] Moreover, public reactions might reflect intensity more than the actual proportion of public support or opposition regarding a particular nomination. The groups or segments of society that feel the most strongly about a particular nomination are also the likeliest to monitor its progress and to express their opinion about it. A partial check on any distortion that mobilized responses might cause is conceivable, but only at the expense of some privacy, that is, people might be required to identify themselves or to be identified (or identifiable) so that Senate staffers can put the feedback received into some coherent framework.

Moreover, it is probably impossible to overestimate the resistance that streamlining the process will meet from representatives in the executive and legislative branches. Some opposition will derive from the many people in each branch who will be unwilling to cede the control they now have to the forces that they perceive will be aggrandized by an Internet-oriented system (including the public and interest groups). At the very least, the opposition that those in power express or exhibit with respect to such a system will speak volumes about their vested interests.

Last, presidents will be required to develop their own Web sites on pending nominations. Such Web sites would be far more efficient for administration purposes than the present system, under which this information is listed separately by departments and agencies. The more diffuse appointments-related information, the more difficult it is for interested parties to retrieve it. Further, a presidential or administration Web site on pending nominations will keep the Senate, interest groups, and the media honest because it will allow each administration to provide the particular information that it wants to make public, and will also allow for direct feedback that it can use to support its campaigns on behalf of its own nominees.

Chapter Ten

ON THE FUTURE OF JUDICIAL SELECTION:

STRUCTURE, RULES, AND NORMS

MOST PROPOSALS FOR improving the federal appointments process focus on reforming judicial selection, particularly the process for choosing Supreme Court justices, and most are predicated on supposed deficiencies in the constitutional structure for making judicial appointments. In the first section I evaluate the most popular proposals (and critiques of judicial review) for reforming judicial selection. My focus is on whether proposed structural alterations are likely to produce a mix of benefits and costs sufficient to merit adoption (because it outweighs the disruption of vested interests in the status quo).

In the second section I examine the need to reform particular Senate procedures and practices regarding judicial selection. Initially, I address the deceptively difficult question of whether the Senate has an institutional obligation to provide final votes on nominees (particularly acute in cases involving the judicial branch, for whose staffing and functioning the Senate is partially responsible). Though I conclude that the Senate has no such obligation, I consider the significance of flux in some norms in the judicial selection process. Such flux signals that norms hold much greater potential for change than any other constraint operating in the judicial selection process. Consequently, I examine how the deterioration of certain norms has impeded judicial nominees' efforts to get full consideration or final action from the Senate. Possible solutions include pitting superior, more resilient, or weightier norms against inferior ones; fortifying degraded norms or developing new norms to govern judicial selection;

and seriously considering some changes in Senate procedures that would be in the mutual interest of presidents and senators while also increasing the chances for nominees to get fuller consideration by the Senate.

The recognition that norms drive the process for making judicial appointments is indispensable for understanding the need and feasibility of reforming judicial selection. The more durable the norms, the greater the resistance to change in Senate practice. Moreover, if similar norms apply to the process for making nonjudicial appointments, as I argue some do, then their resilience and popularity need to be taken into account in considering the feasibility of generally reforming the federal appointments process.

RETHINKING THE CONSTITUTIONAL STRUCTURE FOR JUDICIAL SELECTION

In this section, I consider the desirability and feasibility of the two most popular suggestions for altering the constitutional framework for judicial selection. The first is eliminating life tenure for federal judges, and the second is requiring a supermajority vote for Supreme Court confirmations. As I explain below, both are problematic.

Abandoning Judicial Life Tenure

Article III provides in pertinent part that federal judges "shall hold their Offices during good Behavior."[1] This language has generally been understood to mean that federal judges will serve for life, unless they have committed an offense requiring removal.[2] Based on inferences from the framers' and ratifiers' discussions regarding Article III and from the constitutional structure, one can discern several purposes served by the guarantee of life tenure for federal judges.[3] The continued efficacy of life tenure depends of course on the continued validity of one or more of these objectives.

First, life tenure immunizes federal judges from direct political retaliations for their decision making. Such immunity grants to federal judges the necessary security to perform their constitutional duties (including protecting minority interests), even if it means frustrating or conflicting with tyrannical majorities. Popularly elected judges are often thought to be overwhelmingly concerned with reelection and the avoidance of conflicts with majoritarian preferences.

Second, life tenure promotes public confidence in the judiciary. When confidence in the impartiality of judicial decisions is weak, people may be less likely to obey or respect those decisions. When judges are perceived as politicians, confidence in the neutrality of their decisions diminishes. Judges who receive campaign contributions from the lawyers and groups that often appear before them are perceived as less impartial than life-tenured ones.

Third, life tenure encourages or facilitates the appointment of competent jurists. Under the present system, the appointment process is the only means by which to ensure that federal judges are minimally qualified or competent. Voter apathy, ignorance, identity politics, issue salience, and party loyalty lead to the election of judges based not so much on their competence as on name recognition, party affiliation, and campaign spending. In contrast, presidents and senators understand that once appointed, federal judges are no longer subject to their direct influence, so that both actors have strong incentives to have confidence in the abilities of the people they appoint.

Fourth, life tenure permits federal judges to accumulate considerable wisdom, experience, and expertise in handling federal constitutional and statutory questions.[4] Moreover, life tenure (or at least judicial service for a relatively long period of time) conceivably promotes predictability or consistency in judicial decision making (though state court systems seem to function relatively well in spite of periodic turnover).

The primary reason for abandoning life tenure is to eliminate the "countermajoritarian difficulty"[5] — unprincipled or self-interested interference by unelected federal judges in the decisions of the people's duly elected representatives.[6] Many critics of life tenure seek to make federal judges politically accountable through such means as limited terms of office,[7] popular election, reappointment, or reconfirmation.[8]

Two other related problems with life tenure have yet to be explored in the literature on federal appointments, though both are relevant to the calculation of its costs to society and the legal system. One possible problem is that life tenure does not work well enough, that is, there is no foolproof method by which presidents and senators can pick justices who, once confirmed, will perform according to the wishes of those picking them. Because federal judges, particularly justices, are prone to institutional,[9] jurisprudential (preferences for flexible standards or rigid rules),[10] and ideological complexity (relating to their conceptions of what constitute relevant sources of decision and how they prioritize those sources), many judges frustrate the expectations of those who appointed them.

The second possible problem is, in the view of some scholars, that life tenure has not produced an independent or courageous judiciary. The political branches more than once have successfully employed various means—such as impeachment attempts or threats[11] or efforts to modify the Court's size or jurisdiction—to pressure the Court into avoiding conflicts with them.[12]

The other possible difficulty with life tenure is that it might work too well. Consider, for instance, an administration's likely reaction to ideological drift, as a result of which, as Kathleen Sullivan suggests, "rights once thought of as having liberal provenance are embraced by conservatives even as liberal attachment to them falters."[13] The possibility of such a transference might invite an administration to adopt a tough litmus test for choosing judicial nominees, who would have rigid or inflexible precommitments to certain outcomes in constitutional adjudication, regardless of the facts of any given case, and would not be prone to adapt their views to changing or unforseen circumstances.

Such a litmus test might challenge senators and other interested parties to determine whether they wanted inflexible, rigid ideologues as judges. It is rare for the latter kinds of nominees to make it successfully through the confirmation process, in part because they are easier targets than nominees whose views are not known or fixed. A nominee picked for the inflexibility of his perspective on constitutional adjudication is usually more easily spotted than one whose views are not fixed or known, because the former is likely (but not always) to have a public record in which his or her rigidity is apparent. Moreover, if given a choice between a nominee with extremely fixed, rigid views and the prospect of one who does not, most senators are likely to hold out for the latter. Of course, senators will support a rigid ideologue if they agree with his or her views or if partisan or interest group pressure or issue salience dictates that they should. Otherwise, many if not most senators will support someone whose views are not fixed or known, because there is a chance that such a nominee may occasionally if not routinely rule as the senators prefer. Thus, the prospect that a judge will serve for life may produce pressure in some quarters to support nominees whose appointments hold out the possibility of performance in the manner preferred by most senators.

Notwithstanding these criticisms of life tenure, it is highly improbable that life tenure will be abandoned. Another book would be required to assess all of the reasons for the inertia against such a political movement. Nevertheless, a few reasons are apparent, each of which illuminates important aspects of the dynamics of judicial selection. To begin with, presidents and senators hold onto the hope that sooner or later the wheel will turn and they will have opportunities to pick the kinds of judicial nominees they prefer. Also, there is no proof (at least yet) that state judges, many of whom are popularly elected, handle federal constitutional questions more competently, credibly, and courageously than their federal counterparts. It makes little sense to abandon the present system without confidence that judges can perform at least as well if not better with different tenure (though of course there will be considerable if not endless debate on what constitutes "better").

Another critical factor is the assessment of precisely what would be lost if federal judges lost their life tenure. More than a few scholars suspect that subjecting federal judges to popular election would rob them, as it has already robbed many state court judges, of the requisite courage to enforce the Constitution's countermajoritarian values.[14] Moreover, the Court's activism over the course of the past fifty or so years has provoked considerable resistance and criticism but even more widespread public support. Though all of the reasons for the Court's continued hold on the public's imagination and support remain a mystery,[15] one thing is quite clear—the most successful efforts to curtail life tenure because of the Court's perceived or actual activism predate *Brown*. The first, most famous instance involves President Roosevelt's ill-fated Court-packing plan, while the second proposal was undone on the eve of the Court's decision in *Brown*. There is perhaps no greater irony in the area of reforming judicial selection than the fact that the Court's decision in *Brown* overshadowed and completely defused the momentum generated by the Senate's passage on May 11, 1954, of a proposed constitutional amendment to compel the retirement of any justice over seventy-five.[16]

The failure of Congress after *Brown* to come anywhere near as close as it did to passing the Court-packing plan of 1936 or the forced retirement scheme of 1954 is attributable in part to the absence of a cause or motivation for public mobilization for abandoning life tenure. Perhaps most people perceive the Court's activism only to have bite or substance when it is bolstered or reinforced by the political branches. Perhaps the public perceives the Court's activism to be relatively infrequent if not inconsequential. In any event, most cases do not involve the hot-button issues of *Dred Scott, Lochner v. New York, Roe,* and *Brown* but instead are almost invisible. The public is oblivious to much of what the Court does (even less to what district and appellate judges do).

Another conceivable reason for the public's complacency about the Court is that, particularly over the past decade, it has come to accept that the engines for social change in our society are not the federal courts but rather the political branches of the federal government and the state governments. If this is an accurate statement of the public's attitude, then it reflects the achievement of the Rehnquist Court, one that it no doubt aimed to achieve. Ironically, this achievement was accomplished by judges who enjoy life tenure, and their success undercuts the claim for abandoning life tenure for federal judges as a means to restore public confidence in the federal judiciary. This achievement might confirm paradoxically that the Court does not pose an immediate threat to individual liberties. In the absence of such a threat, the public is not likely to support a revolt against the Court, and no revolt is likely to be successful without public support.[17]

A Supermajority Requirement for Supreme Court Confirmations

One provocative proposal is to adopt a constitutional amendment requiring a supermajority Senate vote for the confirmation of Supreme Court justices. Bruce Ackerman has given perhaps the most extensive arguments in support of such a proposal.[18] First, he argues that the proposal is designed to make the selection of Supreme Court justices more democratic by changing the dynamics of Court appointments. In his view, the proposal would ensure that appointments are likely to come from presidents who are extremely popular or command considerable public support. Moreover, the requirement would prevent "an ideological President with a weak mandate [from using] a slim Senatorial majority to ram through a constitutional revolution."[19] In addition, the proposal would force presidents "to consult with the political opposition and select distinguished professionals who would adopt an evolutionary approach to constitutional interpretation."[20] Other scholars support the proposal because they believe it would force presidents not so much to find justices who would adopt any particular approach to constitutional interpretation but rather who would be consensus candidates, that is, Court nominees with impeccable credentials who could easily win confirmation and avoid contentious hearings.[21]

The proposal would undoubtedly change the dynamics of Supreme Court confirmation proceedings because each senator would know that his or her vote would have added weight under the new system. The alteration in dynamics would, however, make the future of Supreme Court confirmation proceedings quite unpredictable. First, a supermajority requirement is not needed to encourage presidents to pick consensus candidates, as reflected most recently in President Clinton's nominations of Ruth Bader Ginsburg and Stephen Breyer, both of whom were easily confirmed. Second, a supermajority vote would not necessarily result in the appointment of superior justices. Conceivably it could have kept a number of eminently qualified people off the Court in spite of their strong records.[22] Third, it is not clear that the supermajority vote would democratize (i.e., enhance or impede popular sovereignty) in the appointments of Supreme Court justices. It is quite possible that a popular president could still fail to win confirmation of his or her well-qualified nominee because of some hostile faction in the Senate.[23]

Moreover, it is not clear why the supermajority requirement necessarily would lead to the appointment of justices who would follow Ackerman's preferred "evolutionary approach to constitutional interpretation."[24] Ackerman fails to show why the proposed requirement necessarily would result in the appointment of justices with some (but not other) kinds of viewpoints regarding constitutional interpretation. Nor has Ackerman shown how the appointment of justices who adhere to an evolutionary approach would represent a vindication of popular sovereignty, for he has not shown that the American people favor this or any other particular approach to constitutional interpretation. In addition, Ackerman assumes the supermajority requirement would dissuade a president from nominating "constitutional visionaries,"[25] but a president disposed to find such a visionary might still find that person in the guise of a nominee who lacks a paper trail reflecting how he or she would perform on the Court once confirmed. The fact that a nominee lacks a paper trail of an ideology does not mean the person lacks certain ideological viewpoints.[26]

Indeed, it is conceivable that the dynamic brought about by the proposal would be more likely to frustrate rather than facilitate the making of meritorious appointments (though, as we have seen, there has historically been considerable disagreement over what constitutes merit). The more accomplished a Supreme Court nominee, the more likely the nominee has done or said something in his or her professional life to stir the opposition of some faction. And the two-thirds requirement empowers a small faction—at least one-third of the Senate—to wield a veto power over Supreme Court nominations. Rather than fulfill Ackerman's (and others') desire to ensure that confirmation of Supreme Court nominees will occur only with overwhelming public support, this proposal would make it easier for a nominee's opponents to block a nomination because they would have to persuade fewer people than they do at present.

The final problem with the supermajority requirement is that it is hard to reconcile with the Founders' reasons for requiring such a vote for removals and treaty ratifications but not for confirmations. The Founders reserved a two-thirds supermajority voting requirement to shift the presumption against certain matters they expected not to arise routinely in order to ensure greater deliberation on them, decrease the chances for political or partisan reprisals on removals and treaty ratifications, and protect an unpopular minority from being abused in Senate votes on these questions.[27] The framers required a simple majority for confirmations to balance the demands of relatively efficient staffing of the government with the need to check abusive exercises of the president's discretion (as well as the composition or direction of the federal judiciary).

I have previously suggested that the constitutional framework allows the development of Senate procedural rules and norms that provide significant constraints on the judicial selection process. These practices raise two important questions. First, does the Senate have an institutional obligation to provide a final vote or action on every judicial nomination? The answer to this question is essential for clarifying the extent to which Senate practices are legitimate. The second question concerns the durability and desirability of these practices—to what extent are they impervious or resistant to change? The answer to this question clarifies the prospects for reforming judicial selection.

The Senate's Institutional Obligation to Take Final Action on Every Judicial Nomination

The argument that the Senate must vote on each judicial nominee is relatively straightforward: the Constitution empowers the Senate to provide advice and consent on judicial nominations; such advice and consent must be given to each nomination; and advice and consent entails an affirmative act—that is, a final vote up or down—on every judicial nomination.[28] A related argument is that in being able to place an unlimited number of temporary holds on any one judicial nominee (or any number of them) for any reason, individual senators (acting alone or in concert with other like-minded members) are able to frustrate the will of a majority of the Senate, not to mention a president's nominating authority. In other words, individual holds reflect the enormous power that the smallest faction conceivable—an individual senator—can wield to frustrate the will of a committee as well as most members of the institution.[29]

The counterarguments to the claim that the Senate has a duty to vote as a body on every judicial nomination are likely to prevail for telling reasons. First, the Senate's delegations of certain authority to committees and individual senators derive from explicit constitutional authority. Article I, section 5 provides in pertinent part, "Each House may determine the Rules of its Proceedings. . . ."[30] Though this authority does not empower each chamber to violate other explicit guarantees of the Constitution (such as the explicit procedures required for lawmaking elsewhere in Article I or the due process clause of the Fifth Amendment),[31] it grants each chamber substantial, unreviewable discretion to make delegations to smaller units within it for the purpose of facilitating the exercise of its official responsibilities.

Such delegations are hardly unique. The Senate routinely delegates fact-finding authority to committees (and empowers individual senators to exercise holds or attempt filibusters, under certain conditions) to assist in rendering judgments on various matters over which the body has exclusive control. Nor has it been unusual outside of the realm of judicial selection for committees, through inaction, protracted deliberation, and delays in scheduling or voting (or individual senators through holds or filibusters), to preclude the Senate from taking final action on matters committed to the whole for consideration.

Treaty ratifications pose an interesting analogy. In fact, it is not uncommon for treaties signed by the president to languish in the Senate and even if they get a hearing in the Foreign Relations Committee, never to be subjected to the Senate for a final vote.[32] If the Senate has not been compelled constitutionally to take final actions on treaty ratifications, it should not be compelled to do so with respect to every judicial nomination.

Three other, related arguments in support of the Senate's institutional obligation to take final action on every judicial nomination cannot be lightly dismissed. First, judicial nominations trigger separation-of-powers concerns not present in many of the other areas in which the Senate does not take final action on matters committed to its discretion. The fate of the third branch is conceivably at risk, because individual senators and committees might be able to impede filling enough judicial vacancies to reach the tipping point at which the quality of justice administered by the federal courts has been seriously compromised or sacrificed. Second, the Constitution embodies a presumption of judicial confirmation, because it requires a majority for approval. In contrast, the Constitution's requirement of a supermajority vote to ratify treaties conceivably embodies a presumption against ratification.[33] Consequently, one could argue that the failure to process a substantial number of judicial nominations frustrates the constitutional presumption that most would be confirmed (in contrast to the expectation that most treaties would not be ratified).[34] The third argument is that the Senate's authority to give its advice and consent to presidential nominations is not just a power but also presupposes or requires a particular process. No other power is quite like that. For instance, the Senate's authority to ratify treaties does not oblige the Senate (at least as a textual matter) to provide any particular kind of process for considering the ratification of treaties. Advice and consent conceivably impose a different obligation on the Senate; they provide a standard by which to measure the adequacy of the Senate's process in considering judicial nominations. The terms *advice* and *consent* conceivably imply not just that the Senate has the authority to consider nominations but also that the Senate is obliged to formulate a process through which it must give its advice and grant or withhold its consent on every nomination.

Though intriguing, these arguments are not ultimately compelling. First, every judicial vacancy will eventually be filled (as long as Congress has not abolished it). To the extent there are delays, they are temporary, though they are likely to harm many litigants who have been precluded from seeking justice or vindication in federal court.[35] The delays will preclude particular confirmations, but they do not ultimately prevent a president from filling the vacancy. The fact that sooner or later the Senate agrees to vote on a nominee for a particular vacancy means that it has fulfilled its obligation to provide its advice and consent with respect to that particular judgeship.

Second, the Constitution sets no time limit on the confirmation process. The Constitution does not prohibit or preclude the Senate from taking its time in considering nominations. Just as the Constitution does not dictate how quickly a president must act in making a nomination, it does not direct how quickly the Senate must act in approving or disapproving it. Perhaps it will take days, maybe months, or even years. In taking its time to act as a body on any particular judicial nomination, the Senate is giving its advice and consent, just not speedily.

Third, the Senate's advice and consent power is analogous to its authority to try impeachments in at least one significant way. The latter authority clearly allows the Senate not only the final, nonreviewable discretion to craft impeachment trial procedures as it sees fit[36] but also to conclude a trial (or even forego a trial) without voting on every impeachment article approved by the House (as was the case with President Johnson). Similarly, the Senate's advice and consent authority includes the discretion to conclude that a particular nomination does not merit further action. In each instance in which the Senate allows a nomination to languish or takes no final action, it is effectively expressing its judgment that no further action is warranted.

Moreover, as a practical matter, there is no chance senators will ever agree to abandon the prerogative of temporary holds. If most senators wanted to do away with this practice, they could; but they have not, because each senator recognizes that allowing colleagues to exercise this prerogative protects his or her own ability to exercise it. Also, senators understand that the exercise of holds is almost never cost-free, for other senators whose interests have been hurt by this practice will be disposed to seek retribution in some fashion. In addition, the exercise of holds has been used for decades, and it seems a little late in the day to decide that it is not permissible. Thus, the only conceivable way to get rid of this practice is to make it in the interest of at least a critical mass of senators to curtail or abandon it. In other words, the challenge is to motivate or encourage senators to develop new or different norms.

Judicial Selection Norms
Over the past several decades, presidents and senators have developed or refined various norms to govern or constrain judicial selection. These norms (some of which overlap with norms applicable to other appointments matters) include senatorial courtesy; Congress's creation of new judgeships for an incoming or newly elected president to fill; individual senators' prerogatives to place any judicial nominations temporarily on hold for any reason; the stalling or paralysis of judicial confirmation proceedings during a presidential election year; committee chairs' implied authority to control the scheduling of hearings, number of witnesses, and timing of votes; the majority leader's authority to control everything that comes to the floor of the Senate; the selection of District of Columbia lawyers for federal court judgeships in the District of Columbia; and the preference evident since the early 1980s for nominating sitting judges (as opposed to distinguished elected or political leaders) to the Supreme Court.

Some of these norms have begun to degrade, and their degradation is one factor that helps to explain the intensification of interbranch conflicts over judicial selection (though the conflicts are another likely cause for the deterioration of certain norms), culminating in higher proportions of delayed and forced withdrawals of judicial nominations during Bill Clinton's presidency as compared to corresponding years in Ronald Reagan's and George Bush's presidencies.[37] One of the more important norms that has begun to degrade is Congress's creation of new judgeships for incoming or newly elected presidents. This was a standard practice for most of the twentieth century, particularly after World War II, but it fell apart during Bill Clinton's presidency.[38] The degradation, no doubt, is related to President Clinton's failure to defend or perpetuate the tradition of making judicial nominations a high priority of his administration. Other deteriorating norms include temporary as opposed to indefinite holds by senators,[39] senatorial courtesy (though this still remains by far the strongest norm, it has begun to weaken, particularly through a process known as norm ambiguation, i.e., the development of a new norm as a result of conflict or argument over the meaning of a norm),[40] and at least two other norms whose degradation has had spillover effects on judicial nominations.[41]

Though the Constitution does not, as I have argued, compel the full Senate to take final action on every judicial nomination, it is possible to develop strategies for using existing norms or developing new norms to ensure that many if not most nominees get fuller consideration, if not final action, by the Senate. Most proposals for reforming judicial selection are directed at either the president or the Senate but not at maximizing the leverage of the other formal participant in the appointments process, the nominee. The strategy draws on norm theory, which I will explore in greater detail in the next three sections. It ensures that the actions undertaken are in the interests of the president and at least a critical mass of senators.

Managing Existing Norms

Generally, nominees have little leverage in facilitating the full Senate's consideration of their nominations.[42] The critical question is, how can nominees make it in the interests of presidents and senators to move their nominations at least to the floor of the Senate? Three related strategies are possible, all of which entail the use of existing judicial selection norms.

The first tactic is to employ senatorial courtesy,[43] by which I mean nominating a senator or prominent member of the House.[44] Though the Senate defeated John Tower's nomination as secretary of defense, Tower did get final action from the Senate.[45] More recently, Carol Moseley-Braun's nomination as ambassador came into conflict with several prerogatives of individual senators (employed by a parliamentary master, Jesse Helms), yet she got final Senate action and indeed was successfully confirmed.[46]

Braun's successful nomination is instructive in other ways. It underscores the degree to which senatorial courtesy outweighs individual senators' hold prerogatives. Consequently, it might prove to be a useful norm in other contexts. For instance, it could be invoked at times when holds are on the rise, such as during a presidential election year. Even though confirmation slowdowns are notorious during such periods, it is never easy for senators to turn their backs on one of their own, particularly someone who is still a colleague at the time of his or her nomination or has only recently left the body.

Moreover, a president's nomination of a senator to the Supreme Court is an effective means for breaking the inertia in the Senate against nominating elected or political leaders to the Court. In fact, it was quite common, until after the nomination of Sandra Day O'Connor to the Court in 1982, for presidents to nominate people directly from significant positions of public or political leadership. The statistics are striking: of the Court's 111 justices, only 24 have had ten or more years of experience as a judge on any court, state or federal; 81 have had significant experience in public service or governmental leadership, and more than half came directly from prominent nonjudicial positions.

Nevertheless, the tradition has died for several reasons. First, there is increasing skepticism that professional politicians cannot appreciate the distinction between policymaking and judging. They have been increasingly viewed as not appreciating, much less having, the requisite skills for judging. Moreover, many prominent justices who had served in political life before joining the Court (Earl Warren, for example) are now viewed by many Republican senators (and conservative interest groups) as having largely been unprincipled in their approach to separation-of-powers and federalism questions. In addition, the stakes in constitutional adjudication have increased enormously, leaving very few senators completely indifferent to or uninterested in the ideological orientations of judicial nominees. If, however, a president believes that nominating someone with a keen understanding of political institutions and policymaking will benefit the Court and the nation, his nominee is more likely to get a sympathetic hearing if the nominee has come from the Senate. Though the nominee still must persuade her colleagues that she appreciates the differences between law and politics and between legislating and judicial decision making, such persuasion might be easier for someone known well by most senators than for someone unknown to them.

Moseley-Braun's successful nomination is also attributable to the fact that the nomination of a former senator focuses media and public attention on the appointments process. When an event is being broadcast by the media, it becomes difficult for senators to rely on dubious or disingenuous grounds for their actions. Instead, public scrutiny pressures senators to show good cause for their actions or to articulate compelling reasons for what might seem cheap shots at a former colleague, whom the public probably believes is qualified for the office in question.

A variation on President Clinton's recourse to senatorial courtesy on behalf of Moseley-Braun is his successful nomination of Richard Paez and Marsha Berzon to the Ninth Circuit. Though of course not planned to unfold as they did, these nominations became high-profile, triggering sensitive election-year concerns. As such, they demonstrate a second important means for checking abusive holds.

Each nomination symbolized an important constituency in the next presidential election, Hispanics for Paez and women for Berzon.[47] Nevertheless, some Republican senators on the Judiciary Committee tried to put an indefinite hold on Paez's nomination to the Ninth Circuit, based on his work as a legal aid lawyer and self-description as a "political liberal." Similarly, some Republican senators tried to thwart Berzon's nomination because of her work as a labor lawyer (and to some extent because she was a former law clerk to Justice Brennan and had done some work earlier in her career for the ACLU). After both nominations cleared the

Judiciary Committee, further efforts were made to place the nominations on indefinite hold, again based on the suspicion that the nominees if confirmed would become liberal activists on the Ninth Circuit. After Senate minority leader Tom Daschle cut a deal to bring the nominations to the floor (to resolve conflicts between President Clinton and Senator James Inhofe over Clinton's exercise of his recess appointment prerogative), the majority was finally put to the test of whether they wanted to defeat these nominations (for whatever reason) and hand a campaign issue to the Democrats for the 2000 presidential election—namely, the Republicans' dubious treatment of women and minority judicial candidates. In the end, the Senate confirmed the nominations.[48]

The common thread in the Moseley-Braun, Paez, and Berzon nominations is a third, related check on the excessive exercise of individual holds—a president's willingness to make judicial selection a legislative priority and thus to put a spotlight on it.[49] The importance of such willingness cannot be overstated. It is no coincidence that President Clinton's public denouncement of the paralysis in judicial selection at the end of 1997, coupled with the Chief Justice's criticisms of the Senate's slowdown in 1997 and 1998, produced some movement, albeit temporary, in the judicial confirmation process.[50] Such public denunciations make a difference because many senatorial norms need to operate below the public radar in order to be effective. The parties who shape or develop such norms are often not prepared to defend their informal agreements publicly. Thus, exposing publicly the dilatory tactics of some senators operates in effect as an effort to impose a shaming penalty on them. Though such shaming penalties are of course not guaranteed to work in every case, they are likely to have some modest effect on dislodging or breaking impasses. For example, it became difficult for Senator Lott to defend Senator Inhofe's attempt to put all judicial nominations indefinitely on hold because of Clinton's alleged breach of another deal governing recess appointments. Although the issue no doubt had salience for Inhofe, it did not have enough salience to outweigh the hesitancy of most Republicans to appear to be overreacting by punishing judicial nominees from two important constituencies in retaliation against Clinton's purported lapses.

Developing New or Different Norms

The previous subsection emphasized the critical importance of a president's willingness to engage in some publicized contests over judicial selection as a significant means for increasing the numbers of judicial nominations that get hearings or final Senate action. Restoring this practice of course requires a commitment from a president to make judicial selection a priority of his administration. The reasons for and implications of President Clinton's failure to do this merits further scrutiny, particularly for the purpose of identifying new or different ways to keep public pressure on the judicial selection process.

President Clinton had at least two important reasons for not making judicial selection a priority of his administration. First, he had other legislative priorities, such as health care and balancing the budget, that he considered more important to the immediate and long-term welfare of the nation. He wanted to devote his leverage as president primarily to the achievement of these other priorities. Second, he believed that by not making judicial selection a priority he would be able to depoliticize it, that is, he was concerned that presidential involvement in judicial selection drew the wrong kind of attention and sent the wrong kind of signal. He thought that his involvement would suggest (wrongly) to senators and interest groups (if not the public) the infusion of political considerations in judicial selection (such as using the federal courts to achieve policy or political objectives not achievable but more legitimately pursued in other fora).

Though laudable, these objectives backfired. Perhaps most important, they made the president's judicial nominations generally vulnerable to an unusually high (some would say unprecedented) degree of delay tactics. In retrospect, it is not hard to see how such circumstances could develop. The Clinton approach was simply a recipe for adversity. On one side of the equation was a president who wanted to use his limited leverage (because he won in his first term by a plurality of votes and was reelected by a bare majority) to fight for legislative priorities other than judicial selection; on the other side of the equation was a Senate dominated by the opposition party (from 1994 through 2000), with most members not sharing the president's legislative priorities and many having the priorities of combating judicial activism and preserving vacancies for the appointments of right-minded jurists. Of the latter senators, many welcomed public contests (because the issue of judicial selection was particularly salient for them), thus taking advantage of one of the president's vulnerabilities (his willingness to cut deals and otherwise take actions to avoid high-profile contests).

If a president under these circumstances wants to ensure his judicial nominees get full or final Senate action, he has limited options, either restoring old norms or developing new ones. First, if he refuses to revise his priorities, he will, as President Clinton has done, broker numerous deals with the Senate, some of which compromise his prerogatives (as he did in trying to secure William Fletcher's nomination to the Ninth Circuit[51] or in agreeing to nominate Senator Hatch's preferred candidate Ted Stewart to a federal district judgeship in Utah).

Second, the president may revise his priorities. If a president is willing to return to the old practice of making judicial selection a priority for which he will fight publicly, he can do so in several ways. I have already suggested that a president can do so by nominating members of Congress, prominent public servants, or others whose status or records trigger concern among interest groups or constituencies disposed to fight for the embattled nominees. By nominating such candidates, a president picks people who to some extent can do his work for him — as public figures, they draw media and other attention, as well as pose challenges to interest groups and other opponents. In a public contest, Senate opposition needs to be grounded on something respectable or neutral-sounding. For instance, the opposition to Paez and Berzon withered once the nominations reached the floor of the Senate, because exposing it to the light of day revealed its grounding almost entirely in dubious suspicions or inferences (i.e., they must be liberal activists because Paez represented indigent clients and Berzon worked for labor unions). Many Republicans were not disposed to defend these conjectures publicly.

Presidents' reordering of their internal organizations or practices for processing judicial nominations can also affect if not increase the chances for nominations to get more complete consideration from the Senate. As I explain below, adopting different practices or developing different norms for presidential decision making on judicial nominations would help to expedite the forwarding of nominations to the Senate and avoid having them accumulate in a presidential election year, when they are least likely to get hearings, much less committee or final votes.

First, it rarely makes sense for a president to make judicial nominations that he is not prepared to defend publicly.[52] Moreover, a president's choice of a consensus candidate has been a surefire way for a quick, uneventful confirmation. This practice depends in part on a president's assembling a competent support staff who are responsible for evaluating candidates and making timely and reliable recommendations to him.[53] However, backroom negotiations between a president and senators might undermine the value of a process that is open and accountable to the public. It is possible, for example, that consultations could produce deals to keep certain harmful information about a nominee from the public or the media. The eventual public reaction to the Senate Judiciary Committee's initial decision not to hold a separate hearing on Anita Hill's sexual harassment allegations against Justice Thomas demonstrates how well such deals can be contained.

Another practice that would expedite the making of judicial nominations is for presidents to direct their staffs to develop lists of viable candidates for each judicial vacancy.[54] This practice is advantageous because it enables an administration to move more quickly both in initially proposing nominations and in those cases when its initial choices failed. The obvious problem is that it could produce delays in making nominations, because developing lists involves an expenditure of both time and resources. Once such lists have been developed, however, the administration can rely on them in filling subsequent vacancies. If an administration develops lists of viable judicial candidates, those names will be at hand should another vacancy arise in the same district or circuit. An administration could, alternatively, identify districts or circuits in which vacancies are likely to arise and develop lists of viable candidates prior to the actual occurrence of a vacancy.

The more quickly presidents move in nominating judges, the more time they allow pressure to build for senators to move on those nominations. Presidents could issue challenges to the Senate Judiciary Committee to move quickly, perhaps within a set period of time, and to explain publicly its reasons for not moving more expeditiously. Obviously, a set time limit provides an incentive for some senators to try to run out the clock. The next subsection considers possible procedural reforms to address unreasonable delays in judicial confirmation proceedings.

Containing or Shaping Norms through Procedural Reforms

The absence of specific procedural rules to govern certain aspects of judicial selection have introduced, no doubt, flexibility in the process. It is also clear that adopting or changing some rules, even if it were possible, would not necessarily alter the dynamics substantially, because some senators would develop informal practices for working around the rules or would learn how to manipulate them to maximize or facilitate their preferred outcomes.

Nevertheless, some proposed procedural changes or rules do merit special consideration if for no other reason than to clarify the areas in which informal practices or norms rather than formal rules will prevail as the primary mechanisms for constraint. Of particular concern are procedural alterations that might be in the interests of both presidents and senators to adopt. I will explore more than a dozen such proposed formal changes. Though all suggested modifications involve Senate practices or procedures, I organize them in terms of the institutions or participants whose interests they are likeliest to implicate.

The Senate. Although many of the proposed procedural changes discussed below can be defended as preserving if not enhancing individual senators' roles in judicial selection, many senators will probably not see it that way. Their resistance is likely to reveal their vested interests in the status quo and their opinions about the stakes involved in judicial selection.

One proposal is the adoption of a rigidly enforced, specific time limit on nomination holds. Divided government has no doubt led to a weakening of a rigid time limit. Of course, senators are unlikely to abandon nomination holds altogether, for holds allow them to protect the interests that they perceive have been jeopardized as a result of some nomination. But they might also resist a time limit as long as stalling nominations is in their interest. Obviously, they are most likely to do so when their party does not control the White House. Nevertheless, putting a rigid time limit on holds might further the interest of every senator. For one thing, when a senator is from the same party as a president, it ensures that the nominations that he or she would like to see fully processed have a greater likelihood of doing so. In addition, putting time limits on holds preempts retaliatory holds from senators who have axes to grind from past confirmation squabbles.

A second possible reform is for senators to abandon their prerogative of allowing each other anonymously to put an unlimited number of nominations on hold temporarily. Publicizing the names of senators who have repeatedly on their own or in tandem placed nominations on hold is one way to try to make them publicly accountable for their actions. In some cases, it might operate as a shaming mechanism, exposing them to the harsh glare of public, interest group, media, and presidential scrutiny. Some senators might think twice about exercising such holds if they are subject to public scrutiny when they do.

The obvious disadvantage of this proposed change is that many, perhaps most, senators would be unwilling to relinquish this prerogative. Though such a change would surely increase the chances for full consideration of judicial nominations, the idea behind anonymous holds is similar to the purpose behind closed hearings—to ensure more candid discussion and judgment about any lingering problems with particular nominations. Moreover, senators are likely to defend the prerogative on the ground that it allows temporary rather than permanent delays. The problem with this defense is that there is no limit to the number of senators who can put a nomination on hold (or the number of nominations on which a senator can place holds), so that as a practical matter the hold can become so persistent or protracted as to be functionally the equivalent of a permanent nullification.

A third suggestion, made by the Miller Center,[55] is that the senators from the president's party should identify viable candidates for judicial nomination even before any judicial vacancies arise. This practice could supplement or perhaps substitute for the norm proposed earlier for presidents to anticipate and develop plans for filling likely judicial vacancies. The Miller Center recommends that once a vacancy arises, the senators could then recommend at least three people to fill it. The obvious advantage is that this practice would give senators a vested interest in filling certain vacancies and thereby help to expedite judicial selection by assisting or facilitating a president's search for suitable judicial nominees. Such recommendations would provide a president with a rich supply of names (to supplement his own lists) to keep in mind when judicial vacancies arose.

The problem with this suggestion is that it might trigger the expectations of some senators that a president would choose nominees from their lists. Difficulty is likely to occur whenever a senator recommends someone in particular for a vacancy in a confirmable office. Ignoring such recommendations puts a president at risk of alienating those senators or putting himself in their debt (to be repaid in making other nominations down the road or in supporting certain legislative initiatives).

Fourth, the Judiciary Committee might follow the example established in the mid-twentieth century when it pressured President Hoover to select Justice Cardozo. The committee strategy was to give Hoover a list of preapproved candidates, indicate that it would refuse to confirm anyone not on the list, and suggest it had a strong preference for the first name, Benjamin Cardozo. This solution is considered one means by which the Senate could force a president bent on doing otherwise to make a merit appointment to the Court. Of course, the effectiveness of this proposal depends on the Senate's ability to stand its ground persistently in the face of presidential opposition, and, as I have suggested, it has rarely been able to do so because so many variables are involved. The likelihood of this suggestion ever working again depends on two convergent circumstances: a vacancy arising on the Court at a time when the Senate could unite behind a particular candidate and an extremely pliable, disinterested, or unpopular chief executive (or one not presently in a position to squander his political coinage).

Fifth, senators could strive for consensus (either in the form of a norm or formalized practice) on the burden of persuasion in Supreme Court confirmation proceedings. The Senate could follow the lead of former Senators Albert Gore Jr. and Paul Simon, both of whom insisted in the midst of the floor debate on Clarence Thomas's nomination that the burden of persuasion should be on those who wished to show the nominee merited a seat on the Court.[56] In the final debate on the Senate floor, Gore and Simon took the position that the burden of persuasion was on the president, Thomas, or both. Senator Simon argued that "the benefit of the doubt" regarding a Supreme Court nomination should be resolved in favor of "the people of this country" and the Constitution.[57] Both senators maintained in effect that the Senate's ultimate fidelity should be to the future generations of Americans who would have to live under the justice's rulings. In short, they maintained that Thomas was asking the committee to give him life tenure to make final interpretations of the Constitution, and the Senate should not entrust the Constitution to him unless it was fully comfortable with that.

It is not likely, however, that this suggestion could be enforced uniformly. Even if most of the Senate or just the Judiciary Committee were to endorse such a burden of persuasion—which is extremely unlikely—other members of the Senate would remain free, in the absence of any practical enforcement mechanism, to apply the standard each thought appropriate.[58]

Sixth, the Senate might consider having professional counsel ask questions for each side to make confirmation hearings more efficient. However, this proposal presents two potential problems. On the one hand, it is based on the premise that senators may not be adequately discharging their constitutional responsibility, in which case we might consider either electing different people or doing away altogether with the Senate's confirmation role. On the other hand, the people hired to ask questions might try to score points in a confirmation proceeding for no better reason than to justify their role.

Seventh, the Judiciary Committee might reconsider how it schedules confirmation hearings. The committee often delays hearings to allow for investigation of a nominee, but that delay also gives interest groups, Senate staffers, and others time to mobilize support for or against a nomination, and the administration time to coach or indoctrinate a nominee on how he or she should approach deciding cases. Moreover, the nominee may feel beholden to the administration because of his or her indoctrination and the assistance he or she receives—particularly during heated hearings—to achieve confirmation. Alternatively, the committee could schedule hearings shortly after a president announces his choice for the Court and focus the hearings primarily on the nominee's public record. More rapid scheduling of Supreme Court confirmation proceedings could encourage the choice of nominees who would probably be more prepared to stand on the merits of their records.

An eighth possible revision to Senate practices is to have the Senate, and in particular the Judiciary Committee, try to define or assess the criteria for evaluating judicial nominees. A variation on this proposal is for the committee or individual senators to give notice before hearings about the particular criteria they will use to evaluate judicial nominees. The typical considerations include a judge's fitness to serve (including temperament, experience, and integrity), theory of or approach to judging, interpretations of particular constitutional clauses (of special concern to some senators, interest groups, or constituencies), and a single issue of overriding concern.[59] Moreover, if ideological orientation or commitments matter (and they plainly do to most senators), judicial nominees (and the president who nominates them and the senators who support them) are entitled as a matter of fairness to know the criteria by which they will be judged.

For example, the majority on the Judiciary Committee could announce at the outset of proceedings that it will not vote for any nominees who give evasive answers to questions about their public records, fail to affirm expressly certain fundamental liberties or freedoms that committee members would like to see endorsed, or fail to demonstrate a level of professional accomplishment that committee members want to see in a federal judge, particularly a Supreme Court justice. If the president were to nominate to the bench candidates with little meaningful experience in the law, dubious temperament, or no apparent propensity to excel in the craftsmanship of judging, then senators could exercise their political judgment and demand nominees with more substantial, credible, and meaningful professional experience and achievement. Although it is possible that a significant number of senators could agree on the relevance of particular criteria in a given case, it is highly unlikely they could reach consensus on the basic criteria for judicial nominations or on the appropriate prioritizing of the relevant criteria.[60]

For instance, in the aftermath of the Thomas hearings, Senator Joseph Biden dared his colleagues to follow his example by agreeing not to support any Supreme Court nominee who failed to accept *Roe* as the law of the land. Such a challenge is likely to be effective only if it is linked to other means (such as logrolling or vote trading) that give the senator issuing the challenge some leverage over his colleagues. Otherwise, as a practical matter, every senator has been free to rest his or her final decision on a judicial confirmation on whatever grounds he or she thinks is appropriate. And this proposal is unlikely to pass, because senators almost certainly would not want to relinquish any discretion in measuring the fitness of judicial nominees.

The nominee. In the absence of the Senate's consensus on formal criteria for evaluating judicial nominees, senators have apparently unrestricted freedom to focus on any aspect of a nominee's record that they think appropriate. For many scholars, the choice of many senators to ask probing questions about how judicial nominees would be likely to rule in cases coming before them poses a serious threat to judicial independence. The concern is that through interaction with administration personnel in interviews for judgeships, and with senators in private meetings or formal confirmation hearings, judicial nominees are pressured to make commitments to certain views in exchange for appointment. These interactions probably do subject judicial nominees to some pressure to conform, if not their views then at least their statements about their views. Although it is true that once confirmed, federal judges are generally immune from direct political reprisals (except for impeachment), they are especially vulnerable to personal or partisan attacks in the appointments process, in which they lack the means available to political figures to defend themselves.

I have already suggested that questioning judicial nominees about their likely ideologies does not pose a serious threat to judicial independence.[61] Nevertheless, concerns about protecting that independence have led scholars to argue for the development of new norms that constrain senators' focus in evaluating judicial nominees. One popular alternative to looking at a nominee's views on judging or on particular constitutional issues is to recommend that senators focus instead on the person's moral character. Both Stephen Carter and Ronald Dworkin, for instance, believe that character, because it is a source of a judge's orientation toward his craft, is a proper focus of a confirmation proceeding.[62] In their view, moral character or disposition is a much more meaningful and reliable indicator of a judicial nominee's likely future performance than his or her expected or declared ideology. Indeed, more than a few senators from both parties seem to agree, as reflected in their opposition in the late 1980s and early 1990s to judicial nominees who were members of country clubs or other private organizations that excluded women and minorities and over the past eight years to some nominees based on inferences drawn from the nominees' clerkships or law practice.

There are, however, several problems with the view that a judicial nominee's moral character constitutes a more appropriate basis for evaluation than the likely judicial ideology. First, a focus on the nominee's moral character is bound to make judicial confirmations much messier because it will invite his or her opponents to do whatever they can to taint the nominee's reputation. One benefit of focusing on a nominee's judicial philosophy, in contrast, is that it usually turns on some sort of documentation. If the focus were on a nominee's moral disposition, much of the debate would be bound to turn on perceptions or even on swearing contests between conflicting witnesses about private conduct with arguably public implications—something, say, on the order of the second phase of the Thomas hearings.

Second, although it might be preferable for a judge to have a good moral character, there is little or no agreement among political leaders and scholars on what constitutes the ideal or preferable moral character for a judge (other than the obvious ingredients of integrity, evenhandedness, and sound temperament, though many would disagree about the appropriate indices for each of these). Further, it is hard if not impossible to determine the extent to which certain personal attributes should take priority over an assessment of the nominee's judicial skills and judgment. Character is undoubtedly relevant as an aspect of a judicial nominee's likely or proven temperament on the bench. Judicial temperament, indispensable to good judging, includes such attributes, in addition to good moral character, as the quality of interaction with colleagues, open-mindedness, patience, even handedness, disposition to listen to all sides of an issue, leadership, and personality.[63] If the nominee has not been a judge, the question is to what degree he or she has shown or demonstrated the propensity to develop these attributes. Some other important measures of judicial performance are proven excellence in a relevant area of the law, demonstrated leadership in some field of law or some legal endeavor, well-developed bargaining or negotiation skills, accomplished writing ability, the quality or sophistication of the nominee's judicial decisions (assuming the nominee has been a judge), and other significant public service.

Moreover, while good moral character would obviously seem to be an important attribute for a high-ranking official, particularly a federal judge, some of the people who have been commonly viewed as great Supreme Court justices arguably lacked the "right kind of moral instincts." [64] For example, Hugo Black had been a member of the Ku Klux Klan and arguably lied publicly about the length of his membership, and Earl Warren has been harshly criticized for his initiative and support as California's attorney general in detaining Japanese-Americans on a dubious basis.[65]

In addition, confirming Supreme Court nominees on the basis of their "strongest moral commitments" will not necessarily make the Supreme Court's controversial rulings easier to swallow or produce greater credibility for the Court.[66] For example, the Warren Court has been vilified in some circles for its activism ever since it decided *Brown v. Board of Education*,[67] despite the fact that over that Court's sixteen-year life span most of its members were well-respected men with substantial experience in public service. The moral characters of the justices who decided *Brown* have not saved the judgment from massive resistance or criticism over the years; and *Brown* is widely hailed today as a courageous and principled decision not because we know that the people who decided it had great moral character or were great "moral philosophers" or visionaries but rather because the vast majority of Americans accept *Brown* as morally sound.[68] Moreover, many of the justices in the majority of *Roe v. Wade*[69] came to the Court with arguably good moral characters that have not (yet) spared *Roe* (or the Court) from vicious attack.

The most powerful reason for focusing on a nominee's character rather than on his or her ideology is expressed in Ronald Dworkin's argument that the time has come for us to accept that judges, particularly Supreme Court justices, interpret the law partly on the basis of their moral convictions or dispositions. That is, because we cannot predict precisely all of the kinds of cases likely to come before the Supreme Court, the appropriate approach in confirmation hearings would be to examine the premises from which the judge's or justice's decisions will later flow.[70]

Numerous constitutional law scholars have expressed their agreement with the basic point that judicial nominees' moral and political judgments about the nature of U.S. society and the judiciary's role within it influence their decisions.[71] Indeed, it is because many presidents and senators have recognized this fact that they have looked beyond a judicial nominee's stated ideology for other indicators of how he or she would perform on the bench. Consequently, the focus on a nominee's moral character already is consistently considered in the judicial confirmation process; it just has never been the system's sole focus.

To be sure, allowing for any portion of a confirmation hearing to examine a nominee's moral fitness to become a judge or justice would certainly undercut the popular belief that judges — or at least good judges — exercise their authority independently of their personal moral convictions and judgment. In other words, a good judge may be someone who would, as Clarence Thomas suggested once he was confirmed to the Court, strip himself down "naked like a runner" prior to making decisions as a judge.[72] The problem with this pronouncement is that it defies reality and thus lacks credibility. It is beyond question that judges bring something of themselves to the task of judging; the critical question is, what do they bring? In answering this, it is relevant to consider not just a person's expressed philosophy of judging but also the source of his or her approach to judicial decision making.

The source of a judge's preferred mode of constitutional interpretation is not, strictly speaking, the Constitution. Perhaps no scholar in recent years has made this argument more vigorously than Jed Rubenfeld. Rubenfeld contends that a theory of constitutional interpretation derives its legitimacy not from the Constitution, which says (and presupposes) nothing about how it should be interpreted, but rather from a political "theory accounting for the revolutionary place of written constitutionalism in democratic self-government."[73] The question is, where does such a theory come from?

The latter question can only be answered fully in another book. For present purposes, a few tentative observations about the nature and likely source of a judge's theoretical foundations for preferring certain modes of constitutional interpretation are possible. As Rubenfeld and others have shown,[74] one source is not how the framers would have wanted judges to perform. The framers largely believed that the meaning of a particular document should be construed independently of the specific intentions of those who drafted it; the language should be construed according to its plain meaning. Making recourse to the views of the framers' generation on how judges should perform as a guide for how contemporary or subsequent judges should perform would be circular, for in each case the judges are looking beyond the Constitution for guidance on how they should perform as judges, even in cases involving the Constitution. The direction in which judges tend to look and what they perceive there are shaped by their fundamental moral and political judgments—a theory of legitimacy, in Rubenfeld's conception—about the judiciary's (and even the Constitution's) role in American society. As Rubenfeld's Yale Law School colleague, Stephen Carter, has suggested,

> The words of the Constitution do not, by themselves, determine everything, and all who must strive to interpret and apply the text, no matter how great their intellectual force or legal sophistication, must at some point make leaps of faith not wholly explicable by reference to standard tools for interpretation. . . . All [constitutional] questions require judgment in the finding of answers, and in every exercise of interpretive judgment, there comes a crucial moment when the interpreter's own experience and values become the most important data. That moment cannot be spotted in advance, any more than the pressing issues of ten years hence can be predicted today. But it is certain that the moment will come.[75]

The question raised by Carter's argument is whether the Constitution or prudence requires decision makers within the judicial selection process to focus on moral character or ideology exclusively or predominately. The confirmation process, however, does not require an exclusive focus on any particular factor, for it allows an ongoing dialogue about how judicial performance should be evaluated or predicted. As with every nomination, each confirmation contest has its own dynamic and achieves its own balance, for better or worse, between questions about a nominee's moral character and those about his or her ideology. Nor is this scenario a bad thing. An ongoing dialogue is ultimately desirable because it allows each generation to rethink the judiciary's function and the relationship between character and judging, and makes presidents and senators address these subjects and account for their attitudes about them.

Though presidents and senators are likely to persist in disagreeing about the appropriate criteria for evaluating judicial nominees, they might be more amenable to persuasion that several possible changes in the nominee's role in the confirmation process are in their mutual interest. First, The Century Foundation and the Miller Center have both suggested streamlining the paperwork judicial nominees must complete in order to have their nominations fully processed by the Senate. This recommendation would not only expedite confirmation hearings but also reduce the unnecessary obstacles or burdens nominees must endure.[76]

Second, senators should consider diminishing the role of the nominee in judicial confirmation hearings. The fact that nominations are often won or lost early in the process could be taken as proof that substantial input from the nominee after the nomination is not necessary for senators to make an informed decision on the nominee's fitness to serve on the Court. This has been true for judicial nominations regardless of whether nominees have had to testify. No doubt, fairness demands that a nominee should be given every opportunity to defend his or her reputation or integrity in a public forum, but if the way has already been paved for a nomination through good-faith consultation between the president and key senators, then limiting the time for the nominee to testify or restricting questions to a nominee's public record could substantially reduce the need for senatorial interrogation of the nominee. Valuable information about the nominee could still be produced for the public record through the testimony of people who know the nominee and his or her record.

In questioning people who know the nominee, the Judiciary Committee is already aggressive in uncovering stances on constitutional issues that the nominee may have communicated privately. For instance, the committee could cross-examine a nominee as to whether he spoke to or communicated with anyone about his prospective nomination or testimony, and, if so, to whom, when the exchange(s) took place, what was said or communicated, and why the contacts or exchanges occurred. Although this kind of questioning could discourage cutting deals with respect to certain nominations, it poses a few possible problems. One is that it encourages tit-for-tat; aggressive searches into the backgrounds of nominees for any clues to their judicial philosophies (or the origins of them) are likely to result in the knocking out of at least a few of them, provoking retaliation when a different majority controls the committee. Moreover, such aggressive questioning would probably be obstructed by claims of attorney-client privilege for any private lawyers who consulted with the nominee on the matter and of executive privilege for any administration lawyers who counseled the nominee on his or her testimony.

Yet another possibility (often mentioned by legal scholars) is to preclude judicial nominees from having to testify altogether. This proposal seems to have no chance whatsoever to be adopted. The Senate has gotten into the habit of having nominees appear on demand and of threatening to delay or permanently stall a nomination if the nominee refuses to testify. Though the Constitution does not require a nominee to testify before the Senate (any more than it obliges the Senate to provide a hearing for or take final action on every judicial nominee), no nominee will have the political clout to refuse a Senate request to make an appearance without having his or her nomination suffer irreparably as a result. Even if for some reason the committee were to return to its practice of not having the nominee testify, it would then be incumbent on the Senate to stop nominees from paying private "courtesy calls" on each senator. Otherwise, the nominees could easily undermine the rationale behind the proposal by making private assurances to senators. If, however, the committee barred nominees from testifying in confirmation hearings but the Senate permitted private "courtesy calls" with each senator, then the committee would have to ensure that any information about the nominee's judicial ideology shared privately with any senator would be made public.

Interest groups. Another possible reform of the judicial selection process is to eliminate entirely or at least severely restrict participation by organized lobbying groups. The obvious concern is that some groups wield disproportionate influence over the process and distort the debate.

The problem with trying to curtail or diminish interest group participation in judicial selection is of course that, as a practical matter, the Senate can do nothing to prevent interest groups from contacting or lobbying receptive members or talking with the media outside the hearing room, for these activities are protected by the First Amendment. It is also unlikely that the Senate would achieve much by barring interest groups from testifying or restricting how much they may testify in confirmation hearings. Even if the Judiciary Committee could reach consensus to modify or do away entirely with most or all interest group testimony, interest groups would still have access to sympathetic senators, and thus their messages would still be heard.

At present, interest groups operate in the appointments process as proxies for different segments of the public. An arguably more effective means for advancing direct public participation in the process (assuming one thinks that is a good thing) is via the Internet. The more the Internet accommodates direct public feedback on nominations and the more people are aware of these accommodations, the less credibly self-described mediators such as interest groups can claim the authority to speak on behalf of the public interest.

Public scrutiny. Periodically, some senators recommend returning to closed-door judicial confirmation hearings. Perhaps some senators feel, based on their experiences in the closed-door deliberations on President Clinton's removal, that public hearings discourage candor and encourage grand-standing. In contrast, closed-door hearings would be less circuslike because there would be no media or crowds for participants to play to and thus a more serious, deliberate, and candid discussion of the nominee's record would occur.

There are three major problems with this suggestion. First, some determination would have to be made as to how much of the hearings would be held behind closed doors. The question would be whether keeping some parts of a hearing behind closed doors would lead to a more responsible, dignified proceeding or to a more fractious or distorted one insofar as the public and media are concerned. Moreover, making some parts of a hearing open but not others allows the opposing sides to make deals that might not ultimately be in the public's or the judiciary's best interests. Such was the case the first time the Judiciary Committee considered Anita Hill's allegation of sexual harassment against Clarence Thomas: after taking statements from both Hill and Thomas, the committee decided behind closed doors not to investigate the matter further; regardless of the merits of that decision, once it became public, it left the impression that a questionable deal had been struck. Second, closed-door judicial hearings, at least insofar as the testimony of the nominee is concerned, do not guarantee that some groups will be precluded from wielding disproportionate influence in or otherwise distort the process. Having hearings held behind closed doors does not necessarily guarantee more elevated debate or less manipulative conduct on the part of senators, their staffs, or interest groups. Throughout the nineteenth century and up until the Brandeis hearings in 1916, many contentious Supreme Court hearings occurred behind closed doors. Indeed, one major reason that Brandeis's supporters insisted (successfully) that his confirmation hearings should be held in open session was the recognition that closed door hearings emboldened dubious attacks on nominees' records or characters and allowed the contending sides to make questionable deals. At the very least, open hearings have operated, as Brandeis later would suggest on the Court, as a disinfectant and exposed much of the process to the scrutiny of the media and the public.

Finally, opting for closed-door hearings on judicial confirmations would not necessarily preclude media campaigns regarding the fates of different nominations. Up until fairly recently, the media functioned as the primary gatekeeper for the release of information on governmental hearings and operations. In this decade, the gatekeeper function has been increasingly taken over by the Internet. Even if hearings are held behind closed doors, information is likely to leak out in a couple of different ways, including anonymous sources who leak data or spread rumors on the Internet or who talk off the record to the press. The leaks are likely to resemble something on the order of the published reports on closed-door, supposedly confidential grand jury testimony regarding President Clinton's testimony and actions undertaken to conceal his relationship with Monica Lewinsky.

Of course, it might be possible to solve the leakage problem by holding all confirmation proceedings in executive session. Under such circumstances, the participants would be obliged under Senate rules to remain silent—or gagged—afterward; however, leaks would still be possible, as was the case throughout the nineteenth century and more recently regarding the initial closed-door hearing to consider Anita Hill's sexual harassment charges against Clarence Thomas.

The ensuing question is whether the American people are prepared to pay the price for holding judicial confirmation hearings in secret, including gagging the participants. This is not done for other confirmation hearings, except for discrete portions of proceedings relating to the confirmation of officials in the national security area, such as the director of the Central Intelligence Agency.

The answer turns on two things. First, it depends on whether the American people have sufficient confidence that judicial confirmation hearings could be conducted responsibly away from the public eye. In other words, how much are the American people willing to trust senators if no one is looking over their shoulders in the process? A second question concerns whether judicial independence is likely to be served or disserved by holding judicial confirmation hearings in executive session.

In some respects, it is conceivable that the choice of open versus closed hearings might make little difference to the maintenance of judicial independence. First, judicial independence seems to be more durable than most commentators concede, as reflected by the absence of any proof of coercion of judicial performance as the result of confirmation antics.

Second, one price of holding judicial hearings behind closed doors (including holding them in executive session) is to remove the judiciary one step further away from public awareness or scrutiny than it is at present. For some, this is indeed a good development, for it reflects the possibility that judicial confirmation hearings, if held behind closed doors, would be less likely to become analogous to referenda. For others, restricting public scrutiny of the process might make it easier for special interests to wield disproportionate influence in the process. The price of such closed-door hearings, which apparently most senators still believe is too high to pay, would be to deprive the public of one of its rare glimpses into federal judicial operations. In other words, defenders of open hearings insist they help to demystify the functions of the federal courts, particularly of the Supreme Court, for the American public.

Ironically, open hearings pressure senators to do an increasing amount of bargaining beyond public scrutiny. Consequently, in the final analysis, it is unclear how much open hearings fulfill their objective to demystify the operations of either the federal judiciary or of the Congress itself.

POSTSCRIPT

PRESIDENT HARRY TRUMAN once observed, "The only new thing in the world is the history you don't know."[1] There is a lot of history that we in the legal academy don't know. Consequently, our analyses of some subjects such as impeachment and federal appointments are limited by our failure to take into account the patterns or practices in past decision making in these processes.[2] These patterns or practices consist, most importantly, of the ways in which major political institutions have tried to effectuate the balance of power, including expanding or protecting their prerogatives while handling others' efforts to enlarge their respective prerogatives regarding federal appointments. Among the key practices are the norms developed by institutional actors to guide their decision making within the enormous gaps in the loose constitutional framework for making federal appointments.

As this book has suggested, the study of these patterns or practices is the province of the emerging field of historical institutionalism. Scholars in this field examine the operations of the federal appointments process in terms of the powers and authorities of and interaction between the major political institutions (and other interested parties) involved. In particular, historical institutionalism explores several interrelated questions: To what degree do norms affect the behavior of political leaders, who learn how to cultivate, work with, and work around these norms in order to achieve their desired outcomes? How have different institutions and actors influenced each other's performances regarding appointments? What is the relationship between structure and organization and outcomes? And what are the external and internal pressures influencing the powers, authorities, organizations, and operations of the major political institutions responsible for federal appointments?

This book has tried to answer some of these questions. Primarily from the perspectives of constitutional law and history, I have attempted to illuminate the internal operations of the federal appointments process, particularly the learning curve for each of the major actors for expanding its influence and checking other actors' efforts to expand or preserve their influence. This is not to suggest that the performances of these actors necessarily improve over time because they learn to do better. Rather, it means that the actors who lead or staff the institutions routinely involved in the federal appointments process ceaselessly try to refine the powers and authorities of their respective institutions in response to and in anticipation of the actions of other institutions in the process as well as various social, political, historical, and economic events. Moreover, those who lead or staff the institutions regularly involved in the federal appointments process inherit and face the challenge of preserving or changing to the advantages of their respective institutions past orderings of powers and authorities regarding appointments matters. Each governmental actor has developed its own institutional memory, with senators, for example, drawing on seniority, parliamentarians, formal procedural rules and prerogatives, congressional records and transcripts, and staff; and with executive branch officials relying on career civil servants, the experiences of staffers or officials in prior administrations, and the records of past administrations. Those who are regularly involved in the process but not formally part of these institutions have access to some of the same records as well as their own recorded experiences or studies of the process. In short, those regularly involved in the federal appointments process build on their own and their predecessors' experiences in trying to shape outcomes in this process.

Some of the most significant challenges confronting the major actors routinely involved in the federal appointments process are to master what others, particularly those who have occupied similar positions, have learned or done with respect to federal appointments and to expand this lore for those who will follow. The learning process includes developing an appreciation of the operative norms, how such norms develop and influence behavior, and the various strategies for circumventing or modifying them. No doubt, the future of the appointments process depends significantly on how much of what these actors learn about the factors influencing outcomes brings the actors closer together or pulls them farther apart. In short, institutional analysis of the internal operations of the federal appointments process suggests that evaluating each actor's performance in and influence over the process depends on identifying two sets of things: (1) the factors that they have learned have the potential to influence outcomes in the process; and (2) the means that they have inherited or cultivated to try to control or manipulate these factors.

Take, for example, the presidency. On the one hand, executive branch leaders have learned that several factors arguably under their control have the potential to influence outcomes in the federal appointments process. These factors include the institutional support that presidents enjoy or lack in the Senate, the quality or nature of their administrations' organizations for handling appointments, the timing (including how quickly presidents assemble skillful advisers regarding appointments and the proximity to midterm or presidential election years), coordination with other competing legislative priorities, the development of sound strategies for maneuvering nominations successfully through the confirmation process, the caliber of a president's bargaining skills, a president's bargaining position or power relative to that of other influential parties, manipulation of the media, and popularity (of the president and various policies at the time a nomination is made). The means presidents have cultivated or inherited for influencing or manipulating these factors include, of course, the nomination power itself (through the exercise of which presidents reward allies or constituencies for their support or service, punish foes, trade for support of other nominations or legislative initiatives or both, unify their administrations, build support for their reelection or for their implementation of certain constitutional or policy objectives, and influence the directions of the Supreme Court and federal judiciary). Other presidential powers and authorities include the bully pulpit (using the office of the presidency rhetorically and interacting with the media to achieve some of the aforementioned objectives); political party leadership; personal interaction with nominees while they have worked in the executive branch or other nonjudicial offices; and drafting policy initiatives, priorities, and objectives (so as to set the terms of debate in confirmation proceedings, the general goals to be achieved programmatically or politically by means of certain appointments, or the possible universe of things with which to bargain).

Of course, presidents also need to appreciate the ways in which other actors may facilitate or impede nominations. Principal among these other actors are senators. The factors under the control of senators include their party's representation in the Senate and the White House, their relative seniority in the hierarchy of the Senate (including their committee responsibilities), their ability to influence or manipulate the media or public perceptions of the president or his nominees, their relationships with other senators, their relationships with their own party leaders (and, if different, the president's party leaders), interest group support or opposition, and their understanding of and expertise in exercising parliamentary procedures. The means (including but not limited to the norms) senators have developed for asserting or preserving their influence over federal appointments include senatorial courtesy, the respective authorities of committee chairs to schedule confirmation hearings and of majority leaders to schedule floor votes, exercising holds over nominations, abolishing or creating confirmable offices (including funding or withdrawing the funding for certain positions), logrolling, interacting with the media, personal contacts with leading administration officials (many of whom might have worked in the Senate prior to joining a president's staff or administration), and influence with or relationship to certain interest groups (to build popular support for or opposition to various nominations).

Historical institutionalism helps to illuminate more than the lessons learned by those formally charged with decision making on appointments matters. It clarifies the influence over the appointments process of other actors, including the media, political parties, nominees, interest groups, and the public. Historical institutionalism also illuminates the capacity of the system for reform, based on the patterns of past change. One important lesson learned by all of the actors routinely involved in the process is that reform or significant change is possible only if the major political actors have incentives for modifying the system. The general history of the operations of the federal appointments process indicates that each of these actors has a vested interest in the status quo. The history of the federal appointments process indicates how much the status quo is structured to resist change (or certain objectives), the pressure or incentive for institutional and other actors to change, and the relative abilities of political leaders to marshal the necessary resources and coordinate the necessary powers to facilitate change or preserve constitutional orderings as they see fit.

Examining how these various elements interact reveals a great deal to participants and observers about the feasibility for achieving various objectives as well as significant changes in the federal appointments process. For instance, one conceivable objective for the federal appointments process is that of the framers, who wanted to avoid certain evils in the process. A majority of the delegates to the constitutional convention and virtually all of the Constitution's defenders in the ratification process especially wanted to avoid at least two major problems: domination by one branch of the system and the appointment of presidential cronies.

To date, the first objective has been partially realized. Different branches have dominated the system at different times in U.S. history, and it is already clear that as presidential power has expanded in numerous areas over the course of this century (including in this realm by virtue of, among other things, the constitutional presumption of confirmation), senators have tried mightily to counteract or counterbalance it through the development or exercise of their own prerogatives.

With regard to the appointment of presidential cronies, many framers feared that such people would be either unqualified for public service or inclined to feel more allegiance to the president personally than to the public's welfare. This problem has been only partially avoided. Every president has been able to appoint a significant number of his friends to important confirmable and nonconfirmable offices. Moreover, many presidents have been embarrassed by the misconduct in office of some of those close friends. These embarrassments have overshadowed the fact that a significant number of close presidential friends have proven to be distinguished public servants. Moreover, Congress has coordinated many of its powers to check the abuse of power by presidential cronies in office. An important question for scholars to consider is whether the Senate's confirmation authority alone or in conjunction with Congress's appropriation, oversight, impeachment, investigatory, and other powers has been sufficient to check abuses of power engendered by presidents' attempts to appoint their close friends to important offices. If the answer is in the affirmative, then the necessity for reforming the federal appointments process to eliminate the appointment of presidential cronies is less acute. If the federal political process lacks sufficient safeguards to preclude the appointment of presidential cronies (at least to the point of precluding significant abuses of power), then one of the framers' objectives regarding the federal appointments process has not been adequately addressed, and this failure provides a good reason to consider serious reform.

Of course, neither the presidency nor the Senate is the same as it was at the time of the founding. The Twelfth Amendment and subsequent electoral reforms have transformed the presidency into a popularly elected office, while the Seventeenth Amendment has radically altered the system by which senators are elected. Consequently, senators have become acutely sensitive to the views of the electorate regarding the exercise of their respective prerogatives. The heightened sensitivity of presidents and senators to popular opinion has allowed the public to exert pressure on the process through such means as interest groups, polling, the media, and the Internet.

Many critics of the federal appointments process believe that the media and interest groups have contributed negatively to the operation of the process. These critics argue that the media have increasingly focused on scandal and speculation rather than reporting actual events. As a result, the public, in their view, has had to discount a good deal of what it learns from the media and look to other possible sources for unfiltered or unbiased information. Moreover, some critics denounce the disproportionate influence apparently wielded in the appointments process by some interest groups. Others, however, believe that interest groups provide a conduit or pathway by which citizens can participate in different aspects of the political process, including confirmation hearings. Moreover, some scholars view the participation of the public in judicial confirmation hearings as putting judicial independence at risk, because such participation transforms the proceedings (undesirably) into popular elections or referenda. Other scholars suggest that direct citizen participation in the process is crucial for maintaining political actors' accountability for their decisions on federal appointments and that such participation might be maximized or facilitated by means of the Internet.

Postscript

Still others complain that the level of discourse in the appointments process has diminished to all-time, or at least thoroughly unacceptable, lows. To be sure, it is by no means clear that the quality of dialogue is problematically low. Political psychologists suggest that even if the media (and interest groups) have succeeded to some extent in creating a culture permeated by what President Clinton has called the "politics of personal destruction," the public has become adept at cutting through such media campaigns and coverage to figure out what it needs to know.[3]

Moreover, it is important not to confuse disjunctures in the public dialogue about federal appointments with a decline in civility. It is popular, at least among some legal scholars, to identify the increasing focus of Republican political leaders on the ideology of judicial nominees, and the corresponding efforts of their Democratic counterparts to denounce such a focus as antithetical to judicial independence, as a decline in the quality of public discourse in judicial confirmation proceedings. The Democrats argue further that the appropriate focus in judicial selection should be on nominees' qualifications rather than their ideologies. The difficulty with the Democrats' response is that it misses the point. For one thing, they appear not to appreciate that many Republican leaders view ideology (often defined as precommitments to reach certain results, whatever the facts or laws of a specific case) as an important qualification. Second, Democrats largely fail to acknowledge that they also prefer certain candidates over others for judicial nominations precisely because of their anticipated approaches to constitutional decision making. Moreover, some senators (on both sides of the aisle) might not have any clear or single meaning of the term *ideology* when they use it, while others may use the term to refer to a person's ideas about justice, about key values like liberty and equality, about basic institutional relations like judicial deference to legislatures, or about core constitutional concepts such as federalism and separation of powers.

During the Reagan and Bush administrations, those responsible for judicial selection often looked to possible nominees' political affiliations and extracurricular activities as reflections of their real convictions and moral dispositions. Judge pickers in those years figured that the judicial records or political activities of candidates told only a part of the story of their dispositions as judges; how these people lived their lives and the people with whom they associated were also important facets of their qualifications to serve as judges. In other words, those responsible for judicial selection in the Reagan and Bush administrations learned that a disposition to favor predispositions as evidenced in lifestyle, political affiliations, and personal attachments presaged performances on the bench.

To be sure, the concern of some Republican senators and conservative interest groups to oppose judicial nominees disposed not to interpret the Constitution or follow the written law but rather to make policy akin to legislation from the bench is a legitimate one. Even some of the Republican senators who complained openly about the motivations for some of the inordinate delays in confirmation hearings for many of President Clinton's judicial nominees quickly added, as did Senator Orrin Hatch, the chair of the Judiciary Committee, that they "will stand firm and exercise the advise and consent power to the best of [their] ability to ensure that President Clinton does not pack the judiciary with activists who will make mincemeat of our Constitution and laws."[4]

The concern is not just about ideology, however it is defined. It is about power. And today's divided government, with a president hurt as the result of his impeachment and losing some of his influence or control over the judicial appointments process, is not unique. A similar thing happened to President Andrew Johnson.

Moreover, the concern that President Clinton may have nominated as judges people who were politically liberal or activist oriented or outside the mainstream of acceptable judicial orientation has been overstated. At least one study has found, for example, that President Clinton's judicial nominees were much more similar in ideological terms and orientation to President Ford's than to those who were nominated by President Carter.[5] Moreover, in assessing the significance of delays in the Senate, including those seemingly based on dubious reasons, one should understand that for many conservative watchdogs of the judicial selection process the qualifications to serve as a federal judge include the right disposition for deciding constitutional cases. Those interested in facilitating or achieving different kinds of or more diverse judicial appointments (in terms of backgrounds and dispositions, if not ideologies) have yet to engage the opposition fully in a dialogue on both the former's and the opposition's differing views of the federal judiciary in U.S. society.

Postscript

332

President Clinton's public denouncement of the Senate's failure to provide his judicial nominees with quicker and fairer confirmation hearings, though belated, was the first significant step in engaging the opposition in a responsible public debate on the matter. President Clinton's public response helped to galvanize the media, in the form of numerous editorials around the country, to denounce the strategic delays of his judicial nominees' confirmation hearings and to proclaim the dangers that such delays posed for the quality of the administration of justice, that is, ensuring that litigants in various circuits hurt by the delays are not further deprived of meaningful opportunities to have relatively speedy, fair adjudications of their claims. The presidential and media pressure produced results. Within a few days the Republican leadership in the Senate altered course and began to schedule hearings and expedite the confirmation process for some of President Clinton's pending judicial nominations. In the absence of any public declaration by the president, it would not have been surprising if the delays and the opposition to his judicial nominees had continued unchecked. Prior to making the public declaration, President Clinton tried to diminish the importance of partisanship in judicial selection by shying away from candidates who made easy targets because of their political activism or express adherence to a controversial judicial outlook and by making diversity and proven excellence his two most important criteria for selection.

At the end of 1997, Chief Justice Rehnquist added his voice to the chorus protesting the unusually long and large number of delays of President Clinton's judicial nominees.[6] In his annual state of the judiciary report, the Chief Justice acknowledged that "[t]he Senate is surely under no obligation to confirm any particular nominee" but warned that "after the necessary time for inquiry it should vote him up or down," allowing someone else to be nominated.[7] He complained that delays in the Senate had left nearly one in ten of the nation's more than eight hundred judgeships vacant. The Chief Justice further warned that "[v]acancies cannot remain at such high levels indefinitely without eroding the quality of justice."[8] Senate Judiciary Committee chair Orrin Hatch contested the latter claim, blamed the administration for inordinate delays in making many judicial nominations, and defended the Senate's actions in guarding against what he regarded as President Clinton's attempt to appoint activist judges. For

Senator Hatch (and a number of his colleagues), the delays in judicial confirmation proceedings do not produce injustice; indeed, they promote a different notion of justice by protecting against the appointment of judges who will interfere with and sap the vitality of democratic decision making and by ensuring the appointment of better judges (requiring, of course, certain attributes).

Subsequently, the judicial confirmation process stalled again throughout the impeachment proceedings against President Clinton in 1998–99. Nevertheless, just before he took over the reins of President Clinton's impeachment trial as the presiding officer, Chief Justice Rehnquist again denounced (in his report at the end of 1998 regarding the state of the federal judiciary) the Senate's inordinate delays of many judicial confirmation hearings, which continued to seriously compromise the quality of justice in several circuits.

The pressure exerted by the Chief Justice and President Clinton to break the logjam in judicial confirmation proceedings is analogous to the shaming penalties that some legal theorists have suggested provide suitable substitutes for the coercive power of law. Some groups also favor applying coercive pressure on presidents and senators by means of lobbying or campaigns directed at presidents' or senators' concerns about their reputations or standing in some circles.[9]

Yet another possible objective of the federal appointments process has been the implementation of a president's (or, for that matter, of senators') constitutional or programmatic vision. Some commentators, including Lloyd Cutler and Bruce Ackerman, have expressed concern that the ease with which the national legislature can frustrate the popular mandates of presidents is contrary to our constitutional allocation of power. As the only political leader elected by all of the people of the nation, a president is entitled, in their view, to a chance to implement what the people elected him to do. Getting his preferred agents to help him implement that agenda is no small part of his ultimate success in realizing his mandate. To the extent that the system frustrates this implementation, it needs overhaul. Thus, these commentators would argue for even greater deference to presidents' choices of executive personnel than they currently enjoy. No doubt, others would argue that presidents already enjoy a good deal of deference in this realm and that more would simply reflect senators' abdication of their duty to determine that a president's executive appointments are not just in his best interests but also in the best interests of the nation and the Constitution.

Another objective some commentators have wanted to achieve in the appointments process is increasing the diversity of the kinds of people appointed to high federal offices. Presidents Carter and Clinton both made this an important priority in making nominations, and both achieved unprecedented representation of minorities and women in confirmable offices, particularly federal judgeships. For example, Jimmy Carter appointed thirty-seven African Americans to federal judgeships, a number surpassing the number of minority appointments made by every president except for the sixty-two African Americans appointed to the federal courts by Bill Clinton.

A popular goal for many critics of the federal appointments process is expedited nominations and Senate confirmation hearings. This objective could be achieved in various ways, including by ensuring that each major candidate prior to a presidential election has assembled a set of first-rate, experienced advisers who can provide the names of possible nominees for key administrative positions soon after the election, if not before; streamlining or reducing the paperwork presidential nominees must complete; reducing the necessity for some nominees to testify; ensuring greater Senate deference to a president's choice of lower-level nominees for executive branch positions; presidential willingness both to respect senatorial courtesy and to make judicial selection a visible priority; and eliminating the scheduling of hearings for most lower-level nominees (assuming there is some degree of consensus on the people who would qualify as such).

Another conceivable objective is to reduce the number of offices subject to the confirmation process. This is not a new goal by any means. In 1937, the President's Committee on Administrative Management recommended that only the people to be chosen for "policy-determining" offices should be nominated by the president and subjected to Senate confirmation.[10] In 1953, Joseph Harris, in his seminal study of the confirmation process, made precisely the same recommendation.[11] In 1996, The Century Foundation made the same suggestion for reforming the whole appointments process.

The failure to reduce the number of confirmable offices (either by eliminating the offices altogether or by eliminating the requirement of Senate confirmation) says a lot about how the people in power feel about the need for fundamental change in the federal appointments process. These people have resisted and indeed ignored the last two bipartisan studies of the appointments process conducted by the Miller Center and Citizens for Independent Courts (a task force of The Century Foundation), respectively.

On the one hand, these failures are ironic given the persistent complaints of presidents about the pressures of having to deal with appointments. President Cleveland, for instance, complained more than once about "the damned, everlasting clatter for office."[12] Yet, President Cleveland was like every other modern president in his steadfast refusal to relinquish any of his prerogatives to appoint people to key positions. He did not back down even when the Senate delayed hundreds of his nominations to offices in retaliation against his unilateral suspension of the previous occupants of those offices. The same could be said of William Howard Taft, who as president once complained to a friend, "You don't know—you can't know—the difficulties of such responsibility as I have to exercise, and how they burden a man's heart with conflicting feelings prompted by duty and personal affection."[13] Nevertheless, Taft as president (and later as Chief Justice) refused like almost every other modern chief executive to relinquish his influence over judicial appointments.

Senators, on the other hand, have rarely been heard to complain about the clatter for federal offices. Instead, they have persistently yearned throughout U.S. history for control of federal patronage, both to increase their influence over policy through the choice of personnel and to reward their political supporters or punish the allies of a president whose policies or politics they have not supported.

Some scholars have suggested increasing the accountability of the officials responsible for making federal appointments. Two means for doing so are conceivable, though neither is without problems. First, the media could cover the appointments process more widely and thoroughly than they presently do. Media coverage would have to include a more thorough recognition and discussion of not just the merits of particular nominations but also the relationship between presidential and senatorial actions in the appointments process to their interaction generally and to their other priorities as well. Expanded coverage increases the pressure on presidents and senators to meet public expectations, to do those things that will increase their stature (and popularity), and otherwise to avoid actions that have the potential to come back later to haunt them. As one might expect, presidents and senators have limited interest in expanded coverage of their actions in the appointments process. Presidents and senators desire greater coverage of some activities or priorities while they prefer to have certain other activities kept behind closed doors.

A second means for improving accountability might be the Internet. Trying to democratize the appointments process further is, however, likely to meet a similar fate as doing away with senators' prerogatives to exercise holds. No doubt, allowing for more direct feedback on pending nominations through the Internet would give citizens more of a voice in the appointments process than they have ever wielded before. The problem is that national political leaders might not want to lose or relinquish some of their influence or control in this process to the public en masse. This is particularly true for judicial appointments. By a long-standing tradition and understanding in the realm of constitutional law, one of the most important functions of the federal judiciary is to exercise the countermajoritarian function of judicial review. The process would become inverted, in the view of many constitutional scholars, if the public were allowed to veto judicial nominees, because the latter serve not at the pleasure of the people but rather exercise a special duty to protect and interpret the Constitution.

A final proposed reform of the federal appointments process involves developing different criteria for evaluating its fairness, utility, and efficacy. No systematic effort has been made to define or clarify these objectives and to assess the constitutional means for achieving them; a multidisciplinary approach such as historical institutionalism is crucial in this regard.

Historical institutionalism illuminates the significance of presidents' and senators' managerial skills in manipulating the appointments process to achieve their respective preferences. Moreover, historical institutionalism illuminates the fact that the federal appointments process is a microcosm of the relations between presidents and senators generally; it is one venue in which presidents or senators work out their respective differences on personnel and policy. This interaction is at the core of the federal appointments process.

It is important to understand what this interaction teaches us about the Constitution and the political institutions it establishes and attempts to constrain. As a dimension of separation of powers, the federal appointments process demonstrates the limits of constitutional constraints in practice. These informal arrangements—those not required or clearly prohibited by the Constitution—have come to define the dynamic in the federal appointments process. The informal arrangements through which the system operates—including senatorial courtesy; logrolling; individual holds; "blue slips"; consultation between presidents, members of Congress, and other interested parties, including judges; interest group lobbying; strategic leaking by administrations, senators, and interest groups; manipulation of the press; the media's efforts to influence the news; and nominees' campaigning—are the sum and substance of the federal appointments process. Studying these arrangements provides even greater illumination than studying Supreme Court decisions or the Constitution itself of how the different branches of the federal government interact on matters of mutual concern.

This is not to say that formal constitutional constraints do not matter or that informal arrangements are somehow superior to or more important than the formal constitutional structure. Identifying and understanding the informal arrangements, including the strategies developed by various actors to develop, work with, and around various norms, are crucial for an accurate assessment of the effectiveness or utility of the formal constitutional constraints. With respect to federal appointments, the relevant constitutional structure merely provides the broad outlines within which significant informal arrangements or norms have developed among presidents, senators, interest groups, the media, nominees, and others.

The informality of much that happens in the federal appointments process helps to camouflage the interactions among the nation's political leaders on appointments matters and other affairs. Even so, the effort undertaken in this book to sketch both outside and inside perspectives of the federal appointments process, particularly how presidents, senators, and others have used, coordinated, tried to expand, or organized their respective formal and informal powers in the appointments process and related areas, is an important step—albeit a single one—on the path to developing a more sophisticated explanation and evaluation of national political leadership generally, including presidential-Senate interactions on issues of mutual concern. Taking this step is important to ensure greater and more meaningful accountability for the decisions made by important governmental actors regarding appointments. It is a step that will demystify this process for many people. Moreover, it is a step that will provide other scholars with evidence of the patterns or practices of the system that they can use in constructing their own frameworks for studying the appointments process. Appreciating the significance and utility of such evidence is crucial for ensuring that the federal appointments process will not remain a mystery to those most interested in its improvement and welfare.

AFTERWORD

AS THIS EDITION goes to press, President George W. Bush has made history. He is one of only three presidents whose party gained seats in both the House and the Senate in midterm elections. (The other two were Franklin Roosevelt in 1934 and Bill Clinton in 1998.) The conventional wisdom is that these gains, including the Republicans' return to control of the Senate in January 2003, guarantee that President Bush can expect little if any trouble in getting his judicial nominees through the Senate. Democrats worry that they cannot stop a tidal wave of conservative ideologues and activists appointed to the federal bench. Without a majority, Democrats have very limited means to defeat particularly troublesome judicial nominations. The blue slip process was one possibility, until Orrin Hatch, the incoming chair of the Senate Judiciary Committee, declared that a Democratic home state senator's objection to a judicial nominee would be noted but not fatal to the nomination's success. Moreover, Democrats had no reason to expect that they could defeat judicial nominations with the support of moderate Republicans, who seemed unlikely to break ranks often if at all from the administration on judicial appointments. Filibustering had limited appeal. Democrats had sufficient numbers in the Senate — forty-eight members — to ensure that they could mount a successful filibuster; however, senators have rarely used filibusters to defeat judicial nominations. It is a weapon to which Democrats could likely resort on only a few occasions before they would be perceived as obstructionist. Indeed, filibusters have not been used to defeat a judicial appointment since 1969, when a bipartisan coalition filibustered President Lyndon Johnson's nomination of Abe Fortas as chief justice of the United States.[1]

For the sake of argument and greater understanding of the federal appointments process, I raise three possible objections to this conventional wisdom. First, it might discount the extent to which Republican senators might resist presidential preferences in order to protect their institutional prerogatives. The conventional wisdom presumes that Republican senators will allow the president to make inroads on such institutional prerogatives as senatorial courtesy, but in the past strong resistance to some presidents' judicial nominees has come not from senators in the opposition party but rather senators in the president's own party. One can expect Republican senators to protect senatorial courtesy with some vigor and thus their prerogative that the president appoint their, rather than his, preferred candidates for judicial offices in their states. It will be interesting to see whether Republican senators will accept the reforms that President Bush proposed in the final days of the midterm election campaigns for streamlining the confirmation process for federal judges. These reforms call upon Republican senators to relinquish some institutional control over the pacing of judicial appointments, and it is risky to presume that such abdication will come easily.

Second, the conventional wisdom does not take into account that public attitudes about social mores can exert pressure on a president's nominating authority. George W. Bush and Republican senators argue that his judicial appointments reflect the preferences of the American people. It is fair to ask whether this is so. Some might question whether the public really cares about judicial appointments and thus imply that the president and Republican senators are banking on the public's indifference to judicial appointments. Others, particularly Democrats, wonder about the public's capacity to mobilize opposition to judicial appointments that threaten the scope of federal rights of concern to them, particularly abortion rights.

In any event, the president and Republican senators clearly appreciate that judicial appointments are of keen interest to the far right, without whose support the president cannot win reelection. At the time this edition goes to press, 25 of the 179 seats on federal courts of appeal are vacant, and Republicans are in the majority on seven of the nation's thirteen circuits. President Bush, Senator Hatch, and Senator Bill Frist (who succeeded Trent Lott as majority leader)[2] have all signaled their willingness not only to make judicial nominations a priority but also to withstand Democratic challenges and negative votes so that the people they want as judges will be confirmed. Indeed, they have all indicated their lack of interest in consulting with the minority party about judicial nominations. Moreover, their rhetoric has been belligerent (in their view justified by the Democrats' obstruction of the president's judicial appointments). They have, for instance, promised to ensure the appointment of two circuit nominees—Charles Pickering and Priscilla Owen—whom the Judiciary Committee previously rejected. In addition, the expectation is that President Bush's judicial appointments will be like those he has already made or promised to make; his appointees have been mostly young, white men whose principal qualification appears to be their ideology. Many have been active members of the Federalist Society or served causes evidencing their commitment to a strong, conservative judicial ideology (including, for instance, a very broad, robust conception of state sovereignty and limited federal power, opposition to abortion rights, and protection of property rights). In fighting for his judicial nominees, the president has risked abandoning his repeated campaign pledge that he was "a uniter not a divider" in exchange for an enduring, sharply rightward shift in the composition of the federal judiciary. In short, the president has staked his legacy at least in part on his judicial appointments.

Lastly, the conventional wisdom accepts, but only implicitly, something obvious about the federal appointments process, namely that in the end federal judicial appointments are driven less by noble or grand ideals than by gritty political reality and strategy. Many political scientists maintain that political actors—including judges and justices—merely manipulate the Constitution and its structure, federal statutes, institutional norms, and Supreme Court precedents to implement their preferred political objectives. In their view, the law is merely a means to an end. This perspective might call to mind the arguments of legal scholars who, in one form or another, have maintained that law merely reflects (if not cements) current power structures within society. In recent years, some prominent legal scholars have argued that the Supreme Court largely if not wholly tracks majoritarian sentiments in constitutional adjudication. The Court tends to go, in their view, with the prevailing political winds. If President Bush gets the judges whom he favors appointed to various federal courts (including the Supreme Court), and those judges perform as he hopes, one will need to wonder whether the congruity is happenstance or purposeful. As one watches Republican senators in the years ahead interact with the president over judicial and other kinds of federal appointments, it might be instructive to monitor the signals that this interaction sends to the public and to those aspiring to judicial and other federal offices, and how these signals are received by judges and particularly justices. It is hard to show, but not to suspect, that judges and justices decide cases or controversies with their political objectives and agendas in mind, including the likely reactions of the institutions affected by their decisions. As readers ponder the future of the federal appointments process, they should consider the possibility, and the extent to which they find appealing, that the federal appointments process will go where the public wants or lets national political leaders take it.

NOTES

Introduction to the Paperback Edition

1   121 S. Ct. 525 (2000).

2   I treat as the nominations approved by close votes or after contentious proceedings those in which at least a third of the Senate opposed the nominees. These nominations include those of Clarence Thomas (1991), William Rehnquist for chief justice (1986), William Rehnquist as an associate justice (1971), Sherman Minton (1949), Charles Evans Hughes for chief justice (1930), Louis Brandeis (1916), Mahlon Pitney (1912), Melville Fuller for chief justice (1888), Lucius Lamar (1888), Stanley Matthews (1881), Nathan Clifford (1858), John Catron (1837), Philip Barbour (1836), and Roger Taney for chief justice (1836). Of course, there have been other nominees, such as Thurgood Marshall, whom the Senate confirmed by wide margins after relatively intense proceedings.

3   The one exception was Stanley Matthews, whom the Senate confirmed by a single vote when he was renominated for the Court by President Garfield. The composition of the Senate at that time was instrumental to his success; it had 37 Republicans, 37 Democrats, and 1 independent. The Senate had failed to act on his previous nomination to the Court by President Hayes, at which time the Senate had 42 Democrats, 33 Democrats, and 1 independent.

4   *See* Kermit Hall, *The Politics of Justice* 5, 29, 62, 90, 131–50 (1979).

5   Sheldon Goldman, *Picking Federal Judges: Lower Court Selection from Roosevelt through Reagan* 8–9 (1997).

6   One study indicates that since 1945 the Senate has confirmed only seven nominations not reported favorably by committee. *See* Robert C. Byrd, 4 *The Senate, 1789–1992: Historical Statistics, 1789–1992*, table 7-2 at 687 (1993).

7   See generally David Yalof, *Pursuit of Justices* (1999).

8   *See, e.g.,* Nancy Scherer, *Who Drives the Ideological Makeup of the Lower Federal Courts in a Divided Government?*, 35 *Law and Society Review* 191 (2001).

9   *Id.* at 191.

10   *Id.*

11   *See generally* Kenneth W. Goings, *The NAACP Comes of Age: The Defeat of John J. Parker* (1990).

12   Analyzing the appointments process in terms of social and institutional norms is fraught with risk. First, the norms are contestable. Second, the appointments process is sufficiently complex that it is difficult if not impossible to determine the points at which normative conflicts occur within it. Third, counter-examples abound. For example, the Senate barely confirmed President Bush's nomination of Clarence Thomas as an associate justice, but it rejected President Clinton's nomination of another African American, Ronnie White, to a federal district court. These outcomes are conceivably reconcilable because race had become an issue front and center in Thomas's hearings whereas it had not in White's. Perhaps more importantly, Ronnie White is the only African American judicial nominee yet rejected by the full Senate.

13   President George H. W. Bush was less successful than his son as a norm entrepreneur. He failed in his efforts to modify the Judiciary Committee's access to FBI reports. Just as the Judiciary Committee was preparing to send Clarence Thomas's nomination as an associate justice to the full Senate for final consideration, someone on the Judiciary Committee had leaked Anita Hill's affidavit to the Justice Department and the press. This leak led to an embarrassing turnaround by the committee, which reopened its hearings, calling Hill and recalling Thomas in dramatic, televised appearances devoted to her sexual harassment charges against him. Though the Senate ultimately confirmed Thomas by an extremely close vote, President Bush announced shortly after the vote that he had issued an order restricting the committee's future access to FBI reports. The order provoked an impasse while the Judiciary Committee refused to process any pending judicial nominations until it could arrange for its own investigation of nominees' backgrounds to substitute for the FBI reports. After three months, the administration changed course by restoring access to the FBI reports for committee members and staff, but with a stricter accounting of who would be allowed to read the reports. The delay was fatal to over two dozen judicial nominations made during the impasse: their earliest opportunities for a hearing did not arise until 1992, by which time the process had slowed almost to a standstill pending the outcome of the presidential election.

14   See March 6, 2002, study of Citizens for Independent Courts.

Introduction

1   See, e.g., Ronald Dworkin, *Freedom's Law: The Moral Reading of the Constitution* 310–11, 324–25 (1996); Stephen L. Carter, *The Confirmation Mess: Cleaning Up the Federal Appointments Process* 99–112 (1994).

2   For some notable exceptions, see Sheldon Goldman, *Picking Federal Judges: Lower Court Selection from Roosevelt through Reagan* (1997); Henry J. Abraham, *Justices and Presidents: A Political History of Appointments to the Supreme Court* (3d ed. 1992); John Massaro, *Supremely Political: The Role of Ideology and Presidential Management in Unsuccessful Supreme Court Nominations* (1990); Joseph Harris, *The Advice and Consent of the Senate: A Study of the Confirmation of Appointments by the United States Senate* (1953); and Calvin R. Massey, "Getting There: A Brief History of the Politics of Supreme Court Appointments," 19 *Hastings Const. L.Q.* 1 (1991).

3   See generally Stephen Skowronek, *The Politics Presidents Make: Leadership from John Adams to George Bush* (1993); Jeffrey K. Tulis, *The Rhetorical Presidency* (1987); *The Presidency in the Constitutional Order* (Joseph M. Bessett and Jeffrey K. Tullis eds., 1980); Ronald C. Kahn, "Presidential Power and the Appointments Process: Structuralism, Legal Scholarship, and the New Historical Institutionalism," 47 *Case W. Res. L. Rev.* 1419 (1997); Stephen Skowronek, "Order and Change," 28 *Polity* 91 (1995); Christopher L. Eisgruber, "The Most Competent Branches: A Response to Paulsen," 83 *Geo. L.J.* 347, 348, 353–55 (1994).

4   Much recent legal scholarship has focused on the relationship between social norms

and regulation. See generally Larry Lessig, "The New Chicago School," 27 *J. Legal Stud.* 661 (1998). Of particular relevance for a study of the federal appointments process is the work examining signaling and social norms, i.e., the ways in which groups try (either as part of or apart from a particular institution) to signal or otherwise attempt to influence or coerce others (including lawmakers) to conform to some of their norms, and the consequences of these activities. See, e.g., Timur Kuran, "Ethnic Norms and Their Transformation through Reputational Cascades," 27 *J. Legal Stud.* 623 (1998); Eric A. Posner, *Law and Social Norms* (Harvard University Press 2000). See also Richard A. Posner, *An Affair of State: The Investigation, Impeachment, and Trial of President Clinton* 193, 215–16 (Harvard University Press 1999).

5　In earlier works I have argued that the confirmation process is a crucial forum for a serious dialogue between the president and the Senate not just on the merits of particular nominations or appointments but also on related constitutional and policy matters. See, e.g., Michael J. Gerhardt, "Toward a Comprehensive Understanding of the Federal Appointments Process," 21 *Harv. J. L. & Pub. Pol'y.* 467 (1998); "The Confirmation Mystery," 83 *Geo. L.J.* 395 (1994); "Divided Justice: A Commentary on the Nomination and Confirmation of Supreme Court Justices," 60 *Geo. Wash. L. Rev.* 969 (1992); "Interpreting Bork," 75 *Cornell L. Rev.* 1358, 1386–91 (1990).

6　See R. Posner, *An Affair of State*, 115–16.

7　In their book *Politics by Other Means: The Declining Importance of Elections in America* (1990), Benjamin Ginsburg and Martin Shefter argue that as a substitute for elections (whose importance, they claim, has been steadily declining in American society) the major parties have developed, with the complicity of the media and the federal judiciary, "a major new technique of political combat—revelation, investigation, and prosecution." Id. at 26. Without stretching the analogy beyond the breaking point, I explore confirmation skirmishes as possibly other fora for "postelection politics" in chapter 6.

8　See, e.g., Dan M. Kahan, "Social Influence, Social Meaning, and Deterrence," 83 *Va. L. Rev.* 349, 373–89 (1997). See also Jeffrey Rosen, "The Social Police: Following the Law Because You'd Be Too Embarrassed Not To," *New Yorker*, Oct. 20, 27, 1997, 170. For criticisms of Kahan's views, see, e.g., James Q. Whitman, "What Is Wrong with Inflicting Shame Sanctions," 107 *Yale L.J.* 1055 (1998).

9　See the Miller Center of Public Affairs, *Improving the Process of Appointing Federal Judges: A Report of the Miller Center Commission on the Selection of Federal Judges* (1996); Citizens for Independent Courts, *Uncertain Justice: Politics and America's Courts* (The Century Foundation 2000).

10　See, e.g., R. C. Ellickson, *Order without Law: How Neighbors Settle Disputes* (Harvard University Press 1991).

11　The respondents whom I surveyed served in one or more administrations as cabinet secretaries, deputy cabinet secretaries, under- and assistant secretaries, attorneys general, deputy attorneys general, assistant attorneys general, chiefs and deputy chiefs of staff, and chief and deputy White House counsels.

1. The Original Understanding of the Federal Appointments Process

1   U.S. Const., art. II, sec. 2, cl. 2.

2   See U.S. Const., art. I, sec. 5 ("Each House may determine the Rules of its Proceedings . . .").

3   See, e.g., Tim Groseclose and David C. King, *Committee Theories and Committee Institutions* (1997); Burdett A. Loomis, *The Contemporary Congress* (2d ed. 1998).

4   See J. Harris, *The Advice and Consent of the Senate*, 19–25.

5   Id. at 19 (footnotes omitted). See also Gerhard Casper, "An Essay in Separation of Powers: Some Early Versions and Practices," 30 *Wm. & Mary L. Rev.* 211, 217 (1989) (the state constitutions adopted between 1776 and 1787 "distributed the power of appointments in various ways, but legislative controls predominated").

6   1 *The Records of the Federal Convention of 1787* 67 (Max Farrand ed., 1966) (hereafter *Records*).

7   See, e.g., Forrest McDonald, *Novus Ordo Seclorum: The Intellectual Origins of the Constitution* 228, 255, 272 (1986); John P. Kaminski and Gaspare J. Saladino, eds., 13 *The Documentary History of the Ratification of the Constitution* 346 (Historical Society of Wisconsin 1981) (recounting George Mason's complaint to Thomas Jefferson about "the precipitate, & intemperate, not to say indecent Manner, in which business was conducted, during the last Week of the Convention"); Goebel, 1 *Supreme Court* at 244 (describing the atmosphere of the final days as "supercharged with discontent"); James E. Gauch, Comment, "The Intended Role of the Senate in Supreme Court Appointments," 56 *U. Chi. L. Rev.* 337, 342 (1989) (noting the haste with which the Constitutional Convention concluded).

8   1 *Records* 21.

9   Id. at 66.

10   Id. at 67.

11   Id.

12   Id. at 244.

13   Id. at 292.

14   2 *Records* 136.

15   Id. at 132.

16   Id.

17   Another resolution provided "that a National Judiciary be established, to consist of one supreme tribunal, the judges of which shall be appointed by the second branch of the National Legislature," and for the appointment of inferior tribunals, the authority for which likewise would be vested in the national legislature. Id. at 132–33. Apparently, the judges to be appointed to the inferior courts were to be appointed by the body creating such courts, but no specific mention of this is made.

18   Id. at 182–83.

19   Id. at 389.

20   Id.

21   Id. at 405.

22 Id.

23 Id.

24 Id. at 314–15.

25 Id. at 315.

26 Id. at 614. Sherman opposed the motion because he believed that "as the two Houses appropriate money it is best for them to appoint the officer who is to keep it." Id. Gorham and Rufus King (also from Massachusetts) contended that the people were "accustomed and attached" to the appointment of the treasurer by the legislature. Id. Pinckney supported the motion, pointing out that in South Carolina, where the legislature appointed the state treasurer, "bad appointments are made and the Legislature will not listen to the faults of their own officer." Id.

27 1 *Records* 119.

28 Id.

29 Id.

30 Id. at 120.

31 Id.

32 Id.

33 Id. (footnote omitted).

34 Id.

35 Id. at 224, 232 n. 12.

36 Id. at 232–33.

37 Id. at 233.

38 Id. at 244.

39 2 *Records* 41.

40 Id.

41 Id.

42 Id.

43 Id.

44 Id. at 43.

45 Id. at 42.

46 Id.

47 Id. at 42–43.

48 Id. at 43.

49 Id.

50 Id. at 44.

51 Id.

52 Id. at 80.

53 William Ross, "The Functions, Roles, and Duties of the Senate in the Supreme Court Appointment Process," 28 *Wm. & Mary L. Rev.* 633, 637 n. 18 (1987).

54 2 *Records* 81.

55 See id. at 44, 82.

56 Id. at 83.

57 Id.

58 Id. at 495.

59 Id. at 498.

60 See id. at 538–39. Pinckney did not want the Senate involved in the appointments process except with respect to the selection of ambassadors, and Wilson opposed any Senate involvement with the making of appointments.

61 Id. at 539.

62 Id. at 539–40.

63 Federalist No. 76 at 492 (A. Hamilton) (Modern Library ed. 1937). Moreover, in Federalist No. 70, Hamilton discusses the need for presidential appointment of executive officials so that the executive can implement the laws and policy with energy and can act decisively, secretly, and quickly.

64 Id., No. 76 at 492.

65 Id., No. 77 at 462 (A. Hamilton).

66 Id., No. 66 at 405 (A. Hamilton). He made the same point twice more in *The Federalist Papers*. See id. at 494 ("The Senate could not be tempted by the preference they might feel to another to reject the one proposed; because they could not assure themselves that the person they might wish would be brought forward by a second or by any subsequent nomination"); id. (predicting that the rejection of one presidential choice would only make room for another presidential choice and that "[t]he person ultimately appointed must be the object of his preference, though perhaps not in the first degree").

67 Id. at 457.

68 Id. at 458.

69 2 *Records* 639. Writing under the pseudonym "A Landholder," Oliver Ellsworth replied that the states that had used executive councils had found them to be "useless, and complain[ed] of them as dead weight." See Paul L. Ford, *Essays on the Constitution* 163 (1892; Burt Franklin 1970). He suggested that the department heads would be able to give the president trustworthy and responsible advice on a variety of matters, including appointments.

70 2 *Records* 638–39.

71 Robert Yates, *Secret Proceedings of the Federal Constitution* 75 (1821; GPO 1909).

72 Paul L. Ford, *Pamphlets on the Constitution of the United States* 298 (1888; Da Capo Publishing 1968).

73 4 Jonathan Elliott, *The Debates in the Several State Conventions on the Adoption of the Federal Constitution* 116 (1888; J. B. Lippincott Co. 1901).

74 Id. at 122.

75 3 *Records* 79.

76 Calvin C. Jillson, *Constitution Making: Conflict and Consensus in the Federal Convention of 1787* 152 (1988).

77 See J. Harris, *Advice and Consent*, 26; but see Gauch, "The Intended Role of the Senate," 348 (arguing that Harris downplays the importance of state rivalries to the outcome of the convention).

Notes to Chapter 1

78   2 Elliott, *Debates,* 466.

79   Id. at 511.

80   For a comprehensive analysis of the historical support for this view, see Martin J. Flaherty, "The Most Dangerous Branch," 105 *Yale L.J.* 1725 (1996).

81   Charles Black, "A Note on Senatorial Consideration of Supreme Court Nominees," 79 *Yale L.J.* 657, 659 (1970). See also Charles M. Mathias Jr., "Advice and Consent: The Role of the United States Senate in the Judicial Selection Process," 54 *U. Chi. L. Rev.* 200, 202–3 (1987) (discussing possibilities for meaningful advice by the Senate).

82   John O. McGinnis, "The President, the Senate, and the Constitution, and the Confirmation Process: A Reply to Professors Strauss and Sunstein," 71 *Tex. L. Rev.* 633, 639–40 (1993).

83   5 U.S. (1 Cranch) 137, 155 (1803).

84   Black, "Note on Senatorial Consideration," 659 n. 3.

85   H. Abraham, *Justices and Presidents,* 74–75.

86   Id. at 88–89.

87   Id. at 81.

88   Jean Edward Smith, *John Marshall: Definer of a Nation* 145 (1996).

89   Letter of George Mason to James Monroe (Jan. 30, 1792), in 4 *The Founders' Constitution* 111 (Philip B. Kurland and Ralph Lerner eds., 1987).

90   McGinnis, "Reply," 644.

91   Federalist No. 66 at 405 (A. Hamilton) (emphasis in original).

92   James Wilson, "Government, Lectures on Law" (1791), in 4 *The Founders' Constitution,* 110. For a sampling of other comments to the same effect, see, e.g., Letter from Gouverneur Morris to Lewis R. Morris (Dec. 3, 1803), in 3 *The Life of G. Morris,* 193–94 (describing the role given to the Senate in confirming appointments as but "a feeble share of the ancient executive power of Congress" and simply a "negative" on appointments to office); Letter from G. Morris to Uriah Tracy (Jan. 5, 1804), in 3 *The Life of G. Morris,* 198 (describing the Senate's authority to give advice and consent on nominations as less substantial than the constitutional requirement of advice and consent for treaty ratifications because the latter required approval by two-thirds of the Senate but nominations required approval by a bare majority of the Senate); Federalist No. 76 at 456–57 (A. Hamilton) ("In the act of nomination, [the president's] judgment alone would be exercised; and as it would be his sole duty to point out the man who, with the approbation of the Senate, should fill an office, his responsibility would be as complete as if he were to make the final appointment); id. No. 77 at 461 (The "blame of a bad nomination would fall upon the President single and absolutely"); 4 Elliott, *Debates,* 134 (comments of James Iredell) ("As to offices, the Senate has no other influence but a restraint on improper appointments. The President proposes such a man for such an office. The Senate has to consider upon it. If they think him improper, the President must nominate another, whose appointment ultimately again depends upon the Senate"); *Papers of Thomas Jefferson,* 379 (emphasis in original) ("The Constitution itself indeed has taken care to circumscribe [the appointments process] within very strict limits: for it gives the *nomination* of the foreign Agent to the Presi-

dent, the *appointment* to him and the Senate jointly, the *Commissioning* to the President"); Letter from Mason to James Monroe (Jan. 30, 1792), in 3 *The Papers of George Mason*, 1255 (emphasis in original) ("There is some thing remarkable in the Ar[r]angement of the Words: 'He shall nominate.' This gives to the President *alone* the Right of *Nomination*").

93   For instance, Gouverneur Morris was one of the convention's most outspoken advocates of executive prerogative and consolidated government. See Theodore Roosevelt, *Gouverneur Morris* 140 (Cambridge: Riverside Press 1888). Hamilton was both a zealous advocate of a strong executive and a critic of legislative supremacy. See Ross, "Functions," 641. Moreover, James Iredell was a leading proponent of ratification in North Carolina. Because the North Carolina ratifying convention was held late in the ratification process (see Michael Lienesch, "North Carolina: Preserving Rights," in *Ratifying the Constitution* 341, 343 [Michael A. Gillespie and Michael Lienesch eds., 1989]), Iredell's remarks distill many of the arguments that the Federalists found effective in other state conventions. For his part, Wilson consistently opposed the Senate's involvement in the federal appointments process. Like all of these others, he was an ardent Federalist whom President Washington would later nominate to important national offices.

94   For example, in requesting confirmation of his first nominee, Washington sent the following message to the Senate: "I nominate William Short, Esquire, and request your *advice* on the propriety of appointing *him*." In 1 *Journal of the Executive Proceedings of the Senate of the United States of America* 6 (June 16, 1789) (1828), reprinted in 2 *Documentary History of the First Federal Congress of the United States of America, 1789–91* 8 (Linda G. De Pauw ed., 1974) (emphasis in original). Washington was acutely aware that his actions would set precedents for future generations. Letter from Washington to James Madison (May 5, 1789), in 30 *The Writings of George Washington* 310, 311 (John C. Fitzpatrick ed., 1939). The Senate then notified the president of Short's confirmation, which reflected that they too might have thought "advice" was a postnomination rather than prenomination function. See 1 *Journal of the Executive Proceedings of the Senate of the United States of America* 6 (June 18, 1789), reprinted in 2 *Documentary History of the First Federal Congress of the United States of America*, 9. This formulation, which the Senate has continued to use to the present day, reflected the first Senate's understanding of the limited nature of its role. For instance, on retiring from the Senate, Senator George Cabot explained that "the power of the senate was in no sense initiative or even active, but negative and censorial, and was never to be exercised but in cases where the persons proposed for office were unfit. I have always rejected the idea of non-concurrence with a nomination merely because the nominee was less suitable for the office than thousands of others; he must be positively unfit for the office, and the public duty not likely to be performed by him, to justify in my mind non-concurrence." Letter from George Cabot to Thomas Pickering (Sept. 23, 1799) in *Life and Letters of George Cabot* 240 (Henry C. Lodge ed., Boston: Little, Brown 1878) (emphasis in original). See also Roy Swanstrom, *The United States Senate 1787–1801: A Dissertation of the First Fourteen Years of the Upper Legislative Body*, S. Doc. 31, 100th Cong., 1st Sess. 98 (1988) (noting that the Senate generally shared this view during the Washington administration).

Washington made known his views on whether the Senate had any formal prenomination role when he wrote in his diary that Thomas Jefferson and John Jay agreed with him that the Senate's powers extended "no farther than to an approbation or disapprobation of the person nominated by the President, all the rest being Executive and vested in the President by the Constitution." Diary Entry (Apr. 27, 1790), in *The Diary of George Washington from 1789 to 1791* 128 (Benson J. Lossing ed., 1860). In a later letter to James Monroe, Washington explained further that "as I *alone* am responsible for a proper nomination, it certainly behooves me to name such an one as in my judgment combines the requisites." Letter from Washington to James Monroe (Apr. 9, 1794) in 33 *The Writings of George Washington,* 321 (emphasis in original). No subsequent president has recognized that senatorial advice prior to nomination is mandatory. To be sure, some presidents have consulted with key senators, but it was done out of comity or prudence and never with a declaration of constitutional obligation. Because the branches are not hermetically sealed from one another, informal interchange between them can be expected and does not require a formal role for the Senate in the prenomination process.

95   See U.S. Const., art. II, sec. 2, cl. 2.

96   U.S. Const., art. II, sec. 1, cl. 8.

97   Federalist No. 76, 494 (A. Hamilton).

98   4 Elliott, *Debates,* 134. See also Letter from George Cabot to Thomas Pickering (Sept. 23, 1799), in *Life and Letters of George Cabot,* 240 (emphasis in original).

99   30 *The Writings of George Washington,* 373–74.

100   Federalist No. 76 at 457 (A. Hamilton).

101   Federalist No. 77 at 461 (A. Hamilton).

102   Id.; see also Joseph Story, *Commentaries on the Constitution,* sec. 791 (R. Rotunda and J. Nowak eds., Carolina Academic Press 1987) (noting that the Senate will bear a heavy responsibility in justifying its rejections to the public).

103   Prior to the direct election of senators mandated by the Seventeenth Amendment, political fallout would have come largely from state legislatures in the form of instructions or recalls (as well as the ire of the media, important financial backers, and party officials). Subsequent to the amendment's passage, such fallout has come largely from the senator's party and constituents, contributors, and supporters, as well as from interest groups and the media. For more on the nature of this fallout, see chapter 6.

104   Few framers speculated about requisite qualifications, and said little when they did. For instance, Oliver Ellsworth, whom President Washington would later appoint to the Supreme Court, mentioned that judges should possess "a systematic and accurate knowledge of the laws" as well as information on the law of Nations." 2 *Records* 73–74. James Madison suggested that "[t]he Legislative talents . . . were very different from those of a judge," 1 *Records* 120.

2. The Structure of the Federal Appointments Process

1   Cf. Craig v. Boren, 429 U.S. 190, 211 (1976) (Stevens, J., concurring) ("There is only one Equal Protection Clause").

Notes to Chapter 2

2   The Supreme Court has considered the question of who qualifies as an "officer of the United States" on several occasions but has yet to resolve the issue definitively. See Edmond v. United States, 117 S.Ct. 1573 (1997); Weiss v. United States, 114 S.Ct. 752 (1994); Freytag v. Commissioner, 111 S.Ct. 2631 (1991); Morrison v. Olson, 487 U.S. 654 (1988); Young v. United States ex rel. Vuitton, 481 U.S. 787 (1987); Buckley v. Valeo, 424 U.S. 1 (1976): Humphrey's Executor v. United States, 295 U.S. 602 (1935); Myers v. United States, 272 U.S. 107 (1926); Ex Parte Siebold, 100 U.S. 371 (1879).

3   For example, in the Senate debate over Clarence Thomas's nomination to the Supreme Court, Senators Al Gore and Paul Simon argued that the burden of persuasion in a Supreme Court confirmation proceeding should be on the president, the nominee, or both to demonstrate that the person nominated merits a seat on the Supreme Court. See M. Gerhardt, "Divided Justice," 993. Senator Simon maintained further that "the benefit of the doubt" regarding a Supreme Court nominee should be resolved in favor of "the people of this country" and the Constitution. Id.

4   Cf. Michael J. Gerhardt, *The Federal Impeachment Process: A Constitutional and Historical Analysis* 113 (2d ed., University of Chicago Press 2000) (discussing the difficulties of enforcing uniform rules of evidence or a uniform burden of proof in impeachment proceedings); Michael J. Gerhardt, "Rediscovering Nonjusticiability: Judicial Review of Impeachments after *Nixon,* 44 *Duke L.J.* 231, 267 (1994) (same).

5   See generally M. Gerhardt, *The Federal Impeachment Process,* 9–10.

6   McGinnis, "Reply," 653.

7   Stephen Carter identifies the focus on disqualifying factors as a major problem with the confirmation process in *The Confirmation Mess,* 159.

8   Traditionally, commentators have concluded that the Senate scrutinizes judicial candidates more closely than nominees to executive or administrative offices. See, e.g., Laurence Tribe, *God Save This Honorable Court: How the Choice of Supreme Court Justices Shapes Our History* 78 (1985).

9   Of course, a president's nominating power is subject to various countervailing political forces, including congressional authority to preempt it by abolishing vacant offices (such as judgeships) before a president has been able to fill them. See Sheldon v. Sill, 49 U.S. (8 How.) 411 (1850). See also Martin Redish, *Tensions in the Allocation of Judicial Power* 21–24 (1980).

3. Historical Changes and Patterns

1   Jeffrey K. Tulis, "Constitutional Abdication: The Senate, the President, and Appointments to the Supreme Court," 47 *Case W. Res. L. Rev.* 1331, 1353 (1997).

2   See generally David Herbert Donald, *Lincoln* 536–52 (1995).

3   H. Abraham, *Justices and Presidents,* 123. See also D. Donald, *Lincoln,* 552 (Lincoln "chose Chase to be Chief Justice because he thought him worthy—but he expected to receive political advantages from his choice. The appointment was part of the broader program of conciliating all the factions within the Republican party").

Notes to Chapter 3

4   Indeed, Lincoln had signaled earlier in his career the kind of approach he thought a president should take in making federal appointments. He had strongly urged President Zachary Taylor, on behalf of whose election he had tirelessly worked, to make party loyalty and service primary considerations in awarding significant federal appointments. See D. Donald, *Lincoln*, 138.

5   Id. at 267.

6   Id. at 551.

7   J. Smith, *John Marshall*, 171.

8   Id.

9   The framers of the Constitution recognized that the Senate would not always be in session to give advice and consent to presidential nominations. Consequently, they made the following provision in the Constitution to authorize the president to make recess appointments to cover these periods: "The President shall have the Power to fill up all Vacancies that may happen during the Recess of the Senate, by granting Commissions which shall expire at the End of their next Session." U.S. Const., art. II, sec. 2, cl. 3.

10   Justice Iredell, who supported Rutledge's nomination as Chief Justice, acknowledged nevertheless that Rutledge's remarks had been "intemperate." See Letter from James Iredell to Hannah Iredell (Aug. 13, 1795), in 1 *The Documentary History of the Supreme Court of the United States, 1789–1800* at 780, 780 (Maeva Marcus and James R. Perry eds., 1985). See also *South Carolina State-Gazette*, July 17, 1795, in id. at 766 (reporting that Rutledge had described the treaty negotiated by John Jay, then the Chief Justice of the United States, as a "puerile production" with the "grossest absurdities" among the terms). Moreover, an opponent of the nomination writing as "A Real Republican" criticized Rutledge's speech because it showed that Rutledge had "no habit of deliberate investigation" and was "deficient in common sense, and without regard to character, which all decent men possess and exhibit upon common occasions." A Real Republican, *Columbian Centinel*, Aug. 26, 1795, reprinted in id. at 785, 786. Then–Vice President John Adams believed that Rutledge lacked proper deportment for a judge when he became "a popular orator." See Letter from John Adams to Abigail Adams (Dec. 17, 1795), in id. at 813.

11   5 U.S. (1 Cranch) 137 (1803).

12   5 U.S. (1 Cranch) 299 (1803).

13   Arthur M. Schlesinger Jr., *The Age of Jackson* 46, 47 (1945).

14   Letter from President Jefferson to Elias Shipman and others, July 12, 1801, in 9 *The Works of Thomas Jefferson* 272–73 (P. Ford ed., 1904).

15   Id.

16   Leonard D. White, *The Jeffersonians: A Study in Administrative History, 1801–1829* 379–80 (1951).

17   Harry Ammon, *James Monroe: The Quest for National Identity* 494–95 (1990).

18   2 *Messages and Papers of the Presidents* (James D. Richardson comp., 1889–1905) 448–49 (Dec. 8, 1829); *Register of Debates*, 22d Cong., 1st Sess., p. 1325 (Jan. 24, 1832). See also Leonard W. White, *The Jacksonians* 318 (1954).

Notes to Chapter 3

19   L. White, *The Jacksonians*, 308.

20   4 *Messages and Papers of the Presidents*, 5–21 (Mar. 4, 1851).

21   Norma Lois Peterson, *The Presidencies of William Henry Harrison and John Tyler* 45–51, 71, 168–69, 197–98, 224–25, 236–41 (1989).

22   See James K. Polk, *The Diary of James K. Polk during His Presidency* 116, 184, 261, 317 (1929).

23   Elbert B. Smith, *The Presidencies of Zachary Taylor and Millard Fillmore* 57–65, 159–63 (1988).

24   Id. at 59, 66, 159–60, 161–63.

25   Larry Gara, *The Presidency of Franklin Pierce* 49–51 (1991).

26   Elbert B. Smith, *The Presidency of James Buchanan* 20–22, 67–68, 84–85, 102–3 (1975).

27   David Herbert Donald, *Lincoln Reconsidered* 71–72 (1956).

28   Id. at 76 (citation omitted in original).

29   See generally Leonard D. White, *The Republican Era, 1869–1901* (1958).

30   See generally N. Peterson, *The Presidencies of William Henry Harrison and John Tyler*, 45–51, 71, 168–69, 197–98, 224–25, 236–41.

31   See H. Abraham, *Justices and Presidents*, 105.

32   See id. at 119–20.

33   See Homer E. Socolofsky and Allan B. Spetter, *The Presidency of Benjamin Harrison* 31–45 (1987).

34   These factors have included the establishment of a large federal bureaucracy; the electorate's increasing concern with personality and issues and decreasing tendency to identify with a single political party; split ticket voting; the Supreme Court's striking down most forms of patronage based on party loyalty as violating the First Amendment; the rise of interest groups; major shifts in the composition and agendas of the national parties; and a shift in the source of presidential authority from personality, parties, and interest groups to independent political apparatuses and mass communications technologies enabling direct appeals to the people. See generally Martin Wattenberg, *The Decline of American Political Parties* (1990) (presenting a comprehensive statistical analysis of the decline of party voting and identification during the second half of the twentieth century); David Mayhew, *Placing Parties in American Politics* (1986); Laura Orren, "The Changing Styles of American Party Politics," in *The Future of American Political Parties: The Challenge of Governance* 31 (J. Fleishman ed., 1982). See also Larry Kramer, "Understanding Federalism," 47 *Vand. L. Rev.* 1485, 1531–37 (1994); Michael A. Fitts and Robert Inman, "Controlling Congress: Presidential Influence in Domestic Fiscal Policy," 80 *Geo. L.J.* 1737, 1741 n. 13 (1992); Michael A. Fitts, "The Vices of Virtue: A Political Party Perspective on Civic Virtue Reforms in the Legislative Process," 136 *U. Pa. L. Rev.* 1567, 1604 n. 14 (1988). Yet another development often cited as a factor contributing to the declining influence of political parties in this century is the Seventeenth Amendment. Moreover, the diminution in party control of the appointments process has coincided with the rise in identity politics, i.e., the tendency for voters, interest groups, and others to support or op-

pose those candidates or nominees identified or associated with particular issues or traits of considerable concern to them.

35   See generally H. Abraham, *Justices and Presidents,* 110–12.

36   See R. McCormick, *The Party Period and Public Policy* 143–96 (1986).

37   See generally J. Massaro, *Supremely Political,* 78–134.

38   Three of William Howard Taft's six appointees were Democrats: Horace Lurton, Edward D. White, and Joseph R. Lamar. One of Wilson's two appointees to the Court, Louis Brandeis, was a registered Republican. One of Harding's three Supreme Court appointments, Pierce Butler, was a Democrat. One of Hoover's three appointees, Benjamin Cardozo, was a Democrat. One of Roosevelt's nine was an Independent, Felix Frankfurter, while another was a Republican, Chief Justice Harlan F. Stone. One of Truman's four appointees was a Republican, Harold Burton. One of Eisenhower's five appointees was a Democrat, William Brennan. One of Nixon's four Court appointments was a registered Democrat, Lewis Powell.

39   See Stephen E. Ambrose, *Eisenhower: The President* 19–24 (1984).

40   The two Democrats were Mrs. Oveta Culp Hobby, a Texas newspaper publisher and influential member of the Texas Democrats for Eisenhower, and Martin Durkin, head of a very powerful national plumbers' union. William J. Brennan was the Democrat whom Eisenhower appointed to the Court.

41   *Diary of Dwight D. Eisenhower* (Jan. 5, 1953, entry).

42   See, e.g., Martin Flaherty, "The Most Dangerous Branch," 105 *Yale L.J.* 1725 (1996); Michael Fitts, "The Paradox of Power in the Modern State: Why a Unitary, Centralized Presidency May Not Exhibit Effective or Legitimate Leadership," 144 *U. Pa. L. Rev.* 827 (1996); Michael Stokes Paulsen, "The Most Dangerous Branch: Executive Power to Say What the Law Is," 83 *Geo. L.J.* 217 (1994); Lawrence Lessig and Cass R. Sunstein, "The President and the Administration," 94 *Colum. L. Rev.* 1 (1994); Michael Froomkin, "The Imperial Presidency's New Vestments," 88 *Nw. U. L. Rev.* 1346 (1994); Steven G. Calabresi and Saikrishna B. Prakash, "The President's Power to Execute the Laws," 104 *Yale L.J.* 541 (1994); Michael B. Rappaport, "The President's Veto and the Constitution," 87 *Nw. U. L. Rev.* 735 (1993); Henry P. Monaghan, "The Protective Power of the Presidency," 93 *Colum. L. Rev.* 1 (1993); Steven G. Calabresi and Kevin H. Rhodes, "The Structural Constitution: Unitary Executive, Plural Judiciary," 105 *Harv. L. Rev.* 1153 (1992). See also *Symposium: The Law of the Presidency,* 48 *Ark. L. Rev.* 1 (1995) (with articles by Cass R. Sunstein, Steven G. Calabresi, Harold H. Bruff, Peter M. Shane, Akhil R. Amar, and Mark R. Killenbeck).

43   Forrest McDonald, *The American Presidency: An Intellectual History* 277 (1994).

44   S. Goldman, *Picking Federal Judges,* 191.

45   In this century, 11 percent of Supreme Court nominations (7 out of 61) have failed thus far. This contrasts rather dramatically with the failure rate of 29 percent (20 out of 70) in the nineteenth century. In the eighteenth century, the failure rate was 12 percent (2 out of 17).

46   Two authors, for different reasons, have concluded that the presidency is the most

Notes to Chapter 3

dangerous branch. See Flaherty, "The Most Dangerous Branch," 1817–28; Paulsen, "The Most Dangerous Branch," 223–24.

47   J. Harris, *The Advice and Consent of the Senate*, 40–41.

48   F. McDonald, *The American Presidency*, 221. Five years after the Fishbourn decision, several senators, including James Madison and James Monroe, tried but failed to talk President Washington into nominating Aaron Burr as minister of France, a position to which the president eventually named Gouverneur Morris. J. Harris, *The Advice and Consent of the Senate*, 42.

49   In the First Congress, Representative James Madison argued that senators had been vested, like the president, with some appointment power because they were "from their nature, better acquainted with the character of the candidates than an individual." 1 *Annals of Congress* 380 (May 19, 1789). A few weeks later, Congressman Benjamin Goodhue expressed his agreement that it was "more probable that the Senate may be better acquainted with the characters of the officers that are nominated than the President himself." Id. at 534 (June 18, 1789).

50   See H. Abraham, *Justices and Presidents*, 144.

51   U.S. Const., amend. XVII.

52   See generally 2 George H. Haynes, *The Senate of the United States: Its History and Practice* 1070–83 (1960).

53   See C. B. Swisher, *Roger B. Taney* 190–288 (1935).

54   See generally Barbara Sinclair, *The Transformation of the U.S. Senate* 188–216 (1989).

55   See J. Harris, *The Advice and Consent of the Senate*, 93–98 (recounting Wilson's difficulties in filling more than a dozen federal positions because of his resistance to patronage, occasional willingness to consult with Republican senators, infighting within the Democratic party, and the business connections of some of his appointees).

56   See id. at 249–55.

57   Id. at 117–19.

58   Robert A. Katzmann, *Courts and Congress* 19 (1997).

59   See B. Sinclair, *The Transformation of the U.S. Senate*, 89, 102–4.

60   See id. at 103; see also C. Lawrence Evans, *Leadership in Committee: A Comparative Analysis of Leadership Behavior in the U.S. Senate* 22–24 (1991).

61   This tracks the so-called exchange theories of interest group influence. See, e.g., K. Schlozman and J. Tierney, *Organized Interests and the American Democracy* (1986); M. Hayes, *Lobbyists and Legislatures: A Theory of Political Markets* (1984); J. Chubb, *Interest Groups and the Bureaucracy: The Politics of Energy* (1983).

62   See, e.g., John W. Kingdon, *Agendas, Alternatives, and Public Policies* (1984).

63   See generally Maneur Olson, *The Logic of Collective Choice* (2d ed., 1971).

64   See Michael J. Klarman, "Majoritarian Judicial Review: The Entrenchment Problem," 85 *Geo. L.J.* 491, 498 n. 38 (1997) (observing that according to public choice theorists, "legislators generally respond not to the will of a majority of their constituents but rather to well-organized special interest groups which offer campaign contributions

in exchange for favorable votes on legislation"); Jonathan R. Macey, "Transaction Costs and the Normative Elements of the Public Choice Model: An Application to Constitutional Theory," 74 *Va. L. Rev.* 471, 490 (1988) (arguing, "[p]olitical parties, recognizing the phenomenon of voter apathy due to rational ignorance, compete for the right to divert resources from the general population to those interest groups most adept at overcvoming the free rider problem").

65   See generally Ethan Bronner, *Battle for Justice: How the Bork Nomination Shook America* passim (1989).

66   Bork's 1987 confirmation hearings were a watershed event insofar as the Senate's interest in preserving *Roe v. Wade*, 410 U.S. 113 (1975), is concerned. Prior to the hearings, *Roe*'s fate was primarily the concern of those responsible for judicial selection in the Reagan administration. See generally Herman Schwartz, *Packing the Courts: The Conservative Campaign to Rewrite the Constitution* (1988). In the Bork hearings, Democrats in the Senate forged an alliance with interest groups interested in preserving *Roe*. Subsequently, *Roe*'s status has figured prominently in Supreme Court confirmation hearings.

67   See R. Katzmann, *Courts and Congress*, 35; Gregory Caldeira, "Commentary on Senate Confirmation of Supreme Court Justices: The Roles of Organized and Unorganized Interests," 77 *Ky. L. Rev.* 531, 536–38 (1988–89). See also Ruth Shalit, "Borking Back: The Right Gets Even," *New Republic*, May 17, 1993, 18 (noting that after the election of President Clinton, conservative groups joined forces to create the Judicial Selection Monitoring Project to lobby for the appointment of conservative judicial candidates and against the appointment of liberal ones).

68   Paul A. Freund, "Appointment of Justices: Some Historical Perspectives," 101 *Harv. L. Rev.* 1146, 1149 (1988).

69   See generally Larry Kramer, "Understanding Federalism," 47 *Vand. L. Rev.* 1485, 1549–53 (1994); see also Richard Davis, "Supreme Court Nominations and the News Media," 57 *Alb. L. Rev.* 1061 (1994).

70   "Surgeon General Gets Cautious Support," *Washington Post*, Feb. 7, 1995, A3.

71   See generally Bill Kovach and Tom Rosenstiel, *Warp Speed: America in the Age of Mixed Media* (Century Fund 1999).

72   See R. Katzmann, *Courts and Congress*, 36 ("Television's power is that it can shape public perception by what it covers, what it culls from the day's [activities] for the evening broadcast, and how it interprets the news"); see also S. Carter, *The Confirmation Mess*, 38 (arguing that the press mishandled this control in covering Lani Guinier's nomination to head the Civil Rights Division in President Clinton's Justice Department by failing to become sufficiently familiar with her writings to be able to keep the American public adequately informed about her qualifications and views and to keep administration officials and senators honest; Carter also argues that this mishandling ultimately posed a fatal problem to Ms. Guinier's nomination).

73   I base the conclusions in this section largely on readings of various primary materials from the nineteenth and twentieth centuries, including congressional hearings and correspondence and presidential speeches, interviews, and diaries. See also Michael J.

Gerhardt, "Toward a Comprehensive Understanding of the Federal Appointments Process," 21 *Harv. J. L. & Pub. Pol'y* 467 (1988); "Putting Presidential Performance in the Federal Appointments Process in Perspective," 47 *Case W. Res. L. Rev.* 1359 (1997). For other sources regarding particular nominees, see particular cites in relevant portions of the remainder of this chapter and subsequent chapters.

74 Political party affiliation is likely to be both a short- and a long-term concern. It is a short-term consideration in the sense that presidents might be concerned (as, for example, was Lincoln) to make nominations that will be good for their party and keep them in good standing with their parties. It is likely to be a long-term concern in the sense that it provides a useful signal for generations to come of the utility of party activity *and* a proxy or indicator of certain political beliefs (particularly compatibility with a president's objectives).

75 For some statistical surveys consistent with this conclusion, see, e.g., Janet M. Martin, "George Bush and the Executive Branch," in *Leadership and the Bush Presidency: Prudence or Drift in an Era of Change?* 37 (Ryan A. Barilleaux and M. E. Stuckey eds., 1992) (citation omitted); John W. Macy, Bruce Adams, J. Jackson Walter, and G. Calvin Mackenzie, *America's Unelected Government* (1983); G. Calvin Mackenzie, *The Politics of Presidential Appointments* (1981).

76 See, e.g., H. Abraham, *Justices and Presidents*, 56–70, passim.

77 It is possible to discern a similar pattern of decision making by other presidents, regardless of the number of appointments each made to the Supreme Court. For instance, Presidents Jackson, Lincoln, Teddy Roosevelt, Taft, Franklin Roosevelt, and Eisenhower made multiple appointments to the Court and clearly had well-defined criteria in mind for sifting through potential candidates (see chapters 5 and 7) but made their final choices with pragmatic considerations in mind. The one possible exception to this pattern was arguably President Jackson's repeated nominations of Roger Taney, but I argue elsewhere in this book that Jackson had several objectives in mind, including ensuring the implementation of certain fiscal policy and constitutional philosophy *and* repaying a loyal political lieutenant (see chapters 5 and 6). In this sense, Jackson's nomination of Taney was not appreciably different from Lyndon Johnson's nomination of Abe Fortas. Both presidents were not only rewarding loyal political aides but also were nominating people about whose constitutional philosophies or orientations they had no doubts.

78 H. Abraham, *Justices and Presidents*, 85–86.

79 See generally Daniel J. Danelski, *A Supreme Court Justice Is Appointed* (1964).

80 Stephen Labaton, "Clinton Is Relying Less on Advisers in Finding Supreme Court Nominee," *New York Times*, Apr. 6, 1993, A18. Reportedly, President Clinton sought a nominee "progressive on social policy, civil rights and privacy issues. He [had] a strong preference for someone who would be able to forge coalitions in a fractured and changing court." Id.

81 Again, I base this conclusion on my review of various materials, including the records of Senate confirmation hearings for cabinet and Supreme Court nominees in the nineteenth and twentieth centuries. The fact that relatively few cabinet nominees have

been rejected supports the conclusion that senators disposed to reject such nominations need to find something more serious to base rejection on than partisan affiliation. For a similar conclusion regarding the Senate's deliberations on Supreme Court nominations, see generally Jeffrey K. Tulis, "Constitutional Abdication," 1331. For more on the Senate's reasons for rejecting cabinet and particularly Supreme Court nominations in the twentieth century, see chapter 6.

82 See E. Bronner, *Battle for Justice*, 98-126.

83 See S. Carter, *The Confirmation Mess*, 24. See also John Hanchette, "Why Can't Clinton Get His Act Together on Nominees?" Gannett News Service, Mar. 15, 1995, available in Westlaw Allnews File (quoting unnamed sources in the Clinton administration and some Democratic members of Congress as describing the resistance to many of President Clinton's nominations as "payback" for the difficulties Democrats gave to President Reagan's nomination of Robert Bork to the Supreme Court and President Bush's nomination of John Tower to become secretary of defense); Ruth Marcus and Ann Devroy, "Another Lesson in Confirmation Pitfalls," *Washington Post*, June 5, 1993, A1 (quoting some administration sources and some Democratic members of Congress as attributing the failed nominations of Zoë Baird and Lani Guinier to political "payback" by the conservative right, who sought a "good nomination fight to avenge . . . the failed Supreme Court nomination of Robert H. Bork").

4. The President's Role in the Federal Appointments Process

1 See, e.g., Richard Tanner Johnson, *Managing the White House: An Intimate Study of the Presidency* xvi-xvii, 54-55, 82-83, 125-27, 211-12 (1974) (discussing how the appointments of Presidents Truman, Eisenhower, Kennedy, and Nixon reflected their personal styles and beliefs). See also Robert Scigliano, *The Supreme Court and the Presidency* 148-57 (1971) (discussing how different presidents' Supreme Court appointments have reflected their personal values and partisan affiliations).

2 See, e.g., Ronald Dworkin, "One Year Later, the Debate Goes On," *New York Times*, Oct. 25, 1992, sec. 7, 1 (noting that the Thomas hearings "taught us much about the character of some of our most prominent officials"); Steven V. Roberts, "In Confirmation Process, Hearings Offer a Stage," *New York Times*, Feb. 8, 1989, B7 (describing the ways senators' performances in confirmation hearings reflect their personalities and agendas); Henry P. Monaghan, "The Confirmation Process: Law or Politics?" 101 *Harv. L. Rev.* 1202, 1207 n. 21 (1988) (suggesting that a senator's decision is the result of the tension between political self-interest and personal principles).

3 Letter from George Bancroft to J. G. Wilson, Mar. 8, 1888, *The Presidents of the United States* 230 (J. G. Wilson ed., 1894).

4 Stephen Hess, *Organizing the Presidency* 77, 81, 185 (rev. ed. 1988).

5 See, e.g., E. Bronner, *Battle for Justice*, 160, 200-203.

6 See, e.g., Maureen Dowd, "In 1994-Model Politics, Loyalty Is Often Optional Equipment," *New York Times*, Mar. 20, 1994, sec. 4, 3.

7 Cf. H. Abraham, *Justices and Presidents*, 15-19. See Michael Oreskes, "Bush's Man

and Mandate on the Line," *New York Times*, Feb. 26, 1989, sec. 4, 1; Timothy M. Phelps and Helen Winternitz, *Capitol Games* 138, 305 (1992).

8   See, e.g., Jane Mayer and Jill Abramson, *Strange Justice: The Selling of Clarence Thomas* 351–54 (1994).

9   See, e.g., James David Barber, *The Presidential Character: Predicting Performance in the White House* (2d ed. 1977) (arguing that presidential character heavily influences performance in office); Henry C. Kenski, "A Man for All Seasons? The Guardian President and His Public," in *Leadership and the Bush Presidency: Prudence or Drift in an Era of Change?* 91 (Ryan J. Barilleaux and Mary E. Stuckey eds., 1992) (discussing the importance of public approval and popularity as a measure of presidential success). Cf. Michael Fitts, "The Paradox of Power in the Modern State: Why a Unitary, Centralized Presidency May Not Exhibit Effective or Legitimate Leadership," 144 *U. Pa. L. Rev.* 827, 872 (1996) (arguing that because the public assessment of presidential performance is based on "a standard of moral assessment appropriate for individuals, rather than for institutions," presidential power is undermined); see also Barbara Hinckley, "Beyond Reform," in *The Presidency in American Politics* 105 (P. Brace, C. B. Harrington, and G. King eds., 1989) (examining the link between presidential performance and public perceptions of the President).

10   See generally D. Baird, R. Gertner, and R. Picker, *Game Theory and the Law* 44 (1994).

11   "The Thomas Nomination: Excerpts from Senate's Hearings on the Thomas Nomination," *New York Times*, Oct. 12, 1991, A12. See also J. Mayer and J. Abramson, *Strange Justice*, 299–300.

12   See generally Sheldon Goldman, "Judicial Selection under Clinton: A Midterm Examination," 78 *Judicature* 276, 277–78 (1995).

13   See Paul Richter, "Clinton Takes More Time on Court Choice," *Los Angeles Times*, May 13, 1994, A4; Carl M. Cannon and Nelson Schwartz, "Clinton's 'Trial Balloon' Strategy Tends to Burst," *Chicago Sun-Times*, June 22, 1993; Holly Idelson, "Clinton Closes in on a Nominee; Choices Winnowed to Two," 51 *Cong. Q. Wkly. Rep.* 1482, 1485 (1993).

14   See generally Baird et. al, *Game Theory*, 171–72, 174, 316.

15   Id. at 316, 171–72.

16   See P. Freund, "Appointment of Justices," 1155. Interestingly, well over half of the fifty-nine respondents to my survey of executive branch alumni cited tit-for-tat or payback as the most common (and least legitimate) reason for senators' opposition to judicial nominees.

17   See Julia Malone, "Sentencing Agency, Lacking Commissioners, Unable to Perform Its Duties," *Houston Chronicle*, May 29, 1999.

18   A great deal of literature suggests that claims of incoherence in group decision making are overdrawn and that groups adopt procedures to alleviate problems of cycling and inconsistent outcomes.

19   Cf. Arthur Schlesinger Jr., "The Ultimate Approval Rating," *New York Times Magazine*, Dec. 15, 1996, 50–51 ("To succeed, Presidents must have a port to seek and

must convince Congress and the electorate of the rightness of their course. Every President stands in Theodore Roosevelt's 'bully pulpit.' National crisis widens his range of options but does not automatically make the man. The crisis of rebellion did not spur Buchanan to greatness, nor did the Depression turn Hoover into a bold and imaginative leader. Their inadequacies in the face of crisis allowed Lincoln and the second Roosevelt to show the difference that individuals can make to history").

20   See generally S. Skowronek, *The Politics Presidents Make*, 28.

21   Id. at 28–29.

22   Id. at 208.

23   Interestingly, Skowronek groups President Clinton together with Presidents Nixon and Wilson as exemplars of "third-way politics." See Stephen Skowronek, "President Clinton and the Risks of 'Third-Way' Politics," *Extensions*, spring 1996, 10. According to Skowronek, "Third-way leaders like Clinton have sought to . . . occupy a new middle ground largely defined by their opponents." Id. Because they "threaten to appropriate much of the field of action carved out by their opponents and to attract disaffected elements within the dominant coalition," the political contest is "framed by the president's purposeful blurring of received identities and his opponents' stake in keeping those established identities intact." Id. at 11. It is therefore in the nature of "third-way politics" to raise questions about a president's "authenticity and credibility" and sometimes, because of the precariousness of the third-way president's balancing act, "to bring [about] a colossal collapse of presidential authority." Id. at 12.

24   This was particularly true on the eve of and in the aftermath of President Clinton's impeachment. See Charles E. Smith, Mary E. Stuckey, and John W. Hinckle III, "Executive-Legislative Conflict and the Nomination-Confirmation Controversy in the Lower Federal Judiciary," *Presidential Stud. Q.*, Oct. 1, 1998 ("Clinton's relations with the media, reflecting institutional changes in media organization, have not been particularly good since his first election and have become increasingly strained as the 'feeding frenzy' surrounding the Monica Lewinsky scandal thus occupied increasing amounts of attention over the past seven months. Moreover, judicial nominations particularly in the lower courts are a low public priority and, in the absence of a strong effort from the president, are not likely to generate much spontaneous public interest. Given the present scandal, the public agenda is almost completely outside of presidential control. Thus weakened by the scandal in terms of controlling the national media, and facing a battle over public opinion with the Congress and in the media, the president has neither the time nor the resources for a public battle over judicial nominations").

25   John McGinnis, "The President, the Senate, and the Constitution, and the Confirmation Process: A Reply to Professors Strauss and Sunstein," 71 *Tex. L. Rev.* 633, 653 (1993).

26   A. Schlesinger Jr., *The Age of Jackson*, 43.

27   Janet M. Martin, "George Bush and the Executive Branch," in *Leadership and the Bush Presidency: Prudence or Drift in an Era of Change?* 37, 53 (Ryan J. Barilleaux and Mary E. Stuckey eds., 1992). See also Goldman, *Bush's Judicial Legacy*, 295, 297.

Notes to Chapter 4

28 Letter from Joseph D. Lerned to Henry Clay, Sept. 27, 1827, 6 *The Papers of Henry Clay* 1079 (Hopkins et. al. eds., 1959).

29 Theodore Roosevelt, *An Autobiography* 379 (1913).

30 See generally John Morton Blum, *The Republican Roosevelt* 42–49, 65, 68 (1972).

31 See S. Skowronek, *The Politics Presidents Make*, 232.

32 Teddy Roosevelt is far from being alone in making a less than perfect choice of a successor. In spite of his many premonitions of his own death, President Lincoln accepted Andrew Johnson as his second running mate. Johnson proved to be a disastrous choice. He lacked many basic leadership skills and failed completely to maintain goodwill with members of the president's party or a good working relationship with congressional leaders or members of Congress generally. Similarly, President Jackson chose his close political ally Martin Van Buren as his successor, but Van Buren proved incapable of leading the nation on the path set by Jackson and, more important, out of its first great depression.

33 In some cases, Wilson chose people with whom he was not personally acquainted. The latter practice brought him into conflict, however, with only one significant cabinet appointee—William Jennings Bryan, who as secretary of state embarrassed Wilson because of his untiring efforts to find offices for many of his friends and supporters.

34 R. Remini, *The Life of Andrew Jackson*, 331.

35 S. Skowronek, *Justices and Presidents*, 46.

36 Id.

37 See, e.g., William N. Eskeridge and John Ferejohn, "The Article I, Section 7 Game," 80 *Geo. L.J.* 523 (1992).

38 See Tim Weiner, "Lake Pulls Out as C.I.A. Nominee," *New York Times*, Mar. 18, 1997, A1, 12.

39 J. Massaro, *Supremely Political*, 55–77.

40 S. Goldman, *Picking Federal Judges*, 318–19.

41 These figures exclude the U.S. Court of International Trade. By September 1, 1998, the Senate had not taken final action on the only nomination pending for the single vacancy on the latter court.

42 See generally John D. Felice and Herbert F. Weisber, "Senate Confirmation of Supreme Court Justices: The Changing Importance of Ideology, Party, and Region in Supreme Court Nominees, 1953–88," 77 *Ky. L.J.* 509, 511–12 (1989) (discussing the correlates between political parties and Supreme Court confirmation votes).

43 R. Scigliano, *The Supreme Court and the Presidency*, 97–98.

44 The irony and significance of Jackson's victory did not elude him. Two days before his second term came to an end in 1837, Jackson wrote to a friend that he was looking forward with deep satisfaction to the "glorious scene of Mr. Van Buren, once rejected by the Senate, sworn into office by Chief Justice Taney, who [had twice] been rejected by the factious Senate." 5 *Correspondence of Andrew Jackson* 189 (J. S. Bassett ed., 1926–35).

45 L. White, *The Jacksonians*, 106–7.

46 William S. McFeely, *Grant: A Biography* 384 (1980).

47 Id. at 385.

48　Dixon Wechter, *Hero in America* 329 (1941) (citation omitted).

49　Letter from C. H. Hill to Benjamin Helm Bristow, Dec. 19, 1873, Bristow Papers (Library of Congress).

50　A. Schlesinger Jr., *The Age of Jackson,* 67–73.

51　Quoted in Dom Bonafede, *The In- and Outers: Presidential Appointees and Transient Government in Washington,* 35 (G. Calvin Mackensie ed., 1987).

52　Sheldon Goldman, "Judicial Appointments to the United States Courts of Appeals," 1967 *Wisc. L. Rev.* 186.

53　Letter from Harold R. Tyler Jr. to author, Oct. 11, 1995.

54　See generally Larry C. Berkson and Susan B. Carbon, *The United States Circuit Judge Nominating Commission: Its Members, Procedures, and Candidates* (1980). See also Elliot E. Slotnick, "Judicial Selection: Lowering the Bench or Raising It Higher? Affirmative Action during the Carter Administration," 2 *Yale L. & Pol'y Rev.* 270 (1983); W. Gary Fowler, "A Comparison of Initial Recommendation Procedures: Judicial Selection under Reagan and Carter," 2 *Yale L. & Pol'y Rev.* 299 (1983).

55　See Michael J. Gerhardt, "The Past, Present, and Future of President Clinton's Judicial Appointments," Vital Speeches, Feb. 15, 1997 (speech to the City Club of Cleveland).

56　See generally H. Schwartz, *Packing the Courts.*

57　Id. at 60–61.

58　Id. (contrasting both presidents' organizations for judicial selection).

59　See generally Victor H. Kramer, "The Case of Justice Stevens: How to Select, Nominate, and Confirm a Justice of the United States Supreme Court," 7 *Const. Comm.* 325 (1990).

60　S. Wasby, *The Supreme Court in the Federal Judicial System* 128 (3d ed. 1988). In yet another study, Segal provided the first multivariate analysis of the historical record, using a probit analysis to study the determinants of the confirmation of appointments. Jeffrey A. Segal, "Senate Confirmation of Supreme Court Justices: Partisan and Institutional Politics," 49 *J. Pol.* 998, 1003–5 (1986). See also Jeffrey A. Segal and Harold S. Spaeth, "If a Supreme Court Vacancy Occurs, Will the Senate Confirm a Reagan Nominee?" 69 *Judicature* 186, 189 (1986). Segal's final model shows significant effects for a number of factors, including whether the opposition party controlled the Senate, whether the nominee was a sitting senator, whether the nomination occurred in the fourth year of a president's term, whether the nominee was a member of the cabinet, how long the nominee had served in the national legislature, and whether the nomination occurred in the twentieth century. Id. Lemieux and Stewart also used logit analysis of the same historical record and found a close proximity between the party mixes on the Court and in the Senate. See P. Lemieux and C. Stewart, "Advise? Yes. Consent? Maybe. Senate Confirmation of Supreme Court Justices" (1988) (paper presented at the Annual Meeting of the American Political Science Association).

61　J. Harris, *The Advice and Consent of the Senate,* 94.

62　See Sheldon Goldman, "Bush's Judicial Legacy: The Final Imprint," 76 *Judica-*

Notes to Chapter 4

ture 282, 284 (1993) ("Traditionally, minimal confirmation activity occurs during presidential years, especially when the Senate is controlled by one party and the White House by another").

63 See id. at 284.

64 Id. at 277.

65 Id.

66 Neil A. Lewis, "Jilted Texas Judge Takes On His Foes in Partisan Congress," *New York Times*, Nov. 16, 1997, A1.

67 See *Cong. Rec.*, S 7238-01, 7238.

68 *Washington Post*, Sept. 14, 1997 (quoting Sheldon Goldman).

69 See Neil A. Lewis, "G.O.P. Begins Clearing Backlog of Nominees," *New York Times*, Oct. 25, 1997, A1.

70 E. Bronner, *Battle for Justice*, 202–3.

71 J. Massaro, *Supremely Political*, 79, 106, 144.

72 S. Carter, *The Confirmation Mess*, 137.

73 Steve Berg, "Clinton Gets Serious Message about Higher Ethics," *Star Tribune*, Jan. 23, 1993, A1; see also Editorial, *New York Times*, Jan. 23, 1993, A20.

74 For an excellent review of the criteria that presidents have employed in nominating Supreme Court justices, see H. Abraham, *Justices and Presidents*, 4–9.

75 Here, as elsewhere in the book (including the remainder of this chapter), the statistical information relating to the composition or characteristics of judicial nominees is based on several different sources, including *Selection and Confirmation of Federal Judges, Hearing before the Committee on the Judiciary*, U.S. Senate, 96th Cong., 1st Sess., 1979, serial no. 96-21, part 1, pp. 123–32; *Judges of the United States* (2d ed., GPO 1983); *Biographical Dictionary of the Federal Judiciary* (Harold W. Chase, Samuel Krislov, Keith O. Boyum, and Jerry N. Clark eds., 1976); *Legislative History of the United States Circuit Courts of Appeals and the Judges Who Served during the Period 1801 through May 1972*, Senate Committee on the Judiciary, 92nd Cong., 2nd Sess. Other useful sources include *Congressional Quarterly Almanac*, state legislative handbooks, newspaper articles about judicial nominees, the responses to a survey distributed to various officials responsible for judicial and other kinds of presidential nominations in administrations from Truman through the present, and Senate Judiciary Committee and administrative staff. Another extremely useful source is Sheldon Goldman, *Picking Federal Judges*, 58–59, 104–5, 147–49, 189–91, 227–29, 276–78, 338–40, 346–65.

76 Neil D. McFeeley, *Appointments of Judges: The Johnson Presidency* 26 (1987).

77 Harold W. Chase, *Federal Judges: The Appointing Process* 51 (1972) (quoting public statement of President Kennedy made May 20, 1961).

78 Campaign speech (Richard Nixon), Nov. 2, 1968, quoted in 27 *Cong. Q., Wkly. Rep.*, May 23, 1969, p. 798.

79 Id.

80 Id.

81 See generally S. Goldman, *Picking Federal Judges*, 252–53. See also Larry G. Berk-

son and Susan B. Carbon, *The United States Circuit Court Nominating Commission: Its Membership, Procedures, and Candidates* 4 (1980).

82   See M. J. Gerhardt, "The Past, Present, and Future of President Clinton's Judicial Appointments."

83   S. Goldman, *Picking Federal Judges*, 274.

84   Id.

85   One should note, however, that with the application of Executive Order 12,866 to independent agencies, President Clinton possibly exercised more continuing control over policy and thus might be less concerned with the initial appointment. See Exec. Order 12,866 3 C.F.R. 638 (1993), reprinted in 5 U.S.C. Section 601 (Supp. 1993). Essentially, this executive order requires, among other things, review of a regulation's equity and distributional impacts. See generally Richard H. Pildes and Cass R. Sunstein, "Reinventing the Regulatory State," 62 *U. Chi. L. Rev.* 1 (1995) (assessing the revolutionary significance of Executive Order 12,866).

86   Some legal and political scholars have argued, however, that the president's control of officers depends less on whether they serve in independent agencies or executive branch departments than on other factors. See, e.g., Geoffrey P. Miller, "Independent Agencies," 1986 *Sup. Ct. Rev.* 41, 82, 83.

5. The Advice and Consent of the Senate

1   See Lynn A. Baker and Samuel H. Dinkin, "The Senate: An Institution Whose Time Has Gone?" 8 *J.L. & Pol.* 21 (1997).

2   See generally Daniel A. Farber and Philip P. Frickey, *Law and Public Choice: A Critical Introduction* (1991).

3   See, e.g., John D. Felice and Herbert F. Weisber, "Senate Confirmation of Supreme Court Justices," 511–12.

4   H. Abraham, *Justices and Presidents*, 144.

5   S. Ambrose, *Eisenhower*, 530.

6   J. Massaro, *Supremely Political*, 73.

7   See generally Katharine Q. Seelye, "With Iron Gavel, Helms Rejects Vote on Weld," *New York Times*, Sept. 13, 1997, A1.

8   See Jeffrey Rosen, "Judicial Bashing," *Dallas Morning News*, May 4, 1997, J5.

9   Professor Fletcher is one of several judicial nominees whose nominations languished in the Senate for more than three years. He was eventually confirmed on October 8, 1998. Another person nominated, Michael Schattman, had been nominated in 1995 to the federal district court in Dallas but withdrew his nomination in mid-1998. Hilda Tagle, a similarly situated nominee to the federal district court in the Southern District of Texas, was confirmed on March 11, 1998. Clarence Sundram, who had been nominated to a federal district court in New York, had his nomination resubmitted January 7, 1997, but had not been confirmed at the time of this writing.

10   See Neil A. Lewis, "Clinton Agrees to G.O.P. Deal on Judgeships," *New York Times*, May 4, 1998, A24.

11 Chief Justice Durham withdrew her nomination so that she would have adequate time to take care of her seriously ill husband. Paul Elias, "Berzon's 9th Circuit Bid Looks Good," *The Recorder,* June 17, 1999, 1.

12 Catalina Camia, "Some Lawmakers Complain about Leisurely Pace," *Dallas Morning News,* Mar. 15, 1998, A14.

13 Tim Poor, "Hardball Politics Creates Gridlock in Southern Illinois Courts; Judicial Appointments Are on Hold in Senate," *St. Louis Post-Dispatch,* Mar. 15, 1998, A11.

14 S. Goldman, *Picking Federal Judges,* 133–34.

15 Among the nominees who had been stalled for more than a year and had to be resubmitted because of various delays engineered by different senators was Marsha Berzon, a widely respected labor lawyer from San Francisco, former law clerk to Justice William Brennan, and former Distinguished Visiting Practicioner at Cornell Law School (coinciding with the author's own visit there). The delays of Berzon's nomination were largely attributable to suspicions that she might be inclined to liberal activism on the bench (based on her having served as a member of the Board of the American Civil Liberties Union, clerked for liberal Justice Brennan, and represented unions for years in high-profile cases). She is reputed to have allayed concerns expressed about her nomination by assuring the Senate Judiciary Committee in her confirmation hearing that as a circuit judge she would faithfully adhere to Supreme Court precedent and treat her personal beliefs about any particular issue as wholly irrelevant to her judicial duties, and that her attitudes about judging or particular constitutional issues were not carbon copies of those of Justice Brennan. See P. Elias, "Berzon's 9th Circuit Bid Looks Good."

16 The Senate voted fifty-four to forty-five to reject White's district court nomination. The most common reason given by those who voted against his nomination, all Republican senators, was that he was "procriminal" and "anti-death penalty." But White voted to uphold 70 percent of the fifty-nine death sentences he reviewed, in contrast to the 75 to 81 percent averages of the five Missouri Supreme Court justices appointed by John Ashcroft when he was governor. See Stuart Taylor Jr., "The Smearing of a Moderate Judge," *Connecticut Law Tribune,* Oct. 25, 1999. The only tangible evidence of White's "procriminal, anti-death penalty" orientation derives from his lone dissents to the Missouri Supreme Court's decisions to uphold the impositions of the death penalty in two cases. See Missouri v. Johnson, 968 S.W. 2d 123 (1998) and Missouri v. Kinder, 942 S.W. 2d 313 (1996). In both cases, White called for new trials based on his assessment of the lower court decisions. In the latter case the trial judge had made "indefensibly racist" comments in a campaign release that raised reasonable suspicion that he could not preside over a case involving a black defendant impartially; in the former case the defendant's lawyer had made a blunder in his opening statement that so "utterly destroyed the credibility" of the defendant's insanity defense as to deny him a fair trial. For Senator Ashcroft, who orchestrated White's rejection, these dissents revealed his lack of fitness to be a federal district judge, while for all the Democrats in the Senate they merely reflected arguments on which reasonable jurists could disagree.

17   Dennis DeConcini, "Examining the Judicial Nomination Process: The Politics of Advice and Consent," 34 *Ariz. L. Rev.* 116 (1992).

18   Id. at 124.

19   Message of Aug. 6, 1789, 1 *Messages and Papers of the Presidents* 58–59 (James D. Richardson ed., 1899).

20   7 Henry Adams, *History of the United States during the Administrations of Jefferson and Madison* 55–60 (1889–91).

21   2 *Senate Executive Journal* 382 (1813).

22   See H. Schwartz, *Packing the Courts*, 58–62.

23   See P. H. Bergeron, *The Presidency of James K. Polk*, 164–65.

24   J. Harris, *The Advice and Consent of the Senate*, 220, 223.

25   Id. at 116.

26   For an excellent discussion of the policy arguments underlying the exercise of "blue slips," see W. Gary Fowler, "A Comparison of Initial Recommendation Procedures: Judicial Selection under Reagan and Carter," 1 *Yale L. & Pol'y Rev.* 299, 328–30 (1983).

27   Ari Hoogenboom, *The Presidency of Rutherford B. Hayes* 52–53 (1988).

28   H. Abraham, *Justices and Presidents*, 242. President Truman also nominated Fred Vinson, a former congressman, to be secretary of the treasury during Truman's first year in office and later, in 1946, to be Chief Justice. Id. at 244.

29   In his first term, President Clinton also appointed former Colorado senator Tim With as counselor to the secretary of state, a nonconfirmable position.

30   See Roger K. Newman, *Hugo Black: A Biography* 240–46, 307 (1994).

31   President Truman was also concerned that Black's nomination as Chief Justice would magnify a rift on the Court due to an ongoing feud between Black and Robert Jackson. Id. at 343–44.

32   J. Harris, *The Advice and Consent of the Senate*, 75.

33   Id. at 84.

34   See Donald B. Chidsey, *The Gentleman from New York: A Life of Roscoe Conkling* 363 (1935).

35   See Ellen Silberman, "Dellinger Wins Confirmation Despite Helms and Faircloth Objections," *Washington Post*, Oct. 13, 1993, 1. Senator Helms's objections were also designed to send a signal to the Clinton White House not to try to nominate Dellinger for any federal appellate judgeship or the Supreme Court. Id. See also "Courtesy and Senator Helms," *New York Times*, Oct. 11, 1993, A16.

36   See Helen Dewar, "Nominees Now Face 'Trial by Fire'; Senate Confirmation Process Has Evolved into Political Warfare," *Washington Post*, Mar. 23, 1997, A10.

37   See James Rosen, "Helms Raises Ire with Court Bill," *News and Observer* (Raleigh, N.C.), Mar. 28, 1999, A1 (quoting Senator Helms as saying, "You go out on the street in Raleigh, North Carolina, and ask 100 people, 'Do you give a damn who is on the Fourth Circuit Court of Appeals?' . . . They'll say, 'What's that?' It matters only to politicians and newspaper editors").

Notes to Chapter 5

38   5 U.S. (1 Cranch) 137 (1803).

39   See Patricia C. Acheson, *The Supreme Court: America's Judicial Heritage* 43–44 (1961).

40   Id. at 44.

41   Id. at 47.

42   H. Abraham, *Justices and Presidents*, 86.

43   Id. at 99–100.

44   Id. at 102.

45   Id. at 125.

46   Id. at 127.

47   See R. Newman, *Hugo L. Black*, 210–13, 236, 239.

48   See Ann Scales, "Politics Cited for Surgeon General Vacancy," *Boston Globe*, Oct. 15, 1996, A3.

49   See Kirk Victor, "Judgment Day," *National Journal*, May 25, 1996.

50   See Editorial, *Washington Post*, July 10, 1996, A16; Jamie Dettmer and Susan Crabtree, "A Judge Too Far," *Washington Times*, Apr. 29, 1996, O6. See also S. Goldman, "Bush's Judicial Legacy," 284 ("Traditionally, minimal confirmation activity occurs during presidential years, especially when the Senate is controlled by one party and the White House by another").

51   David G. Savage, "California and the West; Study Will Delay Bid to Split Up Ninth Circuit," *Los Angeles Times*, Nov. 13, 1997, A3.

52   See Rex Bossert, "The Call for Dividing the 9th Circuit Grows; Some Call the Courts Too Big; Others Say Study the Issue," *National Law Journal*, May 5, 1997, A1.

53   See David Skidmore, "House Passes Bill Applying Federal Labor Laws to White House," Associated Press, Sept. 24, 1996; Cynthia Hanson and Yvonne Zipp, "The News in Brief," *Christian Science Monitor*, Sept. 26, 1996, 2.

54   United States v. Hartwell, 73 U.S. (6 Wall.) 385, 398 (1868).

55   United States v. Germaine, 99 U.S. (9 Otto.) 508, 511–12 (1879); Auffmordt v. Hedden, 137 U.S. 310, 326–27 (1890).

56   United States v. Mouat, 124 U.S. 303, 307 (1888).

57   424 U.S. 1 (1976).

58   Id. at 126.

59   90 Stat. 475, sec. 101 (1976).

60   *Buckley*, 424 U.S. at 137–38.

61   42 U.S.C. section 1975(b)(1)(B)(C).

62   478 U.S. 714 (1986).

63   487 U.S. 654 (1988).

64   501 U.S. 868 (1991).

65   Id. at 880–82.

66   Id. at 888–90.

67   Id. at 892.

68   114 S.Ct. 752 (1994).

69   Id. at 756–60.

70   Id. at 759.

71   117 S.Ct. 1573 (1997).

72   Id. at 1582.

73   U.S. Const., art. I, sec. 6, cl. 2.

74   Id.

75   For two excellent discussions of these and other situations in which Congress has tried to pass special legislation to allow certain of its members to be appointed to federal offices in spite of their having served in Congress at the times the salaries for those offices were increased, see Louis Fisher, *Constitutional Conflicts between Congress and the President*, 24–26; Michael Stokes Paulsen, "Is Lloyd Bentsen Constitutional?" 46 *Stan. L. Rev.* 907 (1994).

76   See G. Paulsen, "Is Lloyd Bentsen Constitutional?" 908.

77   For similar conclusions, see R. Katzmann, *Courts and Congress*, 11–12; L. Fisher, *Constitutional Conflicts between Congress and the President*, 35–37.

78   Federalist No. 76 at 386.

79   2 J. Story, *Commentaries on the Constitution of the United States*, sec. 1526.

80   President Coolidge's appointments included the following: Frank Kellogg, whom he appointed as secretary of state and who later shared the Nobel Peace Prize with Coolidge's vice president, Charles Dawes; Herbert Hoover, whom Coolidge kept as secretary of commerce in spite of the persistently tense relations between the two men; Owen Roberts, one of two special prosecutors in charge of investigating the Teapot Dome scandal; Henry Stimson, who served as Coolidge's special envoy to bring peace to Nicaragua and served as secretary of war under President Taft from 1911 to 1913 and in 1940 under President Franklin Roosevelt; and Dwight Morrow, who won fame for his remarkably effective embassy to Mexico.

81   David E. Rosenbaum, "Clinton Withdraws Nomination for Secretary of Veterans Affairs," *New York Times*, Oct. 25, 1997, A8.

82   See, e.g., James D. King and James W. Riddlesperger Jr., "Senate Confirmation of Appointments to the Cabinet and Executive Office of the President," 28 *Soc. Sci. J.* 189, 192–95 (1991).

83   S. Carter, *The Confirmation Mess*, 8.

84   Id.

85   See Pamela Fessler, "Gates Confirmed to Lead CIA into Post-Soviet Era," 49 *Cong. Q. Wkly. Rep.* 3291–92 (1991).

86   S. Carter, *The Confirmation Mess*, 8n.

87   Tim Weiner, "Clinton Picks Acting CIA Boss to Run Agency," *Plain Dealer*, Mar. 20, 1997, A1, 14. Tenet received the nomination after Anthony Lake withdrew his nomination to head the agency. Influential Republican senators had delayed the Senate vote on Lake's confirmation indefinitely because of their concerns about his management record as President Clinton's national security adviser and his possible involvement in dubious fund-raising activities on behalf of the administration. See Tim Weiner, "Lake Pulls

Out as C.I.A. Nominee," *New York Times*, Mar. 18, 1997, A1, 12. Lake would have succeeded John Deutsch, who was confirmed as the head of the agency after Michael Carns withdrew his nomination in 1995 following reports that he had violated immigration laws to hire a Filipino servant. Id.

88 See T. Weiner, "Lake Pulls Out as C.I.A. Nominee," A1, 12.

89 Id.

90 See Tom Baum, "Battle over Rights Nominee a Standoff," *Plain Dealer*, Nov. 14, 1997, A22.

91 Id. at 34.

92 See H. Abraham, *Justices and Presidents*, 127–28.

93 See C. Massey, "Getting There," 11–12.

94 H. Abraham, *Justices and Presidents*, 201.

95 Id.

96 Id. at 205–6.

97 See D. Donald, *Lincoln*, 296, 319, 360, 370–71, 390, 492.

98 Id. at 326–27, 332.

99 Carl von Clausewitz, *On War* (Michael Howard and Peter Paret eds., 1976); Sun Tzu, *The Art of War* (trans. Thomas Cleary, 1988).

100 Sun Tzu, *The Art of War*, vii.

101 C. von Clausewitz, *On War*, 69, 87, 605.

102 Benjamin Ginsberg and Martin Shefter, *Politics by Other Means: The Declining Importance of Elections in America* 26 (1990).

6. The Nominee's Functions

1 U.S. Const., art. II, sec. 2, cl. 2.

2 H. Abraham, *Justices and Presidents*, 288–89.

3 Id. at 176. See also id. at 14–15, 287. Although the double nomination of Fortas and Thornberry could have been viewed as an act of expediency, the president's long-standing political relationship with Thornberry, including his having arranged for Thornberry's appointments as both a federal district judge and a circuit court of appeals judge, indicated that Thornberry's nomination was "obviously dictated by personal and political friendship." Id. at 290.

4 See generally E. Bronner, *Battle for Justice*, 66–97.

5 S. Carter, *The Confirmation Mess*, 48.

6 Id. at 48 (quoting Gary Wills, *Under God: Religion and American Politics* 262 [Simon and Schuster 1990]) (quoting from then-Judge Bork's speech before the Federalist Society). See M. Gerhardt, "Interpreting Bork," 1386–91.

7 See J. Mayer and J. Abramson, *Strange Justice*, 29–32; Richard L. Berke, "The Thomas Hearings: In Thomas' Hearing Room, Spirits of Hearings Past," *New York Times*, Sept. 11, 1991, A25; see also Gerhardt, "Divided Justice," 971, 977, 981.

8 Sara Fritz, "Nominee Called Trailblazer Who Kept Low Profile," *Los Angeles Times*, June 15, 1993, A1 (quoting President Clinton).

9   Charles Warren, *The Supreme Court in United States History,* vol. 1, *1789–1835* 129 (1937).

10   E. Bronner, *Battle for Justice,* 98 (citation omitted).

11   Clint Bolick, "Clinton's Quota Queens," *Wall Street Journal,* Apr. 30, 1993, A12.

12   See Bradley Graham, "Ralston Ends Candidacy for Military Chief," *Washington Post,* June 10, 1997, A1.

13   See J. Massaro, *Supremely Political,* 52–55.

14   See id. at 6, 79–93.

15   See Ann Devroy and Walter Pincus, "Carns Withdraws as CIA Nominee; 'Abusive Accusations' Cited; Deutch New Choice," *Washington Post,* Mar. 11, 1995, A1. Carns stated that his purpose in providing false information to the government had been "humanitarian" and that he had not realized the nature of the documents he had signed or the extent of the misrepresentations made in them to the INS. Id.

16   David G. Savage, "California and the West; Study Will Delay Bid to Split Up Ninth Circuit," *Los Angeles Times,* Nov. 13, 1997, A3.

17   See, e.g., Graham Button and Kerry A. Dolan, "Warning Flags: How Far Can You Get as a Slick-Talking Investor with a Spotty Record?" *Forbes,* May 3, 1999, 142; David Lightman, "Moffett Backed for Post in Argentina," *Hartford Courant,* June 23, 1999, A4.

18   See Nadine Cohodas, "*Senate Judiciary Rejects Reynolds Nomination,* 43 *Cong. Q. Wkly. Rep.* 1261 (1985).

19   See C. Massey, "Getting There," 5–7.

20   Neil A. Lewis, "Jilted Judge Takes On His Foes in Partisan Congress," *New York Times,* Nov. 16, 1997, A22.

21   Yet another example is Richard Paez, whom President Clinton nominated and twice renominated for a seat on the U.S. Court of Appeals for the Ninth Circuit. He provoked strong opposition from Republican Senator Jeff Sessions, among others, who threatened to filibuster the nomination because of the nominee's support for affirmative action. See David Rosenzweig, "Three Selected for Federal Judgeships: Clinton Nominates Gary Fees and Resubmits Richard Paez and Virginia Phillips," *Los Angeles Times,* Jan. 27, 1999, B3.

22   J. Massaro, *Supremely Political,* 79–93.

23   See Holly Idelson, "Breyer's Business Risks," 52 *Cong. Q. Wkly. Rep.* 1932 (1994).

24   See Holly Idelson, "From 'Wealth of Talent,' Clinton Picks Breyer," 52 *Cong. Q. Wkly. Rep.* 1213, 1215 (1994).

25   See Editorial, *Washington Post,* July 10, 1996, A16; J. Dettmer and S. Crabtree, "A Judge Too Far." See also S. Goldman, "Bush's Judicial Legacy," 284.

26   See Tom Carter, "Atwood Won't Seek Post in Brazil, Says He Can't Resolve Dispute with Helms," *Washington Times,* May 19, 1999, A13.

27   See J. Massaro, *Supremely Political,* 108–16.

28   See S. Carter, *The Confirmation Mess,* 33.

29   Sidney Blumenthal, "Adventures in Babysitting," *New Yorker,* Feb. 15, 1993, 58.

30   See, e.g., "The Thomas Nomination: Excerpts from Remarks by Members of

Senate Judicial Panel on Thomas," *New York Times*, Sept. 28, 1991, 8 (recounting doubts about Thomas's qualifications raised by Senators Metzenbaum, Leahy, Kohl, and Heflin).

31   Joan Biskupic and Helen Dewar, "Senate OKs Judge after Two-Year Delay but Another Nominee's Case on Hold," *Washington Post*, Feb. 13, 1998 (quoting Senator Orrin Hatch).

32   J. Harris, *The Advice and Consent of the Senate*, 55–57.

33   C. Swisher, *Roger B. Taney*, 198–220, 317–25.

34   Gary Lee, "Administration Mobilizes behind Foster; Embattled Surgeon General Gets Support from Panetta, Shalala," *Washington Post*, Feb. 13, 1995, A5.

35   See "Weld Deserves a Hearing on Mexico Nomination: The Battle Is Mostly Politics, but Principle Is at Stake Too," *Los Angeles Times*, July 29, 1997, B6.

36   Peter Baker and Helen Dewar, "Clinton Taps Weld for Post Despite Helms Objection," *Washington Post*, July 24, 1997, A1.

37   Id.

38   "Weld Steps Down as Governor; Faces Battle for Diplomatic Post," *Plain Dealer*, July 29, 1997, A6.

39   See Lori Santos, "Two Top Justice Officials Resign; Departures Are Linked to Meese and His Legal Problems, Sources Say," *Seattle Times*, Mar. 29, 1988, A1.

40   Andrew Cain, "Gay Activist Hormel Is Sworn In," *Washington Times*, June 30, 1999, A1 (quoting Secretary of State Albright).

41   The votes against all of President Jackson's nominees to the directorship of the National Bank were divided along "the usual Bank versus anti-Bank lines." J. Harris, *The Advice and Consent of the Senate*, 58. In fact, the Senate rejected the nominees in spite of considering each one's qualifications to be "above question." Id.

42   Id. at 66. After breaking with the Democrats to run as Whig presidential candidate William Henry Harrison's vice president and with the Whigs in Congress after ascending to the presidency, Tyler was "a President without a party." Id. Many of Tyler's nominees subsequently paid a price for his politics.

43   Eva Rodriguez, "Most Ginsburg Critics Lay Down Their Arms," *Legal Times*, July 19, 1993.

44   See Holly Idelson, "Clinton's Choice of Ginsburg Signals Moderation," 51 *Cong. Q. Wkly. Rep.* 1569–71, 1574.

45   Gerald Gunther, *Learned Hand: The Man and the Judge* 561–62 (1994).

46   See id. at 458–60, 561–66.

47   See Richard Benedetto, "Fallout Continues in and out of White House: Wood, Baird Cases Different, Most Say," *USA Today*, Feb. 9, 1993, A4.

48   See Nadine Cohodas, "Ginsburg Hurt Badly by Marijuana Admission," 45 *Cong. Q. Wkly. Rep.* 2714–16 (1987).

49   Id.

50   Id. at 2715.

51   Id. at 2716.

52   See E. Bronner, *Battle for Justice*, 90.

Notes to Chapter 6

53 Id. at 220–76.

54 Id. at 241–46.

55 See William E. Gibson, "Guinier Nominated for Civil Rights Job," *Harrisburg Patriot & Evening News*, Apr. 20, 1993, A10.

56 Guinier, *The Tyranny of the Majority: Fundamental Fairness in Representative Democracy*, 2 (1994).

57 Alpheus T. Mason, *Brandeis: A Free Man's Life* 465–508 (1956).

58 J. Harris, *The Advice and Consent of the Senate*, 158.

59 See "Nomination of David Lilienthal," 3 *Cong. Q.* 105–6 (1947).

60 David McCulloch, *Truman* 537–38 (1992) (citation omitted).

61 See David G. Savage, *Turning Right: The Making of the Rehnquist Court* 349–58 (1992).

62 See Sheldon Goldman, "Reagan's Judicial Legacy: Completing the Puzzle and Summing Up," 72 *Judicature* 318, 319–20 (1989) (suggesting that the Reagan administration was "arguably . . . engaged in the most systematic . . . philosophical screening of judicial candidates ever seen in the nation's history"); Sheldon Goldman, "The Bush Imprint on the Judiciary: Carrying on a Tradition," 74 *Judicature* 294, 297 (1991) (noting that those in the Bush administration responsible for making recommendations on judicial nominations were instructed by the White House to ensure that the nominees recommended were, among other things, highly qualified and philosophically conservative and sensitive to the need for judicial enforcement of strict separation of powers).

63 H. Abraham, *Justices and Presidents*, 420.

64 See id. at 80 (Adams), 84–87 (Jefferson), 88–91 (Madison), 91–92 (Monroe), and 93–94 (J. Q. Adams).

65 Id. at 95–103.

66 See id. at 107–12.

67 Id. at 116.

68 Id. at 140–47 (Cleveland), 147–52 (Harrison), 152–55 (McKinley).

69 Letter from Theodore Roosevelt to Henry Cabot Lodge (July 10, 1902), *Selections from the Correspondence of Theodore Roosevelt and Henry Cabot Lodge, 1884–1918* 519 (Henry Cabot Lodge and Charles F. Redmond eds., 1925).

70 Id.

71 Quoted in Henry F. Pringle, *Theodore Roosevelt: A Biography* 183 (1931).

72 Presidents Franklin Roosevelt, Richard Nixon, Ronald Reagan, and George Bush each pledged to make certain kinds of judicial appointments. See H. Abraham, *Justices and Presidents*, 212 (Roosevelt), 298 (Nixon), 337 (Reagan), and 365 (Bush); L. Tribe, *God Save This Honorable Court*, 71 (Nixon), 134 (Roosevelt), 77 (Reagan) (1985); see also S. Carter, *The Confirmation Mess*, 56, 69–71 (describing Presidents Reagan's, Bush's, and Clinton's campaign pledges regarding Supreme Court appointments).

73 This process describes the criteria for the Reagan and Bush administrations' nominations of Chief Justice Rehnquist and Justices O'Connor, Scalia, Kennedy, Souter, and Thomas. See *Advice and Consent: The Selection of United States Supreme Court Justices*,

Notes to Chapter 6

4–9 (remarks of then–Solicitor General Kenneth Starr), 41–44, 46 (remarks of former assistant attorney general Brad Reynolds) (A. Darby Dickenson ed., 1993).

74   J. Woodford Howard Jr., *Courts of Appeals in the Federal Judicial System* 90 (Princeton University Press 1981).

75   See Linda P. Campbell and Max B. Baker, "Fort Worth Federal Caseload Growing, Not Booming," *Fort Worth Star-Telegram*, July 25, 1997, B1.

76   Robert A. Carp and C. K. Rowland, *Policymaking and Politics in the Federal District Courts* 165 (University of Tennessee Press 1983).

77   Id. at 166.

78   Id.

79   Id. at 168.

80   J. Harris, *The Advise and Consent of the Senate*, 118–19 (citation omitted in original).

7. Public and Interest Group Participation in the Appointments Process

1   See G. Gunther, *Learned Hand,* 130–33.

2   See "Baird Is Ko'd by the Punch of Populism," *Plain Dealer,* Jan. 24, 1993, 2C; "The Baird Nomination," *Washington Post,* Jan. 24, 1993, C6.

3   See, e.g., S. Carter, *The Confirmation Mess,* 98–99.

4   See generally C. Massey, "Getting There, 5–7.

5   See Erwin Chemerinsky, "Ideology, Judicial Selection, and Judicial Ethics," 2 *Geo. J. Legal Ethics* 643, 646–53 (1989) (discussing the rejections of Supreme Court nominees John Parker, Clement Haynsworth, and Robert Bork). Supreme Court nominees confirmed after close scrutiny of their judicial ideologies include Justices Brandeis, Thurgood Marshall, Rehnquist, Kennedy, Souter, and Thomas. See Gerhardt, "Divided Justice," 973–76.

6   See, e.g., Peter Schuck, "Against (and for) Madison: An Essay in Praise of Factions," 15 *Yale L. & Pol'y Rev.* 553 (1997); Einer R. Elhauge, "Does Interest Group Theory Justify More Intrusive Judicial Review?" 101 *Yale L.J.* 31 (1991).

7   See, e.g., Dennis Mueller, *Public Choice II* (1989); Russell Hardin, *Collective Action* 68, 72–73 (1982); Mancur Olson, *The Logic of Collective Action* 45 (2d ed. 1971); Elhauge, "Does Interest Group Theory Justify Intrusive Judicial Review?" 34–43 (reviewing the literature on interest group theory).

8   See, e.g., T. Kuran, "Ethnic Norms and Their Transformations through Reputational Cascades"; E. Posner, "Symbols, Signals, and Social Norms in Politics and the Law"; B. D. Benheim, A Theory of Conformity, 102 *J. Pol. Econ.* 841 (1994).

9   See generally Eric A. Posner, "Efficient Norms," *New Palgrave Dictionary of Economics and Law* 19–24 (1999).

10   In an influential study conducted in 1981, political scientists Kay Schlozman and John Tierney found that 53 percent of all registered interest groups sought to influence appointments outcomes in all types of presidential nominations. K. Schlozman and J. Tierney, *Organized Interests and the American Democracy* 92 (1986).

11   Some scholars would contest this assertion, contending that individual citizens sel-

dom exercise much influence in politics; political activity is group activity. So the increase in interest group activity actually empowers the individual citizen, who can realistically participate as a member of a group. See, e.g., P. Schuck, "Against (and for) Madison: An Essay in Praise of Factions," 553. The degree to which these scholars are correct depends on the accuracy or meaning of several of their underlying assumptions. For instance, what does it mean to suggest that interest group activity empowers citizens, who as a practical matter can participate in the group's activities? Does it mean that the number of individual citizens empowered by interest group activity is conditioned on wealth, spare time, or the intensity of their agreement with the group's objectives or norms? Moreover, recent polling suggests that most of the public views "special interests" as a wedge rather than a conduit between themselves and the federal government. As a practical matter, for which particular (and for how many) citizens do interest groups operate as a conduit rather than a wedge?

12   At the time he authored this study, Robert Katzmann was a law professor at Georgetown University, a fellow at the Brookings Institution, and president of the Governance Institute. In 1999, Senator Daniel Patrick Moynihan persuaded President Clinton to nominate Professor Katzmann to the Second Circuit. Senator Moynihan's relationship with Katzmann extended back to the days when the latter was Moynihan's student at Harvard. Subsequently, Katzmann had advised Senator Moynihan on a wide range of issues and had been enlisted by Moynihan, among others, to assist then-Judge Ruth Bader Ginsburg in her Supreme Court confirmation hearings. The Senate confirmed Katzmann to the Second Circuit in 1999.

13   R. Katzmann, *Courts and Congress,* 18.

14   Id. at 18–19.

15   For a book chronicling the transformation of Supreme Court confirmation hearings into the functional equivalent of political campaigns, see John Anthony Maltese, *The Selling of Supreme Court Nominees* (Johns Hopkins University Press 1995). As the author explains in his introduction, "[I]nterest groups quickly recognized the power of the Supreme Court to influence public policy and therefore sought to influence the appointments process.... [T]he 1881 nomination of Stanley Matthews serves as a case study of early interest-group involvement in the Supreme Court appointment process . . . that appears to have been quite successful.... [T]he ill fated nominations of John J. Parker in 1930 and Clement Haynsworth in 1969 . . . serve as examples of the new power that interest groups began to exert over the confirmation process." Id. at x.

16   Id. at 95–97.

17   Id. at 154–55; J. Massaro, *Supremely Political,* 139–40.

18   See generally S. Goldman, *Picking Federal Judges,* 310–11.

19   See id. at 311–12.

20   See Robert Shogan, "The Confirmation Wars: How Politicians, Interest Groups, and the Press Shape the Presidential Appointments Process," in *Obstacle Course: The Report of the Twentieth Century Fund on the Presidential Appointments Process* (1996). Shogan concludes: "The interest groups that have proliferated across the spectrum, both as cause

Notes to Chapter 7

and effect of the erosion of parties, increasingly have become a force in the appointments process, second only to the president. The interest groups cannot always decide who gets confirmed and who gets rejected, but they can determine who gets contested—and that is sufficient to give them plenty of weight with both the executive and legislative branches." Id. at 91.

21   For example, in a speech before the Eighth U.S. Court of Appeals Judicial Conference, Justice Thomas identified the most serious threat to federal judges as "the role of interest groups in the nomination and confirmation process. I think they have sorely distorted the process, and they have driven it from a respectable and respectful course." Speech of Associate Justice Clarence Thomas to the Eighth U.S. Court of Appeals Judicial Conference, July 9, 1999. In his speech, Justice Thomas also clarified for the record that no one in President Bush's Justice Department, nor President Bush himself, ever asked him anything about his ideology or how he would rule in particular cases if he were nominated and confirmed as an associate justice. He had been asked only "perfunctory questions" about whether anyone had ever criticized him for his interracial marriage, whether he and his family could survive a confirmation fight, and whether if confirmed he could "call them as [he saw] them." Justice Thomas praised the process by which he was nominated as excluding any "litmus test" and concluded that in his opinion confirmation proceedings generally "should be that respectful [of judicial independence]—that you respect the independence prior to the appointment, and it will be respected after appointment."

22   See generally Marian Lief Palley, "Elections 1992 and the Thomas Appointment," *Pol. Sci. & Pol.,* March 1993, 28–31 (noting that of the 11 women who ran for the Senate, four new women senators were elected, while of the 106 women running for the House of Representatives, the election produced twenty-four new women representatives).

23   M. Silverstein, *Judicious Choices,* 158.

24   Id. at 39–41.

25   Id. at 50–77.

26   373 U.S. 335 (1963).

27   Id. at 50–55.

28   See Elliott Carlson, James Bishop Jr., and William J. Cook, "The Cabinet: Is Stan the Man?" *Newsweek,* Apr. 21, 1975, 81; Robert T. Nelson, "Urban vs. Rural West: A Balancing Act for Clinton," *Seattle Times,* Apr. 13, 1994, B3.

29   See Lauren M. Cohen, "Missing in Action: Interest Groups and Federal Judicial Appointments," 82 *Judicature* 119, 122 (Nov.–Dec. 1998).

30   Id. at 123. The study does acknowledge that the decline in formal participation by interest groups does not necessarily mean that they have been absent from the process. At the very least, they can be quite busy lobbying the media and senators (or their staffs) informally. For example, interest group activity might differ depending on whether the nomination or appointment in question was to an executive or judicial office. The strategy employed by the group might differ in each case as well. For instance, many interest groups interact regularly with executive branch officers (as well as agency officials) and will be in a position to offer jobs to such officials once they leave office. Obviously, the relationship

between a federal judge and interested parties is different. The fact that such groups will likely not interact to the same degree with a judge after his or her confirmation increases the chances that they will want to ensure as best they can that such interaction will not be necessary in order for that judge to perform in the manner they prefer.

31   See supra note 12.

32   See Council for Excellence in Government, "Survey on Public Alienation from Government," released July 12, 1999 (indicating, among other things, that 54 percent of the public believes that the American government is no longer "of, by, and for the people"; and that a plurality blames this on "special interests"). The outcome of this poll reinforces the conclusion of two law professors who have argued on the basis of their own, separate data that special interest groups exert disproportionate influence in the democratic process. See John O. McGinnis and Michael B. Rappaport, "Supermajority Rules as a Constitutional Solution," 40 *Wm. & Mary L. Rev.* 365, 379–80 (1999).

33   See, e.g., *Reasoning and Choice: Explorations in Political Psychology* (Paul M. Sinderman, Richard A. Brody, and Philip E. Tetlock eds., 1991); John Ferejohn, "Information and the Electoral Process," in *Information and Democratic Processes* 1 (J. A. Ferejohn and J. H. Kuchlinski eds., 1990).

34   See N. McFeeley, *The Appointment of Judges*, 22–24.

35   E. Bronner, *Battle for Justice*, 205–6.

36   See T. R. Goodman, "Rallying around Reno: Women's Groups Move Quickly to Support Clinton's AG Pick," *Connecticut Law Tribune*, Feb. 22, 1993, 10.

37   See Felix Frankfurter, "Chief Justices I Have Known," in *Of Law and Men* 129 (Phillip Elman ed., 1956).

8. The Impact of Media and Technology on the Federal Appointments Process

1   For a classic formulation of this criticism, see Stephen Hess, *News and Newsmaking* 128 (Brookings 1996) (lamenting that the financial pressure of the bottom line has led to an increasing tendency of the media to engage in sensational reporting, "where journalism ends and fiction begins").

2   See B. Kovach and T. Rosenstiel, *Warp Speed*, 5.

3   Id. at 4.

4   See generally Charles H. Koch Jr., *Administrative Law and Practice* sec. 4.33, at — (Supp. 2d ed. 1999). See also Peter Strauss, "The Challenges of Globally Accessible Process," in George Berman, Matthias Hergeden, and Peter Lindseth, *Transatlantic Cooperation* (1999) (observing that several administrative agencies experienced significant increases in public comments in response to formal administrative requests); Marshall Breger, "Government Accountability in the Twenty-first Century," 57 *U. Pitt. L. Rev.* 423, 426 (1996) ("There can be no doubt that the task of maintaining openness in government becomes far easier in the computer age").

5   See generally Stephen M. Johnson, "The Internet Changes Everything: Revolutionizing Public Participation and Access to Government Information through the Internet," 50 *Admin. L. Rev.* 277 (1998).

Notes to Chapter 8

6   See R. Posner, *An Affair of State*, 78–83.

7   See E. Bronner, *Battle for Justice*, 274.

8   U.S. Const., amend. I.

9   Besides the speed with which stories or reports need to be done, another obvious pressure for the media is to keep readers interested. In the past this has understandably led to personalizing the appointments process. First, as I have previously suggested, describing appointments matters in personal terms is natural, given that the rise or fall of a particular individual—the nominee—has been the focus of the appointments process; second, this practice has provided a convenient hook to grab a substantial audience because the general public is prone to be more interested in reading, listening to, or watching stories that cater to their emotions, particularly their feelings of empathy, sympathy, envy, and hostility. Moreover, the personal angle helps to educate the public about the personalities, backgrounds, and values of the critical players involved in the appointment. The personal angle helps to build support or opposition to a particular nomination. In addition, describing appointments in personal terms is relatively easy for reporters because it does not require any special training.

10   See, e.g., S. Carter, *The Confirmation Mess*, 45 (discussing some of the misrepresentations made by the press about Judge Bork's record).

11   Id. at 39, 44, 211 n. 17. There might be several objections to the assertion that the Internet is likely to exacerbate the quality of the media's coverage or discussion of appointments, all of which tell us something about the objector's attitudes about the appointments or legislative process. For instance, one might claim that it is unrealistic to expect members of Congress to familiarize themselves firsthand with all of the subjects that come before them. They can rely on their staffs, panels of experts (including the media?), and perhaps even interest groups. The question becomes, How do we evaluate such reliance? How do we evaluate the information provided?

Another argument might be that there has probably never been a period in our history in which those acting as the media could be said to have studied as much or as well as they should have to report the news. Moreover, one should not overlook the significance of the fact that one major feature of the Internet is the unprecedented opportunity it allows for direct (or relatively direct) interaction between citizens and their representatives, without the media operating as the middleman. The function thus increasingly performed by the media, as suggested by Kovach and Rosenstiel, is as digestor rather than purveyor of information. Political psychologists believe that most people seem to be able to cut through the morass of information to get what they need in order to form their opinions. See, e.g., *Reasoning and Choice: Explorations in Political Psychology* (Paul M. Sinderman, Richard A. Brody, and Philip E. Tetlock eds., 1991); John Ferejohn, "Information and the Electoral Process," in *Information and Democratic Processes* 1 (J. A. Ferejohn and J. H. Kuchlinski eds., 1990). Thus, the remaining question is whether the opportunity made available by the Internet for people to bypass the media to get information will pressure the media to move away from purveying data and toward entertainment. At the very least, the odds are that the media have now become just one more source of information to which people turn to understand events.

12 Walter F. Murphy and Joseph Tanenhaus, "Publicity, Public Opinion, and the Court," 84 *Nw. U. L. Rev.* 985 (1989).

13 Id.

14 Id.

15 See J. Mayer and J. Abramson, *Strange Justice,* 178 (quoting the leaders of liberal interest groups acknowledging that the nastiness of the Thomas hearings was largely their fault because their efforts to "lower the standard" in their fight against Bork had simply inspired conservative groups to do the same in fighting for Thomas).

16 Id. at 201.

17 Id. at 336, 345.

18 See, e.g., B. Kovach and T. Rosenstiel, *Warp Speed,* appendix 1 (methodically examining news broadcasts, newspapers, and magazines regarding their relative mix of speculation and factual reporting in several stories relating to the president's impeachment); appendixes 4–7 (identifying seven major threads in major news outlets); id. at 177–78.

19 Id. at 83.

20 Id.

21 See Stuart Taylor Jr., "Clinton Comes Out Loser in the Supreme Court Derby: The President's Process of Serial Leaking of the Names of Potential Nominees Is Undignified, Demeaning to the Candidates, and Unnecessary," *Connecticut Law Tribune,* May 23, 1994, 24.

22 Id.; see also Tony Mauro, "The President Decides: No (New) Cancer on the Court; Is It Right That Judge Richard Arnold Be Disqualified by Illness," *Connecticut Law Tribune,* May 30, 1994, 20; Taylor, "Clinton Comes Out Loser," 24.

23 Id.

24 See Richard Lacayo, "By Selecting Breyer as His Nominee, Clinton Bypassed His Favorites and Opted for a Quick Confirmation," *Time,* May 23, 1994, 24.

25 S. Carter, The *Confirmation Mess,* 37–44.

26 See Susan Page, "Clinton on Defensive; Under Attack on Cabinet Jobs," *Newsday,* Feb. 9, 1993, 7; Mark Thompson and Angie Cannon, "Double Standard Seen with Inman; Women's Groups Note that Male Appointees Have Survived Problems that Sank Baird and Wood," *Orange County Register,* Dec. 21, 1993, A22.

27 S. Carter, *The Confirmation Mess,* 20–22, 24, 30–31, 159–78.

28 Id. at 8, 171.

29 See William H. Freivogel, "We've Become a Nosey Press and Nation," *St. Louis Post-Dispatch,* Mar. 1, 1993, B1; Jill Smolowe, "Rush to Judgment," *Time,* Feb. 15, 1993, 30; Ellen Goodman, "When Character Becomes Caricature," *Boston Globe,* Feb. 10, 1993, 11; Anna Quindlen, "Kimba Wood Is Paying for Zoë Baird's Sins," *Dallas Morning News,* Feb. 9, 1993, A13.

Notes to Chapter 8

30   See Randall Kennedy, "The Case against Civility," *American Prospect* 84 (Nov.–Dec. 1998).

31   It is hard to settle on examples because there are so many. Nevertheless, a few should be illustrative. For instance, Senator Charles Sumner was nearly caned to death on the Senate floor for a speech urging abolition. Moreover, a report widely circulated around Washington society during James Buchanan's presidency was that his vice president, frequently referred to in news reports as "Mrs. Buchanan," was his homosexual lover. Many people treated this allegation as a fact, though to this day it remains pure speculation. President Andrew Johnson was foul-tempered and regularly cursed his opponents and crowds, and he inspired much antipathy from the press and his political opponents. To this day, it is popular to think of President Grant as an alcoholic, but his biographers remain uncertain just how much and how frequently he did drink. This was a charge made by Grant's detractors.

32   B. Kovach and T. Rosensteil, *Warp Speed*, 77–78.

33   R. Newman, *Hugo Black*, 91–93, 114–15.

34   See J. Mayer and J. Abramson, *Strange Justice*, 251–56; see also Susan Page, "Thomas Case Subpoenas; Senate Wants to Question Reporters on Leaks," *Newsday*, Feb. 4, 1992, 15.

9. The Need for Reform

1   See generally Robert A. Dahl, *Dilemmas of Pluralist Democracy* (1982); *Polyarchy* (1971); *Who Governs?* (1961); *A Preface to American Democracy* (1956).

2   See, e.g., Gary J. Miller, "Formal Theory and the Presidency," in *Researching the Presidency: Vital Questions, New Approaches* 289 (George C. Edwards III et al. eds., 1993).

3   Twentieth Century Fund, Obstacle Course: *The Report of the Twentieth Century Fund on the Presidential Appointment Process* 14–16 (1996).

4   The Miller Center of Public Affairs, *Improving the Process of Appointing Federal Judges: A Report of the Miller Center Commission on the Selection of Federal Judges*, 9 (1996).

5   See, e.g., Patrick M. McFadden, *Electing Justice: The Law and Ethics of Judicial Election Campaigns* (1990); Susan B. Carbon and Larry C. Berkson, *Judicial Retention Elections in the United States* (1980).

6   The idea that adopting or clarifying the basic mission that an actor is pursuing in the system tracks one of the basic recommendations made by David Osborne and Ted Gaebler for reforming government generally. See David Osborne and Ted Gaebler, *Reinventing Government: How the Entrepreneurial Spirit Is Transforming the Public Sector* 108–37 (1993).

7   See Richard P. Wulwick and Frank J. Macchiarola, "Congressional Interference with the President's Power to Appoint," 24 *Stetson L. Rev.* 625 (1995).

8   President Nixon had sent no nominations to the Senate for the National Advisory Council on Indian Education or for deputy commissioner of Indian education, in an attempt to destroy a program established by Congress. Eventually, a federal court ordered Nixon to fill the positions and implement the program. See Minnesota Chippewa Tribe v. Carlucci, 358 F. Supp. 973 (D.D.C. 1973). According to the federal district judge in that

case, June L. Green, the implementation of the program in question—the Indian Education Act—would have been "impossible or impractical" unless the president appointed the Council. Id. at 975. She also stated that although it was clear that the president could appoint whomever he chose to the council, he lacked "discretion to decide if the Council should or should not be constituted." Id.

9   See, e.g., Parsons v. United States, 167 U.S. 324, 343 (1897) (unanimously upholding President Cleveland's removal of a U.S. Attorney on the ground that a president has the authority to remove an officer "when in his discretion he regards it for the public good, although the term of office may have been limited by the words of the statute creating the office").

10   See Shoemaker v. United States, 147 U.S. 282, 301 (1893) (rejecting the view that, "because additional duties, germane to the offices already held by [certain officers], were devolved on them by the act, it was necessary that they should be again appointed by the President and confirmed by the Senate. It cannot be doubted, and it has frequently been the case, that Congress may increase the power and duties of an existing office without thereby rendering it necessary that the incumbent should be again nominated and appointed").

11   See generally L. Fisher, *Constitutional Conflicts*, 83–86.

12   See, e.g., Memorandum for the General Counsels of the Federal Government, 20 Op. O.L.C. — (May 7, 1996).

13   See, e.g., In re Investment Bankers, Inc., 4 F.3d 1556, 1562 (10th Cir. 1993) (noting that the argument that an extension of the tenure of an office raises problems under the Appointments Clause "has been rejected by every court that has considered it"), cert. denied, 114 S. Ct. 1061 (1994); In re Benny, 812 F.2d 1133, 1141 (9th Cir. 1987) (holding that a statutory extension of tenure "becomes similar to an appointment" only "when it extends the office for a very long time").

14   The key cases are Edmond v. United States, 117 S.Ct. 1573 (1997); Weiss v. United States, 114 S.Ct. 752 (1994); Freytag v. Commissioner, 111 S.Ct. 2631 (1991); Morrison v. Olson, 487 U.S. 654 (1988); Young v. United States ex rel. Vuitton, 481 U.S. 787 (1987); Buckley v. Valeo, 424 U.S. 1 (1976): Humphrey's Executor v. United States, 295 U.S. 602 (1935); Myers v. United States, 272 U.S. 107 (1926); Auffmordt v. Hedden, 137 U.S. 310 (1890); Ex Parte Siebold, 100 U.S. 371 (1879); United States v. Germaine, 99 U.S. 508 (1879); United States v. Hartwell, 73 U.S. (6 Wall.) 385 (1868).

15   Twentieth Century Fund, *Report*, 10.

16   Id. at 8–9.

17   Once created, some offices demonstrate extraordinary resilience to abolition. For instance, both the Interstate Commerce Commission and the Federal Trade Commission have been widely criticized throughout most of their existence, but each continues to function.

18   5 U.S.C. secs. 3345–3349 (1994).

19   See U.S. Const., art. II, sec. 2, clause 3.

20   See Rogelio Garcia, *Acting Officials in Positions Requiring Senate Confirmation in Executive Departments, as of February 1998,* Congressional Research Service Report,

Mar. 11, 1998, at 1, 5–9 (suggesting sixty-four such appointments have been made in the fourteen executive departments in violation of the requirements of the Vacancies Act).

21   28 U.S.C. secs. 509–10 (1994).

22   5 U.S.C. sec. 509–10.

23   Id., sec. 510.

24   See Michael A. Carrier, "When Is the Senate in Recess for Purposes of the Recess Appointments Clause? 92 *Mich. L. Rev.* 2204 (1994).

25   112 Stat. 2681, 5 U.S.C. secs. 3345–49 (1998).

26   U.S. Const., art. II, sec. 3.

27   Omnibus Consolidated Appropriations Act of 1999, Pub. L. No. 105–277, secs. 3345–3349d, U.S.C.C.A.N. (105 Stat. 2681)611, also S. 2307, 105th Cong. (1998), H.R. 4328, 105th Cong. (1998).

28   5 U.S.C. sec. 3346 (1998).

29   The other provisions of the new law accomplish several of the stated objectives of some of the more outspoken critics of the amended Vacancies Act in the Senate, and particularly with the Clinton administration's partial compliance with it. First, section 3345 states that it applies to all officers of executive agencies whose appointments must be made by the president, subject to the advice and consent of the Senate. Moreover, a person filling a vacant office must be, with certain specific exceptions set forth, the first assistant or must come from an office that requires a presidential appointment, subject to the advice and consent of the Senate. This section does not specifically exempt the Office of the Attorney General; nor does any other part of the statute. Section 3347 specifies that this bill is the exclusive process for temporarily filling a confirmable office in an executive agency, with two narrow exceptions (a statute that expressly supersedes the Vacancies Act or an appointment made pursuant to the president's constitutional authority to make recess appointments). Section 3348, with certain explicit exceptions set forth, limits the extent of the "function or duty" that a temporary appointee may exercise to those created by the statute or by regulation in effect within 180 days before the vacancy arose. It further provides that unless the FVRA procedures are followed, the vacant office must remain vacant. Moreover, section 3348 provides that any action performed by an invalid acting officer will have no force or effect. Nor can any action by the latter be given effect afterward by means of ratification. Section 3349 requires an agency head to notify the comptroller general and each house of Congress of vacancies requiring Senate confirmation. It also requires the agency head to submit the names of temporary appointees and the dates when they first assumed their temporary offices; the names of any nominees sent to the Senate and when the nominations were sent; and the dates of a nomination's rejection, withdrawal, or return.

30   See Bob Egelko, "Critics Want to Break Up Ninth Circuit," *Plain Dealer*, Aug. 16, 1997, 6A.

31   *Report of the Commission on Structural Alternatives for the Federal Courts of Appeals,* Dec. 18, 1998.

32   S. Carter, *The Confirmation Mess,* 166.

33   272 U.S. 52 (1926).

34   Id. at 265–74 (Brandeis, J., dissenting).

35   W. McFeeley, *Grant,* 406.

36   See L. White, *The Republican Era.*

37   A. Hoogenboom, *The Presidency of Rutherford B. Hayes,* 127–51.

38   Id. at 127–31, 244.

39   Margaret Leech and Harry J. Brown, *The Garfield Orbit* 244–45 (1978).

40   L. Fisher, *Constitutional Conflicts,* 26; F. McDonald, *The American Presidency,* 325.

41   F. McDonald, *The American Presidency,* 326.

42   Id.

43   D. Osborne and T. Gaebler, *Reinventing Government,* 125.

44   116 U.S. 483, 485 (1886).

45   See "Senate Confirms Barshefsky as Trade Representative," *Baltimore Sun,* Mar. 6, 1997, 2A.

46   R. Dworkin, *Freedom's Law,* 37–38, 320.

47   S. Carter, *The Confirmation Mess,* 13–15, 19–20, 25–31, 37–53, 166–69.

48   L. Tribe, *God Save This Honorable Court,* 88.

49   60 U.S. 393 (1856).

50   Although some might argue that this conception of law is an illusion and masks what judges, lawmakers, and lawyers really do (see, e.g., Mark V. Tushnet, "Critical Legal Studies: An Introduction," 52 *Geo. Wash. L. Rev.* 239, 239–42 [1984]), it still might be a popular perception of the Court.

51   See chapter 8, note 4.

52   At present, interest groups have varying abilities to move quickly to influence the confirmation process. Accordingly, the amount of time between the moment a nominee's identity is made public and the Senate's confirmation vote is crucial to determining which groups will participate in the process. If the delay is minimal, only currently organized groups with established avenues of communication will be able to participate extensively; a longer period allows groups to form and grassroots campaigns to begin. It seems plausible that executive branch appointments are more likely to concern already formed interest groups (although that may no longer be the case as some issue-oriented groups, like the Institute for Justice, focus on judicial appointments). The critical question relates to the obstacles or impediments to collective action (and the extent to which the Internet will exacerbate or relieve those problems). Classic studies of collective action suggest that large, diffuse groups face greater obstacles to group petitioning than small groups with concentrated interests in lawmaking. See generally Elharge, "Interest Group Theory," 36–39. These studies suggest further that by virtue of their organizational structures, certain groups enjoy advantages over wealthier or more populous groups that enable them to exercise "disproportionate" influence on politicians and regulators and thus secure laws that favor their interests even when those laws injure larger groups (e.g., the general public) and impose a net loss on society. See Mancur Olson, *The Logic of Collective Action* 27–28 (2d ed. 1971); George Stigler, "The Theory of Economic Regulation," 2 *Bell J. Econ. & Mgmt. Sci.* 3, 10–13 (1971); James Q. Wilson, "The Politics of Regulation," in *The Poli-*

Notes to Chapter 9

tics of Regulation 369–70 (James Q. Wilson ed., 1980). This means, in the views of these theorists, that many statutes or regulations are enacted (or defeated) not to benefit the general public but to help a special interest group exact economic rents from the larger society. Other theorists argue, however, that noneconomic factors such as altruism and ideology do play at least some role in political participation and decision making, and that the preferences of regulators and the general public sometimes prevail over the preferences of interest groups. See Daniel A. Farber and Philip C. Frickey, "The Jurisprudence of Public Choice," 65 *Tex. L. Rev.* 873, 912–14 (1987); Herbert Hovenkamp, "Legislation, Well-Being, and Public Choice," 57 *U. Chi. L. Rev.* 63, 88, n. 56 (1990); Mark Kelman, "On Democracy-Bashing: A Skeptical Look at the Theoretical and 'Empirical' Practice of the Public Choice Movement," 74 *Va. L. Rev.* 199, 214–23 (1988); Edward L. Rubin, "Beyond Public Choice," 66 *N.Y.U. L. Rev.* 1, 2, n. 3, 12–45 (1991). The latter theorists suggest that interest group theory, even if qualified to account for one or more interest groups' incomplete capture of a committee or agency, cannot offer a complete theory of regulation. The questions posed by these different theoretical perspectives on interest group participation in the political process have to do with which theoretical perspective best fits not only the patterns of interest group participation in the federal appointments process but also the likely changes that the Internet will have on such participation.

53   See generally Lawrence Lessig, *Code and Other Laws of Cyberspace* 79–82 (1999).

10. On the Future of Judicial Selection

1   U.S. Const., art. III, sec. 1.

2   There has long been disagreement among scholars about whether the constitutional language "during good Behavior" does more than establish life tenure for federal judges. Some scholars construe the language as establishing both life tenure and a separate standard—good behavior—on which federal judges may be removed from office. Others, including this author, have suggested the phrase merely uses terms of art to contrast the unlimited term of federal judges from the fixed terms of the president, the vice president, and members of Congress. Otherwise, the phrase does not constitute a basis on which federal judges could be removed more easily than other "officers of the United States," who can be removed only for committing impeachable offenses. See generally Michael J. Gerhardt, *The Federal Impeachment Process: A Constitutional and Historical Analysis* 83–84, 96–97 (2d ed., 2000).

3   See generally "Symposium, Judicial Independence and Accountability," 72 *S. Cal. L. Rev.* 723 (1999).

4   S. Carter, *The Confirmation Mess*, 200.

5   Alexander Bickel, *The Least Dangerous Branch: The Supreme Court at the Bar of Politics* 16 (2d ed., 1986).

6   See infra note 14.

7   Republican Senator Bob Smith is the most recent in a long line of members of Congress who periodically propose abandoning life tenure. In March 1999, Smith, joined by Republican senators Richard Selby from Alabama and Jesse Helms from North Carolina,

formally proposed restricting federal judicial tenure to a ten-year term. See also "Federalist Society Panel Discussion: Term Limits for Judges?" 13 *J.L. & Pol.* 669 (1996); J. David Rowe, "Limited Term Merit Appointments: A Proposal to Reform Judicial Selection," 2 *Tex. Wesleyan L. Rev.* 335 (1995).

8 In some jurisdictions, such as Florida, the alternative is a hybrid system, in which the governor chooses a judge from a list assembled for him by the state assembly. In others, such as Virginia, the state assembly chooses judges from a list compiled by the governor or a commission over which he wields significant influence. See also Gerry Spence, *O.J.: The Last Word* 247–50 (1997) (proposing term limits for federal judges, who would be chosen by lottery); David Garrow, "Mental Decrepitude on the Supreme Court: The Historical Case for a 28th Amendment," 67 *U. Chi. L. Rev.* — (2000) (discussing the constitutional amendment approved by the U.S. Senate on May 11, 1954, prohibiting any justice from serving on the Supreme Court past the age of seventy-five).

9 These institutional factors include relative insulation from political pressure and protection from salary cuts as well as concerns about maintaining the credibility and legitimacy of their respective courts and community, collegial, and peer pressure.

10 See generally Kathleen Sullivan, "The Supreme Court, 1991 Term: Foreword— The Justices of Rules and Standards," 106 *Harv. L. Rev.* 22 (1992).

11 Two examples illustrate the arguable effectiveness of impeachment attempts or threats made against judges. In the most notorious impeachment effort ever undertaken against a judge, Associate Justice Samuel Chase was not the same man after he had been impeached by the House but acquitted by the Senate. Chase simply did not demonstrate the same pro-Federalist, anti-Republican fervor from the bench after his impeachment as he had before it.

More recently, District Judge Harold Baer seemingly backed down in reviewing a motion to suppress after he had been threatened with impeachment. After Judge Baer had granted a motion to suppress based on his finding that federal agents had conducted an illegal search (United States v. Bayless, 913 F.Supp. 232 [S.D.N.Y. 1996]), Bob Dole, then the Republican candidate for president, threatened Baer with impeachment. Don van Natta Jr., "Judges Defend a Colleague from Attacks," *New York Times*, Mar. 29, 1996, B1. President Clinton, who had appointed Baer, indicated that he was considering whether to ask Baer to resign. Alison Mitchell, "Clinton Pressing Judge to Relent," *New York Times*, Mar. 22, 1996, A1. Though several Second Circuit judges denounced the threatened impeachment as a violation of Baer's constitutionally protected judicial independence ("Second Circuit Chief Judges Criticize Attacks on Judge Baer," 215 *New York Law Journal* 4, Mar. 29, 1996), Baer reversed himself. United States v. Bayless, 921 F.Supp. 211 (S.D.N.Y. 1996). Not surprisingly, Baer's reversal of his prior order gave rise to the suspicion that the external pressures affected his decision making.

12 See S. Carter, *The Confirmation Mess,* 108–12. See also Barry Friedman, "The History of the Countermajoritarian Difficulty, Part One: The Road to Judicial Supremacy," 73 *N.Y.U. L. Rev.* 333 (1998) (arguing that political reprisals against the Court will flourish during a period when the Court is asserting that its decisions are binding not only on the

parties to the case at bar but on future litigants and the other branches of the federal and state governments).

13 Kathleen Sullivan, "The Jurisprudence of the Rehnquist Court," 22 *Nova L. Rev.* 743 (1998).

14 S. Carter, *The Confirmation Mess,* 99–108. Cf. Paul D. Carrington, "Judicial Independence and Democratic Accountability in Highest State Courts," 61 *Law & Contemp. Probs.* 79 (1998) (discussing the extent to which popular or retention elections of judges threaten the quality of the nation's highest state courts).

15 See, e.g., Tom R. Tyler and Gregory Mitchell, "Legitimacy and the Empowerment of Discretionary Legal Authority: The United States Supreme Court and Abortion Rights, 43 *Duke L.J.* 703 (1994) (discussing the need for further empirical data to substantiate the authors' initial finding that the legitimacy of the Court is premised on the public's perception of its decision making as derived from or grounded in neutral sources and principles).

16 See D. Garrow, "Mental Decrepitude on the Supreme Court."

17 It might strike some as ironic that public confidence is essential for the Court to maintain its countermajoritarian status. Yet, the Constitution contemplates that no radical overhaul of the Court is possible without some serious public support. To begin with, the nominating, confirming, and jurisdiction-stripping powers are all vested in authorities that are directly accountable to the citizenry. Moreover, a constitutional amendment that is directed at the Court is not likely to be achievable by stealth; it will almost certainly be given so much coverage and scrutiny by the press and elicit presidential and congressional responses that it is not likely to escape public attention or consideration.

18 See, e.g., 2 Bruce A. Ackerman, *We the People: Transformations* 407 (1998).

19 Id.

20 Id.

21 See, e.g., S. Carter, *The Confirmation Mess,* 198; C. Massey, "Getting There," 15 (acknowledging that the supermajority vote for Supreme Court confirmations "would inevitably increase the impact of special interest groups because they would be able to block any nomination if they could garner the support of one third of the Senate's members plus one").

22 Conceivably, this rule might have led to different outcomes in the confirmation proceedings for some distinguished but controversial nominees, including Charles Evans Hughes (for chief justice), Louis Brandeis, and Melville Fuller (for chief justice), each of whom was confirmed by barely two-thirds of the Senate. See Lee Epstein et al., *The Supreme Court Compendium: Data, Decisions, and Developments* 322–38 (2d ed., 1996). Other controversial nominees who were confirmed by less than two-thirds of the Senate were Clarence Thomas, William Rehnquist (for chief justice), Mahlon Pitney, Lucius Lamar, Stanley Matthews, Nathan Clifford, John Catron, and Roger Taney (for chief justice).

23 The converse seems equally plausible, that is, a very popular president does not need the supermajority requirement to secure the confirmation of his Supreme Court nominees. Supreme Court nominees of popular presidents are probably destined to get

floor votes (e.g., in this century, only Supreme Court nominees Fortas (for chief justice) and Ginsburg failed to get floor votes, neither of whom had been nominated by a president who was extremely popular at the time of his nomination). Once nominations have reached the floor, the president can use his popularity to break down the opposition of an obstinate faction, which will probably not succeed in defeating a popular president's nomination without a compelling reason. Thus, the supermajority rule might make it easier to defeat a popular president's nominees or might not make any practical difference in the fates of the latter; neither outcome is preferred by the rule's proponents.

24 B. Ackerman, *Transformations*, 407.

25 Id.

26 For further discussion on possible problems with Ackerman's defense of the supermajority requirement, see Michael J. Gerhardt, "Ackermania: The Quest for a Common Law of Higher Lawmaking," 40 *Wm. & Mary L. Rev.* 1731, 1787–90 (1999).

27 M. Gerhardt, *The Federal Impeachment Process*, 12–13.

28 *See*, e.g., Dennis DeConcini, "Where Are the Judges?" *Boston Globe*, Mar. 1, 1998; Yvette Barksdale, "Advise and Consent," 47 *Case W. Res. L.Rev.* 1399, 1408 (1997). See also M. Cooney and E. Acheson, "Pro and Con Government Relations Forum," 51, 55.

29 Two recent controversies, discussed later in this chapter, demonstrate this problem. The first involves Senator Helms's unsuccessful efforts to defeat the nomination of former senator Carol Moseley-Braun as an ambassador (see infra note 46 and accompanying text), and the second involves President Clinton's successful nominations of Richard Paez and Marsha Berzon to the Ninth Circuit (see infra notes 47 and 48 and accompanying text).

30 U.S. Const., art. I, sec. 5.

31 See United States v. Ballin, 144 U.S. 1, 5 (1892) ("each house . . . may not by its rules ignore constitutional restraints or violate fundamental rights, and there should be a reasonable relation between the mode or method of proceeding established by the rule and the result which is sought to be attained. But within these limitations all matters of method are open to the determination of the house, and it is no impeachment of the rule to say that some other way would be better, more accurate or even more just. . . . [This rule-making power is] within the limitations suggested, absolute and beyond the challenge of any other body or tribunal").

32 See, e.g., John H. Jackson, *The World Trading System: Law and Policy of International Economic Relations* 35–38 (1999) (recounting the failure of the Senate to take final action on the International Trade Organization [the precursor to the World Trade Organization], whose charter was submitted to Congress in 1949 but withdrawn by President Truman in 1950 after a year of inaction). More recently, the Senate failed to take final action on the comprehensive test-ban treaty signed on behalf of the United States by President Clinton.

33 Similarly, the Constitution's supermajority requirement for removal embodies a presumption against conviction and removal. See Michael J. Gerhardt, "The Perils of Presidential Impeachment," 67 *U. Chi. L. Rev.* 293, 307 (2000).

Notes to Chapter 10

34   It is important to recognize that one critical difference between treaty ratifications and confirmations is that treaty ratification constitutes only one of the recognized
ways for approving or implementing international agreements, whereas the confirmation
process is the only means by which a person may be approved as an Article III judge. This
difference arguably helps to account for the different threshold in treaty ratifications; the
supermajority requirement should not be viewed as a presumption against ratification, because the Constitution conceivably allows other means to achieve similar objectives. One
difficulty with this perspective is that scholars vehemently disagree over the legitimacy
of implementing international agreements in any way other than treaty ratifications; no
doubt, formalists would view treaty ratification as the exclusive path, while functionalists
would recognize other informal means for implementing such agreements. Moreover, federal judges may be appointed by at least one other method—albeit temporarily—as recess
appointments.

35   The obstruction in judicial selection might have salutary effects that cannot easily
be dismissed. First, they might encourage settlement. Moreover, if federal courts worked
too efficiently, it is conceivable that parties would be encouraged to file their disputes in
federal rather than state courts. (The phenomenon would be analogous to the findings of
some transportation specialists that the more roads that are built and the more cars that
are made, the more people drive.) Lastly, the obstruction of judicial selection might call
attention to the possibility that perhaps we have more federal courts than we need or that
federal courts are largely unnecessary or obsolete.

36   See Nixon v. United States, 113 S.Ct. 732 (1993).

37   These differences have been identified in prior chapters, principally chapters 3, 4,
and 5.

38   Congress's failure to expand the size of the federal judiciary from 1990 to the
present (with a few minor exceptions noted below) is the longest period in more than fifty
years that it has failed to create new judicial seats. Only nine federal judgeships have been
created since President Clinton took office in 1993: three federal district judgeships for
the District of Arizona; four district judgeships for the Middle District of Florida, and
two federal district judgeships for the District of Nevada. All nine were created by the
1999 Omnibus Appropriations Act, Public Law no. 106-113, Nov. 29, 1999, 113 Stat. 1501.
Prior to the enactment of this law, several bills had been proposed to create new federal
judgeships but they failed to pass in Congress (e.g., the Florida Federal Judgeship Act of
1998, the Federal Judgeship Act of 1997, the Wisconsin Federal Judgeship Act of 1997—
a reproposal of a failed 1995 bill—and the Temporary Federal Judgeships Act of 1995).
Meanwhile, six other bills attempting to create new judgeships were introduced in 1999,
but all of them are stalled in committee or subcommittee. For most of the past ten years,
the Judicial Conference—with no formal declaration of support from the Clinton administration—has repeatedly requested an expansion in the size of the federal judiciary to deal
with the more than 23 percent increase in the number of cases filed in district courts during
that same period.

39   In chapters 5 and 9, I recount efforts, particularly in recent years, to effect indefi-

nite rather than temporary holds. One obvious way to accomplish this is for senators acting in sequence to put holds on a nomination.

40   See, e.g., Lawrence Lessig, "The Regulation of Social Meaning," 62 *U. Chi. L. Rev.* 943 (1995).

41   These two norms are agreements regarding recess appointments and the willingness of political appointees to offer their resignations to a newly elected president from the opposite party, who then has the choice of accepting the resignations or retaining the appointees. I discuss the relationship between agreements on recess appointments and judicial selection in the previous chapter on reform of the federal appointments process. The degradation of the second norm became apparent when some sitting U.S. attorneys balked at offering to resign their posts once Janet Reno was confirmed as President Clinton's Attorney General. Reno had merely requested something she thought was pro forma; indeed, the practice was honored at the outsets of the Carter, Reagan, and Bush administrations. The refusals to tender resignations embarrassed (indeed, probably were intended to embarrass) Janet Reno, though she was not doing something by any means unprecedented.

42   See generally chapter 6.

43   It is important to recognize that senatorial courtesy has degraded over the past few decades. The reasons include the decline in the influence of political parties, the decline in civility or collegiality in the Senate (due to various causes, including issue salience, identity politics, and the disappearance of the moderate middle in the Senate), and norm ambiguation (conflict over the meaning and scope of the norm). Nevertheless, senatorial courtesy is still the strongest norm in the appointments process. Its strength derives in part from the structure of the process, in which the Senate is empowered to give its advice and consent on nominations and senatorial courtesy constitutes one of the means for giving advice.

44   I discuss the different meanings of senatorial courtesy in more detail in chapter 5.

45   There are numerous examples of senators' deferring not just to a president's choice of one of their colleagues for a confirmable office but also former House members. One recent example is President Clinton's decision in June 1999 to nominate as ambassador to Argentina Toby Moffett, who served as a U.S. representative from Connecticut from 1975 to 1983. The Democratic and Republican leaderships of the Senate quickly expressed their support for Moffett's appointment, and all signs indicated that he would be quickly (and perhaps unanimously) confirmed once his background check had been completed. Though there were no signs whatever of anything problematic in Moffett's background, he nevertheless withdrew his nomination in early January 2000 when it became clear that the background check was far from over and required more time. He explained that there was little, if any, upside to uprooting his family for a position that might last only a few months.

46   The two dissenting votes came from Senator Helms (who had tried to block confirmation hearings as well as a committee vote) and Senator Peter Fitzgerald (who had tried, with Helms's support, to block a floor vote, because of concerns raised initially in his successful campaign to replace her in the Senate).

Notes to Chapter 10

47　A related point is that Paez and Berzon had the added advantage of a senator (namely, Barbara Boxer from California) fighting for them. Paez and Berzon were nominees in whom Boxer felt a vested interest, because they had been recommended to her by her Ninth Circuit nominating commission. Nominees who do not have a senator (or a group of senators, as did Paez and Berzon) fighting for them are not likely to fare as well in the judicial selection process.

The difference that a senator's intense support can make for nominations is apparent when one contrasts Paez's and Berzon's fates with the present status of the nomination of Elena Kagan (a former University of Chicago law professor and Clinton White House official) to the federal court of appeals for the D.C. Circuit. Nominated by President Clinton for the post in 1999, Kagan is yet to have a committee hearing, much less a committee vote or final action by the Senate. One problem with Kagan's nomination is that it did not comport (in the views of some senators with particular interest in the composition of the D.C. Circuit) with the apparent bargain, struck almost a decade before by the president, the local bar association in the District of Columbia, and interested senators, to nominate a local lawyer (or judge or academic) to the D.C. Circuit. The deal was made to avoid having members of the D.C. bar underrepresented on D.C. courts (or effectively nullified from being considered for judgeships because of their domicile).

Moreover, Kagan's nomination presented an especially easy case for payback. Ever since the Judiciary Committee stalled and effectively nullified more than a dozen of President Bush's judicial nominations in 1992, some Republican senators (notably Iowa's Charles Grassley) have been determined to retaliate. One nomination commonly cited by these Republicans as having been improperly scuttled is that of John Roberts. Like Roberts, Kagan was under forty at the time of her nomination to the federal court of appeals. Also like Roberts, Kagan is a Harvard Law School graduate with prestigious clerkships but not a record of long public service or substantial litigation experience. Perhaps most important, these problems with Kagan's nomination have been exacerbated by the fact that the District of Columbia has no senators. Thus, there is no senator disposed to spend substantial political coinage to salvage her nomination.

48　The Senate confirmed Paez 59 to 39, and Berzon 67 to 31.

49　Indeed, the president's willingness to make judicial selection is one of the classic conditions for limiting the abuses of judicial nominees. The second is that the president and a majority of senators are from the same political party. If a president's party controls the Senate, his nominees have a much better chance to get hearings and final action. The third condition is that a president should establish clear, relatively easily implemented directives to the administration officials responsible for judicial selection. The fourth condition is that the president should assemble a competent staff to process judicial nominations and coordinate interaction with senators over them. The final condition is the choice of confirmable people, that is, people who do not make easy or obvious targets.

As one might expect, these five conditions are rarely all in place at the same time. When they are, judicial selection obviously tends to proceed more efficiently, as it did during most of President Franklin Roosevelt's time in office and the first six years of Ronald Reagan's

Notes to Chapter 10

presidency. In the latter two instances, the norms operated in large part to facilitate a president's objectives in judicial selection.

In contrast, the absence of one or more of these conditions allows for existing norms to function more as impediments than facilitators. Thus, it has not been terribly surprising to find, after the midterm elections of 1994, that the norms have worked against the efficient processing of President Clinton's judicial nominations (at least from his or their perspectives) for several reasons: the Republicans took control of the Senate, he had no desire to make judicial nominations a priority, he adopted criteria for selection that became difficult to fill in some instances (involving gender, ethnic, or geographic diversity as well as other concerns), and he had a high rate of turnover on his staff. Given these factors, President Clinton's appointment of 346 Article III judges as of March 10, 2000, is no mean feat, though how he accomplished it sheds considerable light on the strategies for dealing with judicial selection norms.

50   I discuss these breakthroughs in chapters 4 and 5.

51   I discuss the Fletcher nomination in more detail in chapter 5.

52   One major exception is the martyr syndrome, which I discuss in chapter 6.

53   I discuss different considerations relating to staffing in chapters 4 and 9.

54   The Task Force for Judicial Selection, sponsored by Citizens for Independent Courts (a division of The Century Foundation), has suggested that a president and other executive branch officials should make judicial selection a priority and should routinely engage in advance planning for possible vacancies on the federal bench. See "Justice Held Hostage: Politics and Selecting Federal Judges," final prepublication manuscript, Sept. 29, 1999, 10–11.

55   The Miller Center of Public Affairs, *Improving the Process of Appointing Federal Judges,* 6.

56   See Senate Debate on the Nomination of Justice Thomas, Federal News Service, Oct. 15, 1991, available in LEXIS (remarks of Senator Simon); Senate Debate on the Nomination of Judge Thomas, Federal News Service, Oct. 8, 1991, available in LEXIS, Nexis Library (remarks of Senator Gore).

57   Id.

58   This would be analogous to the practice in impeachment trials of allowing each senator to decide for himself or herself the appropriate burden of proof, rules of evidence, and applicability of the Fifth Amendment due process clause. See generally Gerhardt, *The Federal Impeachment Process,* 113, 115–16.

59   I consider the grounds on which senators have evaluated judicial and other kinds of nominees in chapter 6: The Nominee's Function. For an excellent overview and commentary on selection criteria for the Supreme Court, see David Yalof, *Pursuit of Justices: Presidential Politics and the Selection of Supreme Court Nominees* (1999).

60   Senators, especially from different parties, are not likely to agree over the extent to which the same criteria should apply to district, courts of appeal, and Supreme Court nominations; the relevance of moral character (or its appropriate indices); which theories of judging are acceptable or dangerous; which substantive interpretations of particular

Notes to Chapter 10

constitutional provisions are especially important; and whether there is a specific issue (and if so, which issue) should take precedence over all others in a confirmation proceeding.

61 See Chapter 4.

62 See R. Dworkin, *Freedom's Law*, 37–38, 314–20; S. Carter, *The Confirmation Mess*, 114, 151–53.

63 For a discussion of the significance of these attributes in measuring the quality of certain judges' performances, see Michael J. Gerhardt, "The Art of Judicial Biography," 80 *Cornell L. Rev.* 1595, 1634–37 (1995) (measuring the degree to which these attributes were measured or discussed in recent judicial biographies of Hugo Black, Lewis Powell, and Learned Hand).

64 S. Carter, *The Confirmation Mess*, 44. Professor Carter quotes approvingly the following passage from Senator Paul Simon's book about the Bork and Thomas hearings: "Supreme Court Justices are not saints any more than Senators." Id. at 44 (quoting P. Simon, *Advice and Consent*, 145). Carter does not, however, appreciate the implications of this observation for his preferred focus in judicial confirmations.

65 *See* G. Edward White, *Earl Warren: A Public Life*, 75–77 (1982) (describing how Chief Justice Warren later expressed regret over the role he had played in the internment of Japanese-Americans).

66 S. Carter, *The Confirmation Mess*, 114.

67 347 U.S. 483 (1954).

68 S. Carter, *The Confirmation Mess*, 152. Indeed, it is unclear how much the public knows about the moral characters of the men who decided *Brown*.

69 410 U.S. 113 (1973).

70 R. Dworkin, *Freedom's Law*, 37–38, 313–15, 319–20.

71 See, e.g., Laurence H. Tribe and Michael C. Dorf, *On Reading the Constitution* 15 (1991); Michael J. Perry, "The Legitimacy of Particular Conceptions of Constitutional Interpretation," 77 *Va. L. Rev.* 669, 718–19 (1991); Erwin Chemerinsky, "The Supreme Court 1988 Term—Foreword: The Vanishing Constitution," 103 *Harv. L. Rev.* 43, 94–96, 100–104 (1989); Richard Kay, "Preconstitutional Rules," 42 *Ohio St. L.J.* 204, 206 (1981).

72 R. Dworkin, *Freedom's Law*, 314 (citation omitted in original).

73 Jed Rubenfeld, "On Fidelity in Constitutional Law," 65 *Ford. L. Rev.* 1469, 1477 (1997).

74 For a classic analysis of this issue, see H. Jefferson Powell, "The Original Understanding of Original Intent," 98 *Harv. L. Rev.* 885 (1985).

75 S. Carter, *The Confirmation Mess*, 151.

76 Streamlining the paperwork for all nominees has long been in order. The recent experience of former congressman Toby Moffett is illustrative. See note 45.

Postscript

1 Merle Miller, *Plain Speaking: An Oral Biography of Harry S. Truman* 69 (1974).

2 In his book on President Clinton's impeachment proceedings, Richard Posner suggests that one reason for the sharp disagreement among scholars on the standard for im-

Notes to Postscript

peaching a president is that these scholars come from fields — law, political science, and history — that are soft rather than hard sciences, i.e., they are fields that lack standards their practitioners agree should be used for interpreting relevant texts or data. The same could be said for the federal appointments process. See Posner, *An Affair of State*, 230–40. Though in this book I have tried to analyze the latter process from the perspectives of law and history, I recognize that neither perspective is a hard science. Consequently, one is left by and large to fill the gaps left by these perspectives with pragmatic considerations, such as policy or institutional ramifications.

3   Arguably, some behavioral economists have reached a similar conclusion. In particular they argue that people generally make decisions about investments based on their own choice of the expert opinion they should follow. In other words, people do not become expert themselves on the issues at hand but rather look for shortcuts to either their desired outcomes or information. See, e.g., Robert Schiller, *Irrational Exuberance* (2000).

4   Michael J. Gerhardt, "The Past, Present, and Future of President Clinton's Judicial Appointments," (citation omitted in original).

5   Ronald Stidham, Robert A. Carp, and Donald R. Songer, "The Voting Behavior of President Clinton's Judicial Appointees," 80 *Judicature* 16 (1996).

6   Political scientist G. Calvin Mackenzie reported on behalf of the Century Fund that "1997 has been the most significant year in the evolution of the modern appointments process. The events of th[e] year . . . accelerated the recent deterioration of the presidential appointment process and further diminished its value as a way to staff the top positions in the federal government." G. Calvin Mackenzie, *Starting Over: The Presidential Appointment Process in 1997* 1 (Century Fund 1997). Mackenzie's empirical study revealed that, among other things in 1997, "the administration as a whole experienced a vacancy rate in appointed positions in the executive branch that frequently exceeded 25 percent"; "one of every eight federal judgeships was vacant"; "[e]fforts by individual senators to block action on nominations reached unprecedented levels"; "[t]he practice of batching appointments to regulatory commissions grew more common and left several of those commissions shorthanded for long periods of time"; and "[t]raditional deference [in the Senate] to presidential authority in the selection of subcabinet appointees virtually disappeared." Id. at 1–2. Mackenzie concluded further that "President Clinton was more passive in defense of his appointees than any of his immediate predecessors. This passivity contributed to significant Senate encroachment on executive prerogatives in the exercise of the appointment power." Id. at 2. Moreover, "Frequent, widely publicized appointment controversies subtracted further from the appeal that these appointments now hold for many talented Americans. Nothing that happened in 1997 will make it easier to recruit presidential appointees in the future." Id. See also, e.g., D. DeConcini, "Where Are the Judges?"; M. Cooney and E. Acheson, "Pro and Con Government Relations Forum," 55; Y. Barksdale, "Advise and Consent," 1408.

7   Neil A. Lewis, "Judiciary Panel Chief Responds to Rehnquist," *Plain Dealer*, Jan. 2, 1998, A12.

8   Id.

9   For recent work on reputational cascades, see Timur Kuran and Cass R. Sunstein, "Availability Cascades and Risk Regulation," 51 *Stan. L. Rev.* 683, 685–86, 727–29
(1999); Timur Kuran, "Ethnic Norms and Their Transformation through Reputational
Cascades," 623.

10   J. Harris, *The Advice and Consent of the Senate,* 389.

11   Id. at 390–94.

12   Henry L. Stoddard, *As I Knew Them: Presidents and Politics from Grant to Coolidge*
196 (1927) (quoting President Cleveland) (no citation in the original).

13   Letter from President Taft to Judge John Warrington, Dec. 6, 1909, Papers of
William Howard Taft, Library of Congress.

Afterword

1   There is substantial precedent for filibustering of other presidential nominations
to other offices. For instance, during Bill Clinton's presidency, Republicans successfully
filibustered and blocked the nominations of Henry Foster as surgeon general and Walter
Dellinger as solicitor general.

2   Bill Frist succeeded Trent Lott as majority leader after Lott resigned the position
amid the controversy over his suggesting that the nation would have been better off had the
segregationist presidential campaign of Strom Thurmond in 1948 been successful. Many
observers wondered whether the condemnation of Lott's remarks by President George W.
Bush and other Republicans signaled a shift in Republican leaders' attitudes about race
and the Constitution.

Subsequent events indicate that the shift, if there was one, had been in the party leadership's rhetoric rather than its views on racial equality (including affirmative action). In particular, president Bush came out in opposition to the University of Michigan's affirmative
action program. Moreover, his renomination of Charles Pickering Sr. to the Fifth Circuit
offended several civil rights organizations, which had opposed Pickering's appointment
from the outset because he had favored probation, rather than incarceration, for a person
who had been convicted of cross burning. An additional reason for Democrats' opposition to Pickering was the unusually high number of his decisions reversed by the appellate
court for failing to follow well-settled law.

INDEX

Jackson, Howell, 57–58

Jay treaty, 51–52, 350n. 10

Jefferson, Thomas, 51, 52, 53, 75, 105, 154, 374n. 94

Johnson, Andrew, 123, 126, 155, 163, 330, 358n. 32

Johnson, Lyndon B.: as president, 10, 107, 126–27, 163, 168, 183, 205, 209, 224, 332, 355n. 77; as Senate majority leader, 138, 141

Judicial independence, 175, 214–15, 314–15, 323, 331

Judicial selection: future, 290–324; norms regarding, 301–5, 309–24; public scrutiny of, 321–23; Senate obligation to take final action on every nomination, 298–301; Senate power regarding, 309–14; use of litmus tests, 293. *See also* Reform of the appointments process

Justice Department, 35, 65, 118–20, 176, 178. *See also* Federal Vacancies Reform Act; Offices

Katzmann, Robert, 68, 219, 372n. 12

Kennedy, Anthony, 58, 370n. 73, 371n. 5

Kennedy, John F., 61, 83, 130, 168, 208–9, 356n. 1

Kennedy, Robert F., 83, 208

Kovach, Bill, 234, 241, 242

Ku Klux Klan, 248, 316

Lake, Anthony, 106, 166, 170, 366n. 87

Lee, Bill Lann, 170–71, 187, 267–70

Lee, Richard Henry, 27

Lessons: learned by major actors in the appointments process, 326, 327; learned by presidents, 7–8, 327–28; learned by senators, 7–8, 328

Levi, Edward, 121

Lewinsky, Monica, 249, 322

Lilienthal, David, 199–200

Lincoln, Abraham, 46–47, 48–49, 55, 57, 59, 61, 89, 95, 97, 99, 145, 148, 155, 174, 202–3, 207, 349n. 3, 349n. 4, 354n. 72, 356n. 19, 358n. 32

Lochner v. New York, 295

Lott, Trent, 142, 167, 305

Lucas, William, 171, 187

Lugar, Richard, 138–39

Lurton, Horace, 69, 351n. 38

Madison, James, 17, 19, 20, 21–24, 30, 31, 51, 53, 94–95, 144–45, 348n. 104, 352n. 48, 352n. 49

Manion, Daniel, 202, 221–22

Marbury v. Madison, 29, 52, 153

Marshall, John, 30, 99–100

Marshall, Thurgood, 84, 127, 163, 164, 184, 219, 371n. 5

Martin, Luther, 22, 25

Mason, George, 17, 21, 23, 24, 25, 26, 30, 32, 33

Matthews, Stanley, 69, 383n. 22

McGinnis, John, 29, 31

McKinley, William, 130, 203, 212, 277

Media, 72–74, 322; campaigns regarding Bork nomination, 239–40; campaigns regarding Thomas nomination, 239, 240; as educator, 235–42; gatekeeper function, 322; impact of expansion of television and cable, 238; impact on the appointments process, 239–49, 330–31, 336–37; and Internet (*see* Internet); as ombudsman, 248–49, 336–37; as participant in appointments process, 242–48; performance during Clinton impeachment proceedings, 234, 235, 239, 240–42; and privacy, 238; responsibility for decline in civility of public discourse, 247–48; role in debate about open confirmation hearings, 321–22. *See also* Reform of the appointments process

Index

401

Meese, Edwin, 120, 192, 269

Miller, Samuel Freeman, 46–48

Monroe, James, 51, 53, 147, 347n. 94, 352n. 48

Morris, Gouverneur: in constitutional convention debates, 17, 20, 23, 24, 25, 32, 33, 346n. 93; as nominee for minister to France, 32, 352n. 49

Morrison v. Olson, 159, 160

Moseley-Braun, Carol, 140, 148–49, 223, 303–5, 384n. 29

Moynihan, Daniel Patrick, 194, 372n. 12

Muskie, Edmund, 148, 162

Myers v. United States, 274

NAACP, 221, 230

Need for reform. *See* Reform of the appointments process

New Deal, 89, 100. *See also* Roosevelt, Franklin D.

New York Customshouse, 276, 277

Ninth Circuit, U.S. Court of Appeals, 109, 139, 140, 143, 156, 272, 273

Nixon, Richard, 58, 83, 107, 117, 127, 130, 148, 161, 177, 188, 190, 205, 207, 222, 225, 263, 285, 351n. 38, 356n. 1, 357n. 23, 370n. 72, 377n. 8

Nominations to offices of the United States. See *surnames of specific nominees*

Nominees: as active agents on own behalf, 194–201; criteria generally for selection, 201–11; demonization, 184–85; impediments to confirmation, 183–87, 188–90, 193; as martyrs, 190–93; measuring skill levels, 189–90; opposition as payback, 188; opposition because of political views, 187–88; problems impeding nominations, 183–84; roles within the appointments process, 180–201; selection criteria for judgeships, 314–20; ways to exploit backgrounds,

185–90. See also *surnames of specific nominees*

Norms, 3–5, 8–9, 16, 45, 46, 60, 116, 226, 253, 255–56, 325, 326; ambiguation, 302; institutional, 8; regarding politicians as judges, 228; relating to judicial selection, 290–91, 301–14, 385–86n. 41, 386n. 43; Senate, 236; shaming penalties, 9; signaled in confirmation contests, 226–28; signaling by interest groups, 216, 220–22, 226–28; social, 8, 10, 227

O'Connor, Sandra D., 228, 238, 303, 370n. 73

Officers of the United States, 61, 62; cabinet-level, 53, 117; case law regarding, 265–66, 348n. 2; Chief Justice of the United States, 47–48; civil rights, 11, 62, 71, 83, 170–71, 220, 221, 222, 223; congressional power over, 265; criteria for filling lower courts, 203–5; definition of, 16, 158–60; director of Office of Management and Budget, 133; environmental, 6, 62, 225; judicial, 43–44, 52, 203–5; national security, 6, 62, 169–70; nonjudicial, 48–49, 74–75, 204; requisite qualifications, 9, 16, 37, 156–57, 348n. 104; subcabinet-level, 61, 117; Supreme Court justices, 2, 47, 52, 55–56, 59, 61, 74–75, 111, 123, 129, 171, 202–3, 352n. 45; United States attorneys, 43. See also Offices; *surnames of specific nominees*

Offices: Civil Rights Division, Justice Department, 83, 126, 166, 170, 171; Office of Legal Policy, Justice Department, 120, 122, 152; Office of Management and Budget, 133, 148; White House Counsel, 102, 121, 122, 157, 174, 247–48. *See also* Justice Department; Officers of the United States; *surnames of specific nominees*

Separation of powers: formal analysis, 156, 157, 162, 262–65, 270–71, 384n. 34; functional analysis, 157, 158, 262–65, 271, 384n. 34

Seventeenth Amendment, 9, 65–66, 212, 213, 214, 330, 348n. 103, 351n. 34

Shefter, Martin, 177, 178

Sherman, Roger, 17, 20, 22, 23, 27, 343n. 26

Short, William, 105, 347n. 94

Simon, Paul, 311–12, 348n. 2

Sorensen, Theodore, 169, 187, 190

Souter, David, 73, 200, 202, 219, 370n. 73, 371n. 5

Specter, Arlen, 72, 223

Spoils system, 52–54, 55

Stanton, Edwin, 49, 173

Starr Report, 237–38

Stevens, John Paul, 39, 121

Stewart, Ted, 141, 307

Stone, Harlan Fiske, 67, 173, 199, 208, 351n. 38

Story, Joseph, 164

Strauss, Lewis, 112, 138, 164, 165

Stuart v. Laird, 52

Summers, Lawrence, 103–4

Supreme Court, U.S., 158, 159, 160, 161, 202–5, 281–83, 324; perception as national policymaker, 281–84; public support regarding, 294–95; Warren Court, 68, 163, 201, 224, 316

Sutherland, George, 76, 148

Taft, William Howard: as Chief Justice, 76, 100, 232–33, 336; as president, 69, 98, 100–101, 123, 129, 130, 161, 212, 277, 278, 336, 351n. 38

Taney, Roger: confirmation as Chief Justice, 10, 383n. 22; nomination as associate justice, 10; nomination as Chief Justice, 10, 47, 359n. 44; nomination as secretary of the treasury, 10, 164, 191;

nominations, 154, 190, 193, 355n. 77; rejection as associate justice, 10, 91, 106, 112, 126; rejection as secretary of the treasury, 10, 66, 91, 105–6, 112, 126, 164, 165

Taylor, Zachary, 54, 349n. 4

Tenet, George, 169–70, 366n. 87

Tenure in Office Act, 53, 54, 277

Thomas, Clarence, 11, 83, 84, 96, 127, 163, 168, 176, 184, 190, 200–201, 213–14, 219, 223, 225–26, 238, 239, 240, 241, 245, 249, 308, 311–12, 315, 317, 321, 322, 348n. 2, 370n. 73, 371n. 5, 372–73n. 21, 377n. 15, 383n. 23, 388n. 64

Thornberry, Homer, 127, 183, 367n. 3

Todd, Thomas, 75, 76

Tower, John, 83, 96, 112, 150, 164, 165, 169, 186, 303, 355n. 83

Truman, Harry, 104, 108, 130, 148, 150, 151, 165, 200, 205, 206, 207, 208, 325, 351n. 58, 356n. 1, 364–65n. 28, 365n. 31

Tyler, John, 54, 56, 57, 58, 104, 106, 107, 123, 149, 164, 165, 193, 369n. 42

United States v. Perkins, 279

Van Buren, Martin: nomination as minister to Great Britain, 92, 149, 150, 176, 190; nomination as secretary of state, 91, 92, 149, 209; as president, 93, 94, 358n. 32, 359n. 44; selection as Jackson's running mate, 92, 113, 358n. 32

Vinson, Fred, 150, 365n. 28

Waite, Morrison, 115–16

Wallgren, Mon, 150, 206

Walsh, Thomas, 199

Ware, James, 186, 187

Warren, Charles Beecher, 113, 164, 165

Warren, Earl, 107, 126, 127, 129, 224, 303, 316

MICHAEL J. GERHARDT is a
Professor of Law at The College of
William and Mary. He is the author of
various works, including *The Federal
Impeachment Process: A Constitutional
and Historical Analysis* (2d ed., 2000)
and (with Thomas D. Rowe Jr.,
Rebecca Brown, and Girardeau Spann),
*Constitutional Theory: Arguments and
Perspectives* (2d ed., 2000).

Library of Congress has cataloged the
hardcover edition as follows:
Gerhardt, Michael J.
The Federal appointments process:
a constitutional and historical
analysis / Michael J. Gerhardt.
p.   cm. — (Constitutional conflicts)
ISBN 0-8223-2528-4 (cloth : alk. paper)
1. United States — Officials and
employees — Selection and
appointment — History.
I. Title.   II. Series.
JK731 .G47   2000
352.6'5'0973 — dc21
00-022721

ISBN 0-8223-3199-3 (pbk. : alk. paper)